T0293078

"For something that is increasingly shaping everybody's lives so profoundly, a market is surprisingly ill-understood. William Jackson provides as thorough an account and understanding of the key, yet elusive idea of a 'market' as has been seen in many years. This treasure of a book is likely to dominate the discussion about markets for years to come."

Wilfred Dolfsma, Professor of Business Management & Organisation at Wageningen University, the Netherlands

"Whatever markets are, two things are clear: mainstream economists cannot theorise them adequately, and any adequate theorisation must be multi-disciplinary. Unfortunately, mainstream economists fail to alert their audience to these things. William provides critics from inside and outside the discipline with the intellectual resources to reject mainstream theories of markets and make a start developing alternatives."

Steve Fleetwood, Emeritus Professor, University of the West of England, UK

"Jackson's excellent new book provides a comprehensive appraisal of how economists and social scientists have explained markets. Critical of the narrow neoclassical approach, it emphasizes the diversity of markets in the real world, and argues a layered, non-reductionist social theory attentive to social and cultural factors offering a better framework for a heterodox view of markets."

John B. Davis, Professor Emeritus of Economics, Marquette University, and Professor Emeritus of Economics, University of Amsterdam, the Netherlands

Markets

Defining markets has never been an easy task. Despite their importance for economic theory and practice, they are hard to pin down as a concept and economists have tended to adopt simplified axiomatic models or rely on piecemeal case studies. This book argues that an extended range of theory, social as well as economic, can provide a better foundation for the portrayal of markets.

The book first looks at the definition of markets, their inadequate treatment in orthodox economic theory, and their historical background in the pre-capitalist and capitalist eras. It then assesses various alternatives to orthodox theory, categorised as social/cultural, structural, functional and ethical approaches. Among the alternatives considered are institutionalist accounts, Marxian views, network models, performativity arguments, field theories, Austrian views and ethical notions of fair trade. A key finding of the book is that these diverse approaches, valuable as they are, could present a more effective challenge to orthodoxy if they were less disparate. Possibilities are investigated for a more unified theoretical alternative to orthodoxy.

Unlike most studies of markets, this book adopts a fully interdisciplinary viewpoint expressed in accessible, non-technical language. Ideas are brought together from heterodox economics, social theory, critical realism, as well as other social sciences such as sociology, anthropology and geography. Anybody seeking a broad critical survey of the theoretical analysis of markets will find this book useful and it will be of great interest to economists, social scientists, students and policy-makers.

William A. Jackson is Lecturer in Economics at the University of York, UK.

Economics as Social Theory

Series edited by Tony Lawson, University of Cambridge

Social Theory is experiencing something of a revival within economics. Critical analyses of the particular nature of the subject matter of social studies and of the types of method, categories and modes of explanation that can legitimately be endorsed for the scientific study of social objects, are re-emerging. Economists are again addressing such issues as the relationship between agency and structure, between economy and the rest of society, and between the enquirer and the object of enquiry. There is a renewed interest in elaborating basic categories such as causation, competition, culture, discrimination, evolution, money, need, order, organization, power, probability, process, rationality, technology, time, truth, uncertainty, value, etc.

The objective for this series is to facilitate this revival further. In contemporary economics the label "theory" has been appropriated by a group that confines itself to largely asocial, ahistorical, mathematical "modelling". Economics as Social Theory thus reclaims the "Theory" label, offering a platform for alternative rigorous, but broader and more critical conceptions of theorizing.

The Philosophy, Politics and Economics of Finance in the 21st Century
From hubris to disgrace
Edited by Patrick O'Sullivan, Nigel F.B. Allington and Mark Esposito

The Philosophy of Debt
Alexander X. Douglas

What is Neoclassical Economics?
Debating the origins, meaning and significance
Edited by Jamie Morgan

A Corporate Welfare Economy
James Angresano

Rethinking Economic Policy for Social Justice
The radical potential of human rights
Radhika Balakrishnan, James Heintz and Diane Elson

Knowledge, Class and Economics
Marxism without Guarantees
Edited by Theodore Burczak, Robert Garnett and Richard McIntyre

Markets
Perspectives from Economic and Social Theory
William A. Jackson

For more information about this series, please visit: https://www.routledge.com/Economics-as-Social-Theory/book-series/EAST

Markets

Perspectives from Economic and Social Theory

William A. Jackson

Routledge
Taylor & Francis Group

LONDON AND NEW YORK

First published 2019
by Routledge
2 Park Square, Milton Park, Abingdon, Oxon OX14 4RN

and by Routledge
52 Vanderbilt Avenue, New York, NY 10017

Routledge is an imprint of the Taylor & Francis Group, an informa business

British Library Cataloguing-in-Publication Data
A catalogue record for this book is available from the British Library

Library of Congress Cataloging-in-Publication Data
Names: Jackson, William A., 1959- author.
Title: Markets: perspectives from economic and social theory /
William A. Jackson.
Description: Abingdon, Oxon; New York, NY: Routledge, 2019. |
Series: Economics as social theory; 47 | Includes bibliographical
references and index.
Identifiers: LCCN 2018059455 (print) | LCCN 2019001683 (ebook) |
ISBN 9781315676593 (ebook) | ISBN 9781138936836 (hardback: alk.
paper) | ISBN 9781138936843 (pbk. : alk. paper)
Subjects: LCSH: Capitalism. | Commerce. | Economics.
Classification: LCC HB501 (ebook) | LCC HB501 .J274 2019 (print) |
DDC 381/.1—dc23
LC record available at https://lccn.loc.gov/2018059455

ISBN: 978-1-138-93683-6 (hbk)
ISBN: 978-1-138-93684-3 (pbk)
ISBN: 978-1-315-67659-3 (ebk)

Typeset in Palatino
by Deanta Global Publishing Services, Chennai, India

To my parents

Contents

Figures

Tables

Preface

Academic work on markets has never been confined to a single discipline. Although they are often seen as economic territory, economists have not been the only scholars to analyse them. Discussion of markets and their consequences can be found in other disciplines, such as anthropology, sociology, geography and history, all of which have thriving economic branches. Nobody could reasonably claim that we are short of academic work in this area – on the contrary, we have multiple literatures dedicated to markets and trade.

For all their profusion, these literatures are fragmented and disparate, hampered by the disciplinary divisions among social sciences. Each discipline generates its own theorising on markets, with few links to relevant theories elsewhere. New terminologies are forged, and internal debates conducted as private conversations between people in the same discipline. Compartmentalised thinking increases the dangers of overlaps, redundant terms, repetition and subjective originality. Parallels with related work are missed, as are opportunities for greater coherence. Disciplinary divisions create unnecessary variety of approach, beyond what is needed to understand markets.

A broad, cross-disciplinary stance would be desirable. By comparing the literatures, we can hope to find common ground and distinguish requisite from superfluous variety. Recognising key themes across disciplines would remove the need for each discipline to start from scratch and devise its own concepts. Harmony among 'non-economic' approaches to markets would strengthen their position against the 'economic' approach of orthodox economics. Many alternatives may give the appearance of no viable alternative, leaving the field clear for the orthodox, neoclassical view. While variety of ideas remains important, it can be counterproductive if it goes too far.

The current book adopts a wider perspective on markets than is common in most academic writing and, in doing so, aims to draw the heterodox and non-economic approaches closer together. It addresses basic definitional matters, considers the historical background to markets and identifies shared features in the different literatures. The potential richness of a coordinated alternative to orthodox economics is emphasised. The book proposes no grand synthesis of approaches but suggests that layered social theory can portray the diversity of trading arrangements. As an antidote to the reductionism of orthodox economics, it can highlight the social and institutional elements crucial to a proper understanding of markets and their place within the economy as a whole.

I am grateful to Tony Lawson for his support and to several anonymous referees for their valuable comments. My thanks are also due to the Routledge editorial and production staff, who have been helpful and efficient throughout this project.

William A. Jackson

Part I

What are markets?

1 Defining markets

Markets and trade have always been central to economic theory. Often the very idea of an economy is assumed to begin with trade that yields mutual gains for all. Economics teaching dwells at length on markets, as in the supply-and-demand diagram, the most widespread of textbook models. Since markets are so prominent, one might expect that they would be well defined. This is not the case, and economists seldom bother to define them or explore their background. They are mentioned frequently but casually, as if their meaning were obvious and required no further explanation.

The absence of an agreed definition sits oddly with the supposed rigour attained by economics. Markets are conflated with exchange, evading a proper definition adopted across the discipline (Hodgson, 1988, chapter 8, 2008; Sawyer, 1993; Sayer, 1995, chapter 4; Rosenbaum, 2000). Theoretical models focus on trade among rational agents and say little about markets *per se*. References to markets crop up randomly as a substitute for exchange or trade, without distinguishing features. Any trade can be classified as a market, which becomes a catch-all term that conveys little useful information. The origins and historical background of markets are not stressed in mainstream economics, nor are the variations in their details and operation. Hazy characterisation of markets opens the door for many inconsistencies.

Attempts to find a definition of markets must start with the linguistic sources of the word and its everyday usage. 'Market' derives from the Latin *mercatus* (trade), its first appearance in the English language going back to the medieval period, around the twelfth century (Davis, 1952; Aspers, 2011, chapter 1; Eagleton-Pierce, 2016, pp. 118–124). Early references to markets had a geographical aspect, such that the market was the physical location of trade. A medieval market town would have one or more open areas (market places) where traders in particular commodities could meet to conduct business. Prior agreement to meet at certain times and places suggests that markets must be organised and do not happen spontaneously. Market trade goes beyond a random encounter of two people who make a one-off trade: it implies regular, standardised trading on a large scale. From the outset, markets have been organised commerce rather than informal exchanges between individuals.

While the geographical meaning of a market can still sometimes apply, it has receded during economic development. Modern trade extends to national or international levels and has less need for a physical location – improved communication allows it to occur without meeting in person to transfer goods or money. The meaning of a market has broadened to cover trading for a particular commodity at any location. Markets are then delineated by the commodity traded, not the place of trade. Relaxing the geographical aspect leaves intact the significance of prior organisation, which if anything becomes more important as the size and complexity of the economy increases. In trying to find an all-purpose definition, one possibility is to regard markets as 'organised and institutionalised exchange' (Hodgson, 1988, chapter 8, 2008; Adams and Tiesdell, 2010). This distinguishes them from casual trading and does not restrict them to a certain place of trade. They become one kind of exchange among others, no longer equated loosely with any exchange.

The organised nature of markets narrows down their definition but remains vague about their structural details (Fourie, 1991; Jackson, 2007b; Fernández-Huerga, 2013; Ahrne, Aspers and Brunsson, 2015). Trade can be organised in different ways, and perhaps only some should be termed a market. Many questions go unanswered. What kind of organised trade do we mean? Does it have to be competitive? Can traders bargain and make personal arrangements? How are prices determined and how do they adjust? Are traders provided with the same accurate information? Can anyone enter or exit the market? Does a higher authority administer the market? A complete account would have to answer such questions and specify the organisation that separates market from non-market trade within the larger economy.

Markets in relation to production and consumption

The basic activities common to all economies are production, distribution and consumption. They are in a temporal sequence: goods are first produced, then distributed, then consumed. Trading is a distributive exercise, in that it does not entail production of new outputs or consumption of existing outputs. When trade occurs, some items are exchanged for others to bring about voluntary redistribution. The traders can be producers, consumers or intermediaries specialising in trade, hence the part played by trade in binding the economy together. Although trade spans the whole economy, it can best be classified as distribution and distinguished from production or consumption.

Distribution takes various forms, only some of which should be labelled as trading; examples of distribution without trade are communal sharing, gifts, governmental allocation and allocation by firms and other organisations. Trading stems from voluntary exchanges of property, whereby traders agree to reassign property rights. Exchange, like distribution, has many variants (Davis, 1992, chapter 2; Biggart and Delbridge, 2004; Hann, 2006). Markets can be interpreted as voluntary exchanges that are organised and institutionalised so as to ease trade. By this interpretation, they are a subset of exchange, which is a subset of distribution. Figure 1.1 shows the overall picture.

Distribution in Figure 1.1 refers to the allocation of goods or other resources among people or groups, irrespective of how this is accomplished. Exchange occurs when voluntary property transfers influence the final allocation – it is commonplace in modern economies but not universal. Much distribution within government, firms and households goes ahead without exchange and without markets. To have agreed, binding exchanges presupposes property rights, so that participants abide by the property transfer. This necessitates both property law, defining the rights of property ownership, and contract law, regulating voluntary transfers of property (Commons, 1924; Prasch, 2008, part 1). Involuntary transfers will break the rules and be declared illegal as theft, burglary, fraud, etc.

Markets in Figure 1.1 are organised and institutionalised exchanges, as distinct from less formal exchanges, such as reciprocal gifts, personal trading relations and bargaining. They have never become so prevalent that they entirely displace non-market exchange. As Figure 1.1 attests, they are less fundamental to the economy than one might think from economics textbooks and should not be accorded primacy.

Defining markets as organised and institutionalised exchange may be too broad to have real discriminating power. Almost all exchange will be organised to at least a minimal degree, and the market/non-market distinction may turn upon the nature of organisation as against its existence. A more satisfactory definition should arguably go further and specify the organisational details that distinguish a market. This is far from straightforward. The fact that few textbook writers address the question, which would seem vital to an introductory treatment of economics, indicates the difficulties.

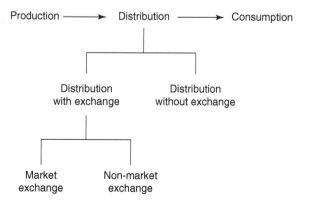

Figure 1.1 Markets, exchange and distribution.

Attributes of markets

What, then, are the organisational and institutional attributes of a market that distinguish it from non-market exchange? Table 1.1 sets out some institutional features often associated with markets. In the earliest definitions of markets, they are a location for trade. At one time, it would have been a physical location; nowadays it may be virtual or electronic, as in financial markets or internet auction sites. Markets should facilitate trade by being accessible to potential traders – closing access off for any reason will breach the spirit of market trading. Each market should generate a known price or rate of exchange for a certain good. Public availability of reliable information on goods and prices is among the main features of a market. Also pertinent is an acceptable and feasible payment method. Transfers of goods on a market must be carried out either at the location of trade or through some other mode of delivery. Regulation ensures that property transfers are lawful; arbitration resolves trade disputes.

Insisting on the features in Table 1.1 would not provide an agreed market definition. What we call a 'market' in common usage may miss out on some of them. Barriers to entry, for example, are legion and deny open access to trade but are treated as compatible with market status. Many markets have differentiated products, no standardised prices and poorly informed buyers. Regulation is another variable. Only a fraction of trade in the real world possesses the full set of market features. There can be no simple checklist of attributes that define a market.

Alternatively, we can look towards the characteristics of market trade, rather than the market itself, as in Table 1.2. Market trade should be voluntary for all participants and a two-way exchange of one item for another. Money is normally the medium of exchange, which enables traders to perform repeatable transactions. Standardised goods are bought and sold at published prices. Nobody should be excluded from trading, which depends only on the ability and willingness to pay. Traders are supposed to care only about the item traded and its price, so they do not form personal relationships with trading partners. The impersonal quality of

Table 1.1 Institutional features of a market

Location	A physical or other location for trade is provided.
Access	Trade is open to anyone wishing to participate.
Pricing	Goods are exchanged at a standardised monetary price.
Information	Accurate details of goods and prices are published.
Payment	There is an agreed and acceptable payment method.
Delivery	Arrangements are made for the delivery of traded goods.
Regulation	Rules are in place for lawful property transfers and good trading practices.
Arbitration	Procedures are agreed and implemented for resolution of trade disputes.

Table 1.2 Characteristics of market trade

Voluntary	Transactions are voluntary, with no compulsion on either sellers or buyers.
Two-way	One item is exchanged for another, so reciprocation is formally required.
Monetary	Money is the medium of exchange and means of payment.
Repeatable	Exchanges are not unique, one-off events and can be repeated.
Standardised	Items traded have common properties and uniform, published prices.
Open	Entry and exit from the market is open to all, subject to ability to pay.
Impersonal	Trading decisions turn on the items traded, not relationships among traders.
Competitive	Traders compete for the best possible deal, especially on price.

market trade opens it up to competitive behaviour, where people switch trading partners to get a better deal.

The characteristics in Table 1.2 are frequent assumptions about markets, though not always explicit. Doubt persists about whether some of the characteristics are necessary for a market definition. Trade without money (barter) would usually be classified as non-market exchange, though the exact meaning of barter has been contentious (Chapman, 1980; Dalton, 1982; Humphrey and Hugh-Jones, 1992; Heady, 2005). Trade described as a market may not have all the characteristics in Table 1.2. Products and prices are often differentiated, so there is no standardisation; entry to an established market can be troublesome and closed off to many; traders may know each other in ongoing relationships; and trading may entail market power that dampens competition.

If we imposed all the characteristics in Table 1.2 as prerequisites for a market, then many exchanges in the real world would not qualify and we would have to find another descriptor for them. A stringent, purist attitude could result in a near-empty set that has few if any members among existing arrangements. Workable approaches should aim for defining characteristics that are not too exclusive and find agreement among economists and the public.

A possible way forward is to have both 'weak' definitions of markets that correspond to everyday language and 'strong' definitions that correspond to ideal markets (Jackson, 2007b). Of the characteristics in Table 1.2, the first four could give a weak definition, as most trading activities termed a market can be said to be voluntary, two-way, monetary and repeatable. These characteristics would not be unduly restrictive and would improve the chances of general agreement. A strong definition would have a longer list of prerequisites, maybe the full set in Table 1.2. This would give a tighter definition but would exclude many trades from market status.

Having weak and strong definitions could resolve some of the tensions and clarify the issues. One should remember, though, that any attempt at a market definition has no official standing and is unlikely to find widespread approval.

Another approach is to avoid having a market/non-market boundary and instead seek a scale of 'marketness' that ranks trading by its market-like features (Heydebrand, 1989; Block 1990, chapter 3, 1991; Storbacka and Nenonen 2011a, 2011b). Cases at the top of the scale would have features typically associated with markets, such as price competition, many participants, anonymous trading, free entry and exit and homogeneous products. Cases at the bottom would have no price competition, few participants, relationships among agents, barriers to entry and customised products. In between the two poles come intermediate cases with some market-like features but not others. A marketness scale recognises the ambiguity surrounding markets by escaping the need for a perimeter wall around them. Observed behaviour is either more or less market-like, without the insistence on a binary division.

Problems remain, however, and assessing marketness is awkward. There will be no consensus on the market-like features to be included in the scale. Several scales could be formulated, whose rankings would not coincide. Inconsistency among marketness scales could be just as great as among market/non-market boundaries. A further problem is that a scale sends the message that the top of the scale is the only true market, all other cases being inferior. The implicit benchmark undermines parity. A market/non-market boundary would, by contrast, give unqualified market status to a wider range of cases.

Theoretical accounts of markets

Difficulties in defining markets create space for variety in theorising about them. If market trade has fluid characteristics, then theorists may pick out different characteristics and portray markets in alternative ways. Diversity among theoretical approaches can be desirable in capturing the complexity and multiplicity of actual trading, since varied subject matter may require varied theoretical responses. This goes against the grain for orthodox economics, which prefers to have a single model of trading based on rational behaviour. Variations in trade are represented as divergences from the ideal and do not lead to alternative theories.

Orthodox theorising about markets rests on a strong definition taking in the full list of characteristics in Table 1.2. The core model assumes rational behaviour, full information, price competition and market-clearing equilibrium. Under these assumptions, neoclassical theory yields a perfectly competitive market with allocative efficiency. The model is often admitted to be rarefied and unrealistic, yet it is still presumed to distil the essence of how markets are constituted and how they should operate. Particular details of markets, such as their institutional background and social context, are omitted and treated as secondary. When actual markets differ from the ideal, the theorist merely drops a few assumptions and turns to imperfect special cases. The pared-down image fosters a logical, axiomatic method capable of mathematical expression. Rigorous formal analysis of a single, adaptable model is the touchstone.

Heterodoxy has favoured weaker market definitions that invoke only some of the characteristics in Table 1.2. Markets are not tied to an ideal case and come closer to everyday language. The institutional background of trade can be highlighted, as can differences in behaviour among traders – there is no template for how we should trade. In place of a single account of markets comes a more spacious view that takes in diverse forms of trade, all of which can be described as markets. A pure competitive market, if it did exist, would be one case among others and have no prestige. Diversity of markets, once properly appreciated, should call forth diversity in the theoretical attempts to interpret them.

The key point here is that no single model can encompass the entirety of trading behaviour. Given that markets have proved so difficult to define, they will not be depicted satisfactorily by an abstract theory. Economic orthodoxy has a vested professional interest in promoting its own approach as the only viable option but has failed to prevent the emergence of many alternatives. Dependence on a core market model has impoverished discussion of markets among orthodox economists and has encouraged false conclusions about efficiency and self-regulation. We can better understand markets by opening up to greater pluralism in how we portray them.

Alternatives to the orthodox account of markets exist in profusion, spread across separate literatures in heterodox economics (institutionalist, Marxian, Post Keynesian, Austrian, etc.) and in branches of other social sciences (economic sociology, economic anthropology, economic geography, etc.). These literatures seldom cite each other or seek a unified stance – division dilutes them and weakens their challenge to orthodoxy. Pluralism of economic theory may be warranted in many respects, but it can give an impression of theoretical incoherence that puts heterodox economics at a strategic disadvantage compared with the monism of orthodoxy (Jackson, 2018). Without wanting to impose a single theoretical scheme, it would be sensible to take stock of the common elements in the alternatives to orthodoxy, build upon them and reduce the duplication of ideas and terminology. Few surveys of market theories have been cross-disciplinary, as most theorists have worked within one discipline or school of thought. The present book offers a broad, comparative appraisal of how economists and others have theorised about markets.

Aims and structure of the book

The main aims of the book are to:

- Emphasise the diversity of markets in the real world, along with their historical background, institutional context and interdependence with non-market sectors of the economy.
- Show the narrowness and inadequacy of neoclassical economic theory as a guide for studying markets.
- Demonstrate the array of alternative perspectives on markets, contrary to the monistic account in orthodox economics.
- Examine the main heterodox approaches to markets, identify common traits and consider the case for a unified alternative to orthodoxy.
- Argue that layered and non-reductionist social theory, sensitive to social and cultural matters, can provide a suitable framework for heterodox views of markets.

The book has four parts. Part I comprises this chapter on the definition of markets and Chapter 2 on the orthodox approach. After giving a more detailed critique of neoclassical theory, Chapter 2 discusses orthodox views that have imperfections and variations on the ideal. While the divergences from the ideal are welcome, the models are hampered by retaining perfect competition as the benchmark.

Part II delves into the historical background of markets. Chapter 3 covers their origins during the pre-capitalist era, while Chapter 4 traces the effects of capitalism in spawning markets for labour, property and finance. Together, the two chapters bring out the long history of market trade, which goes back much further than capitalism or economic theory.

Part III evaluates alternatives to the orthodox approach, classified under the headings of social/cultural, structural, functional and ethical. These four categories are not intended to be mutually exclusive (so some theories may belong to more than one category) but reflect prominent themes in how heterodox economics and other social sciences have handled markets. Chapter 5 deals with approaches sceptical of a self-contained theory of markets and arguing for a historically specific outlook attuned to social and cultural context. Chapter 6 examines theories that see the institutional and social structure of markets, not rational individual agency, as the platform for theorising about them. Chapter 7 addresses theories that revolve around the functions of markets – it considers the purpose of money and prices, the decentralisation made feasible by markets and their value in coordinating information and stimulating entrepreneurship. Chapter 8 broaches the ethical implications of markets, the moral limits to trade and consequences for inequality and economic development.

Part IV offers further discussion of the variety and context of markets. Chapter 9 ponders the prospects for using a layered or stratified scheme based on non-reductionist social theory to embrace diversity in trade. Chapter 10 places markets within the total economy, investigates their connections with non-market and informal economic activities and considers their relation to the macroeconomic level of the economy as a whole.

2   The orthodox approach

The orthodox approach to markets is based on the neoclassical theory that first appeared in the late nineteenth century and came to dominate economics in the twentieth century (Screpanti and Zamagni, 2005, chapter 6; Arnsperger and Varoufakis, 2006; Rima, 2009, part 4; Lawson, 2013; Morgan, 2016). Despite being abstract and stylised, neoclassical ideas supposedly sum up economic behaviour at all times and places. Rational individual agents pursue their own interests; their actions are coordinated through voluntary exchange under competitive conditions. Exchange becomes the kernel of the economy, and the resulting 'markets' have strong equilibrating tendencies. Market-clearing equilibrium is the solution concept for neoclassical theory, on which many formal theorems depend.

This approach has not always been dominant and differs from that adopted by Adam Smith, David Ricardo and other classical economists (Screpanti and Zamagni, 2005, chapters 2 and 3; Rima, 2009, part 2; Stilwell, 2011, part 3). Classical political economy emphasises production and reproduction, rather than exchange or resource allocation, and argues that prices converge on natural or normal levels that maintain factor incomes and permit a surplus. Changes in demand may shift prices away from the natural level, but an eventual supply adjustment restores the natural price (Garegnani, 1998; Martins, 2014, chapter 1). There are no independent supply and demand curves and no market-clearing equilibrium. Any equilibria are weaker than the neoclassical ones, attained by capital mobility that equalises the profit rate but does not remove the surplus or market power. As the surplus is the source of capital accumulation and economic growth, competitive trading will never eliminate profits: the abnormal profits of neoclassical terminology are normal in a classical model. With supply-and-demand analysis missing, markets no longer have the neoclassical properties of market clearing and allocative efficiency.

Modern orthodox economics says nothing about classical political economy, on the premise that neoclassical theory has replaced classical. Teaching of economics proceeds in the style of natural sciences, where later theories supersede earlier ones as the discipline evolves. Classical political economy has been relegated to the history of economic thought, a minority, specialist interest (Blaug, 2001; Kurz, 2006). Heterodox economists have queried the rejection of classical theory, together with the belief that neoclassicism represents an improvement (De Vroey, 1975; Nell, 1980; Birken, 1988; Milonakis and Fine, 2009). From their standpoint, neoclassicism succeeded in taking over the economics profession but was never the best way to theorise – its professional success was for practical as against fundamental reasons (natural science emulation, desire for mathematical methods, imposition of disciplinary boundaries, dislike for Marxian versions of classical theory, avoidance of awkward political issues, etc.). Hence, even at this late stage, we should rethink the foundations of economic theory. The present chapter examines in further detail the orthodox approach to markets, along with the problems identified by critics and the limited attempts within the mainstream to address these problems.

The neoclassical view of markets

From the outset, we should note that the neoclassical view is not a theory of markets as such, given that they remain poorly defined. Orthodox theorists have devoted little effort to explaining what markets are, how they originated, why they endure, how they operate in practice, why they may be diverse and how they relate to the rest of the economy. The chief concern has been to apply neoclassical theory to trade, buttressing the neoclassical perspective. Any particular market must be a microcosm of the broader vision, perhaps with a few quirks or imperfections but portrayable using neoclassical theory. At the heart lies instrumentally rational behaviour such that agents pursue fixed ends in a consistent, efficient manner represented as the maximisation of an objective function (Hodgson, 1988, chapter 4; Hargreaves Heap, 1989, chapter 3; Zafirovski, 2003a). This account of rationality, coupled with individualism, engenders the model of 'economic man', the wellspring of all economic behaviour. Markets are no exception and, indeed, constitute the main channel for rational choices.

Two elements govern market trading in neoclassical eyes. The first is the decision on which goods to sell or buy. Rational agents are assumed to have fixed preferences across the full range of goods and services, so that they can allocate their resources to maximise utility. They will not make mistakes, change their minds or be swayed by random impulses and emotions. Modelling is timeless, as if confined to a single period, and the 'black-box' method ignores the biological and social processes of ageing (Jackson, 1991, 1998, chapter 3). Since the origin of preferences goes unexplained, the cultural background to trading plays no part in the analysis. Agents have enough information about the items being traded to make accurate decisions. External pressures from trends and fashions are absent, as are influences exerted by advertisers, marketers and salespeople. Advertising, if it has a place in orthodox modelling, must be an information source that permits better-informed decisions without creating or changing preferences (Nelson, 1974; Stigler and Becker, 1977). The individualistic method implies that rational traders exist independently and do not interact to change each other's preferences. Rational agents making decisions alone become the foundation for market models.

The second element is the price at which trades are conducted. Rational traders seek the best available price for a particular item: sellers the highest, buyers the lowest. The decision on price is distinct from the decision on goods traded, so prices should not hint at unobservable characteristics of goods. Traders already have full information about goods, which lets them make proper comparisons and select the best prices for homogeneous items. Rational decisions on price are vital to the price competition so important for the neoclassical model. Wherever traders seek the best price, it will be difficult to sustain price differentials: all traders will converge on the best trading option, and inferior alternatives will wither away. By the 'law of one price' a single, distinct price should emerge for each good being traded (Isard, 1977; Richardson, 1978; Miljkovic, 1999). Multiple prices would suggest irrational behaviour or a market imperfection.

Rational agents should, in theory, drift spontaneously towards trade. Recognising the potential gains, they will go ahead and transact. Gains are predicted to be almost universal (theory of comparative advantage), so failure to trade is irrational or due to some impediment. Markets derive from collectively rational behaviour driven by the preferences of the traders themselves. The impulse to trade, which covers all goods and services, should be omnipresent. Nothing much is said about the property rights and other institutions that underlie markets: the theory overlooks them. Any institution that interfered with rational trading decisions would be harmful, for it would threaten the gains from trade and reduce the volume of trading. Markets are synonymous with trade or exchange, the terms being equivalent – there is no systematic distinction between market and non-market exchange. All rational trading gives rise to a 'market'.

Decisions by rational agents in response to prices underpin the theoretical models. For any single good, trading decisions can be aggregated into supply and demand curves – supply increases with price as rational sellers seek higher prices, and demand decreases as rational buyers seek lower prices. In the familiar textbook diagram, the two curves intersect at a market-clearing equilibrium that equates supply with demand. The equilibrium will be stable as long as excess supply leads to a fall in price and excess demand to a rise in price. Agents on both sides of the market are price takers who trade only by price and act independently, with no collusion or cooperation. This is the partial equilibrium model, set out by Alfred Marshall (1890–1920) and used endlessly in the orthodox literature. The partial nature of the model confines it to a single market. Price effects across different markets must be negligible.

Interdependencies among markets extend the analysis from the single-market case with partial equilibrium to the many-market case with general equilibrium (Walras, 1926; Van Daal and Jolink, 1993). A fully adjusted outcome should now be a set of equilibrium prices that clears all markets simultaneously. The possibility of prices in one market affecting supply and demand in other markets makes this far more intricate than the partial-equilibrium case: proving existence and stability of general equilibrium has always been a challenge (Ackerman, 2002; Ackerman and Nadal, 2004; Kirman, 2006). If a well-behaved general equilibrium can be attained, then it represents the ideal of an exchange economy with rational trading and coordination through markets.

Efficiency of rational trading is expressed in the notion of perfect competition, which disseminates the features of pure competitive trading to all markets across the whole economy (atomistic traders, homogeneous products, rationality, full information, price taking, free entry and exit, zero transaction costs, market clearing) (Stigler, 1957; McDermott, 2015). By the fundamental theorems of welfare economics, perfect competition is Pareto efficient (first theorem) and can reach any Pareto-efficient position, given the ability to reassign resource endowments (second theorem) (Blaug, 2007). The normative results link competitive trading with allocative efficiency, encapsulating the neoclassical arguments for exchange through markets. Anything that hampers competitive markets will be harmful, as it causes Pareto inefficiency that erodes the gains from trade.

In perfect competition, everybody trades at the equilibrium price for a particular good and nobody has market power. Any trader diverging from the efficient price (sellers trying for higher prices, buyers lower prices) would be ejected from the market, as their competitors offer better terms. All traders must abide by the equilibrium price, which emerges from the separate, uncoordinated decisions of autonomous traders. Factors of production in this exchange economy are priced like any other goods and receive just enough return to guarantee their continued supply. Firms make normal profits sufficient to maintain the supply of capital but cannot make a surplus or abnormal profit.

This is a major difference from classical political economy, which emphasised the surplus as the source of capital accumulation (Garegnani, 1987; Ciccone, 1994; Bortis, 1997, chapter 3; Martins, 2014, chapter 1). From the classical perspective, an economy whose surplus was wiped out by price competition would be unable to invest or accumulate capital – economic growth would grind to a halt. The neoclassical ideal of a surplus-free economy is hard to reconcile with the expansion of capital that characterises any capitalist system. In their basic assumptions, classical and neoclassical theory are at odds with each other. Table 2.1 summarises the differences between them.

Classical political economy was concerned with economic development at the national level (the 'wealth of nations'), for which it needed

Table 2.1 Classical and neoclassical economic theory contrasted

	Classical	Neoclassical
Main focus	Economic reproduction and growth	Resource allocation
Primary economic activity	Production	Exchange
Core theoretical element	Economic classes	Individual agents
Economic surplus	Permanent and normal	Abnormal
Nature of competition	Capital mobility and non-price competition	Price competition
Equilibrium concept	Profit-rate equalisation	Market clearing
Properties of equilibrium	No efficiency properties	Pareto efficiency

to examine the factor distribution of income between wages, profit and rent, with profit as the source of investment and capital accumulation. Profits come from the surplus, so competition cannot go as far as to put the surplus in danger. Capital will move into existing profit centres, leading to profit-rate equalisation, but will be drained by price competition that would lower the total surplus. The surplus is ongoing, with no tendencies for it to be removed in the interests of allocative efficiency.

Neoclassical theory is in some ways diametrically opposed to classical. It focuses on exchange, not production or development, and begins with individual agents, not factor shares or economic classes. Markets interpreted loosely as exchange provide the venue for competition through pricing, which in equilibrium generates market clearing and zero abnormal profit. The static modelling portrays the economy as an efficient mechanism for allocating resources. Although markets take centre stage, they are perceived in a thin, simplified manner that relies heavily on the benchmark of perfect competition. Increased attention to markets is cramped by a narrow theoretical vision.

Problems with the orthodox approach

The axioms of neoclassical theory were first put forward as modest and tentative abstractions. John Stuart Mill, said to be the inventor of 'economic man', was circumspect about the concept and admitted its limitations (Blaug, 1992, chapter 3; Persky, 1995). Alfred Marshall, who popularised the supply-and-demand model, was wary of overextending it and sought to maintain ties with biology and other disciplines (Thomas, 1991; Hodgson, 1993, chapter 7). Léon Walras, the founder of general equilibrium theory, was careful to qualify its relevance and avoid exaggerating its applicability to the real world (Jaffé, 1975; Cirillo, 1984; Jolink, 1996, chapter 2). This early ambivalence has been lost – ideas once speculative have solidified into core doctrines enshrined in textbooks and taught to students as the only way to practise economics (the 'economic way of thinking'). As their originators surmised, the core components of neoclassical theory are questionable even in their primary application to market exchange.

Pivotal to the orthodox approach is the rational individual trader attaining the best possible outcome. To model this formally requires strong assumptions that clear the path for optimal choices on a small number of dimensions. The method is to assume homogeneous goods in a market, holding the quality constant and allowing a simplified trading decision based on price alone. Rational trading becomes a straightforward exercise in finding the best price, with other criteria removed from the decision, so the informational background shrinks to the price dimension. Everything else is debarred.

If other dimensions vary, as they do in reality, then trading is nowhere near as simple, and rational trade becomes blurred (Prasch, 1995). Among non-price dimensions of trade are characteristics of the goods traded, traders' knowledge of these characteristics, the identities of the traders, relationships between traders, means of payment and timing of payment. People do not trade by price alone, so rational trading must compromise between many variable factors, not all of which are easily knowable. Trading will be diverse – what is rational for some traders will not be rational for others. Greater complexity implies that traders, discouraged from deliberating about every decision, resort to habits or routines (Biggart and Beamish, 2003). Orthodoxy presumes that markets are the epitome of rational economic behaviour, but experience will not necessarily bear this out. A fuller account of market trade would tone down the insistence on rationality.

Agents in orthodox modelling have fixed preferences that predate involvement in the market and remain unaffected by trade. Markets can then become the arena in which traders express their preferences independently to secure mutually beneficial results. Sellers and buyers make uncoordinated decisions; the market itself is the only coordinating mechanism, allegedly the best. Nothing is said about the origin of the fixed individual preferences, which is not seen as crucial to an understanding of markets. In an implicit sequence, preference formation comes before participation in trade. Neoclassical theory abstracts from the cultural questions of how social context moulds individual behaviour and views this as the province of other social sciences (Davis, 2003, chapter 2, 2011, chapter 1; Jackson, 2013). Fixity of preferences during trade is a dubious assumption. Marketing of products makes a conscious effort to influence preferences and create demand. Advertising goes far beyond improving information for rational consumers and aims to change consumer attitudes by playing upon reason, habit and emotions (Galbraith, 1969, chapter 11; Stanfield and Stanfield, 1980; Hodgson, 2003b; De Mooij, 2011, chapter 5). As against responding to existing preferences, markets may be the result of preference formation by traders. Whenever sellers and buyers interact consciously, they may be engaged in persuasion that hopes to influence the preferences of their trading partner. The extent of this will vary, but it is widespread and should not be brushed aside.

Coordination of individual trading decisions in the neoclassical framework occurs through market-clearing equilibrium, a further problem area. Even if all traders did behave in the approved fashion, markets might not equate supply and demand. At the level of abstract theory, the existence and stability of market-clearing equilibrium have been hard to prove in general (Kirman, 1989; Rizvi, 1994; Katzner, 2001, 2008; Lee and Keen, 2004; Hahnel, 2007; Benicourt and Guerrien, 2008). A theory that works poorly under its own stylised assumptions is unlikely to be a reliable guide to reality. In the neoclassical benchmark, every trader must be a price taker who has no market power and just reacts to equilibrium prices. Because nobody sets the prices, it remains unclear where they come from, other than the mysterious invisible hand.

Critics of neoclassicism stress the prevalence of market power and price setting by traders (Sawyer, 1993; Lee, 1998; Downward, 1999; Lee and Keen, 2004; Jo, 2016). Competitive pricing in the neoclassical ideal would drive the surplus made by producers/sellers down to zero, eliminating abnormal profit. Yet actual producers make regular profits over long periods, thanks to market power, product differentiation, brand loyalty, etc. As proponents of a surplus approach have always maintained, the surplus is normal to capitalist economies (Garegnani, 1987; Ciccone, 1994; Martins, 2018). A permanent surplus overturns many features of the ideal neoclassical world: market power is the norm, markets do not clear, supply and demand are ill-defined, resources are not scarce relative to productive capacity and unemployment persists.

The orthodox approach asserts that competitive markets, if left alone, are efficient. Such conclusions rest on the flimsy foundations of perfect competition, subject to all its difficulties. Taking the neoclassical ideal too seriously leads one towards *laissez-faire* and market deregulation. The perils from such policy advice have been illustrated by the recent global financial crisis and its aftermath. Deregulation of financial markets in the 1980s was justified by orthodox theory through the 'efficient-markets hypothesis': financial markets relieved of government intervention would, it was said, yield stable, efficient outcomes (Crotty, 2009; Kotz, 2009; Keen, 2011, chapter 11). Instead of calm, efficient trade, the reforms ushered in a frenzied expansion accompanied by growing financial instability that culminated in the 2008 crash and subsequent recession. Far from being self-regulating, the financial system had to be rescued by government intervention and underwritten by tax revenues (Davidoff and Zaring,

2009; Mishkin, 2011). These policy errors – a repeat of earlier ones in the 1920s and 1930s – would not have happened if the neoclassical fantasy of pure competitive markets had been rejected.

Many mainstream economists, conceding the unrealistic character of perfect competition, wish to insert greater realism into orthodox modelling. The ideal competitive case is not abandoned, retaining its honoured place as an exemplar in textbooks, but takes a back seat when theory is applied to practical issues. In order to cope with the complexities of the real world, the theory has to be adapted from its purest form by relaxing the less plausible assumptions. The two main strands of qualified orthodoxy are imperfectionism, where various imperfections are added to the neoclassical model, and mainstream pluralism, where standard components of neoclassical theory are temporarily omitted.

Imperfectionism

Whatever its theoretical attractions, perfect competition exists only as an abstract ideal divorced from reality. Actual market trading is never perfect in any sense. If neoclassical theory is to be more realistic, it must recognise market imperfections or failures. This style of analysis, sometimes termed 'imperfectionism' in the heterodox literature, fuels much theoretical work in applied orthodox economics (Eatwell and Milgate, 1983; Eatwell, 1987b). Allowing for imperfections reduces the emphasis on perfect competition but keeps faith with the neoclassical model of trade. Imperfect cases are inferior to perfect ones, so gains could be made if the imperfections were removed.

A prime example of imperfectionism is the structure-conduct-performance framework, which has been central to industrial economics (Bain, 1959; Scherer, 1980). Several market structures are assumed to exist on a scale from perfect competition at one pole to monopoly at the other, with imperfect competition and oligopoly as intermediate cases (see Figure 2.1). Analysis of an industry or market starts by selecting the right market structure on the scale, determined by the number and size of the firms involved. Most markets fall into the categories of imperfect competition or oligopoly, such that firms possess market power but are not monopolies. Once the market structure has been selected, the next step is to examine the conduct of firms within that structure – firms outside perfect competition are no longer price takers and interact consciously with their rivals in price setting and other decisions. With knowledge of structure and conduct, the analyst can assess the industry's performance, in a sequence from structure to conduct to performance. The benefit of this approach for orthodoxy is that it accommodates realistic special cases and yet stays within the orbit of neoclassical economics.

Among the problems of the structure-conduct-performance framework is that it does not classify market structures neutrally: the perfectly competitive

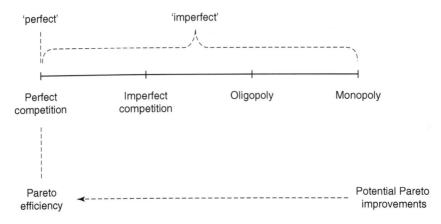

Figure 2.1 Market structures and imperfectionism.

pole must be the best outcome, as it is the only one that displays Pareto efficiency. All other market structures are imperfect and cause efficiency losses. In Figure 2.1, a movement from right to left towards perfect competition brings a potential Pareto improvement in which everybody can be better off. Notwithstanding the admission that perfect competition is rare, it stands acclaimed as the universal benchmark. The other market structures, far more common, are downgraded to being flawed special cases.

Terminology that juxtaposes perfection with imperfection is especially unhelpful and clashes with the initial meaning of 'imperfect competition'. The term was coined by Joan Robinson (1933, 1953), who produced a general theory of competition under market power – in her usage, all competition is imperfect. This was lost on orthodox economists, who preferred to see perfect and imperfect competition as alternative cases on a scale. For heterodox economists, perfect competition should be discarded as misleading and tendentious, whereas orthodoxy wants to keep it at the core of economic analysis.

Another drawback of the structure-conduct-performance framework is that it gives a static view of markets with fixed categories (Sawyer, 1985a, chapter 10). There is no history of how markets emerge and evolve within a capitalist economy. Market structures are the setting for trade but remain exogenous. Rivalry and competition among firms occurs within stable market structures that may survive for long periods. Possibilities for firms to gain or lose market power receive little attention, so the same firms apparently have a permanent presence. This differs from the heterodox literature, where increasing returns to scale are taken to be widespread; in monopoly capital models, for example, competition evolves towards oligopoly as large firms win the battle and crowd out smaller firms (Baran and Sweezy, 1966; Sawyer, 1988; Foster, 2014). Increasing returns will impart a motion from left to right in Figure 2.1, the opposite direction from that implied by gains from trade in a neoclassical model. Competition may induce fluid outcomes characterised by rapid technical changes, new products and shifting market power.

All versions of imperfectionism add restrictions to neoclassical theory and make it more complicated. The imperfections are dealt with one at a time under the assumption that all else remains the same (*ceteris paribus*). While this method may make formal analysis feasible, it has little value as a guide for interpreting the real world. According to the 'theory of second best', efficiency conditions derived under particular restrictions will have no relevance beyond the case in question (Lipsey and Lancaster, 1956; Davis and Whinston, 1965, 1967; Lipsey, 2007). Results for one-at-a-time imperfections cannot be extended to cases with many simultaneous imperfections. In reality, imperfections do not arise one by one, and multiple divergences from the ideal will preclude general results. The real world is too complex to be handled adequately by mathematical modelling, but orthodox economics, in thrall to mathematical methods, seems unlikely ever to acknowledge this.

With perfect competition as their ideal case, imperfectionist models may implant a bias towards *laissez-faire* policies. If we take the models at face value, then the recommended policy would be to get as close as possible to the perfectly competitive pole by lifting regulations on trade and letting markets operate freely. Such arguments can be seen in Chicago School libertarianism, which utilises neoclassical theory and plays down the practical importance of market failures (Friedman, 1962; Van Horn and Mirowski, 2009; Emmett, 2010). Most orthodox economists do not travel this far and regard market imperfections as major issues that warrant government intervention. Neoclassical theory in its imperfectionist mode can support various political stances, as is clear from the policy disagreements among orthodox economists.

The neoclassical model of market trade does, nevertheless, have the inbuilt property that the perfectly competitive case is superior to the others. Anyone arguing for government intervention will have to use imperfect special cases, whereas free-market economists can use the general model and merely argue for removal of imperfections. The models required to justify intervention will be tortuous, inelegant and second-best, as compared with the simple elegance of perfect competition. Orthodox economic theory makes life easier for libertarians than those of other political persuasions.

Mainstream pluralism

Awareness among mainstream economists of the faults of neoclassical theory has led to a broadening out in recent years, seen in the willingness to relax assumptions and explore different ideas. Several new branches of mainstream economics have arisen, which stay in touch with neoclassical theory but move away from standard assumptions: examples are behavioural economics, new institutional economics, experimental economics, neuroeconomics and game-theoretical approaches. Described as 'mainstream pluralism', they adopt pluralistic language without going as far as to part company with the mainstream (Colander, Holt and Rosser, 2004; Davis, 2006, 2007; Cedrini and Fontana, 2018). Mainstream pluralists are anxious to avoid any taint of heterodoxy. The ideas invoked permit internal pluralism that does not break the mould of orthodox theory, leading to adaptations rather than outright rejection. External pluralism, by contrast, cannot be housed within mainstream economics, and reaches out into heterodox economics and the other social sciences.

Will mainstream pluralism overhaul the orthodox treatment of markets? Rethinking assumptions does, in principle, give room for a less blinkered view. If instrumental rationality is relaxed, then there can be variety in how agents trade and how they engage with markets. If the institutional context is considered, then the nature of markets and their interplay with non-market institutions can be modelled more satisfactorily. Such initiatives are a step in the right direction but do not amount to a genuine alternative. Mainstream pluralism is still tethered to the neoclassical reference point, which preserves its mainstream status and will not change how markets are portrayed. To illustrate this, it is worth briefly looking at behavioural economics and new institutional economics, two prime examples of mainstream pluralism.

Behavioural economics seeks psychological insights into economic behaviour that can improve upon instrumental rationality (Kahneman, 2003; Camerer and Loewenstein, 2004; Thaler, 2017). Experimental evidence from studies of decision making (along with casual observation) suggests that people do not always act optimally (Simon, 1959, 1986; Gintis, 2000; DellaVigna, 2009; Karacuka and Zaman, 2012). The capacity for consistent, accurate decisions, as if an objective function was being maximised, may be slender, so that people have bounded rationality. They simplify their decisions through heuristics or rules of thumb, attaining adequate but not necessarily optimal outcomes (Tversky and Kahneman, 1974; Kahneman, Slovic and Tversky, 1982). Perceptions of a complex reality are framed through simplified images and stereotypes that mirror aspects of the real world but do not give a complete picture (Tversky and Kahneman, 1981). The movement away from instrumental rationality brings non-rational, habitual and emotional behaviour into economic decisions, casting doubt on the neoclassical model. Even if people are encouraged to be rational, they fail to match 'economic man'.

When applied to markets, doubts about economic rationality disturb the prospects for competitive trading. In place of well-informed rationality focused on prices, we may have various modes of trading, not all of them rational or efficient. The net outcome may be at odds with the stable, efficient equilibria predicted by neoclassical theory. Such reasoning can be found in behavioural finance, which has queried the reliance of financial theory on rational trading, in favour of a richer portrayal of behaviour (Shleifer, 2000; Barberis and Thaler, 2003; Bloomfield, 2008). Practical experience shows that financial markets do not operate in a stable, orderly manner and are often turbulent. Traders make systematic errors. With behaviour below the rational ideal, the market will not settle down to a single, efficient price. Behavioural finance pays heed to the psychology of traders in explaining bubbles and crashes as well as stable equilibria. The wilful responses of traders may be due to bounded rationality among investors, overconfidence during boom periods, imitation of other traders (herding behaviour) and idiosyncratic decisions (noise trading). Admitting these influences offers a more satisfactory account of finance, capable of embracing the frequent cases when things do not adjust smoothly and errors are made. Analysis has to be localised and piecemeal, given that financial markets do not fit a global template.

While it can address some inadequacies of neoclassical theory, behavioural economics has trouble providing a thoroughgoing alternative. Its vision remains individualistic, as it seeks to improve upon the neoclassical account of individual behaviour but does not stretch much further. The interdisciplinary outreach is slim, confined to a few strands of psychology that mesh with individualism. Little is said about social structures or how society moulds individual behaviour, and the analysis is not integrated into a structural approach. For all its critical commentary on neoclassical theory, behavioural economics stops short of making a clean break from orthodox economics (Sent, 2004; Dequech, 2007; Santos, 2011). Individualism stays intact, with the only changes being different assumptions about behaviour. This may shed light on trading and improve upon the neoclassical model, but it is not going to transform how we understand markets.

The new institutional economics responds to the perceived lack of institutional detail in neoclassical theory. Starting with the standard neoclassical model, it asks how economic decision making may be influenced by institutions, which are defined as informal social norms or formal legal rules (Williamson, 2000; Ménard and Shirley, 2005; Brousseau and Glachant, 2008). Theory augmented in this way can appreciate many social and institutional facets of economic behaviour otherwise missing from orthodox analysis. Items that can be added to the modelling include varied organisational and contractual forms, asymmetric information, bounded rationality, social norms and values, strategic interactions and external governance. The added elements create adapted models for particular cases without leaving mainstream economics: the aim is not to overturn the mainstream but to upgrade it to incorporate institutions. New institutionalism can be contrasted with the older version in the spirit of Thorstein Veblen and John Commons, who overtly rejected neoclassical economics and sought inspiration elsewhere (Hodgson, 1989, 2000;

Dugger, 1990; Rutherford, 1994, 2001; Lawson, 2005). Old institutionalism, unlike the new, wanted no truck with neoclassical economics.

A theme of new institutionalism has been the rationale for markets in relation to non-market arrangements, spurred by the famous observations of Ronald Coase (1937) about the absence of trade or markets within firms. Whether markets emerge will depend on the transaction costs incurred, so we cannot take for granted that markets are the most efficient kind of economic organisation. According to transaction-cost economics, a market will be optimal only if the costs of trading are low enough; otherwise, an administrative hierarchy (as in most firms) may be more efficient (Williamson, 1979, 1985; Tadelis and Williamson, 2013). Such arguments query automatic assumptions about market efficiency and clarify that a whole economy cannot be organised through markets alone. The new institutional economics is open to a more realistic depiction of markets with its institutional details and recognition of diverse trading behaviour.

The embellishments to neoclassical theory do not redraw how markets are represented. Theorising remains individualistic, instrumental rationality marches on and the theory has orthodox foundations; unlike its older counterpart, the new institutionalism offers few clues on how economic behaviour is institutionalised and moulded within society (Hodgson, 1989, 2000; Dugger, 1990; Zafirovski, 2003b). Markets may diverge from the competitive ideal, but they still affirm economic rationality in the neoclassical vein. Explanations of market and non-market arrangements typically have a functionalist hue – a market or firm comes forth whenever it is the best option for efficiency and transaction costs (Dow, 1987; Vromen, 1995, part 2). The message is a qualified reiteration of the neoclassical belief that markets can best be comprehended through their efficiency properties. Regardless of the institutional features added to its modelling, the new institutionalism depends on the neoclassical image of markets as voluntary trade among rational individual agents with fixed preferences. Its view of institutions is narrow, based on constraining individual behaviour, with scant appreciation of how individual preferences may be socially determined. The resulting analysis of markets is an elaborated imperfectionism that grafts an enhanced set of institutional impediments on to the neoclassical model of efficient trade.

Mainstream pluralism does point out some deficiencies of orthodox economics and makes a partial attempt to rectify them. It refrains from full-blooded critique, as it acquiesces in the neoclassical vision as essentially sound – amendments may be needed but not wholesale replacement. The mainstream can be patched up to tackle its problems internally, without looking for external help. A broader viewpoint and a higher degree of pluralism would require dropping the neoclassical benchmark and leaving the mainstream behind. Much theorising about markets has been undertaken in heterodox economics and the other social sciences, and these genuine alternatives deserve a hearing.

Part II
Historical background

3 Markets before capitalism

The earliest human beings survived by hunting/gathering. Each tribal group was self-sufficient and did not generate surplus resources. Material possessions were few and property was held communally: ceremonial transfers within a tribe differed from what we normally understand as trading. Nomadic lifestyles gave freedom from ties to villages, towns or plots of land. Occasional exchanges of goods took place between tribes, though their origins cannot be dated precisely (Curtin, 1984, chapter 1; Clarke, 1987). Any such exchanges were minimal compared with later periods.

Trade was at first external, undertaken with other tribes, and did not impinge on the internal organisation of hunting/gathering (Weber, 1923, chapter 14; Swedberg, 2003, chapter 6). With its limited extent and negotiated outcomes, this primeval trade should not be described as occurring through markets. The hunting/gathering era lasted from the arrival of the human species until the beginnings of agriculture in the Neolithic period, a time span of several hundred thousand years (Cipolla, 1978, chapter 1; Livi-Bacci, 2017, chapters 1 and 2). Organised trading did not exist for the vast majority of human history, so it is recent on an evolutionary time scale. The past dominance of hunting/gathering tells us that markets are not universal and emerge only under particular circumstances.

Economic theorists have seldom shown interest in hunting/gathering societies, seeing them as the province of anthropology or history. The premise is that they cannot have a proper economy, for they lack the expected attributes: organised production, employment, prices, markets, saving, investment and capital are all missing. By the logic of orthodox economics, which thinks primarily in terms of exchange, a non-trading hunting/gathering society does not qualify for the attention of economists. If we define the economy to embrace social provisioning, then a wider outlook will ensue (Gruchy, 1987; Dugger, 1996; Jo, 2011; Jo and Todorova, 2018). Hunting/gathering, a form of social provisioning, does then count as economic activity. The incidence of a non-trading economy shows up the historical specificity of trade and fends off the exaggerated claims made on its behalf. Despite its ubiquity in modern economics, it is not present in all economies.

Another stock assumption is that hunting/gathering must be inferior to economic arrangements involving trade. The evolutionary sequence goes from hunting/gathering to agriculture to industry, every stage more advanced than the previous one. Hunter/gatherers, stuck at the first stage, are written off as laggards who struggle to eke out a meagre subsistence. Such conclusions may seem self-evident, thanks to the vast increases in material welfare offered by agriculture and then, most dramatically, by industry. Qualifications should still be made, however, and a cautious assessment would not draw sweeping conclusions.

Hunting/gathering societies display low productivity and have few material goods but may suffer little poverty or dissatisfaction: people will be happy if their material consumption matches expectations (Sahlins, 1974). While a hunting/gathering lifestyle depends on the local environment, it may under favourable conditions be sustainable without toil or hardship. Varied diets, frequent exercise and low population densities can yield better health than in agricultural societies – the Neolithic demographic transition that accompanied the beginnings of agriculture seems to have reduced life expectancy, height and physical strength (Spooner, 1972; Cohen, 1989; Gage and DeWitte, 2009; Livi-Bacci, 2017, chapter 2). Paradoxically, the introduction of trade in the early civilizations led to a worsening of health, even if it did bring material and cultural benefits. From a relativist angle, hunting/gathering can be viewed as having had advantages as well as drawbacks.

The emergence of trade and money

There are no records of when and where trading first appeared, so discussion of this must be speculative. Hunting/gathering gradually became more organised, leading to greater yields. Agriculture came about when specialised practices evolved away from hunting or gathering into the cultivation of crops and breeding of animals (Maisels, 1990; Ellen, 1994; Barker, 2006). It permitted a drastic increase in output for a narrow range of produce, with the surpluses stored for future use or exchanged for other items. Organised trading became possible, and production was specialised with trade in mind. Agriculture first appeared in the Middle East during the period 12000 to 7000 BC, before spreading to North Africa, India, China and Europe (Smith, 1995; Lev-Yadun, Gopher and Abbo, 2000). Settled and organised societies marked the birth of civilisation, such that people lived in villages, towns or cities and were no longer nomadic. Trade on a large scale began in these early civilisations at an unknown date.

Another trait of the early civilisations was the development of property and property rights (North and Thomas, 1977; Kennedy, 1982; Weisdorf, 2005). Exchange entails transfer of property ownership, so agreement about the nature of property is a prerequisite, along with rules to resolve disputes. Early types of exchange are assumed to have adopted a gift or barter form that did not rest upon money (Davies, 2002, chapter 1). Although a pure gift is a one-way transfer, many gifts have been offered in anticipation of being reciprocated. Gifts may be a normalised exchange with the custom that a return transfer should be made. Various gift arrangements are possible, but most tend to be two-way transfers. Barter is a formal agreement for the direct exchange of goods without monetary payment – in this case the return transfer is an explicit part of the agreement and not left to expectations or customs. Gifts and barter are hampered by their unique, one-off character, in which trade has no medium of exchange.

The significance of gifts and barter in fostering trade has been a matter of debate, stirred by doubts about whether they were ever on a large enough scale (Chapman, 1980; Dalton, 1982; Humphrey, 1985). Reference to a 'gift economy' or 'barter economy' may overstate things. Gifts, requiring personal contacts and mutual obligations, are confined to irregular transactions between limited groups. Barter faces the double-coincidence-of-wants problem, which gives it a random aspect and means that it goes ahead only by chance. These impediments suggest that gifts and barter were too localised to have been responsible for the extended trade in early civilisations. Trade at high volumes may have had a medium of exchange from the outset; money could have appeared simultaneously with it or even preceded it. Gifts and barter might then be the earliest forms of organised exchange, but not the driving force behind the expansion of trade during the Neolithic period.

Large-scale trading turns upon commodities, in other words goods produced to be traded, not consumed by the producer (Gregory, 1982; Lapavitsas, 2003, chapter 2). Gifts or barter can be based on goods useful to all the participants and proceed without a quantitative yardstick. Commodities are useful to the buyer but not necessarily the seller. Trade will be smoother if one commodity becomes the medium of exchange and unit of account with general acceptability to all potential traders – such a medium would be 'commodity money' that allows goods to be exchanged for money, which can then be exchanged for other goods. Discussion of the emergence of trade has always been tied to the kindred issue of the emergence of money. While organised commodity trading without money is feasible, large-scale trade normally revolves around money as a medium. Most definitions of a market presuppose monetary transactions (see Chapter 1).

Analysis of the origins of money has been marked by a binary division between exchange theories (metallism) and state theories (chartalism) (Ingham, 2000; Bell, 2001; Peacock, 2013, part 1). In exchange theories, money arose spontaneously as a medium of exchange, its original and most important purpose. Organisation by central authorities was not crucial, and government regulation came later. An argument of this type was made by Adam Smith in *The Wealth of Nations* (1776, book 1, chapter 4), where he pointed out the inconvenience of barter and the incentives to agree on a medium of exchange. The classic statement of the exchange theory is by Carl Menger, the founder of Austrian economics as well as an early contributor to neoclassicism. According to Menger (1892), money emerges out of barter when traders adopt certain goods before others as a vehicle for trading: the goods selected will be the ones most acceptable to numerous traders. Eventually the process converges on a single good with general acceptability that becomes the medium of exchange – precious metals were the most common choice. Plausible as it may seem, this viewpoint is hard to demonstrate empirically from the scant evidence available and marred by theoretical flaws. A pitfall is the first-mover problem: the initial adopters of a medium of exchange risk trading losses if their chosen medium proves not to be recognised by other traders (Tullock, 1975; Hahn, 1987; Tymoigne and Wray, 2006). The risks could be reduced through collective agreement on a medium, but this overturns the spontaneity cherished by the exchange theorists.

State theories of money argue that central authorities were the first to introduce money, before its use in organised trade or markets (Knapp, 1924; Peacock, 2013, chapter 2; Douglas, 2016, part 3). The early empires of the Neolithic period were sustained by taxes and tributes paid to the ruling state by citizens, vassals and conquered peoples. With such a wide range of people and produce, the central authorities introduced a uniform payment method to assist the comparative assessment and collection of tax liabilities. In that case, the initial motives for money would have been as a means of payment and unit of account, rather than a medium of exchange, and trade is less prominent in the origins of money than neoclassical and Austrian economics would have it. A unit of account implemented by the state could easily become a medium of exchange, but this is secondary and conditional on payment/accounting. Though unpopular with the economic mainstream, state theories have been welcomed elsewhere (Ingham, 1996a; Wray, 2014). Empirical evidence seems to support state theories, as the earliest appearances of money in the historical and archaeological records are to do with taxation as against trading (Hudson, 2004; Peacock, 2013, chapter 3). The evidence has not been decisive, and debates about the origins of money have never reached a consensus.

The close links between a means of payment, unit of account and medium of exchange ensure that all these purposes for money were present at an early stage and none has obvious precedence. An intermediate position is to accept this and demur from making strong claims about a sole, original purpose. In Marxian analysis, for example, organised trade can take a pre-monetary form but becomes widespread only when money is introduced as a universal equivalent with a monopoly on the ability to buy (Marx, 1867, part 1; Williams, 2000; Lapavitsas, 2003, chapter 3, 2005; Dos Santos, 2012). Money is then a medium of exchange from the outset, vital to the expansion of trade, without being a remedy for the problems of earlier gift or barter economies. As the universal equivalent, money would also be a unit of account to measure goods for trading or taxation. Endorsement of money as an accounting device by the central authorities cemented its status but could have relied on existing use among traders, propelled by merchant classes who specialised in trade. On this view, payment, accounting and exchange came forth simultaneously, so none of them can be the unique rationale for money.

Debates about the origins of trade and money have persisted for many years and are probably incapable of definitive resolution. What does seem clear is that monetary trading arrived during the ancient civilisations and became integral to their economic development. Other exchange like reciprocal gifts or barter predated and coexisted with monetary trading (and have survived to the present day) but had a lesser part to play.

Figure 3.1 sets out the approximate sequence of how trade and markets emerged in pre-capitalist times. The earliest trade is unrecorded but assumed to date back to the Palaeolithic period, long before agriculture and industry. This trading was casual, sporadic and small-scale. Organised commodity trading, with items produced deliberately for exchange, began during the Neolithic period when people settled in towns and switched

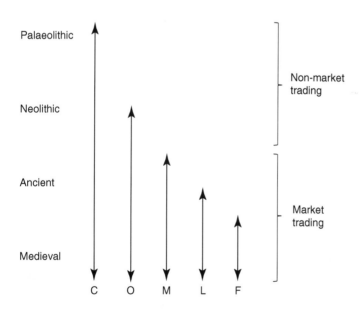

C = Casual exchange   L = Labour markets (in rudimentary form)
O = Organised commodity exchange   F = Financial markets (in rudimentary form)
M = Monetary commodity exchange

Figure 3.1 Trade and markets before capitalism.

from hunting/gathering to agriculture. The way was then clear for the use of money to facilitate trading. The origins of monetary exchange remain hazy, though it seems to have arisen after organised exchanges had begun and perhaps after money had been introduced as a unit of account.

When did markets first appear? If we identify them with organised monetary exchange, then they came about only in the later stages of the Neolithic period – earlier trading is then classified as non-market exchange. The historical span of non-market exchange, which penetrates far back into the Palaeolithic, greatly exceeds that of market exchange, which started late in the Neolithic, so markets are latecomers on this time scale. It is misleading and historically inaccurate to describe all trading as a market. Labour and financial markets are more recent than commodity markets. Early forms of labour market are traceable back to ancient Greece and Rome, as well as the medieval period, but were peripheral and did not determine the allocation of labour. Working practices were dominated by slavery in the ancient world and feudalism in medieval times, neither of which encouraged open trading of labour power and working time. Financial markets too have ancient precursors, though modern banking and finance arose only in the late-medieval period. Two features should be emphasised: trade came before markets and markets before capitalism. Even the trade most distinctive to capitalism – in labour and finance – had forebears in pre-capitalist times.

Markets in the ancient world

Many studies of early economies adopt the categories used by Karl Polanyi in his work on economic anthropology (Polanyi, Arensberg and Pearson, 1957; Humphreys, 1969; Dale, 2010, chapter 4). According to Polanyi, the ancient economies incorporated three distributive activities in different proportions: reciprocity, redistribution and markets. Reciprocity is non-monetary exchange through gifts with the implicit or explicit obligation to return the favour. Redistribution is direct allocation of resources by central authorities through compulsory means such as grants, taxes and tribute payments. Markets are organised, voluntary exchanges of commodities for monetary payment. All three were present in the ancient world, none having supremacy.

Scholars of ancient economies have tended to play down market trading and draw a stark contrast with modern times. Max Weber (1909), for instance, argued that ancient economic organisation was dictated by political and social structures, which hemmed in the realm of markets. Karl Polanyi (1944, chapter 4) took a similar line in arguing that the scope for markets in the ancient world was small and that they were embedded in strong social structures restricting their extent. No ancient civilisation ever reached a point where markets were pre-eminent. Academic views of the ancient economies have been sceptical about parallels with more recent times, stressing the non-commercial values, sparse entrepreneurship and slow technical change (Finley, 1999; Cartledge, 2002; Morris and Manning, 2005). Despite the social and cultural advances made in early civilisations, economic growth was sluggish by modern standards and rapid economic change was not a top priority.

Ancient writings about economic matters reflect the lack of focus on markets. The terms 'economy' and 'economics' derive from the ancient Greeks, whose usage differed from the modern. In its original sense, economics comes from the Greek *oikos* (house) and *nemo* (manage) to give the idea of *oikonomia* or household management. The earliest writings on economics, by Greek authors such as Xenophon and Aristotle, were devoted to good management, rather than trade or commerce (Finley, 1970; Gordon, 1975, chapters 1–3; Lowry, 1979; Blaug, 1991a; Amemiya, 2007). Planning and management took precedence over trading, which is reduced to a supplementary role external to the household or state. Aristotle was well aware of goods produced to be traded (commodities) and discussed the appropriate conditions for trading, but these were secondary to management (Meikle, 1997). For the ancient Greeks, economics was really about the best way to manage a household or state.

The offhand treatment of markets, along with the keenness on management and planning, puts the ancient Greeks out of step with neoclassical theory preoccupied with exchange. As a result, they seldom get credit from the economics profession for their economic writings. Most histories of economic thought dismiss the Greek contributions (a less than generous verdict, given that the Greeks invented 'economics') and trace the true beginnings of the subject to the Enlightenment, when markets and free trade came to the fore (see, for example, Schumpeter, 1954). Economic thought did, nevertheless, start in the ancient world with no fixation on markets and trade, which had their due place but were not the main concern.

From modest origins, trade in ancient times expanded until it covered the known world. Transport by river and sea permitted exchange of commodities in large amounts over long distances within organised trading systems (Couper, 1972, chapter 1; Bernstein, 2008, chapters 1 and 2; Smith, 2009). Trade was mostly in foodstuffs and raw materials – productivity in manufacturing was low by modern standards, as were the associated trade volumes. Even the largest cities possessed little major industry: they were 'consumer cities' with political and cultural influence but reliant on goods from rural areas (Weber, 1921; Finley, 1999, chapter 5). The outstanding case is Rome during the imperial period, which fed its huge population through agricultural imports financed by political, not industrial, power. Such transfers were crucial to Rome's subsistence, and trade became more than just supplementary. Records of large-scale, well-organised trade in ancient times has prompted some scholars to suggest that the term 'market economies' may be warranted (Hopkins, 1980; Silver,

1994; Temin, 2001, 2013). While market trade was significant for ancient societies, calling them a market economy goes too far in overlooking the non-market components. A better description is to view them as mixed economies with markets as one essential element among others.

Ancient markets differed from modern concepts of the competitive ideal. Markets as a trading location may have evolved from 'silent trade', in which people left items for exchange at an agreed place on the outskirts of a settlement, but the extent and feasibility of this have been disputed (Polanyi, 1963; De Moraes Farias, 1974; Knorr Cetina, 2006; Dolfsma and Spithoven, 2008). External trading spots were later accompanied by markets in towns, which led to livelier trading with direct encounters among traders. Personal contacts were important, so trade bore little resemblance to the anonymity of an idealised competitive market. The spread of trade often depended on specialist merchants who travelled with their goods and made social bonds in new markets (MacMullen, 1970; Reed, 2003, chapter 1). Some societies (such as the Phoenicians) specialised in seaborne trade as their chief economic activity (Curtin, 1984, chapter 4; Cameron, 1993, chapter 2; Aubet, 2001). Markets were far from uniform, and details of trading varied across time and place. Any narrow definition of markets, insisting on impersonality and competitive trade, would deny ancient trading a market form. It seems reasonable, though, to opt for a looser definition, in which case ancient trade occurred through markets.

Trade was eased by the consolidation of money, which acquired a distinct identity through standardised and regulated coinage. Coins first appeared in the Greek settlements of Asia Minor during the eighth century BC and then spread across Europe, India and China (Galbraith, 1975, chapter 2; Howgego, 1995, chapter 1; Schaps, 2004, chapter 7). Usually minted by the central authorities who acted as guarantors, coins provided a convenient way to trade over a wide geographical span – the more generally acceptable the coinage, the greater the opportunities for trading. Most coins were made of gold, silver or other precious metals, with an intrinsic value decided by the constituent metal. The monetary system was prone to debasement if the central authorities chose to dilute the precious-metal content of the coinage – episodes of this kind happened repeatedly, yet things worked well on the whole (Howgego, 1995, chapter 6; Schaps, 2004, chapter 2). By the time of the Roman Empire, a single currency issued by the imperial authorities was used for trade across most of Europe and the Middle East. Successful implementation of coinage is a further indicator of the importance of organised trade in the ancient world.

Widespread as they were, markets in ancient times did not penetrate far into the organisation of production – work was organised mostly on administrative, hierarchical principles (Polanyi, 1944, chapter 4; Finley, 1999). If production makes up the foundation of an economy, then this leaves much activity from which markets were excluded. In Marxian, materialist arguments, the economic system is characterised by the mode of production and undergoes major changes only when production is transformed. Modes of production in the early civilisations were variable and have been open to debate but are usually categorised as the Asiatic mode or the slave (classical) mode (Marx, 1857–58; Hindess and Hirst, 1975; O'Leary, 1989; Banaji, 2012). The Asiatic mode, prevalent in the civilisations of the Middle East, was a collectivist society headed by military and religious elites that oversaw production by administrative command and maintained ownership throughout. The slave (classical) mode, found in ancient Greece and Rome, differed in that it allowed individual ownership of slaves, giving slave owners the right to command and organise production – under chattel slavery, a market can emerge for human beings traded as objects. Both these modes of production have been queried as general concepts to portray ancient economies (Hindess and Hirst, 1975; Dunn, 1982; Banaji, 2012). The non-market nature of production is not at issue, only the precise form that it took. Early versions of labour markets did exist in the ancient world, though they were marginal and offered little security (Temin, 2006). Free wage labour could be less secure for poor people than slavery, with inferior long-term prospects.

Markets in the medieval world

The modern image of the medieval world has been negative, for it is perceived as a stagnant interlude between the triumphs of classical learning and their revival with the Renaissance. In economic matters the demise of the Roman Empire and loss of its institutions and infrastructure imply that earlier trade would have been unsustainable, so markets must have been diminished or wound up. Since the ancient civilisations were themselves ambivalent about commerce, any step backwards would be a serious reverse to trade, which lasted through the so-called Dark Ages and was relieved only partially in the late-medieval period. The story of medieval decline sharpens the contrast with the economic success of the modern age.

Assumptions about a collapse of trade after the end of the Roman Empire have been challenged, and the shortage of reliable evidence makes assessment difficult. An alternative to the standard view comes from the 'Pirenne thesis' that the barbarian rulers who took over the Roman Empire preserved its institutions and infrastructure, allowing trade patterns to survive more or less intact – a big disruption to trade occurred only several hundred years later, when Islamic invasions excluded northern and western Europe from Mediterranean trade and forced its slow, separate development as a distinct economic region with its own merchant cities as trade centres (Pirenne, 1925, 1936, chapters 1 and 2; Havighurst, 1976). While the Pirenne thesis has not been universally accepted, it raises doubts about the end-of-empire effect on trade volumes. Commerce seems to have suffered less severely than one might infer from the poor reputation of the medieval world. In late-medieval times, trade underwent an expansion stimulated by new developments in finance sometimes termed a 'commercial revolution' (Lopez, 1976; Spufford, 2002, chapter 1). Debates about trade volumes will never be fully resolved, but markets did endure into the medieval period and ultimately began to grow.

Medieval thought in Europe adhered to Christian doctrines that frowned on commerce, especially when it had a competitive or acquisitive hue. Trade was rebuked if it brought personal gain to some people at the expense of others, hence the Christian disavowal of usury and profiteering (Bolton, 1980, chapter 10; Mews and Abraham, 2007). Christianity had traditionally favoured the poor and humble over the rich and proud, with selflessness encouraged in preference to self-interest: charity was one of the three theological virtues and greed one of the seven cardinal sins. Such attitudes have been construed as blocking economic progress, until a change of values ushered in capitalism (Weber, 1904-5; Tawney, 1926). Yet Christian thought was hostile only to certain types of trade, not trading *per se*, and most medieval commerce went ahead without censure. The Christian position on trade was formalised in the scholastic philosophy of writers such as Thomas Aquinas, who took an ethical view resting on a Christian adaptation of Aristotle (McGee, 1990; Blaug, 1991b; Koehler, 2016). Trade at a normal or customary price, without bias towards either side, would be morally acceptable. Large trading profits were unacceptable, apart from exceptional cases where they were used for public or charitable purposes.

As in the ancient world, a medieval market denoted a physical location for organised trading, usually in a town acting as a regional centre (a 'market town'). Trading was regulated, so that legal permission to hold a market at a certain time and place (the 'market place') had to be granted by the Crown or relevant local authorities (Southgate, 1970, chapter 2; Postan, 1972, chapter 12; Casson and Lee, 2011; Davis, 2012). Markets were held at fixed intervals (seldom daily) and were often dedicated to specific commodities (meat, fish, wool, etc.). Buyers could attend without payment, but sellers wanting a market stall would require prior permission with payment of tolls and fees ('stallage'). Trade hinged on negotiations between seller and buyer, with witnessed agreements for major deals, so it was not anonymous. Regional or international commerce took place in fairs as opposed to markets (Verlinden, 1963; Epstein, 1994). Fairs for particular commodities were huge annual events, attended by merchants, not the public, but augmented by many ancillary activities and trades.

In medieval economies, as in ancient ones, markets did not reach far into the sphere of production, which was organised by non-market criteria. The mode of production in Europe shifted away from slavery towards the feudal system based on land ownership, military service and mutual obligations (Coulborn, 1956; Banaji, 1976, 2012). Under feudalism, all land is owned by the Crown but made available to others as tenants in return for services. The Crown granted pieces of land ('feuds') to the nobility, who could hold this land in perpetuity on the understanding that they would maintain local order, organise agricultural production, and provide military service to the Crown when needed. The local nobility in turn, acting as lords of the manor, offered protection to serfs and small plots of land in return for labour on the manorial lands. Serfs were not free to move, being bound to work on the manor and nowhere else, though they were free in other respects and were not slaves. The only wage labour on the manor was by people outside the feudal system, who had fewer obligations than serfs but were usually worse off because they were excluded from agricultural production and had to rely on insecure, low-paid casual labour (Postan, 1972, chapter 9). This did not constitute a fully fledged labour market, and wage payments were seen as inferior to the feudal arrangements.

The manor was an agricultural organisation unsuited for manufacturing or trade – a well-managed manor was self-sufficient in most respects and did not yield large quantities of produce for external trading (Southgate, 1970, chapter 1; Postan, 1972, chapters 5 and 6; Bolton, 1980, chapter 1). In medieval times, trade and manufacture were concentrated in towns. This was to have important long-term consequences, for it boosted the growth of towns into economic centres, beyond what they had been in the ancient world. Ancient 'consumer cities' had commanded agricultural imports without offering much in return, whereas medieval 'producer cities' generated their own output with less reliance on the countryside (Weber, 1921). Many towns were initially under manorial restrictions but gradually increased their freedoms by the grant of charters and privileges. Merchants and craft-workers were concentrated in towns and free to move between them to find customers. Residents of towns had greater legal freedom than serfs, though this gave no assurance of greater prosperity.

Medieval economies were distinctive in organising trade and work through guilds (Thrupp, 1963; Southgate, 1970, chapter 3; Postan, 1972, chapter 12; Bolton 1980, chapter 8). The ancient world had no close equivalent to guilds; in the modern world, they have disappeared or lost their influence. Guilds were cooperative associations of merchants or skilled workers in a town or city aimed at regulating economic activity, attaining high standards, overseeing entry into the profession and looking after the interests of guild members. Merchant guilds monopolised trade in a particular town for a certain commodity, permitting outsiders to trade only upon paying a fee, and sought to ensure fair trading at reasonable prices with no profiteering. As communal organisations, they discouraged competition among their members, and trading gains made by any individual member were (at least in principle) supposed to be shared. Craft guilds controlled the production of a specific commodity in a particular town, trained new apprentices and guaranteed high standards. Again, the ethos was communal, with differences of grade (masters, journeymen, apprentices) without the capitalist division between employers and employees. Organisation and functioning of guilds were locally variable, and their degree of monopoly over trading has been queried, some scholars claiming that competition was greater than it appears on the surface (Richardson, 2001, 2004; Epstein, 2008). Whether or not *de facto* competition existed, the spirit of the times was communal rather than individualistic, and market trade was no exception to this. Having cooperative organisations at the heart of trade was at odds with the modern emphasis on competition.

The late-medieval world witnessed the onset of specialist finance and banking (De Roover, 1963; Postan, 1973, chapters 1 and 2; Spufford, 2002, chapter 1). Borrowing/lending and trade credit went back to ancient times but had remained limited and did not become a true banking sector. In the mercantile atmosphere of late-medieval cities, the need to lubricate international trading led to formal borrowing and lending organised on a big scale and classified as a distinct economic activity. This was against the grain of Christian doctrine, which had declared lending money for interest an immoral act (usury), done mostly by Jews and other non-Christian groups. Moral scruples were waived once finance came to be accepted as normal, with benefits as well as disadvantages. Banking in a recognisable modern form first appeared in the north Italian city states around the fourteenth century, when merchants started to undertake finance in its own right, disconnected from commodity trade (Lopez, 1979; Kindleberger, 1984, chapter 3; Baskin and Miranti, 1997, chapter 1). Finance was organised under the guild system, subject to its rules about sharing profits and not making undue gains. A modern financial sector was still a long way from emerging, although the seeds had been sown. Specialist finance and banking was a contributory factor (among many others) to the rise of capitalism.

Markets acquired increasing prominence during the medieval period but never reached a point where they dominated the economy. Agriculture was the chief economic activity, with production geared towards self-sufficiency of local communities. People living in rural areas had little exposure to markets in their everyday life; people living in towns had more exposure, but it was modest by today's standards. Most trading was carried out by merchants and organised through the guild system on cooperative lines. Even the most highly organised trade came nowhere near a pure competitive market – in referring to medieval markets, one must adopt a looser definition that does not insist on anonymous competitive trade. As with the ancient world, economic arrangements in medieval times should not be termed a market economy: markets were significant, but only as a component of a mixed economy. Further expansion of markets happened only with the arrival of capitalism and was pivotal in the transition from the medieval to the modern world.

4   Markets under capitalism

Capitalism is often characterised as a 'market economy', with markets the defining feature, and anything that reduces their scope is apt to be seen as a threat or impediment to the system. This gives the impression that markets have a bond with capitalism and only came to the fore during the capitalist era. Yet markets were well established in pre-capitalist economies and are not uniquely capitalist, so a market interpretation of capitalism will fail to distinguish it from other economic arrangements. The extended realm of markets was building upon organised trade that had existed for many centuries.

Commodification under capitalism brought previously untraded goods and services within the ambit of commerce. Markets had greater allure than previously, championed by the *laissez-faire* doctrines of classical economics, and were applauded as the source of economic benefits. Free trade became a lodestar and rallying call for progressive economic opinion. None of this went as far as to create a pure market economy, and many activities continued to be organised on non-market principles. Rather than being just the spread of markets, capitalism imposed wider social and economic changes from new ownership structures, production methods, work discipline and consumption patterns. Compared with earlier periods, the capitalist era stands out for its rapid capital accumulation, technical change and manufacturing industry, as against the growth of commerce. Pre-capitalist economies had local and global trade but never experienced industrialisation. Whatever the essence of capitalism, it cannot be markets alone – a broader perspective is needed.

The nature and origins of capitalism

As its name implies, capitalism draws upon the economic sense of 'capital', which first appeared in the English language around the seventeenth century (Williams, 1988). Derived from the Latin *caput* (head), capital refers to physical or financial assets that can be counted by the head (as in 'head of cattle') and accumulated into a capital stock owned by some person or organisation. 'Capital' would later evoke the idea of a 'capitalist' as a person who holds a large stock of assets in private ownership and exercises the power and influence associated therewith. The word 'capitalist' dates only from the early nineteenth century (Williams, 1988; Eagleton-Pierce, 2016). This was the term used by Marx, who refers frequently to capitalists but only rarely to capitalism as a system, which is implicit in his work but discussed less overtly (Wood, 2012). 'Capital' and 'capitalist' were intended as general concepts that could pertain at any time or place.

Discussion of 'capitalism' as a particular economic system under specific historical circumstances dates only from the late nineteenth century (Williams, 1988). It fits neatly into Marxian analysis and other historically grounded treatments of the economy, but was not initially used in classical economics and sits uneasily with neoclassicism, which claims to be universal and ahistorical. Routine references to capitalism began only a hundred years after the birth of modern capitalist industry.

Markets have never been pivotal to the definition of capitalism, as their pre-capitalist origins provide little assistance in distinguishing capitalism from earlier economic systems. While capitalism sponsored new markets, it has no unique affinity with market trade, which predated it by thousands of years. Changes in the scale of trade have been proposed as the badge of the capitalist era, an argument found in world-systems analysis (Wallerstein, 1974, 2004; Chase-Dunn and Grimes, 1995). According to this viewpoint, capitalist modernity can be traced back to the sixteenth century, when European nations started to trade competitively on a global scale. The competitive ethos, coupled with international specialisation, created world markets operating to the benefit of the European nations with the most advanced technologies and highest capital intensity. On this interpretation, capitalism began with the expansion of trade after the end of the medieval period, at least 200 years before mechanised industry. Novel trading practices (as against trading *per se*) could then be among the factors that spurred the later burst of capital accumulation and technical change. Others have traced the roots of a world trading system as far back as ancient times (Schneider, 1977; Rowlands, Larsen and Kristiansen, 1987). It remains doubtful whether the origins of capitalism should be linked so strongly to trade – putting the onus on trade detracts from capital itself as well as from other social and cultural changes.

Capitalism is marked by private ownership of the means of production, along with the social and economic institutions that make this possible. The capitalist era stands out from earlier ones in the vast acceleration of (private) capital accumulation and the rapid technical change that led to huge productivity gains through industrialisation. Growth of trade occurred in parallel with capital accumulation, and both processes were aided by the climate of *laissez-faire* and competition. Markets were augmented, especially for labour and finance, without being introduced from scratch. The real novelty was the speed of capital accumulation, which had as much to do with production as trade. An understanding of capitalism should begin with capital, not markets, and its description as a 'market economy' is imprecise.

On a more conservative assessment, the capitalist era can be identified with the period since the Industrial Revolution, which started in Britain during the eighteenth century and spread across the developed world (Ashton, 1997; Mokyr, 1998; Mathias, 2001). Precursors of capitalism can be detected in earlier periods – capital itself has existed since Neolithic times – but the profound transformation induced by capitalism dates back no further than 300 years at the most. Alongside the economic changes surrounding industry have come many changes in institutions, public policy, social customs and culture. Reasons for the emergence of capitalism have always been a topic of debate (Flinn, 1966; Hartwell, 1967; Hudson, 1992; Mokyr, 2008). Materialist explanations in a Marxian style give priority to the economic base and the material forces of production in propelling economic development, though the exact meaning of these terms has been fluid (Rigby, 1998). Despite the inconsistent terminology, the overall picture is that production methods changed first, followed by institutional and cultural changes transforming the economy and society.

An alternative, idealist style of explanation looks towards prior cultural developments that fertilise the soil for private capital and industry: examples are the arguments of Max Weber (1904–05) and R.H. Tawney (1926) about the role of Protestantism in removing Christian objections to commerce and praising hard work, commerce and thrift. Many causal influences will have been present simultaneously and interacted with each other, so that causality was complex and irreducible to any single, monocausal account. Mixed in with these influences was the introduction of new market forms that eased the growth of private capital and its extension to manufacturing.

The markets most distinctive to capitalism are for labour, property and finance (Hodgson, 1999, chapter 7). Capitalist development relied upon transfers of labour from agriculture to industry. Feudalism, in which people were assigned to specific locations and plots of land, was incompatible with the rural-to-urban population movements demanded by industrialisation. The preferred alternative was to have labour markets that (at least nominally) freed people to move around and choose their occupations. Employment contracts are among the defining attributes of a capitalist system (Screpanti, 1999). Markets for varied kinds of labour became widespread, as did markets for other factors of production. Enclosure of land and its sale on markets was another drastic departure from feudalism. Only in the capitalist era have markets for labour and property been so central to the economy.

Swift accumulation of industrial capital required expansion of borrowing and lending, assisted by financial institutions. Earlier qualms about the morality of interest payments were swept aside to allow big increases in investment financed by borrowing (Persky, 2007). As private capital multiplied, so did capital markets that allowed easy transfers of financial assets upon payment. Instead of being concentrated on commodity exchanges, markets covered the organisation and finance of production. This is not to say that markets became universal, and important parts of capitalist economies stayed outside the market realm.

Also distinctive to capitalism was the accent on competition among the entrepreneurs at the vanguard of industrial development. Industrialists, compelled to make profits in order to stay solvent and maintain their investment, had to keep up with their rivals. Competition occurred in many dimensions that included prices, costs, technical changes, product design and customer relations. The competitive streak in capitalism influenced how markets were expected to operate: cooperative and relational trade were de-emphasised. Markets had long existed without much insistence on competition but were now being labelled as competitive.

Under ideal conditions, commodity and factor markets were supposed to exhibit price competition in an open arena with free entry and exit. In practice, capitalism has never matched its competitive ideal – the disparity was realised by Adam Smith (1776, book 1, chapter 7), who was well aware that private producers have a collective interest in collusion and will be reluctant to indulge in price competition that would harm their profits. Despite its dubious relevance to the real world, the faith in price competition has persisted and still pervades orthodox economic theory.

Capitalism's connection with markets has never been entirely harmonious. Inherent in capitalism is that markets move away from their most obvious applications and operating modes. Organised trading of physical commodities – the original terrain of markets – had started centuries before capitalism and continued on a larger scale during the capitalist era. Novel with capitalism was the desire to push markets into less familiar terrain previously outside the reach of organised trade. Both labour and financial markets traded non-physical items (working time and financial assets), which were harder to deal with than physical commodities and could yield troublesome relations between sellers and buyers. Atop this came the pressure for trading to be competitive, launching traders into eternal strife with each other. Earlier operating modes, less insistent on competition, were to be replaced by competitive ones. The new trading relations, instead of oiling trade, would increase the likelihood of frictions and instability.

The spread of labour and financial markets, so long after markets had first appeared, was by no means spontaneous. Changes of this magnitude were possible only at the behest of the state (Polanyi, 1944). Labour and finance had been held aloof from market trading in pre-capitalist societies. Markets were extended only when governments lifted the erstwhile barriers and approved new forms of trading. Likewise, competitive trading did not come about of its own accord and had to be promoted, a campaign supported vociferously by orthodox economics (Dowd, 2004; Stilwell, 2012).

If competitive labour and financial markets were as natural as we are often led to believe, then they would have arisen much earlier in the history of markets.

Labour markets

Hired wage labour had existed in pre-capitalist economies and was not unique to capitalism. Before the capitalist era, the bulk of manual work had been done by slave or serf populations, with wage labour on a smaller scale. For labour markets to attain supremacy, it was necessary to remove the institutions that previously determined the organisation of work. Slavery had already been superseded by serfdom during the medieval period, so the key transition was from feudalism centred on serfdom to capitalism centred on wage labour (Martin, 1983; Holton, 1985; Sweezy et al., 2006). Since feudalism relied on land allocations in return for tied labour, the crucial reform was to relax the ties and allocate labour and land by different methods. Without feudal obligations, workers could offer their services on a labour market to any employer willing to pay wages. Their prosperity was not guaranteed, as it fluctuated with labour demand relative to supply, but they could move elsewhere in search of better-paid work. Land was no longer allocated in feudal plots and had to be converted into tradable form through the introduction of property markets. The institutional changes, which overturned centuries of tradition, happened through government action in response to wider economic changes. Industrial capitalism could flourish only after feudalism had been set aside and the path was cleared for wage labour hired by capitalist firms.

During the Industrial Revolution, population shifted from rural areas into towns, where they made up the labour force for the new factory system. Strong labour demand during industrialisation kept workers' wages high enough to attract the net inward movements from rural areas, despite the otherwise poor quality of life in industrial towns (Lindert and Williamson, 1983; Crafts, 1997; Mathias, 2001, chapter 6). Wage labour, no longer a residual category, became the income source for the average worker. Working time in industry was measured and monitored to a greater degree than it had been in agriculture, a trend that led to a fixed working day, factory discipline and hourly wage payments (Pollard, 1963; Thomas, 1964; Thompson, 1967; Rubery et al., 2005). Productivity gains from technical change would eventually yield higher material living standards, even if secure employment could not be assured. The end of feudalism also meant that agricultural workers depended on wage labour, which was the chief income source across the whole economy, in both urban and rural areas.

Because labour exists in many varieties, it has always been hard to pin down as a well-defined commodity. In most labour markets the workers sell their working time, rather than precise services. Marxian theory portrays this through the distinction between labour power (capacity to work) and labour (work actually performed) (Lazonick, 1990; Tinel, 2012). Labour power is the commodity traded on labour markets. When they seek employment, workers offer their time to an employer who acquires the property right over their activities during the agreed working hours. People themselves are not commodities – there is no chattel slavery – and the workers are not performing specific, one-off services. Work in a capitalist firm entails an ongoing relationship between employer and employee, such that the employee must be available for work and the precise duties are negotiable.

Formally, labour markets rest upon employment contracts that delineate work responsibilities in return for wages (Freedland, 2005; Riley, 2016). Given the diversity of work, employment contracts can never set out an exact list of duties for the employees to perform. Among the various contractual forms in trading, employment contracts leave the most room for manoeuvre. Workers carry out tasks that are not codified and vary from day to day. The schedule of required activities is left out of the contract and agreed informally between employer and employees. This is a prime example of how contracts can never be pure or complete (Hodgson, 1999, chapter 7). Issues such as working conditions, work intensity and managerial control remain open, to be resolved by the relative bargaining strengths of capital and labour.

By contrast with feudalism, an economy organised through labour markets allows workers to enter or leave employment when they wish and to move around. Work is voluntary, with no compulsion to work at all, and everyone can in principle make choices about the work they undertake. Freedom to choose sounds attractive, although the real choices open to workers in a capitalist economy are much narrower. Apart from the small class of *rentiers*, most people depend on employment as their income source and must work to make a living. Widespread unemployment excludes many people from working, reduces the bargaining power of labour and curtails the wages paid to those who do have jobs. The downside of voluntary, unregulated arrangements is that work is not guaranteed and may be insecure when it is obtained. Free movement and chances for higher rewards come at the expense of potential loss of livelihood.

Labour markets create the image of a symmetrical transaction between seller and buyer, voluntary on both sides and capable of being terminated by either side at any time. As critics have long observed, the apparent symmetry is misleading and conceals the underlying dominance of capital over labour (Purdy, 1988, part 1; Fine, 1998; Fleetwood, 2006, 2011). Workers who sell their labour power are ceding control over their activities to the employer during the specified working hours: the detailed working arrangements are negotiable, but the typical outcome is that the employee must do the employer's bidding and has only limited say in working practices. The asymmetry is accentuated when management takes a top-down, Taylorist form, in which specialist managers make all the decisions and workers are low-skilled functionaries who follow rules and obey their seniors (Braverman, 1974; Wood, 1982). Such a stark difference between rule makers (owners/managers) and rule followers (workers), inscribed into the everyday functioning of the capitalist firm, stands far distant from any equal relation between independent sellers and buyers. Property rights under capitalism mean that the physical outputs of work belong to the capitalists, not workers, permitting a large surplus of property incomes in excess of wage payments. Workers can try to organise collectively through trade unions to bargain for higher wages and better working conditions, but their ability to do so is hindered by chronic unemployment.

While labour markets may seem to resemble other markets, a view encouraged by the orthodox economic literature, they are in fact distinct (Purdy, 1988, chapter 3; Sawyer, 1989, chapter 3; Fine, 1998; Sallaz, 2013). The traded object is labour power, as against a physical product, and the relationship between the buyer (employer) and seller (employee) is crucial. Pure, anonymous, competitive trading – seldom encountered in any market – is an impossibility for labour markets, which never come anywhere near the neoclassical ideal of perfect competition (Kaufman, 2007). Employers and employees must know each other and interact closely in addressing the problem of how to organise production. Many labour markets operate in a non-competitive fashion that shelters some workers from external competition and allocates work on hierarchical principles, as documented in the literatures on dual and segmented labour markets (Gordon, Edwards and Reich, 1982; Doeringer and Piore, 1985; Rebitzer, 1993; Fine, 1998, part 3; Leontaridi, 1998). The administrative quality of much work organisation has led to arguments that the title 'labour market' may be unsuitable and that alternative terminology, such as 'labour allocation', would be more accurate (Hodgson, 1988, chapter 8). A market does exist insofar that labour power is being bought and sold within an organised setting, although the differences from other markets should be appreciated.

Labour markets are a somewhat awkward, artificial construct, without the simplicity of trade in physical commodities. They emerged fully only within the last few hundred years, thousands of years after the first organised trade, and never exist independently of how production is organised. Economic, social and cultural changes surrounding the nature of work spill over into the structure and functioning of labour markets: debates about the transition from Fordism to post-Fordism provide an example (Amin, 1994; Nolan, 1994; Thompson and McHugh, 2009, chapter 12). If employment and work organisation vary over time or between activities, then the same will be true of seller-buyer relations within labour markets. A single template borrowed from commodity markets is inadequate in portraying labour markets – they are not solely about distribution or exchange but intertwined with production.

Financial markets

A financial sector is among the core elements of a capitalist economy. Borrowing and lending increase the volume of commodity exchanges, as well as speeding up capital accumulation by helping entrepreneurs borrow in order to invest. A longer time horizon becomes feasible, for short-run costs can be borne on the promise of long-run returns. Capital markets support transactions in private capital, which can be bought and sold in a manner similar to commodities. The resulting increase in capital mobility enhances investment opportunities and permits capitalists to switch their asset ownership across different parts of the economy. Finance and banking are not unique to the capitalist era, with origins traceable back to ancient and medieval times (Postan, 1973, chapters 1 and 2; Thompson, 1982; Spufford, 2002, chapter 1; Temin, 2004). The burgeoning of a huge and semi-independent financial sector is, nevertheless, peculiar to capitalist economies.

Informal borrowing and lending arise from commercial (or trade) credit between sellers and buyers. Whenever a potential buyer has cash flow problems, the seller might be willing to let the transaction proceed on the understanding that a deferred payment will be made later. Effectively the seller has made a loan to the buyer, even when the agreement is not described as such. The seller must trust the buyer to make the promised future payment within the period specified. Trust is most readily sustained when the seller and buyer know each other in an ongoing relationship and will be more precarious for a casual purchase. Commercial credit jars with the anonymity of competitive markets, though it can be reconciled with the looser definitions of a market considered in Chapter 1. Its expansion facilitated commodity trading but did not transform the economic system. The financial arrangements with a stronger capitalist odour are those that entail banking and formal borrowing/lending as a specialised economic activity.

Banking credit differs from commercial credit in that it need no longer be bound to commodity exchange and can be purely monetary: a specialist lender can make funds available to a borrower on condition that the debt will be repaid with interest inside a set period (Lapavitsas, 2003, chapter 4). Unlike commercial credit, the lender and borrower will not usually have ongoing trading relations or personal knowledge. Risks to the lender may be greater than with commercial credit but can be offset by the scale and variety of lending, as well as by the specialist lender's experience of economic affairs. The earliest banks in a recognisable modern form go back to late-medieval times, when specialised lenders and formal accounting practices emerged in northern Italy and Flanders (Lopez, 1979; Kindleberger, 1984, chapter 3). Growth of credit provision predated the capitalist era and did not usher in capitalism, though it did make capital accumulation more straightforward. As economies were transformed by manufacturing industry, capital and banking expanded to finance the changes (Deane, 1979, chapters 10 and 11; Mathias, 2001, chapter 13). Notwithstanding its pre-capitalist origins, specialised banking became one of the pillars of a modern capitalist economy.

Along with a formal banking system came money markets in which loanable capital could be obtained on condition of repayment with interest (Howells and Bain, 2000, chapter 5; Fabozzi, Mann and Choudhry, 2002; Pilbeam, 2018, chapter 5). The main participants in money markets were the banks themselves, as they sought to bolster their reserves by borrowing in the short run from other banks and then using the enhanced reserves as the foundation for further lending. Aggregate credit could be increased, and the economy could grow at a faster rate, provided that the credit remained secure and there were no financial crises. Extended credit relied heavily on confidence in financial institutions whose reserves were partially reliant on borrowed funds – the system could be stable on average, but only if bank runs were avoided and risky lending was uncorrelated. The inherent dangers should, in principle, be counteracted by the experience of specialist bankers in assessing the risks attached to particular loans.

Further security can stem from a central bank, which coordinates the borrowing and lending between the banks (Itoh and Lapavitsas, 1999, chapter 7; Moenjak, 2014; Mishkin, 2016, chapter 14). As the focal point of inter-bank transactions, it can monitor the financial situation and act as guarantor of rectitude. Its primacy comes from its links with the state, for it acts as the government's bank and handles the nation's currency reserves – the security of its operations is assured in the last instance by the government's ability to tax. Capitalist economies call forth a complex web of credit relations that rely on the central bank (and thereby the state) as lender of last resort.

Other key components of a capitalist economy are capital markets to assist transfers in the privately owned means of production (Neal, 1994; Itoh and Lapavitsas, 1999, chapter 5; Howells and Bain, 2000, chapter 6; Obstfeld and Taylor, 2004). As the former craft guilds declined, production was increasingly undertaken by capitalist firms controlled by private owners hiring wage labour. Fluid ownership became widespread with the onset of the joint-stock company, disaggregated into numerous ownership shares that could be traded (Hunt, 1936; Schmitthof, 1939; Ekelund and Tollison, 1980; Deakin, 2009). Any such firm is, in effect, continuously up for sale and exposed to adjustments in ownership and control if large shareholdings change hands. The firm is enmeshed with markets both as a legal entity that can sell or buy in its own right and through the ongoing market transactions in its ownership shares.

Similar changes pertained to the ownership of land, which also became transferable through markets. Previous feudal relations with land owned centrally by the Crown were dissolved and replaced by private enclosed land, exchangeable holdings and hired agricultural labour (Chambers and Mingay, 1966; Hudson, 1992, chapter 3; Overton, 1996; Mathias, 2001, chapter 3). While fixed in supply and sometimes sold only infrequently, land was susceptible to the same market trading as any other private property. Capitalism releases as many assets as possible to private ownership and opens them to market exchanges.

During the capitalist era, the scale and influence of financial markets has increased. Industrial capital in the physical guise of machines and buildings has been accompanied by financial capital in the immaterial form of stocks, shares and other financial assets. Capitalist firms can be bought and sold by people with little concern for the day-to-day running of the organisation; speculators in financial capital can make fortunes without ever being entrepreneurs or industrialists. The ballooning of financial markets, along with their sovereignty over the industrial sector, has been termed 'financialisation' (Crotty, 2003; Epstein, 2005; Krippner, 2005; Orhangazi, 2008; Lavoie, 2012; Palley, 2013; Polanyi-Levitt, 2013; Davison, 2015; Toporowski, 2015). Economies with a large financial sector are prone to episodes of furious credit expansion and overconfidence, followed by an eventual crash and retrenchment, until the next bout of expansion. According to the financial instability hypothesis, this unstable, boom-and-bust pattern is a trait of modern capitalism (Minsky, 1994; Keen, 1995; Charles, 2016). The financial sector has been the driving force behind business cycles that affect all other economic activities. Initially a humble provider of services to traders and industrialists, it has swelled to immense size and acquired a life of its own.

Financial markets, despite their turbulence, have come to be perceived as exemplars of purity and efficiency. The belief that they are the quintessential markets is strange, as they arrived late in the history of market trade and did not come about easily. They might have appeared earlier, but pre-capitalist societies never felt happy with borrowing and lending at interest, put off by its overtones of exploitation and undeserved rewards. Capitalist finance could unfold only after centuries-old moral scruples were relaxed and lenders were permitted to make large returns without reproof. Likewise, the capitalist firm could be introduced only when things previously deemed untradable were opened up to trading. Collective arrangements embodied in feudalism and craft guilds had to be replaced by transferable private ownership and hiring of paid labour. The changes were implemented deliberately with state backing. Far from being straightforward, financial markets extended trade into difficult areas traditionally viewed as unsuited to commerce.

Non-market elements of capitalism

Capitalism fosters commodification that turns goods and services into items produced for sale (Strasser, 2003; Williams, 2005; Carvalho and Rodrigues, 2008; Albritton, 2012). As commodification proceeds, the share of organised trade in the economy will expand. It is tempting to extrapolate this trend to an apex where everything becomes commodified in a pure market economy. To predict purity is to neglect the non-market elements of capitalism, which are integral to its functioning and complement the market elements (Hodgson, 1988, chapters 7 and 11). A capitalist economy, like any other economic system, rests upon necessary impurities that give it the diversity needed for survival.

The non-market elements of a capitalist economy, holding out against commodification, are substantial (Ekins and Max-Neef, 1992, chapter 5; Sayer, 1995, chapter 4; Hollingsworth and Boyer, 1997, part 1; Lane and Wood, 2009). Institutions such as firms, governments and households make little use of organised trade in how they operate. For all the attention paid to markets, much distribution and exchange in the modern world takes place without monetary payments. The non-market sector is far from being a tiny enclave that can be safely omitted from economic analysis. On the contrary, it assists trade and capital accumulation, to the extent that capitalism could not exist without it. Choosing to dwell on markets alone gives a crooked portrait of capitalism prioritising trade over production and (bizarrely) over capital itself. The expansion of trade witnessed under capitalism would have been impossible without wider institutions outside the commercial domain. While these institutions take on a capitalist form, they stand apart from the markets that supposedly underpin capitalism.

Private profit-making firms, the productive kernel of capitalism, trade externally in commodities and hire wage labour. Internally, however, they do not trade and prefer a hierarchical, administrative structure. The contrast has been perplexing for orthodox economists, belying their presumption that trade is beneficial. In answer to Ronald Coase's famous query – why do firms exist? – the orthodox literature appeals to transaction costs which, if high enough, overturn the advantages of trade and make administration more efficient (Coase, 1937; Williamson, 1979, 1985). The juxtaposition of market trading and administered firms is less of an issue for heterodox economists, whose faith in efficient markets is weaker. Top-down administrative control of firms is hardly surprising, as the sale of labour power and the nature of the employment contract give the employer discretion over the use of working time (Lazonick, 1990; Tinel, 2012). From the beginning, capitalist firms have had hierarchical management, which is just as integral to the capitalist system as market trading.

Governments have been construed as playing a minimal, *laissez-faire* part in capitalist economies, yet they take up a big and often increasing proportion of total economic activity in developed countries (Tanzi and Schuknecht, 2000; Lamartina and Zaghini, 2011). The standard pattern is to have a mixed economy with interacting, mutually dependent public and private sectors. Outputs of the private sector are saleable commodities, but public services are tax financed and may have no marketed outputs. State education and health care, for example, are large-scale activities accounting for a significant fraction of national income that have a public-service remit and only limited involvement with markets. Social policies within the welfare state have been decommodified in order to protect them from the commercial pressures of private provision (Esping-Andersen, 1990, chapter 2). While currently under assault from neoliberalism, non-marketed public services and benefits seem set to endure. As with large private firms, the internal organisation of public-sector organisations has been on hierarchical principles without markets.

Families and households provide a further example of economic activity outside the market. Much of everyday life is conducted within the household, including day-to-day subsistence, housework, care of children, care of the elderly and leisure pursuits. Even in a capitalist economy, most housework and social care are provided free of charge by family members (Wheelock and Oughton, 1996; Folbre and Nelson, 2000; Himmelweit, 2007; Hill, 2018). These time-consuming tasks would constitute a major sector of the total economy if paid for at average wage rates. Since money does not change hands, they are consigned to a shadowy informal sector that goes unrecorded in the national accounts. Difficulties in measuring the output of informal domestic work have meant that its substantial contribution to the economy has been underestimated (Wheelock, 1992; Goldschmidt-Clermont, 1992; Himmelweit, 1998). Marketed outputs are well recorded by the national accounts, so their relative contribution to the economy tends to be exaggerated. Domestic work has been under-recorded, undervalued and largely invisible but represents a vital component of capitalist economies.

When assessing non-market activities, we might be inclined to see them as less capitalistic than market ones. This is understandable, but it wrongly suggests that market trade is the bedrock of capitalism, in line with orthodox doctrine. If capitalism is interpreted as a complete economic, social and cultural system, then the non-market aspects are no less important than markets in maintaining the system as a whole (Gardiner, 1976; Himmelweit and Mohun, 1977; Lazonick, 1991, chapter 2; Fine, 1992; Lapavitsas, 2003, chapter 5). The state preserves the property relations underlying capitalism, the private profit-making firm organises production and the domestic sector reproduces labour. All these ingredients of capitalism are as significant as markets, which are not intrinsically capitalist institutions. Rather than market trading, the novelty of capitalism was the surge in capital accumulation and technical change; the term 'capitalism' is well chosen in describing this, as compared with 'market economy'. The markets that did come to fruition under capitalism – for finance, property and labour – were the ones that promoted private capital accumulation and the capitalist firm.

Ambiguities about capitalist economies are illustrated by debates over the welfare state (George and Wilding, 1994; Pierson, 2006). At face value, many welfare measures have a non-capitalist flavour, as they are state organised, planned centrally from above, funded by tax revenues, run on a non-profit-making basis and guided by explicit welfare goals. Helping the poor will raise the bargaining power of labour against capital. Such considerations have prompted claims that, as the public sector and welfare provision expand, the economy will gradually evolve away from capitalism towards socialism. Evolutionary arguments in this vein were made by writers who disliked the changes, such as Joseph Schumpeter (1987), and writers who welcomed them, such as Richard Titmuss (2001). Welfare provision seems to create a non-capitalist zone within the larger context of capitalism.

A different interpretation, expressed by Marxian writers, is that the welfare state offers no alternative to capitalism and is part of the capitalist system (Gough, 1979; Mishra, 1981, chapter 5; Offe, 1984). By making small concessions to working-class interests, welfare provision discourages dissent among the labour force and dampens revolutionary ardour. Measures that benefit labour in the short run act against its long-run interests by preventing or delaying the transition to a non-capitalist system. The various interpretations of welfare provision are hard to prove or disprove, although gradual evolution towards socialism seems implausible in the current atmosphere of neo-liberalism, privatisation and welfare retrenchment. Whatever its non-capitalist properties, the welfare state has never seriously threatened the capitalist component of mixed economies.

Instead of being antagonistic to capitalism, the non-market elements are best seen as being encompassed within the system (Albert, 1993; Crouch and Streeck, 1997; Hollingsworth and Boyer, 1997; Block, 2000; Chang, 2002a). They do represent an alternative to market allocation, disproving the universality of markets, but this stabilises the system and ensures its reproduction. A pure trading economy, if such a thing could exist, would lack the coordination and planning carried out by governments and firms; swathes of production, distribution and consumption would simply be missing. Competitive trading would also generate arbitrary, unequal outcomes and rule out the cooperation required for welfare measures. Planned and non-market activities have softened the harsh edges of capitalism by redistributing incomes and providing care. Even though competitive trade is supposedly the hallmark of capitalism – a view accentuated by orthodox economics – the non-market elements have been indispensable.

Part III

Alternative perspectives on markets

5 Social and cultural approaches

Economic theorists have often sought universal theories similar to those in natural sciences, with the result that historical specificity has been swept aside (Hodgson, 2001). Classical political economy rested on general principles but did at least mention key characteristics of capitalist economies: factor shares, the surplus, capital accumulation and capital mobility all got due attention (Bortis, 1997; Milonakis and Fine, 2008, chapter 4; Martins, 2014, part 1). The theory had latent historical specificity through its analysis of the emerging capitalist era. Classical economists were much criticised at the time by Romantic and other authors for their neglect of social and cultural matters (Ryan, 1981; Löwy, 1987; Löwy and Sayre, 2001; Jackson, 2009, chapter 3). Their theory did, however, possess enough institutional content to heed the distinctiveness of capitalism.

With the arrival of neoclassicism, the sparsity of historical detail in economic theory became more obvious. Schools of thought urging historical specificity (the German historical school, American institutionalism, Marxian economics) were outweighed by neoclassical orthodoxy during the twentieth century (Hodgson, 2001, part 3; Fine and Milonakis, 2009). Unlike classical political economy, neoclassical economics presents a single model of economic behaviour supposedly true at all times and places. The theory purports to be exhaustive, so we have no need for other theories or piecemeal studies. With orthodoxy setting itself against historical specificity, arguments stressing the social and cultural variations in economic affairs have had to be made in heterodox economics and the other social sciences, such as anthropology, sociology and geography.

The current chapter examines accounts of market trading that have highlighted its historical and cultural specificity. Each section covers a common theme: arguments dwelling on spatial and temporal variation; arguments that look towards social and cultural influences on trade and arguments that see markets as reflecting material production.

Spatial and temporal variation in markets

The long history of trading, recounted in Part II, offers plentiful evidence of its diversity and intricate social background. Anyone conscious of this history would be wary of venturing into universal theories of the market. Approaches outside orthodox economics have been sensitive to historical and geographical variations in trade. From this angle, no single model can embrace all trading behaviour, and piecemeal, localised analysis is required. Common features of trade may be discernible but will not cohere into a single formal model.

Three main examples are considered here. The first is economic anthropology, which has always valued case-specific study. The second is economic geography, which has expanded in recent years and put forward alternatives to neoclassical thought. The third, unlike the other two, lies within the economics discipline, namely the heterodox tradition of institutionalism.

Economic anthropology

Anthropology is usually defined as the study of mankind, with emphasis on ways of life among different human populations (Eriksen, 2004). This broad definition includes economic arrangements to guarantee subsistence and provide material goods. Most research by anthropologists has concentrated on primitive and pre-industrial societies, partly for their intrinsic interest and partly for comparisons with modernity. Economic anthropology as a sub-discipline appeared from the 1940s onwards with the work of writers such as Karl Polanyi (1944, 1957). An initial dilemma was whether it should mesh with existing theories in economics or strike out on its own and find new methods.

The issue came to a head in the formalism/substantivism debate that began in the 1950s and lingered on for several decades (Isaac, 1993; Spencer, 2009). Polanyi (1957) had identified two ways of defining economics: a formal definition that equates it with the rational-choice individualism of neoclassical theory, and a substantive definition that sees it as addressing social and material provisioning, untethered to any general theory. Formalism drew upon orthodox economics and used the alleged insights within anthropological discussion. Substantivism was unconvinced by neoclassical theory and preferred a piecemeal, case-by-case method. Economic anthropology became split between those happy with orthodox economics and those who rejected it.

Formalists borrowed theoretical foundations from orthodox economics, maintaining contact with majority opinion in the economics profession (Firth, 1951; Herskovits, 1952; LeClair, 1962; Cook, 1966; Schneider, 1974). When formalism first appeared, orthodox economics was increasingly adopting the Robbins (1932) definition of the subject as the study of scarcity and choice, which gave priority to allocative questions. Formalism accepted this definition and endorsed the neoclassical viewpoint: since neoclassical theory distilled the essence of economic behaviour, anthropologists should use the same ideas. They might have to adapt the standard model but could base their work on it. With heavy reliance on neoclassical

theory, the drawbacks of formalism resemble the drawbacks of the orthodox approach discussed in Chapter 2. A single core model goes against the
grain of the cultural and evolutionary thinking that has traditionally dominated anthropology (Davis, 1992, chapter 6; Eriksen and Nielsen, 2001;
Applbaum, 2005). Formalists chose to stand apart from the mainstream
of anthropology in order to come closer to the mainstream of economics.

Substantivists, by contrast, remained faithful to cultural relativism
(Polanyi, 1957; Dalton, 1961; Bohannan and Dalton, 1962; Sahlins, 1974).
With no template for economic behaviour, each case must be considered
separately and regarded as potentially unique. Common features might
become apparent, but from comparisons between cases, not from a prior
theoretical scheme. Instead of being universal and timeless, economic
behaviour is culturally specific and variable over space and time. Each
society may have its own economic way of life. Theory might still be warranted, if tailored to specific cases and allowed to be comparative. Such
an approach takes the anthropological definition of culture as a way of
life and then focuses on the economic dimension as its specialised field. It
harmonises with the wider definitions of economics favoured outside the
economic mainstream.

In discussing markets, substantivists proclaim the diversity of trade,
whether organised through markets or not. They query the need for markets, as viable human societies have existed without much trade. A classic
statement of this is the work of Marshall Sahlins (1965, 1974), who discussed economic activity in societies at the earliest stages of development.
Exchange is here for social reasons, a means to cement relationships. Links
between trade and production are weak, since the items exchanged are
not commodities produced specifically to be traded. Desire for mutual
gains from trade, presupposed by neoclassical theory and formalist
anthropology, is a cultural artefact of societies at later stages of development. Primitive societies are self-sufficient, so they have no dependence
on trading, which is peripheral. Although these societies are poor by modern standards, with low productivity and few material goods, they are not
poor by their own self-assessment and may have better life satisfaction
than 'advanced' societies (Gowdy, 1998, part 1; Sahlins, 2000). Relativist
arguments illustrate the cultural specificity of attitudes to trade.

Rather than conforming to a single pattern, exchange has taken multiple
forms that defy description under a single heading. Gift exchanges were
originally spurred by relations among kinship groups and distinct from
trading for mutual gain (Mauss, 1925; Strathern and Stewart, 2005; Yan,
2005). Economic development led to greater variety in types of exchange.
A threefold distinction has often been made in anthropology between
exchanges with generalised, balanced and negative reciprocity (Sahlins,
1965; Narotzky, 1997, chapter 2). Generalised reciprocity has a loose
expectation of even exchange over time but no formal records; balanced
reciprocity implies an expected return of specified value at a particular

time and place; negative reciprocity is motivated solely by one-sided trading gains, perhaps at the expense of the trading partner. Societies at lower levels of development display generalised reciprocity and informal gift exchanges among tightly bonded kinship groups who know each other well and interact frequently.

Economic development weakens kinship ties, leading to formal types of exchange. Goods produced for exchange (commodities) enter the scene, alongside greater motivation towards personal gain. Gift exchanges, with delayed transactions, inalienable goods, dependent actors and qualitative relations, can be set apart from commodity exchanges, with immediate transactions, alienable goods, independent actors and quantitative relations (Gregory, 1982). Contrasting types of exchange might suggest a contrast between 'gift economies' and 'market economies', although this is liable to be oversimplified. Varied trade may exist within the same society, a possibility acknowledged by anthropologists through 'spheres of exchange' (Sillitoe, 2006). Certain goods or commodities, such as staple foodstuffs, may be traded within a separate environment, subject to moral regulation and limited price variation. Subtleties can be brought out by culturally sensitive anthropological work unhampered by a single model of market trade.

The drift towards commodity exchange reached a pinnacle in capitalist modernity. Ubiquitous commodity trade, including labour, property and financial markets, did not happen spontaneously and was promoted by the state, at great social cost for some of the people affected. Polanyi (1944) depicted the process as an effort to separate markets from the social relations that had characterised gift giving and other non-market exchange in pre-capitalist societies. Pure competitive markets were planned to be an economic realm kept apart from the run of human life. The plan for impersonal exchange was never completed, as gifts and other personal exchanges have persisted (Offer, 1997). Capitalism is peculiar in its suppression of the social dimensions to trade. Other systems locate trade within social relations that may vary between different cases but must always be present.

'Culturalist' critics of substantivism have taken the relativist case one step further. They accuse the substantivists of still depicting trade within general models that include greater institutional content than the formalist versions but represent a similar exercise (Gudeman, 1986, 2001, 2016; Billig, 2000). Modelling of trade will echo the presuppositions of the investigators and their cultural context, even when attempts are being made to capture diversity. The alternative would be to look towards the local interpretations and models within each society. Pushing cultural relativism as far as it can go would lead to bespoke, localised studies that do not extend beyond their remit and cannot be fitted into any global scheme.

Economic anthropology has been divided among formalist, substantivist and culturalist approaches. The formalism-versus-substantivism debate lasted until the 1970s when it petered out for want of any clear outcome (Lodewijks, 1994; Wilk and Cliggett, 2007, chapter 1). Economic anthropology now takes a pluralist stance, eschewing an orthodox position, and scholars exercise their own judgement on whether a theoretical framework is needed. Compared with the economics discipline, anthropology has been awake to cultural variations in trade: even the formalists have heeded cultural influences in a way seldom seen among orthodox economists. Substantivists and culturalists have openly made cultural variations in trade the keystone of their thinking, the only dispute being the role of theory in portraying this variation. Whatever its internal quarrels, economic anthropology has been a prime source for culturally specific analysis of trade.

Economic geography

The central concern of economic geography is the location and spatial distribution of economic activities (Clark, Feldman and Gertler, 2000; Leyshon et al., 2011; Barnes, Peck and Sheppard, 2012). Markets have always had a geographical aspect as a physical place for trading among people from different regions or countries. Geographical studies of trade have a long pedigree, and the sub-discipline of economic geography is expanding rapidly, with a variety of contrasting approaches. As in anthropology, debates have arisen about whether regional differences should be explained within a single formal framework or dealt with through case-specific arguments responsive to cultural diversity. Both approaches are represented in current economic geography.

Approaches seeking a theoretical rationale for industrial location and trade patterns have an affinity with formalist anthropology in their wish for an analytical scheme linked with orthodox economics. An example is location theory, founded on the early contributions of J.H. von Thünen (1826) and Alfred Weber (1909), which aims to explain industrial location by appealing to the economic logic of profitability and cost minimisation: industries will gravitate towards sites with the lowest labour, transport and trading costs. Later versions of location theory come under the heading of 'regional science' and use mathematical techniques (Isard, 1975). This analysis resonates with neoclassical economics and depicts trade in similar fashion, as the result of instrumental rationality conveying the benefits of comparative advantage. Location theory, like formalist economic anthropology, declares its kinship with neoclassical economics in aspiring for a general theoretical explanation applicable in all cases.

Connections with economics have become clearer through the 'new economic geography', which has brought renewed interest in locational questions among mainstream economists (Krugman, 1998; Neary, 2001; Venables, 2010). Although it raises doubts about comparative advantage and introduces broader locational influences, it remains committed to the rational-choice methods of economic orthodoxy. It adds extra institutional detail to formal modelling but poses little real challenge to orthodoxy. The formalist strands within economic geography use similar concepts to those of neoclassical theory and uphold the same view of trade based on mutual gains among rational agents.

Other strands within economic geography are less satisfied with formal modelling and critical of the 'new economic geography', preferring more varied and culturally informed arguments (Martin, 1999; Amin and Thrift, 2000). From this viewpoint, geography requires a rich array of theoretical, empirical and interpretative methods, not a single core theory. Economic geography has been capable of accommodating alternative perspectives, with a diversity sometimes summarised by the plural term 'economic geographies' (Lee and Wills, 1997; Thrift, 2000; Yeung, 2003; Hudson, 2005). From the 1980s onwards, economic geographers have drawn ideas from various disciplines and been influenced by critical realism, regulation theory, post-structuralism and Marxian political economy (Harvey, 1982; Sayer, 1982; Gibson-Graham, 2000; R. Martin, 2000; Hudson, 2005). While critical of global narratives, these geographers are not anti-theoretical and hope to see augmented and stratified theories capable of encompassing economic and cultural diversity.

A major theme is that capitalism has never been a complete, uniform system with a common development path. The pace of development differs among countries and regions, yielding varied outcomes. Pre-capitalist and non-capitalist arrangements continue in some parts of the world. Even within capitalism, local differences should be recognised, as in the 'varieties of capitalism' literature and related research (Albert, 1993; Hall and Soskice, 2001; Amable, 2003; Peck and Theodore, 2007; Hancké, 2009). Economies which at face value are commercialised and capitalistic can still be internally diverse, with big non-commercial sectors. Any theory that plays down local differences, or explains them through efficient locational decisions, will oversimplify things. The alternative is to put social and cultural issues at the forefront, so as to trace how they interact with economics: we then have political, social or cultural economy rather than pure theory expressed in mathematical form.

According to the conventional picture, a country undergoing development should include more of its economy within the ambit of formal market transactions. Countries or regions with the tiniest informal sector will have the highest output, fastest growth and largest real incomes per head. This picture has been queried in recent years, with the continued importance of regional variations in advanced economies and the prosperity of regions that do not fit the mould of centralised, top-down production and formal markets. In place of the 'traded interdependencies' from markets, some regions have prospered through 'untraded interdependencies' from personal contacts, exchanges of information and informal networking (Storper, 1995, 1997; Boggs and Rantisi, 2003; Scott and Storper, 2003).

The competitive spirit of capitalism fades, giving way to a mixture of competition and cooperation among organisations willing to work together in clusters.

As informal cooperation flourishes, it opens up an 'associational economy' distinct from the usual capitalist relations (Cooke and Morgan, 1998). Within a capitalist frame, the regional variations show the internal diversity of capitalism and its capacity to evolve and adapt. Informal cooperation has affinities with pre-capitalist methods, such as craft production by skilled members of a guild. If centralised production and formal trading relations are less widespread than previously assumed, then scholars will have to study the new modes of organisation.

Alternative types of economic activity could decentre capitalism and transform it (Amin and Thrift, 1995; Morgan, 1997; Graham and Marvin, 2001; Pratt, 2004). Once centralisation recedes, space is created for novel initiatives. Some of these impinge on production, including flatter, non-hierarchical work organisation, improved skill levels among employees, greater differentiation of products and sharing of information among producers. Information technology makes it easier to organise production differently and disperse it across many locations. Parallel changes in trade imply a shift towards relational exchange where traders communicate readily and reach informal agreements. In place of formal market trade, there may be local currencies, local exchange trading systems and credit unions. Starting on a small scale, the new activities could expand to change the economy as a whole (Leyshon, Lee and Williams, 2003; Williams, 2005; Gibson-Graham, 2008; Healy, 2009). The full extent of these developments remains debatable. Economic geographers have, all the same, asked telling questions about the nature of capitalism and its possible future.

Varied trade under capitalism reinforces the value of local case studies but also prompts a quest for suitable typologies. A particular goal has been to get away from the unified discourse of formal markets towards a new language capable of portraying diverse, intersecting trading practices. In the 'iceberg model', for example, formal trading is the visible tip of an iceberg made up of informal trading and production methods going largely unnoticed yet of great significance for the day-to-day functioning of the economy (Gibson-Graham, 2006, chapter 3; Mackinnon and Cumbers, 2011, chapter 12). Among the unseen components are gift exchange, barter, self-employment, unpaid social care and domestic work, charity, moonlighting, illegal trade, producer and consumer cooperatives and informal lending. Although unrecorded, these activities should not be ignored. Standard economic analysis, fixated on formal market trade, distorts our perception and biases our conclusions. Analysis needs to be broadened out through a new language and framework that includes the informal sector.

Refusing to be an isolated, self-contained discipline, economic geography has welcomed cross-disciplinary ideas. The curiosity about local economic activity has affinities with substantivist economic anthropology. Bonds are strong with institutional and heterodox economics as well as with Marxian thought. Unlike orthodox economists, economic geographers have been receptive to wider trends in recent scholarship, notably postmodernism, post-structuralism, the 'cultural turn' and related ideas. Work by economic geographers offers an example of economic thought that engages critically with other social studies and does not live behind an external wall.

Institutional economics

Within the economics discipline, the case for a social and cultural approach to markets has been made by American institutionalism, which reacted against neoclassical methods (Rutherford, 1994, 2001; Hodgson, 1998, 2004b). The major flaw of neoclassicism was felt to be its neglect of institutions, not only as a setting for economic activity but as an influence on behaviour: culture in the sense of the social formation of the individual was a core institutionalist concept (Mayhew, 1987, 1994). Institutionalism was an important thread in early twentieth-century American economics, sometimes even regarded as the dominant school of thought. Things have changed dramatically since then, as neoclassicism has swollen to become the mainstream and institutionalism has lost ground (Hodgson, 2004b, chapter 18; Milonakis and Fine, 2008, chapter 10). The 'old institutionalism' now lies on the heterodox borderland of the economics discipline, its ideas chiming with economic research in other social sciences.

Among the formative influences on American institutionalist thought was the German historical school. From the early nineteenth century, German economists such as Friedrich List (1841) had queried the assumptions made by classical political economy about the benefits of free trade. According to List, free trade would not automatically confer gains on everyone, the role of the state being vital if an economy was to establish new industries and markets. Social and political context was essential to a proper understanding of trade, which could not be obtained merely from universal principles. This way of thinking was nurtured by the German historical school in the late nineteenth century and early twentieth century, exemplified by the work of Wilhelm Roscher, Gustav Schmoller, Werner Sombart and many others (Hodgson, 2001, chapters 4 and 9; Tribe, 2003). Members of the school championed historical specificity in economics, with case-by-case studies and customised theory. In the *Methodenstreit*, the German historical economists stood against the Austrian/neoclassical plea for universal, individualistic theorising (Louzek, 2011). There is no direct line of succession from the German historical school, as its German nationalism made it politically toxic after the Second World War (Hodgson, 2001, chapter 9). Its ideas remain relevant, however, and persist in different garb through heterodox economics and the non-economic social sciences.

Another influence on institutional economics has been anthropology (Neale and Mayhew, 1983; Hamilton, 1991). Institutionalists reject universal economic behaviour and look towards the cultural backdrop; their focus has been modern industrial economies, but the interest in institutions extends to the pre-industrial and localised arrangements studied in anthropology. Ideas derived from substantivists, especially Karl Polanyi, have been used to explain the origins and development of capitalist economies (Stanfield, 1980, 1986). The work of John Commons (1924) was seminal, as he delineated the legal foundations of capitalism in private, transferable property rights defined and implemented by the state (Rutherford, 1983). From this perspective, the whole edifice of a capitalist economy depends on state compliance. Instead of being a brake on capitalism, the state has been the bedrock of its existence.

Under the alternative title of evolutionary economics, institutionalism has argued for an evolutionary perspective and lamented its absence from orthodox theory. This has implications for how we understand markets, as it recognises that they can evolve. Even though the legal foundations of trade are set out in advance by the state, trading at any given time and place will be culturally specific (Lowry, 1994). Traders follow norms, routines and habits so as to reduce uncertainty and ease trade. Norms remain constant in the short run but adapt in the long run if the environment changes. Trading attitudes are culturally specific, without innate preferences or universal rationality. Markets are contingent on circumstances and adhere to no single model of efficient trade. The evolution envisaged by institutionalists is open-ended and non-teleological: it has no final destination of ideal trading outcomes; things can get worse as well as better (Hodgson, 1993, chapter 3). Theorising about markets should not idolise them as the perfect allocation mechanism.

For institutionalists, the legal foundations of property have a constitutive purpose in deciding the nature and extent of the economy (Commons, 1931; Samuels, 1994). Exchange requires a voluntary transfer of property rights upon payment, abiding by property and contract law. Any good traded on formal markets must be open to private, transferable property ownership. Usually this is taken for granted, but it surfaces in debates on whether a certain item should be traded. Decisions about what can be tradable private property govern whether a market can emerge. Incentives to trade become stronger once laws are in place and people are aware that trade is officially sanctioned and regulated; the desire to trade will not be independent of the institutional setting. Trade outside the formal economy can also occur, without official approval but with similar trading relations. The institutionalist emphasis on the legal framework for trade draws attention to activities outside the framework that might otherwise be overlooked.

As well as demarcating tradable assets, the legal system may call into being the agents who trade (Deakin, 2006). Much trade is carried out by firms defined as legal entities: the trader is the firm, rather than the people working within the firm (Hodgson, 2002; Gindis, 2009; Deakin et al., 2017). If the traders in a market are institutions, not individuals, then the orthodox model of rational individual agents becomes dubious and the internal composition of the firm should be examined. Institutionalists have analysed the complex motivation of modern business corporations, an issue frequently missing from neoclassical theory (Berle and Means, 1932; Penrose, 1959; Nelson and Winter, 1982). Employment of managers means that day-to-day control of the firm lies with management, while formal legal control lies with owners who may be disparate shareholders with limited voting power. Objectives of owners and managers may differ: owners want profits and dividends, managers want salaries, power and scale. Assumptions about rational traders with a single objective are unhelpful, and a different approach will be needed. More suitable are approaches that allow for multiple, coexisting objectives within a firm and address them by satisficing and routinised behaviour, as against optimisation (Cyert and March, 1963; Nelson and Winter, 1982; Simon, 1997; Augier and March, 2008). Corporate trading entities may bear little resemblance to the rational trader of neoclassical theory.

Another contribution of institutional economics has been to investigate market power and price setting in modern industrial economies. Dismissing the invisible hand as mythical, institutional economists have concentrated on price setting where traders have different degrees of market power. Gardiner Means (1935, 1939), for example, distinguished between market prices, which undergo frequent and substantial changes, and administered prices, which are set by firms and change only rarely (Goode, 1994). Most manufactured goods have administered prices, given the producer's ability to control supply, while agricultural produce and natural resources have market prices, as supply hinges on external events. Neither market nor administered prices correspond to the perfect price flexibility and market-clearing equilibrium in neoclassical models. Pricing should be studied case by case in a cautious empirical approach.

Institutionalism criticises neoclassical orthodoxy for its oversimplified market models and proposes more variety and subtlety. Scepticism about pure theory has sometimes been interpreted wrongly as an anti-theoretical stance (Rutherford, 1997; Hodgson, 1998). Theorising remains possible, but should embrace the institutional background of trade. Institutional features to be noted include price setting, market power, trading relations, location and mode of trading, distribution and transport of goods and regulation by government. These variable features, poorly handled in neoclassical theory, bring diversity to trading behaviour. Different combinations of features spawn a multitude of market types, yet scope remains for comparative analysis. The appropriate response is to seek a deeper, richer theory attuned to the complexity of market trade.

Social and cultural influences on markets

Cultural approaches to markets ask how culture affects trade. This starts with the impulse to trade, which is not inherent in human nature and relies on culture – the human species for most of its existence undertook little organised trade (see Chapter 3). Culture shapes the manner of trade, in areas like competition or cooperation, advertising and marketing, payment method and degree of regulation. Our ideas about markets become formalised as institutions.

The implicit causal stance here is idealist: it regards ideas as causing economic change. Allowing for such causality may not go as far as pure idealism, where ideas are the prime mover behind everything, but it does accept their place in causal explanations. A contrast can be drawn with materialism, in which the prime mover is material production, with ideology derivative. Idealism has downward causality from ideas to the material world; materialism has upward causality from the material world to ideology. The two can be reconciled in a non-reductionist outlook, though most causal interpretations lean to one side or the other. Arguments tending towards idealism are considered in the present section and materialism in the next section.

Two examples of arguments with an idealist flavour will be considered. First is Max Weber's work on trading cultures and the character of markets. Second is Karl Polanyi's work on the embeddedness of markets and the drive to create a market system distinct from earlier trade.

Max Weber on the cultural aspects of markets

As a scholar who roamed the boundaries between economics and sociology, Max Weber was conscious of the complexities of markets, their variety and the difficulties in defining them (Swedberg, 1998, chapter 2; Zafirovski, 2001). In line with the traditional view, he associated them with a location for trade. He paid attention to the structured relations between traders, through the prior existence of social structures. Yet the physical and structural dimensions of a market, essential to its existence, were insufficient to explain trading behaviour. A given market structure left room for different types of trade, with diverse interactions among the participants. To understand markets fully, we would have to interpret the attitudes of the traders themselves in the context of the wider culture.

For Weber, scientific study of trading should aim to identify the motives of traders. This reflects his general argument that social sciences rest upon interpretative understanding of individual human actions (*Verstehen*) (Outhwaite, 1986; Gerrard, 1993; M. Martin, 2000). Knowing the reasons for human behaviour is integral to causal explanation, as well as differentiating social sciences from natural sciences. The accent on the individual seems to commit Weber to methodological individualism, though he treats the individual not as an isolated agent with innate goals but as a member of a particular society swayed by its values. Instead of being unalloyed individualism, this is a cultural approach with culture as a process that forms individuals within society (Jackson, 2009, chapter 2). Understanding the human agent cannot then be achieved without being sensitive to the cultural surroundings. Behaviour of traders, along with other agents, will be culturally specific.

Weber followed the long-standing custom of dividing economic activity into the two categories of 'householding' and 'profit-making' (Swedberg, 1998, chapter 2). Aristotle and the ancient Greeks had distinguished between activities aimed at efficient household management and activities (such as trading) aimed at making a profit (Finley, 1970; Lowry, 1979, 1987; Meikle, 1997; Pack, 2008). For the Greeks, the main economic interest was management and planning – profit-making was a subsidiary pursuit. Trading and profit-making were present in the ancient world but never on a scale that eclipsed management. In Weber's perspective, the relative importance of householding and profit-making varied among societies and guided economic attitudes. Members of a society based chiefly on household production and self-sufficiency within managed organisations display few of the attitudes bound up with competitive trade. Members of a society with extensive profit-making are inclined to search for trading gains and participate in markets. The tenor of an economy will turn on the balance between householding and profit-making.

Although Weber avoided a rigid evolutionary scheme, he recognised the cultural evolution of economic attitudes and the increased significance of profit-making. Capitalism, in his eyes, was not unique to the modern world but had taken vestigial form during the ancient and medieval periods (Weber, 1923, chapter 28; Swedberg, 1998, chapters 1 and 2). Profit-making motives, capitalistic in spirit, had been evident thousands of years before capitalism as an economic system. In place of a divide between pre-capitalist and capitalist eras, Weber referred to a gradual expansion of profit-making. Capitalistic behaviour, initially viewed as ethically suspect, became acceptable and won state approval. He summarised the cultural evolution as the expansion of the economic sphere, delineated by the growth of trade and the spread of a calculating, acquisitive and rationalist motivation (Weber, 1946, chapter 13). A capitalist economy emerged once the economic sphere had prevailed over less acquisitive values.

As Karl Marx had observed, capitalism was revolutionary in upsetting previous economic arrangements founded on social hierarchies and personal relationships (Weber, 1922, part 1, chapter 2). The logic of profit-making is that deals should be made for commercial advantage, regardless of the parties involved, and that personal ties are irrelevant or detrimental. This cuts across the traditional pattern of householding, which connects everyone through social relations and personal knowledge. For much of human history, profit-making was marginal and did not impinge greatly on the economy. With capitalism, it expands until it undermines the previous way of life. Any institutions or beliefs that stand in the way of profit-making will be challenged and overthrown. Time-honoured social hierarchies give way to new commercial realities that (at least in principle) require open, anonymous treatment of all participants. Former regulations on trade are relaxed. Religious and ethical beliefs founded on duties, social solidarity and caring for others are replaced with self-interest and competition.

Another feature pointed out by Weber (1922, part 2, chapter 10) was the tension within capitalism from difficulties in attaining its full competitive programme. The openness and anonymity of the market ideal, while offi-cially acclaimed, does not correspond to actual markets. Successful trad-ers will not want their advantages eroded, so free entry and exit will be hard to maintain whenever the incumbents can impose barriers to entry. Market power will be accompanied by loss of anonymity and conscious interaction among traders: they may be rivals but collude to preserve their trading privileges. They reduce uncertainty by discouraging the risk-tak-ing of new entrepreneurs willing to innovate. Markets, which supplant earlier hierarchies, create new ones founded on market power. Capitalist economies seldom if ever live up to their imagery of impersonal trading, openness and untrammelled competition.

Attitudes observed in commercial profit-making were characterised by Weber as rational self-interest. The 'ideal type' was the instrumentally rational trader, a concept that has had much traction in subsequent eco-nomic theorising (Weber, 1981). It should be remembered that this was one ideal type among others and not universal or natural. Commercial profit-making was culturally specific and visible only in a subset of human behaviour: even after the establishment of capitalism it did not cover the whole economic way of life. Weber's use of instrumental rationality may appear to endorse neoclassical theory, especially as he was sympathetic towards individualistic methods and the Austrian/neoclassical econom-ics of Carl Menger (Hodgson, 2001, chapter 9; Parsons, 2003). Yet he never intended it to be a blanket assumption for all economic behaviour. On the contrary, he drew a contrast with other modes of behaviour in a diverse picture.

The prominence of ideas in Weber's work gives it an idealist tint, with-out going as far as to advocate causal idealism. He was keen to avoid overt idealism and never portrayed economies as following an overall blueprint or predictable evolutionary road. Ideas were not the sole driv-ing force behind economic development, but they were contributory. The salient example is his argument about the stimulus of Protestant religion in the early stages of capitalism (Weber, 1904–5; Swedberg, 1998, chapter 5; Hamilton, 2000). Beliefs linked with Protestantism weakened the ethi-cal qualms about profit-making and brought an atmosphere conducive to commerce. A capitalist economy ensues when economic behaviour tips towards profit-making and away from householding, though it never reaches a pure profit-making case. Impersonal, atomistic behaviour with instrumental rationality is too rarefied ever to pertain to society as a whole.

Karl Polanyi on the disembedding of markets

As a major figure in substantivist economic anthropology, Karl Polanyi was well aware of the cultural specificity of economic attitudes, including those towards trade. His historical perspective was similar to that of Marxian thought and he was a friendly critic of Marx, but never convinced by historical materialism, which in his view overstated the causal influence of production (Litvan, 1991; Block, 2003). For Polanyi, causality was not always upwards from material production and could easily be downwards from beliefs that affect the material world (Polanyi, 1947). While he had a stratified theoretical scheme similar to the Marxian one, with material, institutional and ideological levels, he picked out the downward influences from ideas. His conscious choice was to move away from stringent materialism towards an upside-down, idealist version of Marx.

Polanyi's idealism comes through in his account of how markets were created during the emergence of capitalism (Polanyi, 1944, chapter 4). The spread of markets was not a spontaneous response to mutual gains from trade, as neoclassical theory would model it, nor was it due to changes in production, as in a Marxian materialist view. The social conditions for labour, property and financial markets had to be promoted through ideas that declared the benefits of free, unregulated trade and played down ethical doubts. Commercial values previously frowned upon were now applauded. Items not traded before – labour, land, money – had to become 'fictitious commodities' and were put up for sale (Polanyi, 1944, chapter 6; Fraser, 2014). The span of this argument was global, so it implied that markets should encroach on all areas, including those from which they had once been excluded. Only through state support and implementation could these changes have happened – pre-capitalist institutions had to be erased (whatever the social cost) and capitalist ones brought in. The labour and capital markets at the heart of capitalism had to be planned and instituted by the state.

In the new cultural climate, trade came to be an activity in its own right (Polanyi, 1944, chapter 5). The ideology of free trade demanded that it should be above outside interference from governments and other bodies so as to permit pure competition among traders. Curbs on trade from any source would squander its advantages and lead to inferior outcomes. Social relations or institutions that impede or distort markets should be removed to leave space for competitive trading. Markets were to be the primary mode of economic interaction raised above all others and kept apart from them: outside social influences would damage the competitive gains.

Polanyi described the campaign for competitive markets as an effort to end the economy's embeddedness within society (Polanyi, 1944, chapter 5; Block, 2003; Dale, 2010, chapter 5). The economy, now identified with profit-making rather than householding, was to be a separate entity distanced from the run of social life. In the economy/society division, the economy was to be organised not by public authorities but by private, profit-making firms trading through competitive markets. Commercial self-interest, mediated by the market, would generate results better than anything achievable by planning or householding. These ideas were elevated into the universal language of a natural order, forgetting to mention the state-organised project to extend markets.

Embeddedness as a concept has been widely adopted, especially in social theory, but has proved contentious (Lie, 1991; Block, 2003; Gemici, 2008; Beckert, 2009a; Dale, 2010, chapter 5; Hodgson, 2017). In Polanyi's usage, the disembedded economy was seized upon by politicians and economists to justify the shift towards commercial values and free trade. As such, it remained a hypothetical goal that might be attained in the future but did not match current experience. Disembedded economies exist as a theoretical vision but not in practice, a subtle interpretation that can easily lead to confusion. Any hint that markets could really be disembedded from their social setting is unhelpful and appears to ratify orthodox economic theory in its account of impersonal competition. Actual markets are contingent on their social context, even when attempts are made to create a self-contained economic domain. If markets can never be wholly disembedded from their social surroundings, then the embedded/disembedded dichotomy loses its force and we are left with trading relationships of different strength. Capitalism may weaken them but cannot remove them entirely.

A system of impersonal competitive markets, if introduced across a whole economy, would have harsh social consequences. Producers would face continuous price competition pushing profits down to zero; workers would face similar downward pressures on wages combined with no job security. The outcomes could be tolerated in the long run only with social protection that relaxed *laissez-faire*. Capitalism was rendered workable through a 'double movement': the spread of competitive markets was accompanied by checks on their operation with respect to labour, land and capital (Polanyi, 1944, chapter 6). Market regulations sheltered people from the starkest realities of competition. Social policies were introduced in the late nineteenth and twentieth centuries as a palliative to competitive markets. State-organised welfare measures were never part of the original design of capitalist economies but came to be essential to the smooth functioning of the system. Certain parts of the economy (education, health care, income maintenance) were taken out of the commercial sector and organised through planning that was closer to householding than profit-making. Since the protective social relations of a pre-capitalist economy had been dismantled, a new form of publicly organised social protection had to be introduced; otherwise the whole capitalist edifice would have been at risk of collapse.

The grand endeavour to forge a competitive economy with disembedded markets was, in Polanyi's view, doomed to failure. It was an example of the 'economistic fallacy', in which market-centred, calculative economic behaviour is viewed as natural and universal (Polanyi, 1977; Stanfield, 1980; Block and Somers, 1984, Adaman and Madra, 2002; Dale, 2010, chapter 3). The fallacy occurs in neoclassical theory and formalist economic anthropology, both of which use models of rational behaviour supposedly applicable at all times and places. False claims of universality have underpinned the case for expanding markets during the capitalist era and discrediting any resistance. Capitalism did lead to markets being expanded into new areas of the economy, but it could never yield the pure, impersonal competition envisaged by its proponents. Disembedded markets, if accomplished, would have destabilised the economy through their cruel social effects. Capitalism has had to be mollified through social relations in trading, limits to price competition and welfare measures to offset the hardship of those at a competitive disadvantage.

Material influences on markets

From a materialist perspective, study of markets should begin with their material background. Manufactured goods must be produced before they can be traded. Some goods are produced for trade (commodities), others for direct consumption, and trade will depend on these prior issues. Materialist approaches seek to clarify the roots of all economic activity (including trade) in material production. Stressing production need not mean that social and cultural matters are neglected, but they are discussed within their material setting, not as separate issues. The current section considers two examples of a materialist perspective on markets: the Marxian tradition and cultural materialism.

Marxian views

All Marxian thinking relies on historical materialism (Rigby, 1998; Perry, 2002; Fine and Saad-Filho, 2016, chapter 2). Historical evolution is propelled by material production through a dialectical process in which technical changes bring about tensions with institutions and culture that eventually provoke institutional change. Material production is the motor of history, the ultimate cause of historical evolution, and institutions fall into line with material interests. Major eras are defined by their economic arrangements (feudalism, capitalism, etc.). We have a stratified theoretical picture, with the economy at the bottom, institutions and social structures in the middle and ideas at the top. Causality acts from the bottom upwards, so that material production has causal priority over institutions and ideas. Under capitalism, private ownership of the means of production gives the capitalists the upper hand not only in economic matters but in politics, society and culture. Other class interests (land, labour) are subordinate.

In appraising markets, Marxian thought has to fit them into the materialist scheme and connect them with production. Markets are distributive, not productive, institutions. Historically, production has been separated from trading, which comes second in the temporal sequence. Even under capitalism, with its extensive markets, most firms are organised on hierarchical, non-market principles. Markets are to be distinguished from production and give rise to 'relations of distribution' as against 'relations of production'. Figure 5.1 shows the scheme. Causality starts with the material forces of production at the lowest level and then passes through the relations of production and distribution. All three elements belong to the economic base, though markets lie only on its upper fringes because they are concerned with distribution rather than production. Above the economic base comes the superstructure made up of general societal institutions and the ideology that justifies the economic arrangements. Causality operates from bottom to top in Figure 5.1, but weaker downward causal effects are often recognised in order to escape reductionism.

Ambiguities remain about the precise content of the economic base, for Marx's writings were vague and inconsistent on the definition (Rigby, 1998). Figure 5.1 follows the earlier interpretations with a wider view of the economic base that includes economic relationships (Marx and Engels, 1846). Later interpretations took a narrower view that covers only the material forces of production (Marx, 1859). Early Marx is less strictly materialist and leaves the door open for the causal effects of productive and distributive relations. Late Marx (and much subsequent Marxian writing) takes a stronger materialist line that focuses on material forces alone.

Marxian theorising begins with the methods of material production in the historical era being studied. Trading relations will not be understood unless we first attend to production. In pre-capitalist economies, most trade was for agricultural produce or goods made by craft methods with little mechanisation and low productivity. Trade patterns came close to simple commodity exchange, in which traders would bring commodities to the market, exchange them for money and use the proceeds to buy further commodities (Marx, 1867, part 1; Fine and Saad-Filho, 2016, chapter 4). This yields the circular flow in Figure 5.2 (a), from commodities (C) to money (M) back to commodities. Production is organised at a remove from markets, through small-scale self-employment, craft guilds, feudalism, slavery, etc.

Under capitalism, labour becomes a commodity. Production is by private firms with industrial capital and mechanised techniques, hiring employees from the labour market. In place of simple commodity

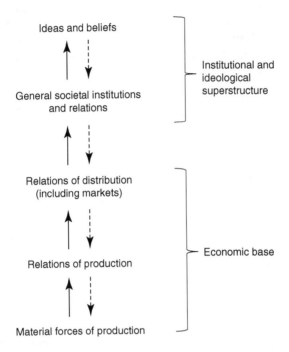

Ideas and beliefs

General societal institutions
and relations

Institutional and
ideological
superstructure

Relations of distribution
(including markets)

Relations of production

Economic base

Material forces of production

Figure 5.1 Markets within historical materialism.

exchange, trade patterns embody capitalist production methods and parallel circular flows for capitalists and workers, as in Figure 5.2 (b). Capitalists invest their monetary capital in the production process to yield commodities and then sell these at a profit to gain a surplus. Workers sell their labour power (L) on the labour market to earn an income and then spend this on commodities. By contrast with pre-capitalist economies, the labour market plays a much bigger part and financial markets are created to help the accumulation and transfer of privately owned capital.

(a) Simple commodity exchange

$$C \longrightarrow M \longrightarrow C$$

(b) Capitalism

$$L \longrightarrow M \longrightarrow C \quad \text{(workers)}$$

$$M \longrightarrow C \longrightarrow M' \quad \text{(capitalists)} \qquad (M' > M \text{ through surplus value})$$

Figure 5.2 Types of commodity exchange.

The key theoretical concept for Marx is not the market but the commodity, in other words goods produced specifically for trading (Marx, 1867, chapter 1). This ensures that markets are never represented in isolation, as in neoclassical models of exchange economies, and are always connected with production. Capitalism is earmarked by the treatment of labour as a commodity through the hiring of labour power and its use in formal employment by private firms. The onset of capitalism brought commodification, which pulled more and more items into the economic realm.

As trade expanded, profit-making replaced householding as the main economic activity. Marx described this as 'commodity fetishism': the desire to buy, sell and make profits was the touchstone (Hussain, 1990; Albritton, 2012; Fine and Saad-Filho, 2016, chapter 3). Pursuit of profit penetrates further under capitalism than ever before, though it never reaches a point at which markets take over the whole economy. Large non-market elements are preserved but enlisted to support profit-making and private capital accumulation (Himmelweit and Mohun, 1977; Lapavitsas, 2003, chapter 2). Capitalism rests ultimately on capital, not on trading *per se*, and trade will be restricted whenever it endangers aggregate profits.

In capitalist economies, producers realise profits through selling output – unsold output gives only potential profit. Capitalists can raise their potential profits by technical improvements, higher intensity of work, lower wages and so forth, but they can convert this into actual profit only when they sell output. Lower prices would raise sales at the expense of lower profit margins and perhaps lower total profit. Better for the capitalist is to boost sales by other means such as advertising and product branding, which bolster market power and sustain demand. The importance of non-price competition has been brought out in later Marxian approaches, notably theories of monopoly capital (Baran and Sweezy, 1966, chapter 5; McChesney et al., 2009; Foster, 2014). Producers encourage demand for their products in advance, instead of meeting the existing demand of customers. They may create their own 'markets' for branded products through advertising and marketing. The result jars with the competitive ideal of the market as a neutral arena in which sellers and buyers interact on even terms. Producers/sellers make every effort to manipulate consumers and guarantee stability of demand, aided and abetted by the advertising industry.

Historical materialism awards causal precedence to material production but does not rule out the influence of ideas. In capitalist ideology, economic rationality and competitive markets have been talismans (Dobb, 1973; Foley, 2004). Even though the internal organisation of capitalist production has little to do with markets, the ideology praises them as the means for social and economic improvement. The chasm between the practice and ideology of markets under capitalism, obvious as it should be, has not displaced the pervasive icon of the pure competitive market. Alongside their practical existence in the material world, markets have acquired a life of their own in the ideology, where they take a rarefied, unsullied form. Virtual accounts of the market feature prominently at the top level of Figure 5.1, so markets impinge on the superstructure as well as the economic base. Marxian thought dismisses the pure competitive market as a depiction of actual trading but acknowledges its ideological role in justifying commodification.

The Marxian view implies that there will be no single theory of markets applicable in all cases. Any attempt to find a universal model, in the manner of orthodox economic theory, will be misguided. Instead of seeking general models, economic analysis should be historically specific and alert to how trade mingles with the material production, institutions and culture in each historical period. Markets under capitalism have a multiple existence as the actual trading of commodities in particular historical circumstances, the institutional framework of property rights and regulations within which trading occurs, and the ideological construct of the ideal market that justifies commodification. Marxian analysis should address all these levels and how they interact.

Cultural materialism

An approach related to Marxian thinking but with a less restrictive view of causality is cultural materialism (Milner, 1993, 2002; Barker and Jane, 2016, chapter 2). Widespread in cultural studies, the humanities and non-economic social sciences, it stays within a materialist scheme but says more about culture than is customary in Marxian arguments and allows ideas to have greater causal influence. All culture must be rooted in material production as a matter of physical subsistence and reproduction, so it makes little sense to speak of culture as disengaged from the material world. The stance is materialist in an ontological respect, for culture needs physical means of expression and material provisioning of the people concerned. Causal materialism would be a far stronger assumption. Culture may not be reducible to material interests, so a cultural materialist view avoids the reductionism in some varieties of Marxism, where the culture and ideology are wholly determined from the economic base. Culture may have causal independence from material production, and ideas may influence the material world.

Cultural materialism exists in two variants, one associated with literary and cultural studies, the other with anthropology (Jackson, 1996). The literary version originated in the 1950s and 1960s, inspired by the New Left and its renewed attention to culture. Seminal was the work of Raymond Williams (1977, 1980, 1981), who had explored the cultural ramifications of capitalism, the resistance to it on cultural grounds, and the growth of mass consumption. For Williams, culture had to be conceived as a whole way of life that included popular culture and the mass media. It relied on material production for its dissemination (the 'cultural industries') but could not be merely a by-product of the economy. Study of popular culture was crucial for a comprehension of modern societies, albeit within a stratified outlook that appreciated its material context. The anthropological version is due to Marvin Harris (2001a and b), who proposed his own materialist standpoint as an alternative to Marxian, functionalist and other theoretical approaches. Again the aim is to recognise the material prerequisites for culture and its ties to the material world in a framework that steers clear of materialist reductionism. While the anthropological and literary versions of cultural materialism appeared at roughly the same time and share many features, the academic literatures on them are separate with hardly any overlap. The current discussion deals mainly with the literary version, which has had a wider impact through its place in cultural studies.

Theories of cultural materialism were not designed as theories of the market. Even so, they have implications for how we perceive markets and how trade fits into the larger cultural frame (Slater, 2002a). Of particular significance is the way that popular culture in modern capitalist societies must be expressed through mass consumption of commodities, a trend usually termed consumerism or the consumer society (Kellner, 1983; Adorno, 1991; Marcuse, 1991; Miles, 1998; Slater and Tonkiss, 2001, chapter 6; Fine, 2002, chapter 8; Stearns, 2006; Cerni, 2012; Baudrillard, 2017). Going well beyond satisfying basic needs, consumer goods define a lifestyle and enter into the consumer's identity. Markets take on cultural importance as the conduit for the goods that define a contemporary way of life. Anyone unable to participate fully in markets will fall below the expected norms of material consumption and face social exclusion. The way of life becomes commodified through its dependence on the purchase of consumer goods. Markets entwine with culture to a degree unseen in neoclassical economic theory or Marxian base-superstructure models.

Cultural materialism retains a material foundation, as it stems from mass production of consumer goods but leaves space for the influence of ideas. Consumerism requires the continuous injection of new trends and fashions, propagated by advertising, to sustain the demand for products and prevent consumers from becoming satiated (Aaker and Day, 1982, part 4; Davidson, 1992; Witt, 2001; Migone, 2007; Pietrykowski, 2009, chapter 5). Far from being left to their own devices, consumers are cajoled into wanting ever more goods, including items not previously available and never before in demand. Expanded consumption, freely chosen as it is, may not be in the consumers' best interests (George, 2001). Commercially successful goods enjoy sales growth as they are integrated into the typical lifestyle, until the market becomes mature and growth tails off. The search is then on for new products to create new demand and keep sales growing.

Markets are the route by which novel trends bear upon society at large. Figure 5.3 illustrates the process. Ideas feed into the consumerist culture to promote new products as a commodified statement of lifestyle and identity ('demand'). Producers take up the ideas and grant them material form as commodities which, if commercially successful, are absorbed into the consumption patterns of the average person ('supply'). Demand and supply in Figure 5.3 are only loosely defined and not independent of each other as in orthodox economic theory – they belong to the same circular causal process. Material production remains vital but no longer has causal priority as in traditional Marxian thought; it is a step in cumulative causation with no obvious starting point. Technical changes (also reliant on ideas) are still a causal influence, alongside the cultural pressures that stimulate product innovation.

Advertising is the most visible expression of consumer culture, as a means to shape consumers' preferences and induce them to buy things. The outcomes may have little to do with well-informed consumer rationality. Modern advertising often appeals to emotion and social conformity rather than instrumental reason. Advertisers have had a deeper insight into human behaviour than orthodox economists, allowing for a stratified view with rational, habitual and sub-conscious levels (Packard, 1991; Huang, 2001; Heath, 2012; Fennis and Stroebe, 2016). Consumers are manipulated by any means possible into consuming as much as possible

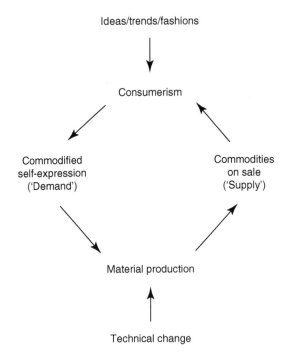

Figure 5.3 Markets and consumerism.

and moving into new areas of consumption. Advertising and marketing have burgeoned on a vast scale to fuel the consumer culture – orthodox economics plays them down or delegates them to other academic disciplines, yet they epitomise modern capitalism. Cultural materialism corrects the omission and accords them their due place in theorising about markets.

A cultural materialist analysis focuses on the cultural forces that inflate commodity demand, including demands that are culturally and historically specific. Beside basic subsistence needs comes an array of wants, desires and social/cultural norms influenced by marketing (Ackerman, 1997; Slater, 2005; De Mooij, 2011, 2014). No longer tied to material subsistence, goods acquire symbolic value as the emblems of a lifestyle and signifiers of social status (Jhally, 1990; Douglas and Isherwood, 1996; Dolfsma, 2002, 2004; Coşgel, 2008; Ravasi and Rindova, 2008). People are encouraged to express themselves through their consumer choices and make consumption crucial to their identity, over and above traditional allegiances (family, religion, social class, etc.). Branding of luxury goods is an example: designer labels, brand names and logos become prime motivators of consumer demand, outweighing the physical attributes of the good itself. Buyers pay a premium for goods with a well-known brand, even when equivalent unbranded goods are available at far lower prices (Farquhar, 1989; Aaker, 1991; Chevalier and Mazzalovo, 2008). Such behaviour differs from pure competitive markets, in which products are homogeneous and consumers seek the lowest price. Modern capitalist economies have no fixed set of homogeneous commodities; new ones are continually added and old ones rebranded and repackaged. Producers cultivate demand for their branded products, so markets will not be a neutral arena to transact a homogeneous commodity.

As consumption swings away from material needs towards culturally induced wants, it may appear that material production has diminished importance. Such arguments abound in certain strands of postmodernism, which speak of a new, dematerialised economy of signs and symbols (Baudrillard, 1993; Lash and Urry, 1994; Fuat Firat, Dholakia and Venkatesh, 1995; Bauman, 2001; Venkatesh, Penaloza and Faut Firat, 2006; Vargo, 2007). Relative decline in subsistence needs suggests that consumption will be driven by symbolic value, with branding and imagery taking over from the physical attributes of commodities. Material goods will become little more than signifiers of cultural status, valued for their symbolic content not their physical nature. Markets will increasingly be for services, meanings and symbolic practices. Trends away from goods towards services seem to confirm this process: the manufacturing sector of developed economies has dwindled in favour of service industries with no material product. It is tempting to extrapolate the drift away from staple consumer goods to paint a picture of a dematerialised economy entirely above the material level.

From the cultural materialist perspective, arguments about total dematerialisation are exaggerated and neglect the continued relevance of material context (Callinicos, 1989, chapter 5; Slater and Tonkiss, 2001, chapter 7; Goux, 2002; Fine, 2002, chapter 8; Slater, 2002c). While symbolic value has become prominent, it should be understood in relation to material forces. We should look at the material conditions for the creation of symbolic value: it does not come about spontaneously and is magnified by advertising and marketing as the means to sell commodities. Signs and symbols do matter in trading behaviour, but are inseparable from the material context. Basic material needs still exist, even if they take up a smaller share of consumption, and physical products must be manufactured, even if their value is a smaller proportion of total income. Cultural materialism implies a layered scheme that pays heed to signs and symbols but only as one level among others. It remains materialist in an ontological sense, because all signs and symbols must be contingent on material reproduction and subsistence.

6   Structural approaches

In response to the varied social context of markets and the difficulties of portraying it theoretically, one might conclude that analysis should go ahead without theory, case by case. This is too pessimistic, as it should be possible for theory to accommodate the social background to markets. Of particular relevance are the structural properties of trade, in other words how traders relate to each other in standardised ways capable of variation but not unique to each transaction. All trade has a structural quality, insofar as sellers and buyers interact within an organised institutional setting.

Structural alternatives to the orthodox view of markets come mainly from the economic branches of sociology and other social sciences (Rosenbaum, 2000; Slater and Tonkiss, 2001, chapter 4; Swedberg, 2003, chapter 5; Fourcade, 2007; Hodgson, 2008; Beckert, 2009b). Heterodox economics has been sympathetic to structural thought but has not produced a structural model of the market to set against the neoclassical account. Another source of structural ideas is the critical realist literature, which seeks a non-reductionist social ontology as a foundation for social science (Lawson, 1997, 2003; Fleetwood, 1999; Lewis, 2004; Pratten, 2015). Structural arguments offer the prospect of a formal yet socially grounded treatment of markets.

The present chapter considers the social structure of markets in the sense of pre-existing roles, as well as wider social relations among traders. Initially the role composition of a market is considered. Discussion then moves on to the social relations behind trading and how they are represented in theories from economic sociology and elsewhere. The chapter concludes by examining a stratified view capable of encompassing the structural and social aspects of trade within a single theoretical framework.

The formal structure of a market

Markets acquire formal structure from the prior organisation needed for regular trading. As a subset of exchange, they rest upon property rights which must exist before organised exchange can appear. A society without property ownership would not give rise to market trade (Commons, 1924; Frankel, 1993; McMillan, 2002, chapter 1). Voluntary legal transfer of property rights underlies the seller and buyer roles in a market: the seller is the initial property owner, the buyer the new property owner. Seller and buyer roles are so well established in modern societies that they get taken for granted, becoming visible only when trade disputes occur. Incomplete trading contracts mean that the roles have gaps and must be accompanied by a general trading culture if markets are to prosper (Rapaczynski, 1996; Aspers, 2009). The roles are always present, though, and should be integral to any theory of markets. To represent them we must have an account of social structure.

As a core concept in sociology and social theory, the notion of social structure has been much debated (Porpora, 1989; López and Scott, 2000). No official view has come forth, but the commonest is the one found in the classical sociology of Émile Durkheim and Talcott Parsons (Durkheim, 1895, chapter 5; Parsons, 1951, chapter 2). In this view, a social structure comprises interrelated roles that are often paired: examples from economics are seller-buyer, creditor-debtor, landlord-tenant and employer-employee. Since none of these roles can exist without its counterpart, they have a necessary relationship and form a social structure (Lawson, 1997, chapter 12; Jackson, 2003; Sayer, 2010, chapter 3). The roles are defined impersonally. If one role occupant replaces another, the social structure will endure, for it is not tailored to specific persons. The analogy is with a theatrical role in which the part has to be played by an actor but is written down in the script and can be performed by future actors. Likewise, social roles must be filled by human agents but remain distinct and exist in their own right.

The chief structural roles in a market are seller and buyer, occupied temporarily during a purchase. Once the sale is complete and property rights have been transferred, the traders leave their roles and cease to participate in the market until the next transaction. For most everyday purchases, trading roles are barely perceptible. People take them on routinely and become so used to them that they appear natural. The social structure is present, all the same, and goes unnoticed only because of its familiarity as the context in which people trade.

Figure 6.1 illustrates the typical structure of a market. Structured social interactions have a threefold character, with seller-buyer (S-B), seller-seller (S-S) and buyer-buyer (B-B) relations (Weber, 1922, part 2, chapter 7; Fourie, 1991; Swedberg, 1998, chapter 2; Jackson, 2007b). At the centre lies the seller-buyer relation, vital for trade. Exchange could take place without S-S and B-B relations but not the S-B relation. All three are potentially competitive. Sellers want the highest possible price, buyers the lowest, so the S-B relation provokes a conflict of interest. Sellers may compete for custom with other sellers in the S-S relation, and the same may be true for the B-B relation. The market structure in Figure 6.1 could be thoroughly

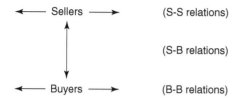

Figure 6.1 The structure of a market.

competitive, such that agents act as atomistic individuals and form no personal bonds with other traders. Competitive assumptions inform much academic work on markets, yet competition in actual markets is variable.

Impersonal seller and buyer roles seem to facilitate anonymous competitive trading. Traders occupy their roles fleetingly and could trade by price alone without knowing their trading partners. Prior, well-defined roles create the setting for price competition among agents who otherwise have no social contact. Markets could apparently come close to perfect competition. The problem is that trading roles are never complete or binding, and they do not snuff out personal and cooperative trading relations. Gaps in social structures and contracts have been widely acknowledged in sociological analysis. Émile Durkheim (1893, book 1, chapter 7) noted the impossibility of pure contract, since any actual contract cannot deal with all possible events in the real world (Hodgson, 1988, chapter 7). Max Weber was careful to admit the tensions between competition and cooperation in a market, with the likelihood of collusive personal trading relations (Weber, 1922, part 2, chapter 2). Even though impersonal roles create the setting for trade, they never dictate the precise character of trading.

Every market sale has a contract between seller and buyer that oversees the property transfer and codifies the traders' legal rights when problems occur. In most transactions, things proceed straightforwardly and legal questions do not arise. The low profile of contractual details has encouraged their neglect in orthodox economics and the tacit assumption that markets can flourish without institutional support. To overlook the legal foundations of trade is misguided, as all markets must be delineated formally if they are to operate well. Three main types of contract underpin trading: sales contracts, contracts for services and contracts of service (Simon, 1951; Hodgson, 1999, chapter 7; Kalleberg, 2000; Riley, 2016). Table 6.1 lists their properties.

A sales contract (top row of Table 6.1) is the most basic contractual form, applicable to manufactured goods, other commodities, primary produce and non-specialised services. The traders usually have limited personal interaction. Although the contract will not be complete in the literal sense, covering every conceivable event, it can cover the most likely problems. Unless they have a dispute, traders will not be

Table 6.1 Types of contract in market trade

	Duration	Personal interaction	Non-contractual elements	Service connection	Structural relation
Sales contract	Fleeting	Low	Few	None	Seller-Buyer
Contract for services	Temporary	Medium	Some	Specific	Hirer-Hired
Contract of service	Permanent	High	Many	General	Employer-Employee

reading the contractual details. The contract permits consistent, equitable resolution of trade disputes, which would normally go through the legal system only when the price of the items is high enough not to be outweighed by legal costs. A sales contract seldom entails a service connection between the traders, except for cases where complex goods may require after-sales services from the seller. The structural relation is between seller and buyer.

A contract for services (middle row of Table 6.1) arises when a client hires somebody to do a particular job or service, such as decorating a house or repairing a car. This is more intricate than buying goods and takes longer, with personal contact and discussion between client and service provider. The intricacy expands the range of things that could go wrong, as well as the number of events not covered by the contract. Compared with a sales contract, a contract of service will be less complete and leave more non-contractual elements that have to be dealt with personally. The service connection between client and provider is explicit and unique to the job being undertaken. In a contract for services, the structural relation is between hirer and hired.

A contract of service (bottom row of Table 6.1) is associated with employment relations in a labour market. The employer is not purchasing any particular good or service but the employee's time for a specified period ('labour power' in Marxian terminology). The employee agrees to serve the employer during fixed working hours, but the tasks to be performed and the working conditions are not set out beforehand and must be negotiated later. Since the arrangement extends into the long run, the parties have to interact personally and build a relationship. Most work practices are decided non-contractually as a result of bargaining between management and workers; the complications ensure that employment contracts are less complete than sales contracts or contracts for services. The service connection is important but not wedded to any specific tasks – the worker is offering non-specific service. In a contract of service, the structural relation is between employer and employee.

All three types of contract leave room for non-contractual relations that generate variety. Sales contracts specify how to settle certain trade disputes but do not tell everyone how to trade. Any traders can interact personally if they wish. Even when they have no direct contact, they may still have virtual relationships through advertising, marketing and brand loyalty. Contracts for services require the traders to discuss the services performed and stay in touch. Contracts of service go further to stipulate a long-term bond between employer and employee, which is not confined to the labour market but spills over into production and work organisation. The informal, non-contractual facets of a market are sometimes hidden, yet they exist in all cases and should be recognised. Theorists aiming for a structural approach will have to look beyond impersonal roles to examine how traders interact socially. Personalised trading has featured strongly in recent economic sociology and social theory, in network and other models.

Personal relations and networks in trading

Economists have been wary of personal relations in trading and viewed them as disturbing the competitive ideal. The ones that get most attention are among sellers with market power who cooperate to reduce price competition and protect profits. Relations among buyers get less attention, as buyers tend to be less well coordinated than sellers. Rarely scrutinised are personal seller-buyer relations. The dictum that supply and demand should be separate from each other colours most economic modelling. Theories that stress personal contact between sellers and buyers have usually been a deliberate contrast with the atomism of neoclassical economics. Two examples are relational exchange and network theories.

Relational exchange

In relational exchange, sellers and buyers know each other and develop a personal bond that reduces the likelihood of seeking other trading partners (Richardson, 1972; Goldberg, 1976, 1980; Macneil, 1981, 2000; Dore, 1983). Participants come to trust one another and stay together, even if better prices might be available elsewhere. The term 'personal' is being interpreted broadly: it does not have to mean individual persons but could refer to firms and other organisations defined legally as agents.

Trading relationships arise for various reasons. They may be due to the complexity of certain goods, for which trustworthy trading partners will reduce risk, or the small number of suppliers and purchasers, which makes anonymity virtually impossible. They could arise through inertia if traders are unwilling to make an effort to find alternative partners. Much literature on relational exchange has come from writers in business studies, marketing and advertising (Dwyer, Schurr and Oh, 1987; Morgan and Hunt, 1994; Lambe, Spekman and Hunt, 2000; Godson, 2009; Kotler and Keller, 2016, part 3). From a business angle, trading relations reflect a firm's desire to promote its products and enter a dialogue with loyal customers.

Most relational exchange would be called a market in ordinary language, which makes no strong distinction between anonymous and personal trading. In academic work, markets are frequently assumed to have price competition and impersonal interaction among the participants. Relational exchange would not then qualify as a market and would be put in a separate category. It is rightly termed exchange, for it transfers property rights upon payment, but it does not possess the price competition often associated with markets. Under a strict definition of competitive markets, it would be non-market exchange, alongside barter, reciprocal gifts and bargaining. It has some market attributes, without having enough of them to be unambiguously labelled a market.

Relational exchange becomes likely when both sellers and buyers have substantial market power. In defence procurement, for example, the only buyers of high-technology armaments are national governments (private purchase is illegal), and the only sellers are the major arms manufacturers (Sandler and Hartley, 1995, chapter 5). Sellers and buyers are in a monopoly or monopsony with few rivals. The complex products require deep discussion before an agreement on price and other details can be reached. Repeated trades take place among the same agents who know each other and form working relationships. Trust based on past experience may be the main consideration, as against price. The personal contacts can lead to perverse incentives, bribes, side payments and so forth. Similar outcomes can be seen in other bilateral monopolies such as health care, where large medical providers transact regularly with a few multinational drug companies and forge trading links (McPake, Normand and Smith, 2013, chapter 13). This can be described as a market only under a loose definition.

Other examples of relational exchange are less obvious because the trading relations are weaker. Most manufactured goods are branded products differentiated to make the seller known to the buyer and foster brand loyalty that will stimulate repeat purchases (Aaker, 1991). Loyal customers develop an indirect relationship with the seller via the brand. Personal contact and interaction are minimal, yet the buyer knows the seller's identity and trusts their branded products (Dick and Basu, 1994; Lau and Lee, 1999; Chaudhuri and Holbrook, 2001; Delgado-Ballester and Munuera-Aleman, 2001). A weak trading relationship has emerged, contrary to the competitive ideal of anonymity and homogeneous products.

Buyers may prefer familiar brands to cheaper equivalents. This is well known to the advertising and marketing industries, anxious to build strong brands that may have little to do with the products being sold (Keller, 2001, 2003). Buyers are urged to see consumer choices as a mode of self-expression and communication, so that certain brands or possessions become part of an admired lifestyle (Belk, 1988, 2013; Douglas and Isherwood, 1996; Coşgel, 1997, 2008). Sellers do market research on customers and try to forge as strong a link with them as possible. Connections between seller and buyer seldom go as far as close personal interaction, but they breach anonymity and contravene the assumptions of a pure competitive market.

Recent technical changes have opened up new avenues for trading relationships. With information technology, markets now churn out vast quantities of trackable data on buyers' behaviour (Fourcade and Healy, 2017). Internet sales and electronic payments have made it easier than ever before to compile databases on people and their buying habits. A technique of modern marketing is 'customer relationship management', which aims for a formal relationship with a known band of loyal customers (Winer, 2001; Chen and Popovich, 2003; Payne and Frow, 2005; Buttle, 2009; Kumar and Reinartz, 2012). Many sellers operate loyalty schemes, where buyers provide personal information and have their purchases recorded by the seller in return for discounts and other privileges. The intended effect for the seller is to reinforce the bond with them clientele, acquire knowledge of their tastes and reduce the chances of them switching to another trading partner. Without physical proximity or face-to-face discussion, seller and buyer have a virtual relationship.

The decline of anonymous trade is barely acknowledged in the orthodox economic literature and has been discussed mainly in management studies and marketing. Even though internet shopping removes the need to attend a market in person and meet a seller, it creates a record of buying behaviour that allows sellers to trace buyers and seek a connection with them. Data from internet usage permit targeted advertising and online marketing centred on the potential buyer's revealed interests, boosting sales and increasing the likelihood of future relational exchange (Gay, Charlesworth and Esen, 2007; Chaffey and Ellis-Chadwick, 2016; Strauss and Frost, 2016). Loss of anonymity in electronic transactions and internet usage is a new blow to the competitive market ideal.

Relational exchange has no clear boundary with markets. If defined narrowly and confined to close personal interactions, then it will be unusual. Most trade will be described as a market, not relational exchange. The anomaly is that these 'markets' include weak trading relations based on brand loyalty, despite being classified as non-relational. If relational exchange is defined broadly to include weak trading relations, then almost all trade will come under the relational heading and markets will shrink to a rump category. Few markets are anonymous in every respect, so there will be an almost empty box for a term common in everyday language. Actual trading is usually relational in some sense but varies greatly in the closeness of relationships, so a nuanced assessment would be better than a market/relational exchange dichotomy. Markets have an impersonal component from the formal buyer/seller roles, as well as a personal one from the interactions of trading agents. Both should feature in a full theoretical analysis.

Network theories

Social network analysis traces relationships among agents involved in social or economic activity. Empirical versions record connections between named individuals, groups and organisations; theoretical versions map out the pattern of relationships through formal models and graphs (Bruggeman, 2008; Prell, 2012; McCulloh, Armstrong and Johnson, 2013; Scott, 2017; Yang, Keller and Zheng, 2017). Networks are structural, as they rely on relationships but emphasise the personal. Priority goes to contacts among people or organisations, which if they endure may become formal and institutional – impersonal roles are derivative of relationships. The analysis can be applied to myriad subject matter.

In portraying markets, network approaches begin with personal interactions among traders, treating these not as aberrations but as normal (Baker, 1984; Lie, 1997; Rauch, 2001; Smith-Doerr and Powell, 2005; Goyal, 2007, 2011). Markets have a social element essential to their operation and not an imperfection or market failure. The positive image of anonymous trading is false – instead of being the exemplar of efficiency, it would be unsustainable. An accurate view of markets should avoid the neoclassical assumption of separate individual traders with fixed preferences and no relationships. The market is a social entity and has to be understood as such, so the appropriate method is relational and the foundation for theory should be trading relations. Study of markets requires formal network analyses of the connections among traders.

The most famous example of a network approach in economic sociology has been the work of Mark Granovetter (1985, 1992, 2017) on embeddedness. This draws from Karl Polanyi's arguments that pre-capitalist economies were embedded in social relationships, whereas capitalism brought the attempt to disembed an economy organised through impersonal competitive markets. For Granovetter, the prospect of a disembedded economy underestimates the extent to which modern capitalist economies are still embedded in social relations. A gulf between a completely socialised economy on one side and a completely non-socialised one on the other is too stark, neglecting the middle ground.

Central to embeddedness is the fact that markets are never governed wholly by their formal setting. Trading depends on people and their relationships. Successful trade means that nobody is deceived or misinformed, goods are of acceptable quality, services performed properly and payments made on time. Regulations can cover these matters partially but never fully. The gaps have to be met informally, such that traders trust each other and trade without complete legal guarantees. Commerce is lubricated when people form bonds and get to know each other; the bonds are not impediments to the market but help its continued operation. Social contacts are often pivotal in the recruitment of employees on labour markets (Montgomery, 1991; Granovetter, 1995). Much information is conveyed not by prices, as in the competitive ideal, but by personal networks among traders. Weak ties with distant acquaintances can be just as important as stronger ties, since distant relationships extend outside one's immediate social circle into different areas (Granovetter, 1983, 2005). Trade without social relations would be unlikely to thrive, regardless of whether the economy is at an advanced stage of development.

Other network approaches, following the contributions of Harrison White (1981, 1993, 2002), have argued that networks create new markets from scratch (Leifer and White, 1987). Markets for manufactured goods do not meet pre-existing consumer demand but are assembled by a network of firms. Each firm aims to find a niche for its differentiated products beside other firms with different niches. A stable market has a clique of dominant producers holding their own niche and happy to maintain the current producer relationships. The market is defined not by a homogeneous product but by a string of interrelated product niches, taking an inherently relational form. Buyers behave only passively, through their endorsement of the differentiated goods on offer from the producers – they can reject products and expose them to commercial failure but have no other influence on what gets sold. Sellers connect with buyers, although the crucial network is among the producers/sellers. Trading relationships are not only assisting trade but make up the fabric of the market, which has no meaning without them.

A variant of network analysis comes from theories that track the clustering of networks (Burt, 1992, 2004; Reagans and McEvily, 2003). Networks often give rise to relationship clusters with strong internal bonds but only weak external bonds to other clusters. As a result, networks can cross an economy or society but leave 'structural holes' in which ties are weak or non-existent. Relationships that span structural holes have special significance, as they exploit gaps in knowledge to find competitive advantages. Empirical study of network clusters can identify structural holes and pick out the distant connections likely to be most important. Economic agents able to mediate between network clusters will have trading opportunities unavailable to those within clusters. An example is the brokerage that becomes possible when one agent has better information than two or more other agents and acts as a broker between them (Burt, 1992, 2002; Stovel and Shaw, 2012; Hannibal and Ono, 2017). Such brokerage is beneficial if it improves information, closes down structural holes and promotes economic development. The broker may, however, maintain the structural hole so as to claim trading gains at other people's expense and play off rival clusters against each other. The consequences of trading networks must be assessed case by case.

Network theorists have discovered trading relationships in markets supposedly competitive and impersonal. The prime example is financial markets, which at first sight display the attributes of perfect competition: homogeneous products, many traders, continuous price adjustments, free entry and exit, etc. Empirical studies of financial markets carried out by economic sociologists show up the personal networks and interactions among traders (Baker, 1984; Abolafia, 1996; Uzzi, 1999; Keister, 2002; Knorr Cetina and Bruegger, 2002; Sassen, 2005; Stearns and Mizruchi, 2005; Preda, 2007). Far from being imperfections that impede the market, networks are a normal part of its trading. Prices are less volatile with close-knit networks than with looser ones. Personal relations spread information that cannot be transmitted by price alone. If trading networks permeate financial markets, then the same should be true of other markets seen as less competitive.

Personal relations in economic affairs are widespread and by no means unique to markets: they are found within firms, governments and other non-market organisations. The influence of networks extends beyond trade into the organisation of production, social capital, research collaboration, innovation and so forth (Powell, 1990; Baker, 1992; Podolny and Page, 1998; Burt, 2000; Inkpen and Tsang, 2005; Smith-Doerr and Powell, 2005; Goyal, 2007). The network aspect of market trade does not characterise markets fully and distinguish them from other economic behaviour. Much recent literature has highlighted the networking propelled by information technology, to the point where we could be entering an 'information society' or 'network society' (Lyon, 1988; Castells, 2000; May, 2002; Van Dijk, 2006; Webster, 2014). If networks are so pervasive, then a network view of markets will come as no surprise and does little to distil the special character of markets in a networked environment. The true place of networks is apt to be less extensive than implied by theories of a network society. Institutions and impersonal roles remain crucial to modern economies, and an account of markets needs to mention institutional context as well as networking. The formal setting for trade leaves space for personal relations but remains distinct from them and essential to the definition of markets.

Further difficulties stem from the narrowness of network theories and their engrossment with social contacts (Stinchcombe, 1989; Bourdieu and Wacquant, 1992, pp. 113–114; Emirbayer and Goodwin, 1994; Fine, 2001, chapter 7; Singh, 2016). Cultural background will shape the attitudes of economic agents and the relations they form, yet network theories often stay silent about this. The intense gaze on a single, relational level of analysis neglects other levels, notably culture and institutions, missing the larger picture (Nee and Ingram, 1998; Spillman, 1999; Krippner, 2001). The approach may be relational and different from pure individualism but does not include social structures in the traditional sociological sense. Social roles, if present at all, emerge from personal relations, so the relational level has priority. This contradicts the usual assumption that roles exist beforehand and normalise behaviour with few opportunities to behave differently. Network models of markets improve on orthodox economics but share its micro emphasis and gloss over the structural or cultural dimensions.

To describe a market as a network can be misleading. Markets do have network properties through the relational side of trading, and network models can shed light on this. The institutional structure of a market does not depend on personal networks, though, so a complete view of a market must stretch beyond networking. Exclusive use of a network approach gives too much weight to the personal qualities of trading and too little to the impersonal structural background that enables trading to take place. Markets cannot be encapsulated by network theories alone and need a wider outlook.

In trying to distinguish markets from networks, some writers go to the opposite extreme and set up a scheme with markets and networks in separate categories: quite common is a threefold scheme based on markets, hierarchies and networks (Thorelli, 1986; Powell, 1990; Thompson et al., 1991; Thompson, 2003). Networks are added to the markets-versus-hierarches dualism adopted in much economic discussion. Treating networks as a category separate from markets can be confusing, as it implies that markets should conform to the pure competitive case and assigns networked relationships to non-market status. The best way forward is a path between the two extremes, so that networks are neither equated with markets nor kept wholly apart from them. Instead, networks should be a feature of market trading, but not the full story.

Performativity in markets

Another way of seeing markets is through 'performativity', in which they are socially constituted by the performances of the actors involved (Callon, 1998; Kjellberg and Helgesson, 2006, 2010; Araujo, 2007; Aspers, 2007; MacKenzie, Muniesa and Siu, 2007; Araujo, Finch and Kjellberg, 2010; Butler, 2010; Braun, 2016). The application to markets derives from broader concepts of performativity within social science. In its weaker sense, performativity implies that a society is made up of never-ending performances by human agents; in its stronger sense, it implies that the performances call society into existence (Austin, 1962; MacKenzie, 2004; Loxley, 2007). Agents who perform in a certain manner construct the social world to match their performances, and a causal link exists between the performances and social reality.

This resembles a self-fulfilling prophecy, where anticipation of an event brings about its occurrence (Merton, 1948; Ferraro, Pfeffer and Sutton, 2005; Felin and Foss, 2009; Marti and Gond, 2018). In economics, performativity suggests that beliefs can be constitutive of the economy. Ideas with little value as an external explanation of things may guide the performances of agents. If we are to understand the economy, we must address the performances directly and not rely on external theoretical templates. An economy exists through the accounting, measurement and marketing activities of its participants, together with the technologies that aid these activities. In studying economics, textbook theories should be replaced with performance or activity-based methods.

The performativity view of markets has been expounded in the work of Michel Callon (1998), emanating from actor-network theory that gives a broad interpretation of science and technology (Callon and Latour, 1981). Science, for Callon, is distanced from the quest for knowledge of an object of study and instead at the heart of how modern societies are reproduced. Markets are the means by which scientific quantification and measurement have been diffused. A market is a social and technical apparatus that allows goods to be compared, quantified, priced and traded – it is created by the accounting and marketing cultures within which actors perform trades (Callon and Muniesa, 2005). Agency, structure and technology are all taken to be interdependent, in a bid to avoid dualism or reductionism.

Trading practices persist by continuous interactions among economic agents within their social/technological setting, hence the affinity between performativity and actor-network theories (Callon, 1999). There is kinship with the network theories of markets outlined in the previous section, though structural analysis of the network takes second place to the cultural and material background. Appreciating the context for the performance of market trading is more important than tracing out the network of traders, as in standard network theories.

Markets from this perspective are central to a larger vision of modernity. Trading motives, accounting procedures and technologies come together to format the 'economy' in its familiar capitalist guise, which appears to be natural but is an artefact of social and technological conditions. The actors in a market are not autonomous individuals pursuing their own separate goals and trading for this purpose alone. They are swallowed up within the culture of calculation and monetary measurement, so that it frames their lives as commercial traders and business people (Callon, 1998; Callon and Muniesa, 2005). Their agency remains intact, but entwined with the cultural environment and expressed collectively through social/technical arrangements (*agencement*). Nobody living in modern societies can escape the calculative logic generated by markets and the technologies behind them. Economists who profess to be neutral commentators are implicated in maintaining the economy. Orthodox economic theory is a manifestation of the status quo, as is clear from its pro-market message and the heavy emphasis on measurement, quantification and mathematics. It both reflects the cultural climate and reinforces the same attitudes and behaviour.

Performativity arguments are supple enough for markets to show diversity within the common logic of calculation and measurement. Empirical case studies have identified various examples of performativity. One area considered is financial markets, where practice has been fitted to economic theories rather than the reverse (MacKenzie and Millo, 2003; Beunza and Stark, 2004; MacKenzie, 2006b, 2009; Svetlova, 2012; Braun, 2016).

Actors steered by a theory and assisted by technological innovations have changed the character of the markets, with consequences for the whole financial sector (MacKenzie, 2006a, 2009; Miyazaki, 2007; Pryke and Du Gay, 2007). Other examples come about if transactions are designed on theoretical principles, as when the auctioning of licences and other items has been informed by models from neoclassical economics and game theory (Callon, 1998; Guala, 2001; Callon and Muniesa, 2005). The performativity in these examples is the stronger variety, such that orthodox theory remakes the world in its own image. Theory becomes a tool to disseminate the calculative culture.

The relevance of the performativity view of markets can be seen in trends towards marketisation and financialisation (Çalışkan and Callon, 2009, 2010; Callon, 2016). Neoliberalism has expanded the reach of markets through privatisation, financial deregulation, contraction of the public sector and decentralisation of firms. With financial markets taking up a higher proportion of the economy, finance has become increasingly influential. Capital mobility on a global scale means that firms and other organisations are available for purchase. Privatisation shifts public services into the private sector and lays them open to monetary pricing. Public policies once treated as qualitative and non-commercial, such as health care and education, are being regulated through quantitative output measures and brought within the calculative grasp of markets. At the same time, marketed goods acquire through advertising an array of qualities not previously associated with them (Callon, Méadel and Rabeharisoa, 2002). In a marketised world, every human activity and institution is measured in money with the prospect of being put up for sale on a market. Markets do not merely facilitate the exchange of fixed commodities; they sow the seeds of quantification and change the world accordingly.

While influential in economic sociology and cultural economy, performativity arguments have faced a good deal of criticism. One problem is that they are descriptive rather than explanatory, as they query the efficacy of outside observation and critique (Fine, 2003, 2005). With no prior conceptual scheme, the emphasis must rest on performances or interactions of agents, in a fashion reminiscent of network theories and with similar drawbacks. The primacy of performances means that other dimensions of markets are pushed aside, to be acknowledged only if they impinge on how agents perform. Viewing markets solely as instances of a calculative culture may lose sight of their character as an organised exchange of property rights (Slater, 2002b). Other levels of analysis, such as institutions, get no independent recognition and are discussed only with respect to performativity. A 'micro' focus on agent interactions, often in small-scale case studies, loses sight of the 'macro' context of culture, institutions and material production. Attention is directed at some capitalist motifs, but little is said about the wider nature of capitalism, which hobbles the capacity for thoroughgoing critique (Roberts, 2012; Christophers, 2014). The outcome is a thin account of certain implications of markets, as against a comprehensive critical overview.

A further difficulty is that performativity arguments overestimate the influence of economic theory on the real world (Miller, 2002; Santos and Rodrigues, 2009). Strong versions of performativity, in particular, tell us that economic ideas call forth the behaviour of economic agents. While this might be true in a few instances, it exaggerates the effects of economic models on the real economy. Allegedly theorists are not studying the economy but creating it, a view that ascribes great power to them – many economists would be surprised to hear their practical sway rated so highly. The case studies that illustrate performativity, which tend to be restrictive special cases, have not always been convincing (Nik-Khah, 2006, 2008). Markets predated economic theory by thousands of years and cannot have been created by it – the markets came before the theory, not the other way round. Despite the claims to be non-reductionist, performativity veers towards an idealism that sees ideas as determining reality. The one-way causality is inferior to a layered perspective that admits complex causality operating in the other direction as well. The prevailing ideology may serve material interests, as Marxian thought has always contended.

Performativity arguments have tacitly endorsed orthodox theory by positing a close match between the theory and reality (Fine, 2003; Mirowski and Nik-Khah, 2007). The match is not because economists have correctly interpreted reality but because the reality has been fitted around the theory. Writers on performativity are not defending orthodox economics and recommend different methods, yet they often treat neoclassical theory as a reliable portrait of reality, if only through it being a self-fulfilling prophecy. This seems unduly generous to economic orthodoxy. The abyss between perfect competition and economic reality is widely recognised, even by orthodox economists, and mainstream economics is forced into imperfectionist mode in order to have a semblance of realism (see Chapter 2). Business leaders and politicians use neoclassical economics as a prop for neoliberalism, not a blueprint for designing economic reality. To depict modern economies as being built from the tenets of orthodox theory is mistaken, apart from a few unusual special cases. The culture of calculation and quantification depends on forces wider than orthodox economics, which has been a symptom as much as a cause.

The structural context of markets

An alternative to adhering to network theories is to stress from the outset the structural context of markets. Sellers and buyers exist within a social setting and hold culturally specific attitudes to trading. Study of markets must address how human agency is interrelated with social structure. Markets are located among other institutions, so we should not be preoccupied with market structures alone. Two structural approaches are considered below: the field theories found mainly in sociology and the stratified theories associated with critical realism.

Field theories

The concept of a field originated in natural sciences and was only later extended to social questions (Hesse, 1970; Mey, 1972; Martin, 2003). Field theories assert the significance of contextual forces, as distinct from the direct linkages highlighted by network theories. In social-scientific applications, a social field is a stable environment within which individuals, groups and organisations interact (Bourdieu and Wacquant, 1992, part 2; Martin, 2003; Fligstein and McAdam, 2011, 2012). The interactions can be cooperative or competitive, but competition in a field must be regulated to ensure that the field survives. Maintenance of a field does not happen spontaneously and is overseen by the government, a regulatory body or the participants. Inside a field the relations are between objective positions, not the agents themselves, and individual behaviour depends to a large extent (though not totally) on occupancy of positions. Agents bring to the field their own cultural background and acquired abilities, which should be noted when appraising how the field operates. Markets can readily be depicted as a social field – they form a structured arena in which socially grounded agents undergo competitive or cooperative interactions.

In social sciences, perhaps the best-known field theory has been the culturally attuned sociology of Pierre Bourdieu. For Bourdieu, a field is a structured setting in which agents interact and hold social positions that bind them together in power relationships (Bourdieu and Wacquant, 1992, part 2; Bourdieu, 2005). A society contains many social fields (economics, politics, the law, culture, etc.), each of which is subdivided into localised fields. Interactions within a field rely partly on the formal social positions and partly on the capacities of the agents, so interdependence of structure and agency is fundamental to Bourdieu's vision. Agents bring to the field their *habitus*, in other words their cultural background and past experience that form their attitudes towards activities comprised by the field (Bourdieu, 1977, chapter 2, 1990, book 1). People who blossom within a field have an extensive *habitus* and various kinds of capital (social, economic, cultural, symbolic), which give them the cultural know-how, reputation and personal contacts needed for advancement. Access to social and other capital correlates with occupancy of senior formal positions in the field, conferring power over other participants. Society as a whole is divided vertically among various distinct but interwoven fields. Cutting horizontally across the fields are the power relations from the stratified class structure.

An economy can be viewed as a field, embracing other fields such as firms, industries and markets. In order to understand the economy, one has to understand its component fields with their structured positions and agents moulded by cultural background and past experiences. Analysis of fields can include a notion of interest (*'illusio'* in Bourdieu's terminology) but sees this as being socially specific and not inscribed in a person's identity (Bourdieu, 1998, chapter 4, 2000, chapter 3). Pursuit of interests is no longer an individualistic matter and has to be situated in the context of the field. A field theory looks not only towards network relations but also towards the cultural background (*habitus*) of economic agents and the formal positions within the field. The aim is for a culturally rich and socially acute picture of the economy.

Markets are among the main economic fields. Positions within a market, engendering market power, depend on its social structures, together with the *habitus* of the traders and their stock of different kinds of capital (Bourdieu, 2005). Economic capital, defined as physical or financial assets, remains crucial for the producers/sellers in an industry or market. Beyond this, Bourdieu points out the relevance of the other kinds of capital that play a part in commercial success (Bourdieu, 2002). Social capital refers to personal trading connections, as in network theories; here they are one item on a larger canvas. Cultural capital reflects the social background and previous experiences of the traders, which may help them fit into the trading environment and obtain better outcomes. Symbolic capital is concerned with how products are perceived by the public, invoking issues of product imagery, branding and customer loyalty. A comprehensive account of markets should ask how economic, social, cultural and symbolic capital affect trading behaviour. Individual interests, social structures and networks should all be duly acknowledged but are only ingredients in a cultural whole. Hopes for a definitive, self-contained theory of markets should be abandoned and replaced with the vision of markets as fields within the wider economy.

Another prime example of field theory is the economic sociology of Neil Fligstein, particularly his work on the architecture of markets (Fligstein, 2001; Fligstein and Calder, 2015). A market in Fligstein's view is not a unique, *sui generis* entity, as in orthodox economic theory, but an organisational field for the interactions of firms and other traders. To be created and sustained it must have the appropriate social setting through property rights, rules of exchange and governance structures. The need for property rights and rules of exchange echo the institutionalist arguments about legal foundations written down in property and contract law: a market cannot exist without prior agreement about property transfers. Governance structures specify the rules for how firms are organised and how they deal with each other. Fligstein (1996) sees markets as being crafted by the participating organisations, so it becomes impossible to theorise separately about trade and organisational matters. Prices will not emerge from competitive trading but will be decided by the dominant traders to suit their interests. Since a market is an organisational field, it can be understood only after examining the relevant organisations and their trading behaviour.

Insights can thus be gleaned from organisation theory (Fligstein and Freedland, 1995; Fligstein and Dauter, 2007). Crucial to any organisation is the ability to reproduce itself, which means that rival organisations in a competitive environment will seek safety. Firms participating in a market aim to control competition and tame the environment in which they interact with other firms and with their customers. Far from being a neutral space in which traders come together, the market becomes a field organised by the participants to secure guaranteed trading returns. Prices must be kept high enough to generate profitability and avoid price competition that could threaten the survival of every firm. Efforts to fix prices and stifle competition are standard properties of markets as an organisational field. Firms set up oligopolies wherever they can and confine themselves to non-price competition that does little damage to profit margins. This prediction of oligopoly as the chosen organisational pattern is consistent with heterodox economics, where market power is the norm, but clashes with the orthodox view of oligopoly as an imperfect special case. The state also plays a part in running markets as an organisational field, through its oversight of the legal system, regulation of trade and intervention at times of crisis (Fligstein, 2001, part 1). Ultimately, each market is organised by its biggest participants under the eye of the state.

Field theories need detailed case-by-case studies. Firms interact in different ways and create different organisational fields that share common properties but are distinctive in how they operate. Both Bourdieu and Fligstein point to practical cases of their field theories. Bourdieu (1996) investigated the market for literary products in France; Fligstein studied trade in the European Union and examined the contributions of multinational firms and national governments in organising it (Fligstein and Mara-Drita, 1996). Empirical study of markets as fields will map out the trading relations as also recorded by network theorists. Field theories need not be incompatible with networks and include personal trading connections when applied to specific cases. The difference is that a field includes more than personal networks, which are parts of a whole. The approach is structural, not interactional, and the impersonal social structures of the market and its participating organisations are paramount. Empirical applications hinge on the social and cultural setting (the field) in which trade takes place.

Stratified and critical realist theories

A stratified social theory results from a wish to avoid reductionism by having emergent powers and multiple levels of analysis, none of which can be reduced to the others (Joseph and Kennedy, 2000; Sawyer, 2005; Hodgson, 2007; Elder-Vass, 2010). Structural approaches, if pushed too far, can lead to structural reductionism that reduces all social outcomes to the structural level, with individual agents having no freedom to behave differently. An example is the structural-functionalism of Talcott Parsons and his followers, which built up large systemic models of society and was often criticised for its reductionist tendencies (Parsons, 1949, 1951; Craib, 1992, chapter 3; Layder, 2006, chapter 2). Orthodox economists have gone to the opposite pole of reductionism through neoclassical models founded on rational individual behaviour. Under methodological individualism, all valid explanations must be at the individual level, and social structures are absent or secondary. A stratified viewpoint seeks to transcend both structural and individualistic reductionism by having a layered theory. At least two interdependent layers are recognised – social structures and individual agents – though further layers can be added.

Similar ideas are found in the literature on critical realism, which has burgeoned in the last few decades across many academic disciplines (Bhaskar, 1986, 1989, 2016; Collier, 1994; Archer et al., 1998; Danermark et al., 2002). Critical realism responds to the excesses of postmodernism, especially ontological relativism that denies the existence of a single objective reality and casts doubt on the possibility of science. It can also provide a naturalistic stance sensitive towards the distinctive qualities of social studies (Jackson, 1995; Bhaskar, 2015). Instead of denying ontology, critical realists address it directly and make explicit ontological assumptions as a foundation for scientific enquiry.

In social sciences, the task for critical realism is to find a non-reductionist social ontology to provide a framework for further investigation. This would constitute a definite object of study, avoiding nihilistic collapse into ontological relativism but being open enough to permit varied social theorising. In aiming to elude reductionism, the social ontology is a layered one with several layers or levels and interaction among them. At certain times, the structural or individualistic layers may predominate, but this can only be a local feature and does not develop into structural or individualistic reductionism. Layered social ontology can justify social sciences while providing a bulwark against reductionist theorising.

Agency-structure duality has been a theme of recent social theorising, with agency and structure conceptually distinct but thoroughly intertwined (Giddens, 1984; Craib, 1992, chapter 7; Fuchs, 2001; Layder, 2006, chapter 8). Rather than being a dualism of contrasted and conflicting opposites, they are mutually dependent: structures are formed and reproduced through human agency; individuals are nurtured and cultivated within a structured social setting. Theorists should discuss structure and agency simultaneously and not let either of them decline into oblivion. The same considerations can be found among critical realists, who also espouse duality (Bhaskar, 1978, 2015; Reed, 1997). Social ontology, if it is to fulfil its intended purpose, must portray structure and agency as distinct, interdependent layers that interact in varied ways. Asserting separate layers in a dualism would not suffice, for it would omit the mutual dependence. Although widely used in social theory, duality-based methods have been criticised for weakening structure-agency distinctions and (paradoxically) increasing the risks of reductionism (Layder, 1987; Mouzelis, 1989, 1995, chapters 6 and 7; Jackson, 1999; Layder, 2006, chapter 11). Proclaiming the duality of agency and structure will not on its own ensure a proper account of their interaction, and duality theorists have to guard against any inclinations to prioritise one layer or the other.

Arguments for non-reductionist social theorising do not cohere into a single theory. Various social theorists have produced their own frameworks with much in common but differences in terminology and content (see, for example, Bourdieu, 1977; Alexander, 1985; Alexander and Colomy, 1985; Munch and Smelser, 1987; Mouzelis, 1995). Stratification is among the shared traits, without a definite prescription about the layers required or how they are connected. Much the same can be said of critical realist theorising, where the case for layered social ontology does not translate into a universal scheme. The foremost critical realist theory is Roy Bhaskar's transformational model of social activity (TMSA), which calls upon agency-structure duality (Bhaskar, 1989, chapter 5). Other critical realists such as Margaret Archer (1995, 1996, 2003) have proposed kindred theoretical schemes. The thrust of critical realist work in economics has been general methodology and the deficiencies of orthodox economics, with its deductive methods, excessive use of mathematics and individualistic theorising (Lawson, 1997, 2003, 2015; Fleetwood, 1999; Downward, 2003; Lewis, 2004). In considering critical realist approaches to markets, one has to adapt these arguments to the study of organised trading.

At the kernel of a stratified view of markets lie the structured roles of seller and buyer created by the institutional setting. If this analytical layer were absent, markets would not have the prior organisation for ongoing trade. The roles of seller and buyer, defined impersonally, are consistent with the role-based notion of social structure usually adopted in sociology (Jackson, 2007b). They are also consistent with the perception of social structure in Bhaskar's TMSA (Bhaskar, 1983, 1989, chapter 5). In taking a structural approach, there should be no need to redefine social structures and shift away from the usual sociological definition. Interdependence of agency and structure should be attainable with standard definitions of these two terms and not contingent on redefining them. Any further structured interactions among traders should be portrayed by adding a new layer rather than replacing one of the existing layers.

The personal trading relations discussed in network theories can be included as an extra level of analysis alongside the structured trading roles. Because formal roles are incomplete and do not dictate trading behaviour, traders can customise the way they trade. Relational exchange may emerge but will not eliminate the formal structure of trading, which still relies on seller and buyer roles. Network theories are too restrictive if they see networking as the sole mode of trading or regard formal structures as mere outgrowths of networking. In a stratified theory, trading networks would be an additional layer centred on personal relations, not impersonal trading roles. A personal trading relation does have a structural quality insofar as it requires the continuous participation of two named agents and would cease to exist if either of them withdrew. Networks can be interpreted as personal social structures (sometimes termed the 'interaction order' or 'figurations'), which may be more ephemeral than impersonal structures but have durability and influence trading (Jackson, 2003). The notion of social structure would then itself be stratified, with personal and impersonal layers.

As well as personal networks, there may be other trading interactions that yield further levels of analysis. An example is product branding designed to reduce anonymous trade and foster brand loyalty from regular customers (Aaker, 1991; Chaudhuri and Holbrook, 2001; Keller, 2003). No longer homogeneous, products are linked to a particular seller and purchasing decisions are prompted by the buyer's connection with the seller as well as the nature of the product. Modern marketing turns on customer relationship management, which aims to stay in touch with loyal customers and forge an indirect relationship with them (Buttle, 2009; Kumar and Reinartz, 2012; Kotler and Keller, 2016, part 3). This is not face-to-face contact but still a personal bond that breaches the anonymity of competitive markets. Information technology makes it simple for firms to compile customer databases, run loyalty schemes and keep track of consumer behaviour (Newell, 2001; Tan, Yen and Fang, 2002; Chaffey and Ellis-Chadwick, 2016; Strauss and Frost, 2016). Customer relations create subsidiary roles of 'regular provider' and 'regular customer', in addition to the seller and buyer roles. Even though the new roles are incomplete and not binding, with people free to switch between sellers if they wish, trade will be channelled into a furrow. The subsidiary trading roles add a new theoretical layer between the seller/buyer roles and personal networks, as in Figure 6.2. Several structural layers coexist, so the social structure of trade has to be understood in a stratified sense.

A stratified theory of markets should treat trading agents as a layer distinct from social structures. Traders are diverse: some are people, others are firms and other organisations defined legally as trading entities. What traders have in common is that they participate in the same institutional arena. They mesh with the social structures and relationships of a market, through formal trading roles and personal contacts with other traders. Different trading agents have different degrees of engagement with trading roles and relations.

For pure competitive traders, as depicted in neoclassical theory, the seller and buyer roles suffice and trade rests on prices alone – there are no subsidiary roles or personal relationships. Such trading behaviour is rare, and markets for most consumer goods include subsidiary trading roles encouraged by product branding and loyalty schemes. Buyers differ on whether they respond to branding or seek the lowest prices. In cases with few participants on both sides of the market, personal relationships

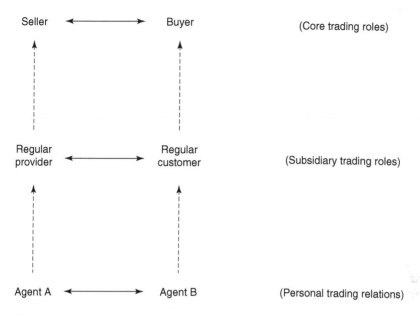

Figure 6.2 Subsidiary trading roles.

are likely to be stronger. The behaviour of trading agents is not wholly determined by social structures and cannot be read off the structure of a market, as in structural reductionism. Agents trade within a structured context but adapt their behaviour and trade in a variety of ways.

Stratified or critical realist theorising leads to a general, non-restrictive account of markets that captures the institutional background of organised trade but leaves open many details of how trade takes place in specific cases. With several layers in the theoretical framework, some layers may prevail at certain times and places, even if they never acquire total dominance. Alongside the framework, a full investigation of markets will require local, case-by-case studies. Analysts looking at specific markets will have to answer specific questions. What is the extent of price competition? How important are subsidiary trading roles? Are traders involved in personal relationships? Dealing with such issues will give each market its unique character. Certain levels of analysis should be emphasised in particular circumstances, but this is within the larger, non-reductionist scheme. A stratified view, pursued sensitively, can combine a wide theoretical vision with variability among particular cases.

The goal in stratified theory is to offer a general perspective on markets, as against a single model. This should be an advantage, though it presupposes that case-by-case studies will actually go ahead. A frequent qualm about critical realism in economics is that its adherents seem preoccupied with philosophical and methodological matters at the expense of practical questions (Nielsen, 2002; Fine, 2004, 2006). They are doing preparatory work ('underlabouring') for a future social science, without moving on to the next step of carrying out detailed research. Critical engagement is less incisive than it might be, since the realism could be compatible with numerous alternative theories and lacks a systemic handle on the whole economy (Sayer, 1997; Hodgson, 2004a; Brown, 2007, 2014). Most critiques of orthodox economics have come from authors who do not work under the critical realist banner. Their arguments are often compatible with the non-reductionist viewpoint that motivates critical realism and could be located within a stratified theoretical scheme. Critical realism has value as scaffolding for diverse heterodox arguments, without supplying a single critical-realist version of economic theory.

7 Functional approaches

As well as looking at the structure of markets, we can look at their functions and characterise them by what they do, rather than what they are. The emphasis is then on the purposes of trading. Why do people trade, and why does trade take a market form? Structures remain relevant but are governed by the functions being fulfilled. From this viewpoint, an understanding of markets should begin with functions, not structures or behaviour. The assumption is that markets emerge and prevail only if they have desirable outcomes for society or at least for the social elite. Theorists should investigate the functions of a market and of related items such as money and prices.

Functional explanation accounts for an institution through its functions alone, with no further causal mechanism (Hempel, 1959; Nagel, 1961, chapter 16). An institution exists because of its functions, so theorists should trace them out. Functionalism has always been controversial, provoking fierce debate (see, for example, Davis, 1959; Dore, 1961; Demerath and Peterson, 1967; Merton, 1968a, chapter 3; Cummins, 1975; Alexander, 1985; Kincaid, 1990). The main problem is that functional approaches may fall short of full causal explanation – merely listing the beneficial consequences of an institution may not be enough to explain how it came about. Functionalist schools of thought have been significant in sociology, anthropology and psychology, though challenged by rival schools. Economists have viewed functionalism with suspicion over its links with non-economic social sciences and never been keen on it. Nowadays the term 'functionalist' has pejorative overtones, so that many academics shun the label. Yet tacit functional arguments are common in economics and elsewhere, even among critics of functionalism (Jackson, 2002). Hard to suppress, functional thought will continue to colour academic debates in economics and the other social sciences.

The current chapter interprets functional approaches broadly to include any arguments that specify functions performed by markets and dwell on what markets do as against how they are structured. Few of these approaches are openly functionalist, despite functions featuring in the discussion. Much more frequent is theorising based on the beneficial consequences of markets, hinting that the benefits justify why markets exist. One can reasonably claim that the orthodox treatment of markets, set out in countless textbooks, has a functionalist character: it includes an elaborate analysis of the efficiency of competitive markets, a universal model light on structural detail and a sparse causal account of how markets originated. The orthodox view has already been examined in Chapter 2 and will not be discussed further as a functional approach. Examples are instead drawn from institutionalism and Austrian economics.

Attention focuses first on the core functions of trade, money and prices, which crop up intermittently in economics, but explicit treatment of them is less prominent than might be expected. Reflection on the functions of markets has been confined mostly to institutionalism, which asks why trade became organised in market form. A different functional strand arises with Austrian economics, which ascribes to markets the functions of gathering information and facilitating entrepreneurship – markets are associated with their functions, and the rosy picture justifies their existence.

Functions of trade and money

Markets are a type of exchange normally using money as a medium. In the history of markets outlined in Part II, the evolutionary sequence appears to have been trade, then money, then markets. Functions of a market derive from functions of trade and money, which have precedence. Since markets are one sort of trading among others, their functional interpretation cannot be kept apart from trade. Likewise, the monetary character of markets means that their functions must be entwined with the functions of money. Before considering the functions of markets, we should consider the functions of trade and money.

Functions of trade

The ability to carry out voluntary property transfers should have priority over other functions of trade. It ties up with the definition of exchange discussed in Chapter 1 and reminds us of the legal roots of trading in the establishment of property rights. Whatever the other consequences of trade, they will depend on how it eases property transfers. Closely related to this function is the argument that trade generates mutual benefits. If economic agents (individuals, firms, groups, regions, countries, etc.) specialise in producing certain goods or services and trade with other agents who specialise differently, then everyone can be better off. The theory of comparative advantage asserts that net trading gains require only comparative (not absolute) advantages in productivity, as will apply in almost all cases (Deardorff, 1980, 2005; Golub and Hsieh, 2000; Ruffin, 2002). Often acclaimed as a universal principle, the theory of comparative advantage sets out the benefits of trading and its economic functions. In practice, the benefits are not always so apparent, and any breach of the standard assumptions (such as increasing returns to scale) can lead to less positive outcomes (Krugman, 1987; Prasch, 1996; Wade, 2004a; Singh, 2011; Whitfield, 2012). It remains true, nevertheless, that the material benefits from trade are vital to its rationale and functions.

Other economic functions of trade can be identified, as in Table 7.1. Specialisation associated with trade may raise productivity, for specialised workers acquire greater skills and expertise. Productivity gains fall within the sphere of production rather than distribution or trade. Whether increased specialisation in production should be encouraged raises thorny issues beyond the remit of the current book and discussed in the literature on the labour process and organisation of work (Braverman, 1974; Lazonick, 1990; Knights and Willmott, 1990; Thompson and McHugh, 2009; Smith, 2016). Specialisation in trade and production are not wholly separable, though, and productivity gains should be mentioned as a potential offshoot of trading.

A further function of trade is to utilise surplus output. Societies that produce more than they consume create a surplus that should ideally have a use. Trade offers one of the uses (alongside saving, investment, etc.) and permits exchange for different goods and services. With the switch from householding to profit-making during economic development, trade is increasingly undertaken by specialist merchants, financiers and others for financial gain alone. Trading may then reallocate an existing surplus for monetary returns, yielding no net advantage – one person's trading profit is another person's loss.

Table 7.1 Economic and non-economic functions of trade

Economic	
Property transfer	Allows voluntary transfers of formally recognised property.
Material gains	Increases the aggregate availability of goods and resources.
Productivity gains	Raises productivity through specialisation associated with trade.
Surplus disposal	Offers a potential use for surplus produce.
Financial gains	Generates financial returns and capital accumulation.
Expanded consumption	Gives access to new goods and services.
Non-economic	
Bonding	Creates and supports social relationships.
Networking	Expands the range and scale of social connections.
Harmonisation	Brings disparate groups closer together.
Information exchange	Spreads information and knowledge.
Symbolism	Generates symbolic value in traded goods.
Political influence	Provides a means of exerting political power.

Other functions of trade stem from its openness and ability to expand consumption. Traders can develop novel products that create new trading opportunities. Trade is not therefore just a distributive exercise but contributes to product innovation. Higher trading volumes are a feature of economic growth; otherwise it is unclear how new goods and services could be introduced and made available to large numbers of people.

Various non-economic or social functions of trade are listed in Table 7.1. Omitted from much economic discussion, they remain important and should not be ignored. The relational qualities of trading, supposedly absent from competitive exchange, have always been there. Trade in its earliest guises was crucial to the spreading of social bonds outside tribal or family boundaries. Without trade it would have been hard to extend connections over the same social, cultural and physical distances. Trade was central to civilisation and urbanisation, and its social aspect should be considered in parallel with its material aspect (Braudel, 1981; Holton, 1986; Dant, 2006). Because it is voluntary and often cooperative, trade has harmonising consequences in bringing people together and deterring strife. In the ancient world, 'ports of trade' emerged to protect traders, maintain peace and reduce the dangers of theft and piracy (Polanyi, 1963). Traders may have conflicting interests, but their willingness to trade makes it less likely that they will clash over resources or other matters (Polachek, 1980; Mousseau, 2000; Gartzke, 2007; Hegre, Oneal and Russett, 2010). Preoccupation with the competitive side of trade can encourage neglect of its cooperative side.

Trading contacts have been a route through which knowledge is spread. Awareness of the technological capabilities of trading partners, as evidenced by the goods and services they produce, prompts a society to improve its own capabilities. Information will be disseminated across the full social and geographical span of trading, far beyond any single community.

Trade has further social functions in the domain of signs and symbols. Access to expensive traded goods and display of these through conspicuous consumption have been a totem of superior social status (Veblen, 1899; Trigg, 2001; Mayhew, 2002; Mason, 2002; Patsiaouras and Fitchett, 2012). The symbolic value of traded goods coexists with their use value and may predominate. Modern advertising relies so heavily on signs and symbolism that the imagery surrounding the brand may count for more than the physical attributes of the product (Williamson, 1978; Zakia and Nadin, 1987; Carruthers and Babb, 2000, chapter 2; Beasley and Danesi, 2002; McFall, 2004; Oswald, 2012). Consumers who seek symbolic value are willing to pay a big premium for designer labels and logos, far exceeding the production cost of the good.

Trade can be deployed to exert political influence on trading partners, especially when economic development is unequal. In commercial forms of imperialism, one trading partner has the power to impose unfavourable terms on the other and may take direct political control (Harvey, 2003; Callinicos, 2009; Ravenhill, 2017, part 5). Expansion of international trade has not shared the benefits evenly, with the most obvious gains accruing to countries already highly developed. Cumulative causation widens the gap between rich and poor countries. The classic expression of this is the Prebisch-Singer thesis, whereby prices of primary products and raw materials have shown a long-term decline relative to prices of manufactured goods and services (Prebisch, 1950; Singer, 1950, 1975; Toye and Toye, 2003). Poorer, less industrialised countries have suffered a shift in the terms of trade against the primary products on which they depend, exacerbated by the market power of multinational companies located in the developed world. Trade has political functions, a fact appreciated in broader analyses of political economy but overlooked in orthodox economics.

Economic and non-economic functions of trade have been remarked upon casually without being enlarged into a full-scale functionalist account. The nearest thing to an overtly functionalist view of trade occurs in formalist versions of economic anthropology that draw parallels with orthodox economic theory (Firth, 1951; LeClair, 1962; Schneider, 1974). Neoclassical models of exchange are hailed as the template for trading behaviour, applicable at all times and places and a reliable guide to why trade is beneficial. Unlike most economists, anthropologists have often been happy to describe themselves as functionalists (Barnard, 2000, chapter 5). The functionalism of writers such as Bronislav Malinowski and Raymond Firth was individualistic, with functions defined through individual interests (Firth, 1955). Theoretical analysis in this vein bore a strong resemblance to orthodox economics. Formalist economic anthropology, on neoclassical principles, is a reminder of the implicit functionalism that permeates orthodoxy. Such reasoning was rejected by many anthropologists, hence the formalism-versus-substantivism debates considered in Chapter 5. Substantivists saw the formalist account of economic benefits from trade as oversimplified and preferred case-by-case studies that embraced the social as well as material dimensions of trade.

The other prime example of functionalism applied to the economy arises from the structural-functionalist sociology of Talcott Parsons and his followers (Parsons, 1949, 1951; Craib, 1992, chapter 3; Holmwood, 2014). By contrast with economic anthropology, his functional arguments cover society as a whole. Economic matters become a subsystem in a larger systemic view and are inseparable from wider social questions. According to Parsons, the central functions of any social system can be summarised by the AGIL scheme: adaptation (A), goal attainment (G), integration (I) and pattern maintenance (or latency) (L) (Mouzelis, 1995, chapter 5; Layder, 2006, chapter 2; Tittenbrun, 2014). Of the four functions, the economy is associated with adaptation, in other words the practical means of meeting goals decided elsewhere. The other three functions are less economic and have more to do with politics, society and culture.

Stressing adaptation allows economics to be perceived in orthodox style as resource allocation and finding efficient means to a given end (instrumental rationality). Neoclassical theory trumpeting the efficiency of competitive trade can find endorsement. The apparent accommodation of orthodox economics reflects the 'gentlemen's agreement' made by Parsons and senior economists to carve out separate territories for the academic disciplines of sociology and economics (Ingham, 1996b; Hodgson, 2001, chapter 13; Milonakis and Fine, 2008, chapter 12). In Parsons's general vision, however, the economy is part of a bigger picture and never separable from society and politics. Economic functions cannot be limited to adaptation alone and extend across the other three functions in the AGIL scheme. The functionalist systemic modelling of Parsons, allegedly applicable to all societies, has been much criticised (Craib, 1992, chapter 3; Layder, 2006, chapter 2). Among the drawbacks are the obtuse theoretical language, over-elaboration, lack of empirical content, disregard of true causal explanation, static image of society and questionable nature of the assumed universal functions. A Parsonian model does, all the same, have merits: it locates the economy within a social context, permits layered analysis and recognises the social dimensions of markets and trade.

Functions of money

Money is amorphous and difficult to define. Economists normally give it a functional definition on the maxim that 'money is what money does' (Ingham, 1996a; Greco, 2001, chapter 4; Davies, 2002, chapter 1). An assessment of the functions of money is therefore required, even if it is not explicitly functionalist. Some but not all functions of money are bound up with trading. The historical ties between money and trade have been a vexed question. As recounted in Chapter 3, the state theory of the origins of money sees money as being connected initially with taxation and only later used for trading, while the exchange theory sees money as having emerged in response to trading needs (Bell, 2001; Peacock, 2013, part 1). The state theory implies wider functions of money, the exchange theory holds a narrower view in which trading comes first. Most economists recognise multiple functions of money, albeit with differences in the emphasis on particular functions. As with trading, various non-economic functions of money can be discerned.

Table 7.2 sets out the main functions of money, grouped into economic and non-economic categories. The economic functions are familiar from the functional definitions of money. Opinions differ as to which was the original function. In the state theory, money originated with taxation and had payment and accounting functions; in the exchange theory, it emerged from trading and had exchange functions. Either way round, all these functions were present early in the existence of money and are crucial to

Table 7.2 Economic and non-economic functions of money

Economic

Payment	Becomes the standard means of payment.
Accounting	Provides a common unit of account.
Valuation	Acts as the yardstick of value.
Exchange	Eases trading as the recognised medium of exchange.
Saving	Offers a store of value that allows people to save.
Borrowing/lending	Assists credit as a means of deferred payment.

Non-economic

Quantification	Provides a general scale for quantitative measurement.
Mediation	Becomes a general medium, not only in exchange.
Reification	Objectifies items traded for money.
Communication	Acts as the language of commerce and investment.
Integration	Indicates and promotes a given social entity.
Individualisation	Encourages impersonal relations between individual agents.

its rationale. Orthodox economics gives precedence to the exchange function, which chimes with its exchange models, though the ideal case of market-clearing equilibrium is defined in real terms and (paradoxically) relegates money to a *numéraire*, accounting function. A criticism of orthodox theory is that it has too restrictive an interpretation of money, reliant on limited functions that do not capture the role of money in modern capitalist economies (Davidson, 2011, chapter 6; Wray, 2012). Adequate treatments of money should look farther.

The saving and borrowing/lending functions ripen in the later stages of economic development, especially the capitalist era. Money as a store of value becomes relevant once people start to save their surplus income and accumulate wealth: it marks the beginnings of financial capital. Such behaviour goes back a long way, predating capitalism by thousands of years, but the vast expansion of private financial capital is distinctive to a capitalist economy. Money as a means of deferred payment eases borrowing and lending. Again the activities have a long history going back thousands of years but have expanded greatly with the onset of capitalism. The ability to borrow and lend, smoothed by monetary transactions, was vital to private capital accumulation. These two intertemporal functions of money are underplayed by the timeless equilibrium modelling of orthodox economics. They have been highlighted in the Post Keynesian literature, which points to the monetary character of Keynesian macroeconomics and the role of money in coping with fundamental uncertainty (Deleplace and Nell, 1996; Rousseas, 1998; Itoh and Lapavitsas, 1999, chapter 10; Lavoie, 2006, chapter 3; Davidson, 2011, chapter 6). The upsurge of credit money confirms that money's intertemporal functions have become pivotal and should be recognised as such.

Money also has social and cultural effects customarily labelled as non-economic and discussed outside the economic literature. The classic reference on the social functions of money is Georg Simmel's *The Philosophy of Money*, a cultural analysis of money and monetary relations in modern societies (Simmel, 1907; Backhaus, 1999; Frisby, 2002, chapter 4; Goodstein, 2002). Simmel deliberately took a non-economic stance, in order to reach beyond the usual perspective of economic theorising. Table 7.2 includes several examples of his non-economic functions of money. Instead of being just a medium of exchange, money in modern societies is a mediator of social relations. Many interactions that would previously have been undertaken without money (or not undertaken at all) are now monetised and subject to payments.

Items available at a price are treated as tradable objects, so money reifies or objectifies things. It thereby has the capacity to change a society, and its consequences span all social activities. The catalyst is the adoption of money as a universal yardstick to quantify everything. As soon as an item has a monetary price, it can be assigned a numerical score and placed on a scale that permits quantitative evaluation. The spread of monetised relations shrinks the qualitative world in favour of quantities that give an aura of exactitude, however imprecise and arbitrary the numbers may be. People will be judged by their incomes and paraded on an income scale with social connotations. Traded objects will be judged by their prices.

By Simmel's interpretation, the social consequences of money may be complex and apparently contradictory, in a dialectic or dualism. Money can extend social connections. It acts as the language of commerce, fostering communication and social links that would otherwise not have happened. Monetary trading has yielded a global network of human interaction. To have a common currency is an emblem of economic, social and political integration within a nation state or other political entity. In these respects, money pulls societies together and fulfils an integrating function – it provides a means of social interaction among people and other agents, with a social and geographical reach never before attained.

Yet counteracting forces are in play. Monetary relations are often impersonal and anonymous, reducing personal interaction: the cash nexus replaces friendship. In a money-based society, people become more individualistic as their family and other social bonds weaken. Simmel's analysis resembles that of Ferdinand Tönnies, who wrote about the shift from personal community (*Gemeinschaft*) to impersonal association (*Gesellschaft*) during capitalist economic development (Tönnies, 1887). The social effect of money is to increase the number and range of connections but cause them to become fragile and less personal. As money interweaves with the fabric of society, it acquires additional meanings in social, cultural and religious spheres not formerly viewed in monetary terms (Zelizer, 1989, 1994; Belk and Wallendorf, 1990; Dodd, 2014). Economic functions of money are supplemented by social functions seldom appreciated in the economic literature.

Not only does money have social functions, it depends on society for its existence, a point made by critical realist writers (Ingham, 1996a, 2004; Lawson, 2016). Exchange without money (barter) can in principle take place without a social setting, between strangers who perchance agree on a one-off transaction. Money, by contrast, can exist only among a group of potential traders who decide to adopt it as a means of payment and medium of exchange. Willingness to use money creates a bond among the traders; otherwise money could never be viable. The social foundations of money have been emphasised by state theories that see the state as the prime source and de-emphasised by exchange theories that see money as arising spontaneously through trade. From the critical realist perspective, all the economic functions of money rest upon the underlying social relations that make money possible. Preconditions for money should be understood through a suitable social ontology that avoids individualism (Lawson, 2012, 2016; Peacock, 2017). The economic/social division then breaks down, and the 'economic' functions of money must begin with social relations.

Close links between money and trade ensure that the functions of money overlap with those of trade without being identical. Money has the bigger set of functions, as it is bound up with measurement, accounting and distributive issues unrelated to trade and critical to how modern societies are constituted. Trading has expanded greatly but does not encompass all economic behaviour; householding and management remain important. Money, meanwhile, pervades formal economic activity and extends outwards into social and cultural matters. Trade in modern societies seldom occurs without money, but monetary calculations are legion, with or without trade.

Functions of a market

Markets, as noted in Chapter 1, can be defined as organised and institutionalised exchange. The institutions vary but generally cover the location for trade, setting of prices, publication of prices, payment methods, regulations for lawful property transfers, arrangements for delivery of goods and services and procedures for handling trade disputes. Trade can occur without these institutions, but insecurely, so a functional explanation must bring out their benefits. It will not be enough to cite the functions of trade and repackage them as functions of a market: a more precise account will be needed. Likewise, the functions of money bear upon market trade but are too broad to be counted as functions of a market. When discussing markets, one should seek functions that relate explicitly to markets as institutions.

Table 7.3 Organisational benefits of a market

Simplicity	Standardised products and prices simplify trading.
Convenience	Circumstances are mutually convenient for buyers and sellers.
Volume	Large volumes of trade can be sustained.
Permanence	The institutional context is durable and allows repeated transactions.
Openness	Anyone can choose to enter or leave.
Security	Regulations protect traders from unscrupulous practices.
Fairness	Prices should be fair and not exploitative.
Competition	Impersonality and neutrality of trade stimulates competition.
Efficiency	Competitive trading can generate efficiency.
Innovation	Free entry fosters product and process innovation.

Table 7.3 lists functions of a market, interpreted as benefits that come from the institutional character of markets and its influence on trade. As with other institutions, markets ease human interaction by providing rules and procedures within which to behave (Neale, 1987; Hodgson, 2006). A market offers a venue for trade that simplifies transactions. Organised trade in a specified location and subject to routines will reduce the uncertainties faced in less organised exchange. Anyone wanting to trade can find trading partners quickly. A market pre-selects potential traders, confining them to those who declare their interest by entering the market. Buyers and sellers still have choices to make, but these are refined choices among genuine traders, as against a random trawl across the whole population. Without a dedicated trading venue, transactions would have to be arranged on a one-off basis and would be much trickier to carry out.

Prices are among the simplifying features of a market. A price can be defined as a publicised rate of exchange between a traded good or service and the monetary medium. It conveys information to potential traders about the terms of trade and assists their decision about whether or not to participate. In doing so, it allows them to communicate and interpret each other's behaviour in a manner that would otherwise be impossible (Ebeling, 1990; Velthuis, 2004; Muniesa, 2007). If prices were not set or published, then traders would have to start from scratch with each transaction and negotiate separate trading terms. Information would no longer be uniform, and some traders would gain advantages over others. The effort from traders would be greater, the uncertainty in trade higher and the risk of unsatisfactory outcomes increased.

For prices to fulfil their simplifying function, they must be an accurate summary of trading conditions and publicised to all potential traders. Since prices are generally attached to well-defined products, they require the products to be distinct. Every market should ideally be dedicated to a single item, known to all and kept separate from the items traded on other markets. Each traded item will have its own market price, which should be public information and not left obscure. Price stability is key: prices that change continuously are less successful in their informational or communicative roles and may confuse trading decisions (Shackle, 1972, chapter 21; Hodgson, 1988, chapter 8). Stable prices act as social norms to underpin calm, consistent trading behaviour, whereas volatile prices distort trade and increase its risks. Trading decisions affected by price movements will not fully appraise the qualities of the items being traded.

Exchange organised through markets can occur in far higher volumes than non-market exchange. Published prices are broadcast to many potential traders who decide only whether the price of a standardised item is acceptable. Payment and product delivery are made as simple as possible. Nobody has to reach customised trading agreements. Trade without markets would entail greater effort in finding trading partners, as well as difficult assessments of the trading terms and goods or services involved. People would be discouraged from participating and the volume of trade would be smaller.

Markets have permanence as an enduring location of trade that permits repeatable transactions. Some traders return to the market to make the same transactions daily or weekly; others return at irregular intervals to make occasional transactions. The market is always present as an institution that facilitates commerce. If markets did not exist, then repeat purchases could not be assured, which would be troublesome. Markets are open to all comers with no entry restrictions, so a market should present trading opportunities for anyone interested. There should be no discrimination between regular participants and those who enter the market rarely or only once. Everyone is welcome to trade if they wish, regardless of how frequently they do so.

Another function of markets is to provide security via a regulated trading environment. As a type of exchange, markets rest on property law and contract law delineating voluntary, mutually agreed property transfers. All formal markets have legal foundations. Atop these, most markets have regulations to ensure good trading practices and impose penalties on traders who provide false information, sell faulty goods and fail to make prompt payments. There may be rules against insider trading, where some traders use private information to gain advantages over the less well informed (Bainbridge, 2000; Beny, 2005; Anderson, 2018). Such rules and regulations would not be present in an unregulated trading environment, and the risks faced by traders would be higher. Anyone wanting to trade would have to have to trust other traders, with exposure to things going wrong and no redress against malpractice. The need for trust is not eliminated by a regulated market, since formal regulations are never complete, but is tempered by rules to protect traders.

Many markets have an ethical dimension, insofar as they are intended to be equitable. Neither sellers nor buyers should have a systematic advantage.

The ethics of trade were salient in pre-capitalist times and remained a feature of markets in classical political economy (Downward, 2009). With neo-classical economics, however, ethics receded before the theoretical vision of efficient, self-regulating markets. Only when markets fail would ethics come into play, as part of an external corrective agency. Treating ethics as external to the market is quite recent in the history of trade and untypical of how markets have traditionally been viewed. The ethical functions of a market should be remembered, despite their neglect in orthodox economics. Chapter 8 discusses ethical issues in further detail.

The organised setting of a market increases the scope for competitive trading. Many sellers and buyers come together in a single venue, so traders can choose among numerous alternatives. If markets are to simplify trade, then the product traded should be uniform and standardised. Competition should focus on prices, not comparisons of different products. The upshot will be pure price competition, a case omnipresent in economics textbooks though harder to find in reality. Competition of this sort cannot happen accidentally and needs an organised market with standardised products and prices. Straightforward price comparisons are possible only if everything else is held constant. For items that are not standardised, choices extend to the nature of the items on offer, which may be similar but distinct enough to be viewed as separate. Sellers may differentiate their products through branding in order to seek competitive advantage. Branded products increase the apparent choices but reduce the market's ability to simplify through standardisation. A unified market may fragment into a host of separate 'markets' for branded produce. Relationships among traders are enhanced, as sellers try to persuade buyers about the brand and turn them into loyal customers (Morgan and Hunt, 1994; Payne and Frow, 2005). Advertising and marketing come to the fore. This all adds to non-price competition, though it upsets the elegance of a single-product market and reduces the chances of price competition.

As a consequence of their competitive attributes, markets are widely assumed to be efficient. The choices available suggest that, as long as behaviour is rational, outcomes will be superior to those without choices. Advantages from the ability to choose are most obvious with pure price competition – buyers are unambiguously better off if they can get the same good for a lower price. Formally, these advantages are pronounced by the orthodox model of perfect competition and the fundamental theorems of welfare economics (Blaug, 2007). Under perfect competition, markets do indeed have allocative efficiency properties. The difficulty, as noted in Chapter 2, is that perfectly competitive assumptions do not translate to markets in practice. The complicating factors in actual markets (differentiated products, advertising, limited information, restrictions on entry and exit, failure of markets to clear, etc.) mean that their efficiency properties are dubious (Sayer, 1995, chapter 5). Choices will be clouded by branding and other extraneous factors and may be manipulated or misinformed.

On the whole, the ability to make choices should be conducive to good trading outcomes, but exceptions and qualifications abound.

Open access to markets lets producers and sellers enter with new or lower-cost versions of existing products or with entirely new products. Incentives towards product and process innovation are built into an open market, with long-term benefits from reduced costs and superior goods and services. New products that differ genuinely from earlier ones (rather than merely through branding and advertising) create new markets and realise the attendant trading gains. A case for markets based on innovation and growth can be contrasted with neoclassical arguments based on efficient resource allocation. Introducing new products will disrupt the standardisation of goods and prices required for perfect competition: it would be an imperfection in neoclassical economics, causing efficiency losses. Multiple prices and products upset the simplicity of a market and dissipate the informational value of a single published price for a well-defined item. In the long run, stable trading conditions are less pertinent, and the receptiveness of markets to change may become an advantage. The capacity for markets to succour entrepreneurship has been a touchstone of Austrian economics, discussed in the next section.

Markets as an outlet for entrepreneurship

Arguments appealing to rapid economic or social changes are seldom regarded as functionalist, owing to the lack of fixed functions. Yet a fluid, lightly structured environment may have the function of allowing change. The Austrian school offers a prime example of such reasoning, with their image of markets not as a static mechanism for allocating resources but as a process that drives entrepreneurship and growth (Hayek, 1948; von Mises, 1949; Kirzner, 1973, 1992; Lachmann, 1976, 1986; O'Driscoll and Rizzo, 1996; Aimar, 2009; Holcombe, 2014). Continuous change takes precedence over stability or equilibrium. Although Austrian economics is not usually categorised as functionalist and does not so describe itself, it makes implicit claims about the functional properties of markets. It will be discussed here as an approach that invokes functions other than the ones mentioned in structural and institutional analyses.

The origins of Austrian economics in the late nineteenth century were entwined with neoclassical economics, to the extent that Carl Menger is credited as both the founder of the Austrian school and an early contributor to neoclassicism (Alter, 1990; Gloria-Palermo, 1999). Austrian and neoclassical ideas shared an individualistic outlook, a premise of rational decision making, belief in universal economic theory and resistance to historical, case-specific studies. In the *Methodenstreit*, Austrian and neoclassical economics stood together against the institutional methods of the German historical school (Louzek, 2011). Differences between Austrian and neoclassical economics were minor compared with their common differences from other schools of thought.

Arguments today associated with Austrian economics date largely from the mid-twentieth century, when the school was relaunched by Friedrich von Hayek, Ludwig von Mises and others – the new version is sometimes called 'neo-Austrian economics' (Shand, 1984; Ioannides, 1992; Screpanti and Zamagni, 2005, chapter 12). It retained the individualism and subjectivism of earlier Austrian economics but broke away from neoclassicism and took on a heterodox complexion. Neo-Austrians were unhappy with the orthodox portrayal of markets, the increasing use of mathematics in economic theorising and the expansion of econometrics. As a challenge to neoclassical theory, they nurtured their own ideas on markets, with many strands. Unlike neoclassicism, Austrian economics eschews axiomatic principles and is susceptible to varied interpretations. There is no single Austrian perspective, so the following discussion addresses generic themes in Austrian economics and its account of markets.

Paramount is spontaneous order, whereby desirable outcomes emerge from uncoordinated decisions of individual agents without external planning (Hayek, 1960, 1979; Sugden, 1989; Fehl, 1994). Efficient rules and conventions do not have to be designed and imposed from above but evolve naturally from experience. The economy can organise itself without central coordination. Markets are the conduit for spontaneous order. Subjective behaviour of separate economic agents comes together in the market to yield results superior to anything attainable by administrative means. If these gains are to be fully realised, markets must be self-regulating and free from outside interference by governments or other corporate interests. Competitive trade should be protected through *laissez-faire* policies. Austrian economics champions free-market doctrines coupled with a wider libertarianism, in a style unlike the pro-market arguments of orthodox economics.

Markets are special in their ability to collate vast amounts of information from disparate people and mediate it to give a positive net outcome (Hayek, 1948, chapter 4; Boettke, 2002). Information on this scale could not be gathered by central planners – any attempt to do so would produce misinformed decisions that suppress the subjective beliefs of economic agents. Top-down planning should, in the Austrian view, be abolished and replaced with unregulated competitive markets. The chief function fulfilled by markets is the processing of diverse information beyond the reach of conscious decision making by planners and administrators. Buyers voluntarily reveal their tastes through their purchasing decisions; producers/sellers respond to these decisions in pursuit of profit. No central authority needs to collect information. As subjective decisions unfold, the market can adjust to them. An unregulated market is a self-organising entity capable of reacting to a changing environment.

The radical subjectivism of Austrian economics rules out the mathematical methods found in neoclassical economics, as well as the static equilibria derived from them, and turns towards the intelligibility of human action (Mises, 1978; Pheby, 1988, chapter 7; Hayek, 1989; Boettke, 1997; Storr, 2010a). Formal theoretical models are absent. Spontaneous order does not give market clearing, nor does it have the allocative efficiency depicted by neoclassical theory. Instead of allocating fixed resources, markets respond to complex, changing information from subjective individual decisions. They adjust continuously and never reach a final end point or steady state, which has no practical relevance. Any concept of spontaneous order stops short of stability that returns a market to its former state after a disturbance. Equilibrating tendencies in Austrian economics are weak: an economy adapts through the market process but never settles down into a static equilibrium.

Markets acquire their dynamic qualities from their openness to entrepreneurship, which has great prominence in Austrian thought (Kirzner, 1973, 1997; Buchanan and Vanberg, 1991; Foss and Klein, 2002; Chiles, Bluedorn and Gupta, 2007; Sautet, 2010; Klein and Bylund, 2014). An unregulated market is the locus for competition, though Austrian economics interprets this differently from neoclassical accounts. No longer based on the pricing of homogeneous goods, competition rests on efforts by entrepreneurs to enter the market with new products and technologies. Successful innovation earns a competitive advantage and temporary market power until the next wave of entrepreneurship. Contrary to the neoclassical wish that any surplus from market power should be eliminated through price competition, the surplus is a necessary reward for entrepreneurship: without it, growth and technical change would grind to a halt. Competitive markets will not remove market power but call forth an ongoing series of entrepreneurs whose market power is fleeting.

The Austrian view of competition was famously described by Joseph Schumpeter as 'creative destruction' (Schumpeter, 1987, chapter 7; Metcalfe, 1998). This oxymoron was not original to Schumpeter and expresses broader philosophies of evolutionary change (Reinert and Reinert, 2006). Creation comes with destruction – the new must stand on the wreckage of the old. While entrepreneurship is creative in introducing new products, promoting new technologies and propelling the economy forward, it is simultaneously destructive in undermining previous entrepreneurs and rendering current practices and products obsolete. It has a dialectical quality, with the capacity to bring about revolutionary economic and social changes, as in Marxian thought (Elliott, 1980). Competition engenders a climate of transformation with no tendencies to converge on any neat, well-behaved equilibrium.

Although Austrian economics proclaims the benefits of competitive markets, its case for them is almost entirely opposed to the orthodox one. In neoclassical economics, a perfectly competitive market is a finely tuned resource-allocation mechanism that cuts out waste through market clearing and achieves Pareto efficiency. Any surplus from market power denotes an imperfection leading to efficiency losses. Profits should be competed down to an absolute minimum. In Austrian economics, temporary market power is crucial for the entrepreneurship and creative destruction that constitute the main advantage of markets. Only the promise of a substantial profit will motivate entrepreneurs to enter the market with new products and technologies. Entry and exit determined by profitability are more significant than price competition among a fixed population of firms who just break even. To wipe out profits would upset the case for markets.

Creative destruction is not going to be efficient in the static, allocative sense of neoclassical theory. It will be messy rather than neat and tidy. Old products replaced by new ones will go unsold, old equipment and buildings will be scrapped, new production facilities will have to be built. All of this is inefficient in the short run, as goods are being produced but not consumed, productive capacities in failing industries are depleted and resources are cast aside and wasted. Markets, from an Austrian outlook, are not justified by their static, allocative qualities but by their value in generating economic change. The focus shifts away from resource allocation towards growth and technical progress, which are the arbiters of economic prosperity in the long run, whatever their short-run wastefulness.

Alongside the contrast with neoclassical economics, Austrian economics also contrasts with institutionalism. For institutionalists the function of markets is to stabilise and organise trading in a regulated environment, which simplifies trade for standard products. Of the organisational benefits of a market listed in Table 7.3, priority goes to the first four: simplicity, convenience, volume, permanence. These are less evident in Austrian thinking than in institutionalism. Pre-eminent for Austrians is the last item in Table 7.3: innovation. They elevate the support for innovation as the highest function of markets, above the many other functions that could be mentioned. This draws attention to aspects of markets that might otherwise be neglected but risks painting an oversimplified picture.

The individualistic method of Austrian economics, with its notion of spontaneous order, gives a false impression that markets and other institutions can somehow emerge from uncoordinated individual actions (Vanberg, 1986; Hodgson, 1991; Rutherford, 1994, chapter 5; Dulbecco and Dutraive, 2001). The theory ascribes little importance to institutions which, if present at all, are liable to be shown in a negative light as impediments to entrepreneurship, especially when government is involved. Overlooked is the structural context of markets: the ability to trade depends on the state setting up property rights and a monetary system. Traders are often large business corporations with an extensive institutional structure. Much innovation in modern economies comes from the research departments of multinational companies, not creative individuals acting alone. Austrian arguments evoke a mythical ideal world, where individual entrepreneurs can enter the market easily and quickly to satisfy the choices of rational, independent consumers. Few markets in modern capitalism tally with this.

According to the strict individualism of Austrian economics, the individual agent should be the foundation for all economic analysis (Christainsen, 1994). Individual preferences may not be modelled in the mechanical fashion of neoclassical theory but are still assumed to be well defined from the outset, with little need to delve into their cultural origins or how they may change. Markets collate information from people who know their own minds; entrepreneurs respond to consumer demands that already exist within the population. This individualistic reductionism hampers a proper treatment of culture as a process shaping people's tastes (Jackson, 2009, chapter 2). Once culture is admitted into theorising, the interdependence of individuals and society becomes clearer and the starting point of fixed preferences recedes. Culturally informed theory should avoid individualistic or structural reductionism. Awareness of culture raises doubts about the Austrian faith in competition and entrepreneurship. Consumer demand may not be firmly founded on preferences and may be prone to external influences from non-price competition, including the cultural pressures induced by advertising and marketing. Entrepreneurship and creativity could be devoted to manipulating people and stimulating frivolous demand rather than obeying sovereign consumers.

Some recent work in the Austrian tradition has been sensitive towards the social and cultural background to subjectivism, interpretative methods and entrepreneurship (Ebeling, 1986; Lavoie, 1990, 1994, 2011; Prychitko, 1995; Prychitko and Storr, 2007; Boettke and Coyne, 2009; Klamer, 2011). The case for interpretative understanding of economic behaviour, if pursued thoroughly, should lead away from individualism towards a non-reductionist stance in which social context receives due attention (Quinn and Green, 1998). Likewise, a thorough account of markets as a process should accommodate culture, which can itself be a process (Storr, 2010b, 2013; Grube and Storr, 2015). Markets then become a social order that kindles relationships among the participants and extends beyond the impersonality of the competitive ideal. The subjective experience of the traders will depend on the trading culture. Any movement of Austrian economics in a cultural direction would strengthen its account of markets and tone down the strident individualism, though it would lose some of its distinctiveness and move closer to other heterodox schools of thought.

An accent on innovation as the prime functional benefit of markets cannot readily be borne out by historical experience. Markets predate capitalism by thousands of years. During most of this time the pace of innovation was slow by modern standards, even though market trade was extensive. The big jump in technical change occurred only with industrial capitalism, which goes back 300 years at the most. Rapid innovation is linked to the institutional setting of capitalism, not markets *per se*, and economic theorising should recognise this. Capitalist economic growth has coincided with a colossal expansion of privately owned and tradable capital, permitted by changes in property rights enacted in the early years of capitalism and promoted by governments. Private firms in a capitalist setting had to innovate to survive, hence the surge in economic growth (Baumol, 2002). Capital markets and labour markets were important, but only as elements in a larger story of institutional change. Entrepreneurship, private capital accumulation and employment of wage labour were contingent on numerous institutional reforms. Markets for goods and services, the axle of Austrian analysis, were not among the new features brought in by capitalism and cannot on their own explain fast rates of innovation. A full treatment of innovation should examine the wider historical and institutional setting.

At any given time, most product markets operate smoothly: the items traded stay the same, prices are constant and well known, and buyers follow normal purchasing patterns. The market is a durable trading arena, and its organisational benefits are those emphasised by institutionalists: simplicity, convenience, volume, permanence. To provide these benefits are core functions of a market under normal conditions. Austrian arguments revolve around the properties of markets under less normal conditions, namely their ability to let new products enter when something novel first becomes available. This facilitates innovation, though the impulse to innovate comes from outside the market: the Austrian approach sees it as the creativity of individual entrepreneurs. In practice, it may be institutionalised through business corporations. An open market does not guarantee innovation and can be consistent with long periods when no innovation occurs, but it gives a chance to sell new products as and when they appear. Innovation will be a brief phenomenon that disturbs longer periods of stability. In everyday trading, major new products are not being introduced all the time, so the function of markets in assisting innovation is only an intermittent one dependent on events elsewhere in the economy. The core functions of most markets at most times are to do with stability rather than innovation. Austrian ideas pick out properties of markets relevant under conditions of change, with large potential effects on long-run growth and development.

8   Ethical approaches

In neoclassical theory, markets are a technical matter outside ethics. Textbooks on microeconomics present formal, axiomatic analysis in mathematical language. Markets are portrayed through a universal supply-and-demand model valid within its own assumptions. Results from microeconomic reasoning are positive, factual knowledge and a toolkit for neutral expertise about the economy. Value judgements should be added at a later stage by politicians or policy-makers: the economist is supposed to act solely as a technical adviser. According to Hume's Law (or Guillotine), a strict fact/value and positive/normative division can be maintained (Blaug, 1992, chapter 5; Gasper, 2008; Barrotta, 2018). Economic theory stands on the factual and positive side.

The division is breached only in the sub-discipline of welfare economics, which becomes normative through a few 'weak' and allegedly uncontroversial value judgements, especially on Pareto efficiency. Even here, there are no grounds for ethical oversight of markets in the ideal case: the fundamental theorems of welfare economics demonstrate that perfectly competitive markets are Pareto efficient. The benefits are a logical outcome of markets under ideal conditions – ethical regulation could not improve things. Intervention, warranted only when markets fail, aims to restore the Pareto efficiency associated with competitive equilibrium.

Such beliefs are common among orthodox economists but differ from how markets have traditionally been viewed. In pre-capitalist economies, markets entailed ethical oversight of trading: the authorities who organised a market and the traders themselves were charged with ensuring proper behaviour and stable prices unbiased against either sellers or buyers. Similar attitudes lingered on into the early nineteenth century, when classical political economy still defined the natural price as a social norm to be distinguished from the short-run fluctuations of market prices (Downward, 2009; Martins, 2014, chapter 1). A sea change occurred with the onset of neoclassical economics, which converted natural prices into market-clearing equilibria. In neoclassical models the equilibrium prices are devoid of ethical oversight or social norms, yet turn out to be optimal.

Arguments for an ethical perspective on markets revive the attitudes held before neoclassical theory. Much academic and other commentary, largely from outside orthodox economics, has made moral judgements about markets and their social effects (Hirsch, 1977; Hirschman, 1982; Zelizer, 1988; O'Neill, 1998, 2009; Carvalho and Rodrigues, 2006; Fourcade and Healy, 2007; Nooteboom, 2014). Instead of yielding stellar results when left alone, the assumption is that they require ethical oversight at all times. Contrary to the neoclassical vision, the normative element must be ingrained in markets from the start and not appended later if things go wrong. Overtly ethical views of trade, despite being overshadowed in orthodox economics, have been widespread in heterodox economics and the non-economic social sciences.

Ethics is, of course, a branch of philosophy, and any discussion of markets hoping to connect with philosophy would have an ethical component. Politics too can scarcely escape ethical questions about social justice and the resolution of conflict, so the original designation of economics as political economy will encourage ethical thought. The non-mainstream traditions of social economics and social economy, while never having much clout in the economics profession, have criticised orthodoxy and its modelling of trade (Dugger, 1977; Waters, 1988, 1993; Lutz, 1999, 2002, 2009; Davis and Dolfsma, 2008). Substantial bodies of academic discourse affirm that markets can be understood only from an ethical vantage point.

The current chapter examines ethical approaches to markets in further detail. It first looks at the ethics of trading as treated in scholarly writings going back to ancient Greek philosophy. Recent arguments for moral regulation and fair trade are considered, including examples from finance and international trade. Discussion then moves on to the ethical implications of a market-dominated society. Further adverse consequences of markets may stem from cumulative inequalities, which are considered in the last section.

The ethics of trading

Ethical appraisal of economic activities dates back to the ancient Greeks. In Aristotle's virtue ethics, the concern was how to flourish and live a good life within a social setting (van Staveren, 2001, chapter 1, 2009; Annas, 2007). Advice on economic behaviour was part of the desire to live well. As noted in Chapter 3, the ancient Greeks divided economic activities into householding and profit-making, with priority to householding, the original meaning of 'economics'. The main ethical task was virtuous management of the household or city state to achieve stability and prosperity. Markets were secondary, confined to the profit-making sphere labelled 'chrematistics' (accumulation of money) rather than economics (Dierksmeier and Pirson, 2009). The ethics of trading depended on chrematistics, not economics.

Natural chrematistics were based on genuine exchanges of useful goods and services; unnatural chrematistics were based on greed and monetary accumulation for its own sake (Aristotle, 1962, book 1, chapters 9 and 10; Crespo, 2009; Sison and Fontrodona, 2012). What marks the trading approved as natural? For Aristotle the key feature was symmetry leading to an exchange of equivalents with nobody making excessive gains. Moral reproof fell upon traders who manipulated the terms of trade to make large returns at the expense of their trading partners. Natural trade mirrored the use values of goods, as against exchange values that could be artificially inflated. A morally acceptable market should align use values with exchange values, such that pricing accurately conveys use values. The 'just price' would be a stable level permitting continuous trading at high volumes with widespread access to useful goods and services (Aristotle, 1953, book 5; Wilson, 1975). Profiteering that reduced trading volumes but enriched certain traders should be discouraged. Aristotle said little about the derivation of just prices, which seem to have been social norms within an organised trading environment. Markets were the physical and social location where traders could come together on neutral ground and equal terms to reach trading agreements with just prices.

Aristotle distinguished between distributive justice and commutative justice (Lucas, 1972; Miller, 1997, chapter 3). Distributive justice is bound up with how we arrange property ownership and what this means for society. It arouses conflicting interests that must be resolved before property transfers can occur. Commutative justice deals with ethical transactions among individuals and includes natural chrematistics, the voluntary exchange of property at just prices. A society possessing both distributive and commutative justice will have well-ordered and ethical property ownership open to fair commerce. Although commutative justice stretches beyond trading to include questions such as taxation, it covers all forms of trading, borrowing and lending. Markets have to be observed through a moral lens.

Medieval views on markets and trade amended the ethics of the ancient Greeks to fit Christian doctrine (Walsh, 2004; Farber, 2006; Davis, 2012). The economy was a human artefact separate from divine law, subject to ethical judgements. There were no maxims for or against trade, but it needed moral oversight and was censured if biased and uneven. It should be an exchange of equivalents with no profiteering or manipulation. A theory of value remained unspecified, though just prices generally reflected production costs, evenness in trading relations or the usefulness of the items concerned (De Roover, 1958; Baldwin, 1959; Hollander, 1965; Walsh and Lynch, 2002; Koehn and Wilbratte, 2012). Ethical trade had price stability so as to avoid disruptions from volatile prices caused by speculators. Markets were monitored ethically and could not be left to the traders alone. A medieval market required the approval of the relevant authorities for trade at a certain time and place as well as rules and penalties to ensure just prices and probity of trade. Exchanges outside this setting would be unreliable, potentially immoral and prone to abuse.

Medieval trade had stern moral regulation to stamp out malpractices. The authorities in charge of markets sought to identify unscrupulous traders and impose penalties on them as a deterrent or exclude them from future participation (Davis, 2012, chapter 2). Trade organisations aimed to discourage unethical trading. Merchant and craft guilds, for instance, operated as cooperatives in which gains were shared and members did not seek advantage over other members; anyone who broke the sharing rules would lose their guild membership and be unable to trade (Thrupp, 1963; Postan, 1972, chapter 12). Unethical trade attempted to manipulate prices for personal advantage, spoiling price stability and upsetting the just price. Trade without a moral compass was motivated by greed, as against proper use of the items traded. Malpractices were analysed in detail and categorised into several varieties, such as *regrating* (buying to sell again in the same market at higher prices), *forestalling* (buying unofficially at lower prices before a market is open) and *engrossing* (buying up stock in order to raise prices artificially) (Herbruck, 1929; Southgate, 1970, chapter 2). The elaborate rules and penalties demonstrate that some traders did not obey trading norms and tried to disrupt them. While officially debarred, malpractices were common, sometimes abetted by the guilds themselves. As in other areas of medieval life, the high moral and religious standards were not always upheld in everyday behaviour.

Christian doctrines of the medieval period took a moral line on borrowing, lending and interest (Noonan, 1957; Bolton, 1980, chapter 10; Mews and Abraham, 2007). The arguments followed Aristotle in querying whether monetary lending could ever legitimately claim an interest return, such that the amount repaid exceeded the amount provided. Money was a social artefact and accounting device – it provided no useful service to be rewarded. While borrowing and lending without interest were acceptable, an interest return on a loan was profiteering. Charging interest was classified as *usury* and added to the list of malpractices. Only in exceptional circumstances could interest be justified, for example, if it was paid as compensation for the breach of a previous agreement about the timing of repayments. Normal borrowing and lending were at zero interest, though interest payments were sometimes made in medieval times, contravening the moral rules (Postan, 1973, chapter 1). Finance was on a small scale compared with the subsequent capitalist era. As Christians were discouraged from offering financial services, the gap was filled by non-Christians such as the Jews, whose religion had fewer objections to interest payments (Shatzmiller, 1990; Lewison, 1999). Medieval banking and finance had to take place under moral suspicion of illicit returns and bias towards the lender.

The ethical views of trade in ancient and medieval times, with their insistence on moral regulation, held firm during most of the history of markets. Arguments that markets require no ethical oversight are more recent, dating from the capitalist era and its allied economic theorising. A change of attitude was propelled initially by the eighteenth-century Enlightenment philosophy of writers such as John Locke and David Hume, who made the case for private property, individual decision-making and freely contracted agreement (Keynes, 1931; Ryan, 1984, chapter 1; Buckle, 1991). Under natural law, this was the ideal for social, political and economic affairs, superior to anything that restricted private decisions, for ethical reasons or otherwise. Contractual freedom became the priority in place of ethical rules, since the best outcomes would emerge spontaneously from voluntary individual behaviour. Similar arguments were taken up and embellished by classical political economy, most famously in Adam Smith's invisible hand (Smith, 1776, book 4, chapter 2). Private, self-interested decisions coordinated only by the competitive market could yield results better than those attainable through ethical, social or cooperative methods. Moral and religious strictures on trading were to be relaxed in favour of *laissez-faire*.

Classical political economy, even though it invoked the invisible hand, did not banish ethics from its theorising and retained a notion of 'moral economy' (Bortis, 1997, chapter 2; Sayer, 2000). Adam Smith (1759) wrote at length about moral sentiments in human conduct, and his views on economic and social behaviour were far subtler than a simple paean for self-interest (Lamb, 1974; Brown, 1994; Montes, 2004). Classical political economy kept markets apart from competitive equilibrium, which was based on capital mobility and profit-rate equalisation rather than market clearing. Trade under ideal conditions brought a natural price still conceived in the ancient and medieval sense. It was a social norm ratified by common practice without the manipulation that would have rendered it unethical. The moral element is present, even if it receives less emphasis than before. There is no impersonal mechanism for determining the natural price, whose normalised character leaves room for ethical assessment.

Economics in its earliest modern form was a 'moral science' that aspired to scientific status but embraced ethics in its theorising on markets and other topics (Alvey, 2000). The breach with ethics was confirmed only with the Marginalist Revolution and the beginnings of neoclassical economics in the late nineteenth century (De Vroey, 1975; Birken, 1988; Milonakis and Fine, 2009, chapter 6). Neoclassicism switched the meaning of natural prices away from social norms to market-clearing equilibria. The market, no longer a social process open to customs and rules, became an impersonal mechanism grinding out desirable results from atomistic behaviour. For the first time individualism was integrated within a standard economic model that omitted social relations and structures (Jackson, 2013). Ethics too was displaced, as self-interested individual behaviour would call forth an economic optimum without ethical supervision. The only ethical judgement was to leave markets alone and let them operate freely lest any intervention (perhaps well-intended) would make things worse. Wherever markets were competitive, ethical appraisal of trade was redundant. The sole exception was second-best cases where market imperfections might need outside intervention to offset their effects. It was impossible to expunge ethics – hence the persistence of welfare economics – yet analysis of markets went ahead with minimal ethical content.

In neoclassical theory, ethical matters are hidden behind a technical vocabulary that plays down any worries about trading. The benchmark model of perfect competition stands unassailable as the ideal: its primacy rests on its Pareto-efficiency properties, an ethical judgement, but the ethics are cordoned off into the separate zone of welfare economics. For the most part, orthodox theorists acquiesce with the perfectly competitive ideal and do not ask awkward ethical questions. Market power remains possible, though for neoclassical theory it is a technical problem of market failure requiring a technical solution. Ethical issues have been transmuted into practical issues of lubricating the market mechanism.

As orthodox economics retreated from ethical discussion, the ethical appraisal of markets became concentrated among heterodox economists and other social scientists. Heterodox schools of thought reject perfect competition, so they do not have the self-regulating market ideal. An ethical perspective becomes necessary, for the same reasons as in ancient and medieval writings and in classical political economy. Balanced trading and fair or natural prices will emerge only with continuous ethical oversight, not from *laissez-faire*. The tradition of an ethical approach to markets has been honoured, albeit outside orthodox economics.

Moral regulation and fair trade

Critical to the *raison d'être* of the modern economics discipline has been the removal of the trade restrictions in pre-capitalist societies. To argue for moral regulation of markets was to argue for slower economic development, less enlightened economic policies and loss of material prosperity. It was acknowledged from the start (notably by Adam Smith) that markets could be twisted to secure market power and biased trading terms (Smith, 1776, book 1, chapters 5 and 6; Bishop, 1995; Elliott, 2000; Kurz, 2016). These difficulties were brushed aside as a rare aberration of the market ideal. Markets were expected to self-regulate, on the grounds that unscrupulous traders would eventually be discovered and go out of business. Competitive trading provided an automatic mechanism to eliminate malpractices, so regulation would be superfluous and hamper competition.

In recoiling from moral regulation of markets, economic orthodoxy has had to throw out the traditional case for ethical oversight. Arguments made for many centuries were dismissed as defunct. Yet self-regulating competitive markets conjured up an abstract image that could never match actual trading. The prevalence of market power, in the long run as well as the short run, means that some traders gain a permanent advantage over others with little chance of this being sapped by competition. Far from being a temporary aberration, biased trading is normal and persists indefinitely in the absence of regulation. Unscrupulous traders may gain permanent competitive advantages. Even if markets did self-regulate so as to expel bad traders, adjustment costs would be high. Malpractices would still occur in the short run, and some people would suffer the consequences.

Outside economic orthodoxy, the moral aspects of markets have been better appreciated. Heterodox economists and other social scientists have maintained the tradition of approaching markets from a moral angle and making the case for moral regulation (O'Neill, 1998, 2009; Kuttner, 1999; Satz, 2010; Halteman and Noell, 2012; Sandel, 2012). This way of thinking is often perceived as a non-economic view. The ideas are economic in subject matter, though, and as germane as ever. Actual markets, unlike the textbook models, depend on a prior legal framework defining property rights and the rules of trading. Contract law, in particular, regulates property transfers and identifies malpractices: this entails moral judgements about what is unacceptable. Moral regulation is embodied in the institutional background of markets, and trading would not proceed smoothly without it. All markets have a moral dimension.

Since trading contracts are incomplete, the legal system can cover most but not all issues that may arise. Issues not covered by contracts require trust among traders so that trading can go ahead without all difficulties being resolved legally. Morality comes to the fore: a trustworthy trading partner will abide by moral principles not legally enforced. Any urge to exploit other traders will be resisted in order to be fair and preserve the trading environment. The self-interest depicted in orthodox economics, which would seize every opportunity for advantage, is moderated by the desire to trade fairly and behave well. Trust tends to be overlooked in orthodox discussion but receives more attention in heterodox economics (Hodgson, 1988, chapter 7; Khalil, 1994; Lorenz, 1999; Lawson, 2001; Nooteboom, 2002, 2009). Generally speaking, trust comes to the fore where contracts are least complete: it plays a larger part with employment (contracts of service) and one-off tasks (contracts for services) than with everyday consumer goods (sales contracts). Legal rules cover as many eventualities as possible but never cover everything, however simple a trade may seem. Moral problems with markets become most obvious when legal resolution is missing and trust among traders is inadequate to fill the gap.

A prominent example arises with financial markets and the frequent crises provoked by them (Kindleberger and Aliber, 2011; Bilginsoy, 2015). At face value, they resemble the self-regulating competitive ideal: they are well organised, have good information, involve many participants, deal with homogeneous products and have free entry and exit. Market-clearing equilibrium should guarantee trading at the right price with accurate information. Competitive trading should reduce malpractices, as does trust among traders (*dictum meum pactum*). Unrestricted competition gets formal approval from the academic literature on finance, which has rested largely on neoclassical economics (Bevan, 2015). According to the efficient-markets hypothesis, unregulated financial markets yield stable and efficient outcomes; external interference from governments or other bodies is unnecessary (Lo, 2008). The orthodox finance literature admits problems with financial markets, but only as market failures in exceptional circumstances. If the markets operate as they should, on textbook principles, then they are predicted to be stable, efficient, reliable and self-regulating.

Practical experience of financial markets has been a long way from this vision of stability and efficiency: financial bubbles and crashes are frequent, with repercussions for other economic activities (Kindleberger and Aliber, 2011). Troubles in financial markets have ethical consequences, given that trading agreements are broken, losses made and some traders benefit at the expense of others. The gulf between financial theory and reality stems from the rarefied models used to predict efficient finance. Actual financial markets cannot always equilibrate smoothly and remain vulnerable to misinformation and mistakes. The theorems claiming that financial risks can be balanced out and offset against each other do not allow for the social interactions and correlated risks during an economic crisis (Crotty, 2009; Kotz, 2009; Keen, 2011, chapter 11). In view of the difficulties, a case for financial regulation to prevent future crises seems clear, with measures such as reserve requirements for banks, separation of speculative from regular lending, curbs on financial innovation and so forth. Such arguments are aired in the wake of financial crises, though it has been hard to make them stick.

Attitudes to financial regulation have been cyclical, as foreseen by Hyman Minsky (1985, 1994) in his financial instability hypothesis. Economic expansion in capitalist economies brings less secure borrowing and financial instability, which culminates in a crash and economic downswing. The aftermath forces a movement back to secure finance, with lip service towards tighter regulation. Once the retrenchment is over and borrowing begins to expand, the sequence starts again with a loosening of regulations and growth of insecure finance prior to the next crash. Easy access to credit is integral to the upswing of the cycle. Despite the strong case for financial regulation, the demands of capitalist growth will interrupt moral oversight of markets.

Wider arguments for a moral stance on markets can be found in debates about international trade and its consequences for poorer countries. While trade has benefited many countries and regions, its advantages are not so obvious for less developed areas whose poverty persists in the face of expanding world trade (Chang, 2003, 2004; Wade, 2004a; Reinert, 2007; Whitfield, 2012; Siddiqui, 2015). The plea for trade justice contends that international commerce under the banner of free trade has favoured the richer parts of the world over the rest. Opening up of trade, coupled with weak international regulation, has allowed richer countries and multinational corporations to set trading conditions for their own advantage. Poorer countries are exploited as sources of cheap labour and raw materials, unable to control production or trade in their own right. Belying the rhetoric of free trade, rich countries support it selectively – they impose protection to defend their domestic markets when it suits them and remove this option for poorer countries (Chang, 2002b, 2007; Wade, 2003, 2017). The global trading environment is a mixture of openness and protection designed to fit the interests of big business. Market power intrudes to upset the balance among international trading partners. The remedy is to aim for fair trade, not free trade, with moral regulation to attain just outcomes. Only with ethical oversight can trade bestow evenly distributed benefits.

The quandary with market regulation on a global scale is how it should be done. There is no international government to act as moral arbiter of trade and enforcer of rules. The international economic bodies that exist (World Trade Organisation, International Monetary Fund, World Bank, etc.) are committed to the free-trade agenda, with intellectual backing from orthodox economic theory. Some traders may choose to respect moral trading norms on their own initiative, but this will be patchy at best. In practice, trade justice has been promoted by non-governmental organisations and campaign groups interested in development and global poverty (Blowfield, 1999; Curtis, 2001; Broad, 2002; Wilkinson, 2007; Pianta, 2014). With little governmental support, the impulse has come from producer and consumer organisations, trade unions, religious groups, environmentalists, charities and aid agencies. Since external moral regulation of markets is absent, the means of promoting fair trade has been to evade and neutralise the market power of the multinationals.

Fair trade networks encourage cooperative and morally responsible trade that reduces the disadvantages of poorer countries and evens out the trading gains (Moore, 2004; Nicholls and Opal, 2005; Linton, 2008, 2012; Nicholls, 2010; Macdonald and Marshall, 2016). Labelling of fair-trade products enables consumers to support poorer countries by purchasing commodities produced under equitable trading conditions. A moral outlook replaces the mantra of universal price competition, even if consumers have to pay higher prices. Stock assumptions about conflicts of interest between sellers and buyers are challenged by the empathy behind ethical trading norms. At present, fair trade accounts for only a small proportion of the total, and its precise details and consequences are debatable (Tallontire, 2002, 2009; Levi and Linton, 2003; Chandler, 2006; Fridell, 2006, 2007; Raynolds, Murray and Wilkinson, 2007; Le Mare, 2008; Utting 2009; Blowfield and Dolan, 2010; Raynolds, 2012; Raynolds and Bennett, 2015). It does, all the same, offer an alternative to the undiluted case for free trade pushed by many business corporations, governments, international bodies and orthodox economists.

Some have claimed that changes in consumer behaviour are moralising markets (Stehr, Henning and Weiler, 2006; Stehr, 2008; Zak, 2008, 2011; Stehr and Adolf, 2010). Consumers in modern societies spend proportionately less on basic needs than ever before and buy for many different reasons, not all of them to do with survival or self-interest. Subsistence is no longer the sole motive for buying. Trading cultures are changing. This opens up space for morality in consumer decisions, as well as making consumption less subordinate to production within the economy as a whole. If buyers make decisions on ethical grounds, instead of seeking the lowest prices, then commodities on sale should eventually adjust and acquire moral content. Ethical values would be inscribed in the goods and services traded, not imposed from outside by rules and regulations. Moralised markets could become self-perpetuating and sustained through new behavioural norms. Rules and regulations would remain but would be less likely to be binding in a market already moral. Small-scale, ethical trading, facilitated by information technology, could promote a 'sharing economy' guided by cooperation, mutuality, sustainability and other non-commercial values (Botsman and Rogers, 2011; Heinrichs, 2013; Martin, 2016; Schor, 2016; Fitzmaurice, Ladegaard et al., 2018). Buyers could exert their power not only as consumers but as citizens, redressing the advantages of the producers/sellers. As yet, ethical consumption is in its youth and variable in extent, influenced by factors such as education levels, income, age, pressure groups, local norms and political climate (Carrigan, Szmigin and Wright, 2004; Harrison, Newholm and Shaw, 2005; Auger and Devinney, 2007; Newholm and Shaw, 2007; Starr, 2009, 2016; Bray, Johns and Kilburn, 2011; Lewis and Potter, 2011). It has far to go before it transforms consumer behaviour and the economy at large. In principle, however, moralised markets could be the dawn of a new trading culture that revives the moral appraisal of trade.

These arguments may overstate the capacity for moral self-regulation in markets and understate the need for external oversight. If markets are given a clean moral bill of health, then we will be less worried about their encroachment on areas previously outside commerce. Advocates of moralised markets, whose goal is to improve the existing market domain, may end up strengthening the case for an enlarged domain. Critics have rebuked moralised markets and fair trade as creatures of neoliberalism and easily subsumed by it (Johnston, 2002; Shamir, 2008; Littler, 2011; Bloom, 2017). Under neoliberalism, markets spread through a two-pronged strategy: public and non-commercial bodies shift towards commercial operation, and private profit-making firms become involved in welfare and other non-commercial activities. Moralised markets may further the second of these changes. Buyers and consumers, acting as internal moral guardians of the market, improve its social outcomes. Firms respond to the moral climate by declaring their corporate social responsibility and aiming to meet the moral standards of their customers (Roberts, 2003; Rowe, 2005; Shamir, 2005; Carroll, 2015). Rather than transforming markets, the marginal changes of behaviour are liable to be exploited by the marketing and advertising industries as a means to sell new products. Moralisation as a process is prone to being captured by big business for its own ends. The well-intentioned desire for moral trade may do little more than provide a smokescreen for neoliberalism, with the false message that markets can be safely expanded without limit.

Ethical implications of the spread of markets

Alongside the ethics of trading, the other main ethical question surrounding markets is their scope and limits. What should be for sale and what should not be for sale? Where should we set the borders to commerce? How far should trading spread across the economy as a whole? Answers have differed over time and place, but it has been accepted that some things at least should be kept away from markets (Walzer, 1983, chapter 4; Anderson, 1990, 1993; Satz, 2010; Sandel, 2012, 2013; Nooteboom, 2014, chapter 3). Items produced for sale (commodities) will presumably be thought suitable to be traded at a market price. Ethical doubts are more likely in the familial, social and political realms, where trading may seem misplaced and harmful. Non-market activities may have to be set apart from market ones. The ethical judgement could outweigh the putative efficiency of trading, so that commerce might be debarred even if deemed efficient.

A market/non-market boundary was inherent in the pre-modern economics of ancient and medieval times. The Aristotelian tradition, still influential in the medieval period, distinguished between householding (economics, the non-market sphere) and profit-making (chrematistics, the market sphere). Specialised trading for gain was different from managing a household or running a city state and subject to different ethical criteria. Management was pre-eminent, trading subsidiary. Good management of a household or state raised its own ethical concerns at the heart of economics. Trading too was viewed ethically with a fair or natural price for traded goods. Markets could be approved only when the authorities were happy that conditions were fit for trade.

Ancient attitudes to the market/non-market boundary sometimes differed from modern ones, the obvious example being the ancient tolerance for slavery, which allowed human beings to be treated as objects and bought and sold on slave markets (Jones, 1956; Garlan, 1988; Bradley and Cartledge, 2011). Modern attitudes see this as abhorrent, a serious breach of liberty and human rights. Such markets are now illegal on ethical grounds, though the modern world includes other commerce that the ancient world found ethically dubious. Trading for speculative gain provides an example: it was castigated as morally suspect by ancient writers but is accepted and often applauded in modern finance. The perception of ethical trading has shifted over time, but it has always been acknowledged that certain activities should be held apart from commerce.

Under capitalism, increased productivity and commodification have greatly expanded the volume of trading and its significance within the economy. Attitudes to trade have adapted accordingly, so that trade is no longer secondary to management or householding. Most goods and services are produced as commodities to be traded, making trade indispensable to economic motivation. Markets for finance and labour cover areas of the economy not previously open to trade. Management and other non-market activities have continued into the capitalist era but are at the service of commercial goals and no longer self-contained. Enhanced prestige for trade broaches the issue of whether it should advance into territory previously off limits.

Modern economic theory arose in parallel with capitalism, under the same impulse towards expanded commerce. Most classical economists championed free trade, both for its inherent benefits and for the stimulus to industrial development. As markets proliferated, the non-market element in economic theory dwindled. The trend peaked in neoclassical theory, whose modelling revolves around exchange above all else. Once neoclassicism had been installed as the orthodoxy, the management/householding problem originally the kernel of economics was relegated to implicit status, lost inside 'black-box' production functions. Production, management and work organisation continued to be discussed in the Marxian and other heterodox literatures, outside the economic mainstream. The attention of orthodox economists had drifted away from management/householding towards trade.

In today's academia, the separation of economics and management has been institutionalised through disciplinary divisions. Management receives plenty of academic attention, but from the specialised disciplines of management or business studies, not from economics. Silence on management in orthodox economics appears to be justified by the fact that it is covered elsewhere. The erstwhile distinction between householding and profit-making has sharpened into a dichotomy, such that management and trading are discussed by separate groups of academics in separate literatures. This is artificial and intellectually unhelpful, as it overlooks the interplay of the two and encourages narrow, blinkered theorising.

The discipline of economics has been redefined as the study of scarcity, choice and resource allocation, a change formalised in the 1930s with the Robbins definition of the subject and dominant by the late twentieth century (Robbins, 1932; Backhouse and Medema, 2009). Recasting economics in this way was somewhat ironic, for it was an exact reversal of the original subject matter and meaning of economics. Management was once the focus with trade marginal; now trade was the focus with management marginal.

Economics as a discipline had abandoned economics (management) and switched to chrematistics (trade). The change had a political dimension through its consolidation of the market-friendliness of orthodox economics. An interest in management/production leans towards planning and non-market arrangements, whereas theory founded on competitive trade can be geared to *laissez-faire* policies. Neoclassical theory, the ultimate eulogy to trade, builds pro-market conclusions into its model of perfect competition.

With theory now conveniently revised, the default setting of orthodox economics was to support competitive markets and resist public intervention. Action to correct market failures remained justifiable, but this was troubleshooting with competitive markets as the reference point. Since trade was so beneficial, it should span as much economic activity as possible. The non-market component of the economy seemed a vestigial trait of pre-modern times destined to wither away. At face value, neoclassical economics would suggest that the whole economy should be organised through markets.

Practical matters were never so simple, and major economic difficulties (notably the depression of the 1930s) confirmed that market failures were on a scale unanticipated by economic orthodoxy. In response, the mid-twentieth century saw arguments for a mixed economy that combined a market sector with a non-market one organised around public ownership, planning and state welfare provision. Certain areas of the economy were decommodified and removed from the market to establish greater diversity (Esping-Andersen, 1990, chapter 2). The size and nature of welfare provision has remained contentious, as has the necessary taxation, resulting in the 'fiscal crisis of the state' (O'Connor, 2002). Public welfare measures have been attacked by neoliberalism in the late twentieth century (Pierson, 2006; McMaster, 2008). Lack of consensus about welfare provision in modern capitalist economies reflects wider disagreements about the domain of markets.

Resistance to the pro-market agenda of orthodox economics has been voiced ever since the beginnings of classical political economy. Romanticism was an early source of doubts, in the Romantic critique of capitalism (Ryan, 1981; Sayre and Löwy, 1984; Löwy and Sayre, 2001; Jackson, 1993, 2009, chapter 3). Various writers and critics outside the economic profession were disturbed by the extension of commerce: examples were Samuel Taylor Coleridge, Thomas Carlyle, William Cobbett, Charles Dickens, John Ruskin, Elizabeth Gaskell and William Morris (Williams, 1958). Among the concerns of these authors was that competitive trading would weaken social bonds and replace them with impersonal monetary transactions (the 'cash nexus', as Carlyle described it). Capitalism dissolved social customs and traditions, yielding a more fragmented, less cohesive society with little sense of identity.

Also problematic for Romantic critics was the mechanistic cast of capitalist commerce, in which everything had to be quantified, measured and put up for sale. Qualitative experiences – the quality of life – would be devalued and lost in a commercialised world that measured things through prices and lost sight of fundamental values (Carlyle, 1829, 1843). Markets would sponsor trade for its own sake, along with wasteful production of superfluous new commodities (Ruskin, 1862). In order to boost trade, producers would have to create artificial wants through advertising, marketing and other social pressures, promoting shallow materialism at the expense of a well-rounded way of life.

Romantic writers worried that markets would obscure the quest for good management once central to economics. This harked back to the ancient and medieval views that put management at the core of economics and trading at the edge. John Ruskin (1863) went as far as to draw up new foundations for political economy that were explicit in wanting to return economics to its ancient roots. His proposals made little headway in the face of vociferous opposition from economists and other commentators, though the strength of the reaction showed how narrow economics had become (Bradley, 1984, pp. 273–295). In sum, the Romantic critics were aghast at the ballooning of commerce under capitalism, together with the apology for this from orthodox economics, and wanted to slow down or reverse the process. They had scant influence on the economics profession but did inform debate about the consequences of capitalism.

A few writers such as Sismondi (1827) attempted to set up 'social economy' as an alternative to political economy, giving attention to the social and ethical matters neglected in standard economic discourse (Lutz, 1999, chapter 2). In the same period, the Ricardian socialists pointed out the divisive social effects of the emerging capitalist economy and used Ricardo's theory to reach radical conclusions (King, 1983, 2003; Burkitt, 1984, chapter 3). A similar path was later followed by Marxian economics, which started with Ricardian foundations and turned them into a critique of capitalism. Unlike neoclassicism, Marxian economics retained the class-based structure of Ricardian theory and did not jettison it for an individualistic method attuned to exchange and trading. Marxian economic theory preserves the traditional, secondary status of trading and takes a sceptical attitude towards it: production has precedence over trade. Labour, not exchange, is the source of value, market prices are surface phenomena distinct from true values, market power is the norm and free and equal exchange under capitalism is an illusion. The ethical thrust of Marxian economics has often been denied – it has prided itself as being scientific and denigrated ethics as utopian, bourgeois idealism at odds with the materialist ethos of Marxism (Kamenka, 1969; Geras, 1985; Lukes, 1985). All critiques are normative, though, and the ethics in the Marxian critique of capitalism are plain enough.

Moral arguments against commodification proved futile during the capitalist era, ending up as eloquent but vain protests. This does not mean that everything has been commodified, and the process was selective in its scope. Various moral limits survived to resist the tide of commerce. Certain areas of social and political life have been held legally apart from trade ('blocked exchanges'), so as to prevent a market (Walzer, 1983, chapter 4; Andre, 1992; Sandel, 2012). First and foremost, human beings should not be objects of trade, and markets for people (chattel slavery) are illegal. Likewise, human relationships among family and friends are not for sale, nor is the right to have children. Welfare provision cannot depend on ability to pay and must be separate from markets, while the destitute are protected from 'trades of last resort' by minimum wages, health and safety regulations, and ceilings on working hours. Artistic, cultural and academic endeavours must keep some distance from commerce if they are to maintain their integrity and freedom of expression.

Many public services do not mesh with commerce and become distorted and corrupted if they are commodified. In health care, for example, the doctor-patient relationship differs from the market relationship of seller-buyer (Pellegrino, 1999; Frank, 2002; Andereck, 2007; Goldstein and Bowers, 2015). Patients are not buyers, customers or consumers in the normal sense: their ill health is not a matter of choice, they have no option but to receive medical treatment, their knowledge of available treatments is sparse and their illness, if severe, will impair their decision-making. Doctors should provide disinterested medical assistance, perhaps under a fixed budget but without commercial motives to make profits or raise fee income. Health care on commercial lines would not be efficient or equitable, and medics would struggle to uphold their professional standards. The unrestricted intrusion of commerce into health care would put its values at risk.

Education is a further example, as the teacher-pupil relationship decays when transformed into a seller-buyer link. Attempts to marketise or commodify education and manage it accordingly will force it into a mould that does not fit and damage its values (Gibbs, 2001; Lynch, 2006; Molesworth, Nixon and Scullion, 2009, 2011; Lorenz, 2012; Natale and Doran, 2012). Pupils are in a bad position to act as buyers – often they are too young and inexperienced to make their own decisions, poorly informed about the object of study, unable to judge the appropriate syllabus and teaching methods, and influenced by the cultural effects of education on their preferences. Teachers are not selling a product and should be aloof from financial interests; they can help pupils to learn as well as possible but this must depend on the pupils themselves (knowledge cannot be bought). Any price for education will never sum up its full benefits, which are incapable of being represented through monetary measures or other quantitative indicators. Market provision, even when commercially successful, would be incompatible with the non-commercial essence of education.

Various other restraints on trading are imposed for ethical reasons. In a properly functioning polity, neither votes nor political offices should be bought, there should be no market for honours and the justice system should be fenced off from commercial interests. Fundamental freedoms of speech, assembly and religion are not for purchase and exist in themselves, irrespective of a person's income or circumstances. Some items are too dangerous to be on sale to the general public, such as military hardware, poisonous substances, addictive drugs and untested medical products. Many professional services cannot lawfully be supplied unless the practitioners have appropriate qualifications or proof of competence. All these activities are kept away from markets, sometimes in defiance of campaigns to commercialise them.

A complicating factor is that a strict ethical dichotomy between market and non-market spheres may be oversimplified. Should markets be given the green light in certain areas, but banned in others? Doubts about such a stark division have prompted debate on whether we should delineate separate spheres or take a more intricate, nuanced stance (Carvalho and Rodrigues, 2008). The separate-spheres view holds that certain items should never under any circumstances be commodified and sold. It puts clear moral limits on markets and protects the non-market sphere (Walzer, 1983; Anderson, 1990, 1993; Sandel, 2012). In doing so, it implies that the market sphere can have unrestricted competitive trading on the orthodox textbook model. An alternative view aims to avoid a market/non-market dichotomy and instead point out the diversity of trade and its interplay with the rest of the economy and society (Radin, 1989, 1996; Folbre and Nelson, 2000; Williams and Zelizer, 2005). Trading labelled as markets includes many 'non-market' elements (trust, relationships, loyalty, commitment, etc.) and incomplete forms of commodification. If the definition of markets is imprecise, then so will be any ethical boundary between market and non-market spheres. Ethical appraisal should avoid dualism and reach out across the hazy boundary to examine the nature and implications of all economic behaviour. To trade or not to trade may be less significant than other issues: commodification impinges on questions of ideology and power that should also be addressed. Preoccupation with the border between separate spheres could deflect from wider moral oversight.

Ethical qualms about markets derive largely from a response to their generic qualities, such as their impersonality, individualism and instrumentality (Anderson, 1990; Cohen, 2003). In their pure competitive form, they deny any personal or sentimental attachments that would dilute commerce and profit-making. Social ties are barriers to their efficient functioning. They cater for individual traders, with no sense of shared or communal interests. Trade is instrumentally conceived as a means to the end of maximising the net gains of the participants. No other goals are pursued. These broad features of idealised markets cut across social and political values. Monetary payments erode the social bonds that exist in non-market exchange and in less commercial ways of living. Markets replace the 'gift relationship' of non-commercial life with a harsher, less caring environment, as famously argued by Richard Titmuss (1970) with blood donation as the example. Monetary motivation changes the tenor of services and taints the relationships among the people involved.

The individualism and instrumentality of markets clashes with many political goals. In the triad of liberty, equality and fraternity, markets can be at odds with all three. Trading through markets jeopardises personal rights and freedoms in areas that should not be open to commerce (personal liberty, voting, access to political offices, etc.). A deregulated, competitive market system generates winners and losers rather than distributing gains equally, an issue that will be examined further in the next section. The individual self-interest fomented by markets leaves little space for fraternal or communal values and pushes them aside to extend commerce. Material benefits from trade will not necessarily compensate for the infringement of political values. Ethical limits have thus been placed on trade even in the most commercially driven societies.

Cumulative effects of markets

A static, neoclassical view of markets sees them as reallocating fixed resources with few consequences other than voluntary redistribution. The short time horizon rules out long-run questions of production, technical change, property ownership and social cohesion. Competitive trading is said to eliminate surpluses, apart from the normal returns needed for producers to subsist. Nobody makes huge profits from trade, so the effects on the personal and class distributions of income will be minimal. Since the traders themselves decide on voluntary redistribution, it will be advantageous to all – from a static viewpoint there is no cause to fret about distributive changes. Inequality becomes a separate issue of resource endowments. Unequal endowments will yield unequal trading opportunities, but this is distinct from the technical functioning of markets. Desire for equality might warrant resource reallocation, which has nothing to do with trade. Any reallocation in a neoclassical model should be done through lump-sum transfers that preserve the relative prices from competitive trading and incur no efficiency losses.

Actual markets have greater social consequences than the static account would imply. Goods and services sold through markets change continuously with the introduction and withdrawal of branded products. Sellers chase profits by marketing and advertising their wares in the hope of recruiting loyal customers. Commercial success yields market power that becomes the norm and has ongoing social effects. Trading surpluses, far in excess of what is needed for subsistence, accumulate into large concentrations of private income and wealth. Instead of being neutral with respect to distribution, markets when unregulated are a motor of sustained and rising inequalities. To depict trade as a voluntary redistribution of fixed resources is misleading. Any individuals or institutions exerting market power can sway distribution in their favour, at the expense of others in a less comfortable market position. Efforts to curb inequalities must tackle market power and cannot be reduced to reshuffling resource endowments.

The long-run consequences of markets exemplify cumulative causation, such that existing trends self-reinforce and get stronger over time (Sawyer, 1989, chapter 13; Fujita, 2007; Berger, 2009; Kregel, 2011). If something is increasing, then it will increase further; if it is decreasing, then it will decrease further. Positive trends intensify into a virtuous circle of cumulative benefits, negative trends into a vicious circle of cumulative decline. Success breeds success, failure breeds failure – the gap widens between winners and losers. Ideas of cumulative causation were put forward by Thorstein Veblen (1898, 1900) as a response to neoclassical economics and later developed by Gunnar Myrdal (1957) and Nicholas Kaldor (1972, 1985) among others. Neoclassical theory pushed orthodox economics towards an equilibrium method: when disturbed, a stable equilibrium changes temporarily but returns to its former state after the disturbance ends. Modelling is static, founded on a concept of logical time that allows former states to be restored (Robinson, 1980; Bausor, 1982; Setterfield, 1995, 1998; Katzner, 2016). Cumulative causation, by contrast, rests upon historical time in which history never repeats itself exactly and we cannot revive the past. When cumulative effects are present, the processes of change are ongoing and do not converge on a well-defined equilibrium.

Two general properties of cumulative causation are worth emphasising. The first is that a cumulative process will persist indefinitely if left alone and not cease of its own accord. It has no internal counterbalances and will be stifled only by external forces that disrupt the causality. This could be some outside event or crisis, or government intervention. Problems from cumulative processes only get worse unless the vicious circle can be broken. The second property is that social changes under cumulative causation tend to become institutionalised. Beneficiaries of a cumulative process face no countervailing pressures and secure their gains in a new institutional environment. They acquire further structural and social capacities from their privileged positions in institutions and relationships that nourish inequalities (Jackson, 2005, 2014). Once established, the social differences become normalised and taken for granted as permanent features of society. The only way that this will change is through external events or deliberate reform.

Cumulative causality within markets has ethical import through the widening of inequalities. An unregulated competitive market throws up winners and losers whose gains and losses have enduring social consequences. Winners consolidate their market power to enjoy a regular surplus that accumulates and can be used to strengthen their market position or build up private wealth capable of being passed on to future generations. Losers may be ejected from the competition, a predicament that threatens their livelihood if alternative income sources are unavailable.

The contrast between winners and losers is stark, with nothing to offset the increasing gap and curtail the uneven distribution of trading gains.

Academic literature has described widening inequality from cumulative causation as the 'Matthew effect': the rich get richer and the poor get poorer in an ongoing process (Merton, 1968b; Wade, 2004b; Rigney, 2010). Markets are by no means the only example of the Matthew effect, which happens in advertising, internet use, scholarly citations, learning processes, celebrity status, etc., but they have special significance because of their impact on incomes and material welfare. A practical test has been the neoliberal policies since the 1980s, bringing a shift from mixed economies towards markets and privatisation – empirical evidence on the personal distribution of income and wealth shows increasing inequalities during this period (Piketty and Saez, 2003; Atkinson, 2008, 2015, part 1; Atkinson and Piketty, 2010). Unregulated markets yield biased, uneven benefits: gains for some, losses for others, and no way for net benefits to be shared.

Alongside the personal distribution of income and wealth, another facet of inequality is distribution among economic classes. In a capitalist economy, asymmetries of income and wealth are rooted in asymmetries of property ownership, given that private ownership of the means of production is legal and privately owned capital can accumulate. Inequality stems from the difference between incomes accruing to property owners (profit, rent, interest) and incomes accruing to workers (wages). This difference underlies classical political economy and Marxian economics. *Laissez-faire* capitalism is associated with persistent unemployment that bolsters the bargaining power of employers and the profit share in national income. Regulatory measures, welfare provision and efforts to reduce unemployment would swing the balance back towards wage incomes, though the asymmetries inherent in capitalism would remain. Neoliberal policies since the 1980s again offer a practical test: deregulation of markets, cutbacks in welfare and disavowal of Keynesian economics have reversed earlier trends and brought a higher profit share in national income (Mohun, 2006; Carter, 2007; Kristal, 2010). Unregulated markets accentuate the advantages of private property ownership and encourage greater inequalities in the factor distribution of income.

Other inequalities occur at the international level. Cumulative causation in a free-market environment has often been argued to cause unequal development and a gulf between richer and poorer countries (Wade, 2004b; Thirlwall and Pacheco-López, 2017, chapter 10). Multinational corporations based in the developed world benefit from market power on a global scale to obtain low-cost raw materials and labour from the less-developed world. Even when manufacturing is transferred to developing economies, corporate control and profits stay in the richer countries. The inability of poorer countries to organise themselves and create countervailing market power is visible in their disadvantageous terms of trade; raw material prices have been in long-run decline, as attested by the

Prebisch-Singer thesis (Toye and Toye, 2003). The gap between rich and poor, created through cumulative causation, has become permanent and institutionalised in a centre-periphery relationship.

Only by interfering with cumulative processes can there be any chance of removing international differences in income, wealth and power. The conventional wisdom of universal gains from free trade would have to be queried and replaced by internal and external intervention, an argument long made by development economists (Thirlwall and Pacheco-López, 2017, chapter 15). Neoliberal attitudes in recent times have reasserted the supposed boon from free markets and deregulation, even for poorer countries (the 'Washington consensus'), though the expected sharing of gains has proved elusive (Gore, 2000; Easterly, 2001; Babb, 2013; Fforde, 2013, chapter 10). Experience of persistent international inequalities suggests that markets do not balance out the trading gains between countries.

Once the cumulative effects of trading are acknowledged, the ethical implications extend outside seller-buyer relations and the just price of the commodities being traded. Commutative justice remains relevant but is supplemented by distributive or social justice. Trading surpluses have been a route to huge accumulations of private income and wealth. Inequalities in trading will soon be reflected in society, through income disparities and social divisions. The divisions become institutionalised and are justified through enabling myths and a culture of inequality (Dugger, 1989, 1998, 2000; Lewis, 1993; Jackson, 2015a). Cumulative causation ensures that the beneficiaries of trade gain more than a temporary advantage and solidify their economic and social status until it becomes permanent. Whether this is deemed a problem turns on ethical judgements about inequality – do the potential gains from trade justify the inequalities from unregulated trading? Egalitarians would note the distributive implications when assessing markets. It will not suffice to look at the prices affecting seller and buyer; also relevant are the incomes from trading and the ramifications for inequality among social groups.

Ethical disquiet about worsening inequalities would vindicate public intervention to slow down, stop and eventually reverse the prevailing trends. Cumulative causation will not cease of its own accord and, left unchecked, will either continue indefinitely to yield ever greater inequality or be halted by some major social crisis or breakdown. Within a capitalist context, the remedy would be a mixed economy with state action to bridle the market power of private capital, control natural monopolies, regulate prices and reduce unemployment. Measures of this kind should limit the income inequalities from trading. Further adjustments to net inequalities can be made through progressive taxation and welfare benefits for those in hardship. These policies, not usually connected with an ethical approach to markets, are a necessary response to soften the harsh social consequences of a competitive economy. Globalised capital may be an impediment, as it hinders policies at a national level and poses the daunting challenge of international policy coordination. Left-wing critics of the welfare state argue that fundamental inequalities are built into the capitalist system, never to be overcome by the welfare measures of a mixed economy (Ginsburg, 1979; Gough, 1979; Offe, 1984). Asymmetries from private ownership of the means of production could be prevented only in a non-capitalist system founded on different property ownership. Whether or not the capitalist context is retained, the redistributive case for intervention remains relevant. The ethics of trading has to delve into distributive as well as commutative justice.

Part IV
Variety and context

9   The diversity of markets

Trading has always been diverse, but has unifying features that can be brought out by general theory and may be overlooked by piecemeal approaches. This is especially true of markets, whose organised nature lends them a robust institutional context. Markets are peculiar as institutions in that they combine a stable structure with an open, fluid population of participants. The market endures as a setting for trade, but the traders are seldom the same across any two periods. A market can evolve in the items traded, the method of payment and other details of trade. It may transform and yet retain its identity, since it exists as an institution apart from particular traders.

Different ways of interpreting markets emphasise their structure or diversity, though both are essential. Many treatments of markets – orthodox and heterodox – view them as a dualism, in which the traders stand separate from and sometimes at odds with the structural environment. One or other side of the dualism is usually given priority. Orthodox economics starts with individual traders and adds structural elements only reluctantly, often as obstacles to trade. Some heterodox economics, keen to reject orthodoxy, follows a structural method and pays more heed to the structural context than to individual behaviour. An alternative to dualism is to invoke duality, in which the individual and structural elements are distinct but intertwined and necessary to each other (Reed, 1997; Jackson, 1999; Fuchs, 2001). In agency-structure duality, the individual trading agents replicate the structural context but depend on it for their ability to trade. Individual traders and the market cannot exist without each other and should be recognised as mutually dependent.

Markets maintain a trading venue while accommodating many different traders and varied behaviour. A single market, persisting over long periods, can witness huge changes in trading volumes, goods being traded, payment methods, information provision and delivery of product. It may reflect as well as reinforce social trends. The upshot is a mixture of stability and change hard to encapsulate in economic theory. A possible answer is duality, so that stability and change need not be opposites. Instead of being a static impediment to change, institutions such as a market may facilitate it by offering an ordered setting that prevents chaos and encourages constructive development. Portraying stability and change as a duality is rare in the economic literature, though not in management studies, where it offsets the tendency to see organisations as merely static (Graetz and Smith, 2008; Farjoun, 2010; Sutherland and Smith, 2011). In a duality perspective, the organisation can endure as a vessel for economic development. Much the same can be said of markets, which may be less structured than firms and other organisations but are still institutions aimed at promoting trade. Neither rigid nor amorphous, they are subtle entities that blend ordered trade with capacity for continuous evolution.

The current chapter asks how we can theorise to distil the complexity and diversity of markets. One option, considered in the next section, is to categorise markets by the item traded – manufactured goods, agricultural produce, housing, labour, financial assets, etc. – and deal with them separately. This highlights the distinctiveness of different markets but struggles to isolate their common elements. How can we theorise to show up both the diversity of markets and their shared foundations? Later sections assess the consistency of heterodox theorising about markets and suggest that it dovetails with layered or stratified analysis. A layered scheme, with depth and internal variety, is the best chance of doing justice to the diversity of markets.

Market types

Economic theorists have traditionally acknowledged the diversity of markets by appealing to different market types according to the items traded. Markets for goods, services, labour, housing and other items are awarded separate treatment in their own theoretical enclaves. This categorises markets clearly, through a visible contrast between traded objects, and allows for varied trading. Analysis can venture away from the supply-and-demand model. In picking out the items traded, the implicit assumption is that other things are less significant. Variation within market types is played down relative to variation across market types. Other sources of variation, such as the institutional setting, market organisation and relations among traders, may be obscured. We could end up with reductionism that reads off market variation from the items traded and sponsors fragmentary, compartmentalised theory. In view of the drawbacks, it may be doubtful whether such classification can differentiate market types. Are the types truly distinctive? Does variety across types outweigh that within types? The rest of this section looks at some of the main market types by items traded.

Manufactured products account for a large slice of the consumer goods bought by the average person. Selling them relies on standard sales contracts that are incomplete but mostly problem-free. Contractual issues become prominent only for complex, expensive goods where the likelihood of faults or misinformation is higher and adverse consequences for the buyer more severe. Products are branded – sellers seek brand loyalty and indirect bonds with buyers as part of relationship marketing (Morgan and Hunt, 1994; Grönroos, 1994; Gummesson, 2008; Godson, 2009). Successful branding brings frequent repeat purchases from loyal customers. Prices of manufactures are cost-determined, as producers can adjust supply at a set average variable cost and preserve a known mark-up of price over cost (Kalecki, 1971, chapter 5; Gu and Lee, 2012). Price competition is avoided where possible (apart from brief 'price wars'); much competition takes a non-price form less harmful to the profits of producers and sellers. Market power among producers/sellers is the norm.

Natural products and raw materials do not undergo a manufacturing process and are supplied directly to the buyer. Standard sales contracts apply and should be little noticed: trade is often in low-cost items for which recourse to law will seldom be worthwhile, even when produce turns out to be faulty. Most products are homogeneous, with less branding than for manufactures. Sellers have only partial ability to control supply, which hinges on climatic, environmental and other external factors. Prices are demand-determined, because demand is more variable in the short run than supply (Kalecki, 1971, chapter 5). The low degree of product branding and market power means that price competition is stronger than for manufactures. Buyers want the lowest price for the homogeneous good, not loyalty to a single producer/seller. Price variability is higher than with manufactures, to the extent that volatile prices may warrant government regulation, as in many agricultural markets.

Housing and property markets rest upon standard sales contracts, but the expense and intricacy of the items traded may cause contractual difficulties. Property deals that go wrong have serious consequences, so the transfer of property rights (conveyancing) is typically overseen by solicitors or other legal experts to reduce the risk of ownership disputes. Hefty transaction costs ensue (Quigley, 2003). Supply conditions resemble those for natural produce, such that supply cannot be adjusted easily in the short run: existing property is more or less fixed in supply and new properties become available only after a time lag for construction or conversion. Demand too is quite invariant, shelter being a basic necessity, and price movements are large, as borne out by the volatility of house prices. Cycles in economic activity correlate closely with fluctuations in housing markets (Leung, 2004; Agnello and Schuknecht, 2011). Property types are diverse but differentiated mostly by physical attributes rather than branding; pursuit of brand identity is rarer than for manufactured goods. While local market power may arise from concentrated property ownership, price competition should be more intense than in many other markets. House buyers make few repeat purchases and have patchy experience, which weakens their market position. Specialist intermediaries such as estate agents can spread information and offer advice, subject to their own commercial interest in boosting sales.

Markets for stocks, shares, bonds and other financial assets are thoroughly organised in formal settings on competitive lines (Howells and Bain, 2000; Mishkin, 2016; Pilbeam, 2018). Sales contracts prevail and should be straightforward as long as the financial asset and its ownership are clearly defined. The conventional image of financial markets is that they are among the most competitive. Such assumptions can be deceptive, as the practical functioning of financial markets does not live up to their image. Regular participants have an informational advantage over others and forge relationships, so they can acquire market power and influence prices. Financial innovation leads to product branding and attempts to create brand loyalty and seller-buyer connections akin to those with manufactured goods. Sale of financial products is prone to over-expansion during a boom, with insecure credit offered in the false expectation of continued growth (Minsky, 1994; Kindleberger and Aliber, 2011). The eventual slump yields financial contraction as lending is reined in and financial transactions scaled down. Finance has lacked the stability of a well-ordered competitive market.

Trade in services can be more complicated than trade in goods, often with one-off purchases. The contractual form moves from a sales contract to a contract for services that is less complete through the inability to codify a service. Sellers and buyers make prior contact to discuss details of the service, timing, cost and so forth, and further contact afterwards to check that the service has been carried out satisfactorily. Price competition is feasible if buyers get cost estimates from several alternative sellers but needs effort and may be modest in scope. Non-price competition also occurs, through advertising, branding and marketing by big service providers. Seller-buyer relationships may emerge when services are repeated and the buyer comes to trust a regular trading partner. For smaller-scale services, past experience and word of mouth can influence the choice of supplier, as with household maintenance, painting/decorating, car repairs, hairdressing, etc. Larger-scale financial and other services have a smaller personal element and more product branding, though trust and reputation remain paramount. Product differentiation is low for generic services but increases with the size and distinctiveness of the service offered.

Labour markets have their own special features unsusceptible to orthodox microeconomic modelling (Fine, 1998; Prasch, 2004; Kaufman, 2007; Fleetwood, 2011, 2016, 2017; Fernández-Huerga, García-Arias and Salvador, 2017; Fernández-Huerga, 2019). Permanent employment gives rise to a long-term employer-employee connection, set out in a contract of service or employment contract. Employees sell their working time or capacity to work, as against any particular services to be performed, so the details of work are not predetermined contractually and must be negotiated. Employment contracts leave room for informal arrangements between employers and employees, who must develop a bond, even if conflicts of interest proliferate. Labour markets vary over wage competition, a difference portrayed in dual labour market theory as the distinction between primary (less competitive) and secondary (more competitive) sectors (Gordon, Edwards and Reich, 1982; Doeringer and Piore, 1985). Wages seldom change rapidly, which would cause economic instability, and employers do not look elsewhere if their labour force is adequate and performing satisfactorily. Product branding and non-price competition are mostly on the buyer side, when employers present their brand and corporate identity to prospective employees. Job applicants promote themselves and compete on grounds other than price, though the degree of organisation is lower than on the buyer side. Price competition and wage variability peak in occupations with low skill levels, low wages and low job security, as in the secondary sector of a dual labour market.

One can readily list various market types by item traded that appear to be distinct. It might seem wise to abandon any general framework for markets and take a piecemeal approach that handles market types separately. Each type could have theories tailored to its own features and informed by empirical evidence. Such localised theory should, in principle, celebrate the diversity of markets in the fullest measure. The pitfall is that the accent on diversity hides the features that the various market types have in common. They are all organised and institutionalised, transfer property rights upon payment, use money as the medium of exchange and have pre-existing trading roles occupied temporarily by traders without dictating every detail of behaviour. Awareness of the shared market traits would be lost if every market type was analysed separately from the others. In place of piecemeal theorising, a better option would be a general framework capable of tracing the common elements of markets but leaving space for diversity.

Orthodox economics claims to possess such a framework through the neoclassical model of competitive markets. Perfect competition is acknowledged as a stylised ideal but still forms the universal benchmark against which markets are judged. Varied market types can supposedly be rendered distinctive by their unique imperfections. A single formal model can be broadened out to cover the multiplicity of markets in practice. Problems with the orthodox approach have been discussed in Chapter 2. The basic difficulty in coping with diversity is that the general case of perfect competition is rarefied and artificial. Given the unattainability of the 'first-best' ideal, all the varied market types must be depicted as 'second-best', imperfect cases marred by efficiency losses. Formal analysis of second-best cases does not abide by the properties of the first-best and yields awkward mathematical outcomes that apply only under unique local circumstances (Lipsey and Lancaster, 1956; Davis and Whinston, 1965, 1967). Second-best cases are so different from the first-best that its relevance as a reference point is dubious, and analysis slides back into piecemeal mode.

Heterodox economists agree on forsaking the neoclassical benchmark of perfect competition. Whatever the differences among heterodox schools, none of them support such a restrictive, 'perfect' view of trade. Space opens up for a less restrictive framework better able to accommodate diversity, which should be possible if not yet fully realised. The rest of this chapter considers what heterodox accounts of markets have in common and what an alternative theoretical framework might look like.

Consistency of the alternatives to orthodoxy

Alternatives to the neoclassical model of markets abound, as Part III has illustrated. They take different angles on trade, in their own language and terminology, without necessarily being incompatible. What, then, do they have in common? They agree that the neoclassical model is inadequate and criticise its oversimplification, excessive reliance on equilibrium, neglect of institutions and insensitivity to culture. These shared criticisms can inspire an alternative framework. Avoiding oversimplification should lead towards a theory capable of embracing complexity. Escaping from thraldom to equilibrium implies a method with weaker equilibria or none at all. Filling the institutional vacuum requires an institutional setting for trade. Allowing properly for culture will recognise it as a process that shapes individual agents and influences their preferences. These responses are consistent with almost all the alternatives in Part III and merit further discussion.

Complexity

A theme of heterodox theorising on markets is that the ahistorical, mechanical and individualistic view propounded by neoclassical theory will never sum up market trade, which needs a subtler vision. Social and cultural approaches point to historical and spatial variations in trade omitted from the neoclassical model – only a less universal and non-reductionist theory could span the cultural diversity. Structural approaches are unhappy with the thin structural content of neoclassical theory and advocate a fuller depiction of structure that, if done carefully, should demonstrate the structural qualities of markets without denying their fluidity, flexibility and variety. Functional approaches draw attention to the manifold functions of market trading, far wider than resource allocation, and give them prominence. Ethical approaches show how the morality of trade, originally at the forefront of economic thought, has been elbowed out by neoclassical theory and make the case for reintroducing it. For all their multiplicity, the alternative approaches converge on wanting a more complex vision of markets.

Complexity has no official definition but is usually understood as the existence of variety and unpredictability within what remains a structured, systemic environment (Rosser, 1999; Hodgson, 2003a). The variety derives from interactions and interconnections within an overall system.

Things are neither wholly disordered nor wholly determined by fixed structures. Markets are a classic example of complexity in this broad sense – they structure the environment for trading but permit large variations of behaviour inside that environment. The systemic quality of markets is supple enough for historical and spatial variations as well as evolution in the nature of trade and the goods or services being exchanged. Any theory of markets should appreciate their complex character. A big flaw of neoclassical theory is that, in place of a complex vision, it opts for mathematical convenience in a simplified model of perfect markets that treats variety as a symptom of imperfections. Unlike neoclassicism, the alternative approaches are comfortable with the complexity of market trade and put it at the heart of their arguments.

In the economic literature, complexity has become associated with a certain class of mathematical and computational modelling that yields unpredictable, apparently random outcomes contrasted with the determinacy of orthodox approaches (Waldrop, 1992; Beinhocker, 2006; Mirowski, 2002, 2007; Arthur, 2010, 2015; Kirman, 2011; Gallegati and Kirman, 2012). Economic behaviour cannot then be explained through its microfoundations, and a richer, layered perspective is required. Computational methods show that even tightly specified mathematical systems may generate unforeseen variety. The real world has more intricate systemic relations than any mathematical model, so the same conclusions apply *a fortiori* to reality. Complexity does not have to be wrapped up in mathematics and, moreover, raises doubts about the use of mathematics in social science. Complex reality will be incapable of mathematical expression, and attempts at this will be futile. Formal structural aspects of reality may be discernible but must accord with diversity and change, otherwise theorising will be too restrictive. A mathematical model of economic behaviour, in the manner of neoclassical theory, will never capture complexity.

Attitudes to equilibrium

Compared with the neoclassical model, alternative approaches to trade are quiet about competitive equilibrium, which reflects a sceptical view of equilibrium in general (Mosini, 2007, part 3). For classical/Marxian economics, competitive equilibrium concerns capital mobility rather than product markets and does not result from competing on price (Eatwell, 1987a; Sawyer, 1989, chapter 5; Salvadori and Signorino, 2013). The equilibrium (profit-rate equalisation) has nothing to do with market clearing and coexists with product markets as profit centres carving out a surplus. Market power is the norm in most markets, supply and demand curves are ill-defined and markets do not clear. For Austrian economics, the market is a process characterised by ongoing changes unlikely to settle down into equilibrium (Kirzner, 1992; Ikeda, 1994; Sautet, 2015). Creative destruction means that the creativity channelled through markets upsets any tendencies to reach stable outcomes, in a never-ending sequence of renewal. Price competition would eliminate the market power that stimulates entrepreneurship. Equilibrium is absent or much weaker than the neoclassical version. Alternative approaches to markets from outside the economics discipline seldom include market-clearing equilibrium within their conceptual language, so it plays little part in their discussion.

Downgrading equilibrium spoils the efficiency properties ascribed by orthodoxy to competitive trade. Market-clearing equilibrium is the source of the allocative efficiency lauded in the fundamental theorems of welfare economics. Perfect competition is Pareto efficient, so the competitive model can be justified on efficiency grounds. The alternative approaches carry no such normative baggage. Competition exists in many guises, and its ethics are ambiguous. Increased competition may or may not be desirable, depending on the form it takes and the activities of the traders. Efficiency is no longer engraved into the definition of competition, and a fairer assessment of its properties can be made.

Institutional background

Orthodox theorising about markets has a minimalist stance on institutions as one of its simplifying features. The alternatives to orthodoxy take virtually the opposite stance. Far from being aloof from institutions, markets are themselves institutions and should be portrayed as such (Hodgson, 1988, chapter 8, 2008; Rosenbaum, 2000). Only through legally enforced property rights can voluntary exchanges of property be sustainable. Markets require organisation in setting up a trading forum for large numbers of participants to trade smoothly and easily – the venue must be arranged, prices set, standardised and published, goods transported and exchanged, services provided, payments made and trade disputes resolved. None of these happen automatically; all have to be organised. Once in place, they get taken for granted, but their importance should be remembered.

Classical/Marxian economics, having never sanctioned the individualism and rational choice of neoclassical theory, has an elastic view of product markets that gives little institutional detail but is compatible with market power and varied trading (Sawyer, 1989, chapter 5). Austrian economics is light on institutional content, given its individualism, though it still needs markets to be the institutional setting within which entrepreneurship can flourish. Alternatives coming from outside the economics discipline are generally founded on social and political theory that bestows higher status on institutions and incorporates them explicitly.

In a true institutional approach, markets enter directly into economic theorising, not as an offshoot of individual agency. They are a pre-existing context inherited by current traders, who could not otherwise trade so easily in large volumes. The formal context lubricates trade without dictating it – there is leeway for varied trading relations, market power, product innovation, free entry and exit, and so forth. Institutional approaches must be careful not to treat trade as wholly institutionalised and leave space for diversity within an ordered but open setting. This implies a non-reductionist perspective, whereby institutions exist alongside trading agents, neither having theoretical sovereignty.

The importance of culture

Culture has never been a standard topic in orthodox economics, which regards it as non-economic and the remit of other disciplines (Throsby, 2001, chapter 1). This neglect of culture extends into the orthodox treatment of markets, where culture barely surfaces. Alternatives to orthodoxy accept greater cultural variation. Examples of trade can be assessed in their own right, with empirical studies and theory tailored to particular circumstances if appropriate. A desire for culturally specific discussion is overt in most economic sociology and in substantivist economic anthropology. Classical/Marxian economics is less overtly cultural, but its weak concept of competitive equilibrium and capacious view of product markets permits case-by-case variation. Discussion is historically specific, focused on capitalist economies and without universal, timeless claims. Austrian economics too is more pliable than neoclassicism and better attuned to historical and cultural evolution.

In general, the alternative approaches can readily fit in with the anthropological sense of culture as everyday behaviour (a way of life) that varies across societies (Jackson, 2009, chapter 2). Culture can also be a process – the formation of individual behaviour within society – and this too meshes with the alternative approaches. Substantivist economic anthropology has studied cultural influences on trading behaviour, while economic sociology depicts markets as being created by producers/sellers, not just meeting the preferences of buyers. Classical/Marxian economics, in querying price competition, leaves the road clear for non-price competition to enter the scene. Advertising and marketing are ubiquitous in modern capitalist economies yet scarcely perceptible in the neoclassical model of trade. The individualism of Austrian economics overlooks social influences on the individual, but the Austrian stress on product innovation is consistent with cultural changes enacted through entrepreneurship. Although the alternative approaches are varied in their appreciation of culture as a process, they have the capacity to embrace it and use it in their theoretical arguments.

The areas of agreement outlined above present opportunities for a unified alternative to the orthodox approach. Any alternative framework should be alert to agency-structure problems and the relevance of culture. Social structures and relationships would have to enter the theory directly, alongside the behaviour of individual traders. The upshot would be a layered or stratified theory in which multiple levels of analysis coexist and interact, none having precedence. Theorising would resemble the 'social theory' in non-economic social sciences, as against the 'economic theory' in orthodox economics. Markets are social phenomena, so a theoretical account based on social theory is sensible and has greater depth than the theory usually adopted by economists. It is worth therefore asking what form a layered view of markets would take.

Layered theorising

Orthodox market models have only a single operative layer, the rational trading agents on whom neoclassical theory is based. The individualistic method insists that valid arguments must rest on individual behaviour, so other layers are missing or reducible to the individual level. In order to get a fuller theoretical picture of markets, it will be crucial to add further layers that exist in their own right. One such layer is made up of the seller and buyer roles created by the legal system and occupied temporarily by agents partaking in trade (Jackson, 2007b). As well as the seller and buyer roles, much trade has various subsidiary roles attached, especially the role of loyal customer engendered by marketing strategies. Another layer is the social and personal web of relational trading where the traders know each other and have an ongoing relationship. Interactions of this kind extend outside formal roles and may affect trade. Individual agents should continue to be one of the analytical layers, but no longer with precedence over the others.

In a layered theory, the layers coexist to give a variety of cases and outcomes. Interdependence of layers is often characterised as a duality among things that are conceptually distinct but entwined (Reed, 1997; Jackson, 1999). Duality contrasts with a merging of layers, which fosters reductionism, and a separation and opposition of layers, which raises the prospect that one layer will win the battle and become dominant. Layered theorising in an anti-reductionist spirit should rule out some layers having lordship over others. While the relative importance of layers may vary, no layer can be expelled – they all have a place in the theoretical analysis. In a stratified scheme, the layers have emergent powers and can affect other layers (Bhaskar, 1994, chapters 4 and 5; Lawson, 1997, chapter 6; Sayer, 2010, chapter 4). Two-way causality makes a clean break with the individualistic reductionism of orthodoxy since it lets structures influence individual agents. Choosing either agency or structure as the foundation of the theory would be arbitrary.

A market is never made up solely of its traders and always has an organised structure: we can name organisation and trade as two basic constituents of a market. Under ideal market conditions they are kept distinct and separate, so as to form a dualism. Organisers of a market, usually the state or other external authorities, are supposed to set up a neutral trading arena with no inbuilt biases towards particular traders. They do not themselves trade and stand above it as a disinterested referee, ensuring good trading practices and acting as arbiter in trade disputes. Market organisers should have no reason to manipulate prices, promote some differentiated products over others or change the items being traded. Their sole purpose is to facilitate trade and prevent malpractice. Traders in a market should likewise be dedicated to trading alone and have no sway in organisation. The sellers and buyers merely decide whether or not to enter a trading arena that already exists and would continue to exist without them. Because they have a vested interest in certain outcomes, they should not be allowed to influence the organisation of trade. As a result, the ideal market should have dualism of organisation and trade, as in Figure 9.1. Organising and trading roles are fenced off from each other. Organisers should not be permitted to trade; traders should not be permitted to organise.

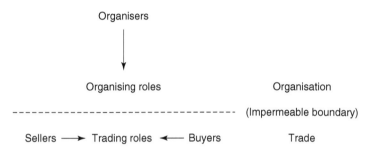

Figure 9.1 Dualism of organisation and trade.

Few actual markets come anywhere near organisation-trade dualism. Organisation falls short of tight regulation of the item traded and does not guarantee uniformity, even standards or complete and accurate information for all participants. The task of organising a market is often dispersed among several agents with varied motives (McMillan, 2002, chapter 1; Ahrne, Aspers and Brunsson, 2015). Traders do not just act as sellers or buyers – they take on larger roles that spill over into organisation. Market power proffers the ability to differentiate products, manipulate prices, collude with rivals, form relationships with trading partners and undertake marketing campaigns. Many producers/sellers devote great effort and expense to managing their customer relationships (Gummesson, 2008; Godson, 2009). If successful, relationship marketing creates subsidiary trading roles of regular provider and regular customer. These new roles, designed and managed by the producers/sellers, demonstrate how traders play an active part in organising the market and changing its structures.

With subsidiary trading roles, the dualism of the ideal market has been breached to yield duality of organisation and trade, as in Figure 9.2. External organisation is present in the legal system governing the transfer

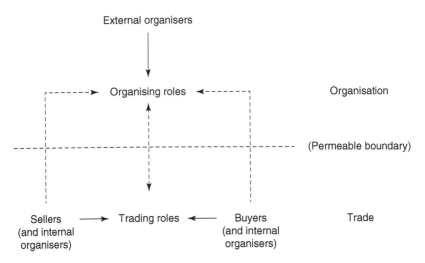

Figure 9.2 Duality of organisation and trade.

of property rights but is partial in coverage and accompanied by the organising activities of traders. Taking on extra roles as internal organisers of the market, traders mould the organisation in their own favour as a stratagem of non-price competition. While they face competitive pressures and do not have freedom to overhaul the market, they can change how it is structured. They act in part as non-neutral organisers, so organising and trading roles mingle, performed by the same agents. The purity and simplicity of organisation-trade dualism has been lost.

Organisation-trade duality blurs the organising roles in a market and makes them less visible. There may be no single body responsible for running the market. Various agents, including the traders, contribute to the organisation, so responsibilities are diluted. The state's role in overseeing property transfers through the legal system remains crucial, but has a low profile in most cases. Duality may create the illusion that markets require little organisation or somehow organise themselves. What really happens is that traders take on much market organisation, which is not perceived as such. It is subsumed in marketing, whereby producers/sellers recast the trading environment. The word 'marketing' gives the game away, as it shows that sellers are building and organising a market, not entering a neutral trading arena (Araujo, Finch and Kjellberg, 2010). Economists should be aware of this, yet show only sporadic interest and leave marketing to be discussed in other academic disciplines. Organising activities of traders give rise to conscious self-organisation by market participants. We can say that markets 'self-organise', but through the deliberate actions of the traders, as against the mysterious invisible hand. Organising agents remain crucial, even if they are not labelled as organisers.

Structured trading roles have repercussions for trade that can also be portrayed through layers and dualities. We have identified three main layers in a market: the trading roles that exist irrespective of particular role occupants, the social relations among traders who know each other, and the attitudes of individual trading agents. All three are interdependent and connected through dualities, as in Figure 9.3. Duality A confirms that trading agents must occupy prior structured roles when they participate in a market, while roles must have occupants if they are to have practical relevance. Duality B arises because the role-based relations in trade, crucial as they are, are never complete and must be supported by less formal relations among trading agents. Duality C stems from the dependence of any social relationship on the agents involved, who will be influenced by the relationship. Taken together, dualities A, B and C yield properties normally associated with the duality of agency and structure. The threefold scheme is richer than a twofold agency-structure duality.

Diverse market types can be accommodated through the relative importance of the dualities in Figure 9.3. Markets regarded as being competitive (such as for finance and generic commodities) have a strong organisational setting with clear seller and buyer roles and trading agents following the roles closely: duality A prevails, though relational trade may also be present. Markets for manufactures see the producers/sellers marketing their products in non-price competition that tries to bond with loyal customers: duality B prevails, without necessarily eclipsing the others. Labour markets founded on employment contracts bring long-term relations between employer and employer in agreeing on work organisation: duality C prevails, again with the others still there. All three dualities will feature in markets, the variation in market types coming from differences in their prominence.

Figure 9.3 does not endorse a favoured mode of trade as the benchmark against which others should be judged. There is no pure or perfect option. All trade mixes structural, social and individual ingredients. Competitive

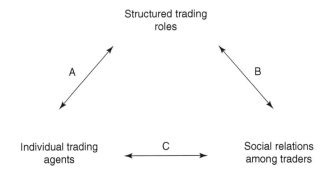

Figure 9.3 Dualities in a market.

cases, always the optimum in orthodox analysis, are one possibility among others and have no special qualities. Much non-price competition entails social relations with customers, so the contrast between asocial competition and social, non-competitive trade is false. Relational trade is an alternative way of trading, not a breach of competitive principles. It would be unfeasible to eliminate the social trading relations of Figure 9.3, and any attempt to do so would be ill-advised, as it would damage the diversity of trade. Variable social relations can make markets and other institutions more flexible through extra dimensions for adjustment (Jackson, 2007a, 2015b). The dualities in Figure 9.3 mean that trading agents can depart from the competitive motives championed by orthodox economic theory. Any trader can choose whether or not to engage closely with trading roles or enter trading relationships. Trading behaviour obeys no single model.

How do dualities A, B and C affect the structure of a market? The seller-buyer relation is no longer direct, as in Figure 6.1, and now is mediated by roles and relationships that call forth several coexisting dualities. Figure 9.4 shows the resulting structure of trade. Instead of anonymous competitive interactions, sellers and buyers now interact through varied trading roles and social contacts. The triangle of Figure 9.3 applies to both sides of the market to give the diamond of Figure 9.4. Core trading roles of seller and buyer, upheld by the legal system, enter the middle of the diagram accompanied by the subsidiary roles from relationship marketing and other trading strategies. Also in the middle come the relationships among traders who know each other, in a duality with the trading roles. Selling and buying agents enter as distinct components of Figure 9.4 but entwined with roles and relations as further dualities. The multiple dualities maintain conceptual distinctions between the elements of trade yet recognise their interdependence. This style of analysis guards against reductionism that collapses trade on to the structural, social or individual dimensions.

As a depiction of trade, Figure 9.4 puts trading roles and relations right at the centre. The core trading roles of buyer and seller must feature in organised trading without being enough on their own to decide how people trade. They are supplemented by subsidiary trading roles and social relationships among regular trading partners. Individual agents make their own voluntary trading decisions, though their choices are now filtered through roles and relations. All the interrelated elements of Figure 9.4 vary in their influence on trading outcomes, leaving space for diversity.

Core trading roles of seller and buyer come to the fore in organised competitive trade. The prime example would be auctions, where sellers and buyers transact in an environment that protects anonymity and encourages price competition. Prices are set through a competitive bidding process, under predetermined rules overseen by an auctioneer – several auction types exist (English, Dutch, sealed-bid, etc.), using different bidding methods to reach the highest possible price for the item being sold (McAfee and McMillan, 1987; Milgrom, 1989; Smith, 1989; Klemperer,

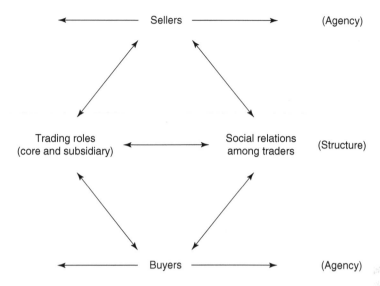

Figure 9.4 Market structure with trading roles and relations.

2004; Krishna, 2010, chapter 1). Price competition is evident on the buyer side, with the highest bidder winning, if less so on the seller side, given the one-off nature of most auction sales. Auctions in practice are subject to social influences that extend beyond the competitive logic of microeconomic theory (Smith, 1993). The market can be said to have cleared in the rudimentary sense that supply of one equals demand of one. Auctions are a fairly close equivalent to the price competition of orthodox economics, hence the invocation of the Walrasian auctioneer in general equilibrium theory (Fisher, 1989). Few actual markets set prices in such an organised competitive manner, and the Walrasian auctioneer remains an imaginary figure. Most markets have incomplete external organisation, price-making by the producers/sellers and market power that suppresses price competition. Core trading roles of seller and buyer are present but joined by many other influences on trading.

Subsidiary trading roles are strongest in cases with product branding, advertising and customer relationship management (Payne and Frow, 2005; Kotler and Keller, 2016, part 3). Producers and retailers create positive roles for themselves in addition to that of mere seller, with parallel roles for the buyers. If brand loyalty can be attained, then the producer/seller takes on the role of regular provider and the buyer the role of regular customer – the new roles gain formal expression through membership of loyalty schemes and other means of contact between seller and buyer. Modern advertising associates product brands with attractive lifestyles or identities and further potential roles for buyers: by purchasing and consuming the product, buyers take on these desirable roles (Meenaghan, 1995; Helman and De Chernatony, 1999; Schmitt, 1999; Kornberger, 2010). Since information is seldom perfect, sellers can also fulfil the role of the best available information provider to the buyer. Such a role should ideally be reserved for a neutral outsider, not the seller, but in the absence of this, the seller may be the only viable option. Trust becomes crucial, as in the well-known example of the market for 'lemons' (Akerlof, 1970). All of these subsidiary trading roles steer trade away from pure price competition to generate varied outcomes.

Social trading relations are most obvious in relational exchange, when a small number of sellers and buyers come to know each other well and form bonds (Goldberg, 1980; Macneil, 1981, 2000). Classic examples occur in defence and health care, with a single buyer (the government) and a handful of sellers (major defence contractors and drug companies) (Sandler and Hartley, 1995, chapter 5; McPake, Normand and Smith, 2013, chapter 13). The traders have few rivals, cannot be anonymous and must negotiate with the same trading partners every time a sale is made. Social interactions among traders determine the volume and pattern of trading. Less direct but still significant trading bonds arise with relationship marketing of manufactured goods and services: sellers maintain contact with customers in order to encourage loyalty (Diller, 2000; Oly Ndubisi, 2007). Information technology and electronic purchasing have made it simple for sellers to compile customer databases and keep track of former buyers. Firms foster an ongoing relationship with their customers via loyalty schemes, discounts, bonuses, newsletters, blogs and after-sales service. Sellers and buyers may never meet face-to-face or discuss things actively, yet they have a passive relationship that influences trade (Jackson, 2019). Wherever buyers become loyal to particular sellers, they forge a social bond based on trust and relax the quest for superior alternatives. Weak trading bonds are ubiquitous in modern commerce and continually pursued by manufacturers and retailers.

Varied trading behaviour

The structural and social facets of trade, while influential, do not determine how any person will trade. Some have closer engagement with trading roles and relations than others, leading to varied behaviour: roles are never complete and wholly binding on the role occupants and relations never commit traders to a single sort of behaviour. Differences among trading agents in Figure 9.4 can be portrayed through different degrees of engagement with core trading roles, subsidiary trading roles and social trading relations.

Suppose that any trader can have either high or low engagement with the two kinds of trading role and with trading relations. This yields eight possible types of trading behaviour, as in Table 9.1. The core roles in all

Table 9.1 Alternative types of trading behaviour

Type of trade	Degree of engagement		
	Core trading roles	Subsidiary trading roles	Trading relationships
Rivalrous	High	High	High
Structured	High	High	Low
Strategic	High	Low	High
Competitive	High	Low	Low
Aspirational	Low	High	High
Habitual	Low	High	Low
Collaborative	Low	Low	High
Casual	Low	Low	Low

markets are seller and buyer. High engagement means that traders stick to seller/buyer roles and transact at the best possible prices; low engagement means that they are less vigilant about the terms of trade. Subsidiary trading roles are mostly the roles of regular provider and customer, nurtured by relationship marketing and product branding: high engagement means that traders participate in loyalty schemes and other formal contacts, and low engagement means that they opt out of these. Social trading relations include face-to-face interactions among traders as well as direct communications through information technology and other media: high engagement means that traders participate in such relations, and low engagement means that they avoid them.

The eight cases in Table 9.1 assume that engagement on the three dimensions varies independently, which may not be the case in reality (if, say, subsidiary trading roles and social trading relations are correlated) but allows coverage of all possibilities. Tentative interpretations of the eight cases are as follows:

Rivalrous trade – Traders identify as sellers and buyers but also participate in subsidiary trading roles and trading relationships, so nonprice competition is extensive. There is rivalry in the sense that traders compete but interact consciously with each other.

Structured trade – Traders engage with core and subsidiary trading roles, but have few trading relationships. Sellers are liable to be dominant through having created subsidiary trading roles for loyal customers who buy in a structured, predictable manner, partly on a perceived basis of value for money.

Strategic trade – The core roles are strong, but subsidiary roles have less significance than trading relationships. Trade is not role-dominated but involves negotiations, which take on a strategic hue given that traders seek competitive advantage.

Competitive trade – The core roles are pre-eminent, with subsidiary roles and trading relationships less influential. This case has the greatest likelihood of price competition, even if it never matches the perfect competition of orthodox textbooks.

Aspirational trade – Traders do not identify closely as sellers and buyers, yet they are fully engaged in subsidiary trading roles and trading relationships. This style of trade arises with luxury goods, where the buyers are not wanting value for money but respond to luxury product branding and its aspirational lifestyle imagery.

Habitual trade – People do not look for bargains or have trading relationships but stay loyal to familiar brands and show little desire for novel experiences. Buyer habits become the key influence on trade, which follows a stable pattern.

Collaborative trade – Trading relationships have precedence over roles, so that trade becomes primarily social. Since the traders do not engage fully with seller and buyer roles, trading will be collaborative rather than competitive, and outcomes will be unstructured and variable.

Casual trade – Low engagement across the board implies that participants in trade have little fondness for it and trade only when necessary. The casual attitude ensures that traders will not be searching for bargains, are not loyal customers and have no desire for trading relationships.

The eight cases in Table 9.1 give only a rough indication of how trading behaviour can vary. Actual traders should not be allocated uniquely among the eight cases, because attitudes can change over time and across different products. Even though the different types of trade may be discernible, they do not amount to separate domains of trade or groups of traders. What matters is the diversity compatible with the structured framework of Figure 9.4. Agents may occupy trading roles and participate in trading relations but retain the capacity to do otherwise and find their own way of trading. Distinctive trading cultures may emerge. Individual behaviour cannot be read off from a structural model and has to be acknowledged in its cultural setting. Trade has common features that should be recognised if we are to understand it, yet it remains complex, fluid and variable.

Variety within a general scheme

Markets can be defined as organised and institutionalised exchange, contrasted with the lesser organisation in non-market exchange (see Chapter 1). A market rests on the core and subsidiary roles set out in the institutional context of trading. When traders enter the market, they take on the core seller and buyer roles as well as any subsidiary roles associated with it.

Roles vary among markets, but the core ones are omnipresent, and subsidiary ones exist for most consumer goods.

In a layered and dualistic perspective, trading roles cannot be treated in isolation and are insufficient to determine behaviour. While they delineate the organised quality of a market, they must be accompanied by the agency of individual traders and the social interaction among these traders. The theatrical analogy is useful. Roles in a play are written out in the script, which provides the words to be spoken by the actors, the details of their actions, their formal connections and the time and place of the events. The script is the codified version of the play that allows it to be performed repeatedly. Every performance will, nevertheless, have unique characteristics. Scripted roles cannot cover every nuance of how the role is performed, so actors in the same role offer their own interpretation and perform it in distinctive ways. Their role playing depends on interactions with other people in the cast, leading to a social as well as individual dimension. Any performance comes from a complex mixture of the roles in the script, the actors playing the roles and the social relations among the actors. Likewise, trading in a particular market comes from the trading roles, the traders playing the roles and the social relations among the traders.

The current layered scheme for a market has three interrelated layers – roles, relationships and agents – or four if we subdivide the trading roles into core and subsidiary. Markets should fit within the scheme while still being open to diverse practices. All layers can vary, as in Table 9.2. Core trading roles reflect the legal regulation of voluntary property transfers but leave space for differences in payment methods, timing of payments, delivery of product, complaint procedures and redress of complaints. Subsidiary trading roles, tied to product differentiation and branding, vary with the great panoply of brands for different products. Trading relationships are distinctive to the traders, whether they undertake face-to-face negotiations or communicate through information technology and other media. Trading agents are individual people and organisations, all of whom have their own attributes and behaviour.

The sources of variation in Table 9.2 admit a vast range of outcomes. When trying to classify them, we can distinguish levels of generality, from more to less general: exchange, markets, types of market, specific market cases. The organised quality conferred by trading roles is enough to differentiate markets from less organised exchange. Variations among markets in their trading roles, relations and agents create different market types at a lower level of generality. Distinctive features of each type can be depicted by variability in one or more of the theoretical layers. Within each market type, further variation yields specific market cases at the lowest level of generality. Manufactures can, for example, be subdivided among different products and brands, labour among different occupations and employers, housing among the varied sizes, ages, design, tenure

Table 9.2 Sources of variation among markets

Market layer	Sources of variation
Core trading roles	Payment method; payment timing; publication of prices; delivery of product; complaints procedures.
Subsidiary trading roles	Brand identity; product marketing and advertising; loyalty schemes; information provision.
Trading relationships	Price negotiations; customised trading; seller-buyer communications; use of social media; after-sales service.
Trading agents	Differences among individual people and organisations; cultural influences on trading attitudes.

and location of properties. Theorising and critical analysis can occur at different levels of generality according to the topic, with the sources of variation in Table 9.2. The theoretical framework is broad enough to harbour detailed case studies of particular markets.

Variations within the layered scheme are unrelated to any benchmark. One can consider different market types without measuring them against a template and finding most of them inadequate. This differs from the orthodox view of markets, which tolerates variability only by considering imperfect special cases that diverge from the competitive ideal. Variability of markets is troublesome for orthodoxy and best minimised, whereas a layered scheme treats it as vital to an adaptable, evolving economy. The lack of a benchmark opens the gate to varied theories and schools of thought. Any of the approaches to markets discussed in Part III are consistent with the layered scheme, as they dwell on different layers of the scheme. They could be pulled closer together if they were to work within a single scheme that accentuates what they have in common without erasing their distinctiveness.

Some issues surrounding markets cannot be resolved by the layered scheme, notably the definitional problems recounted in Chapter 1. The scheme assumes a broad definition of markets as organised and institutionalised exchange, leaving space for variation in how they are organised and how they function. It chimes with the wide usage of the word 'market' in everyday language but clashes with the narrower usage in economic theory. Competition is relegated from the essence of markets to a possible feature among others. Social relations are no longer condemned and take their place among the standard characteristics of trading. A strict distinction between anonymous markets and relational exchange will be redundant, since much market trade has weak trading relations that fall between these extremes (Jackson, 2007b, 2019). Whether the intermediate cases should be termed markets remains moot and goes back to the etymology of markets. The layered scheme implies that relational trading does not remove market status and that many trading relations (especially the weaker, less direct ones) can be included in the definition of markets.

Another difficulty with the layered scheme is that, by treating all traders the same, it has an aura of symmetry. Actual trade brings forth large asymmetries between sellers and buyers: the sellers may be huge multinational producers and retailers who have market power consolidated through marketing and advertising; the buyers are likely to be individuals or families who trade on a smaller scale with far less organisation and power. Firms may be able to 'domesticate' their markets with managed customer relations that consolidate their position and act as barriers to entry (Arndt, 1979, 1981; Redmond, 1989, 2013; Layton, 2007, 2011). General conceptual schemes risk overestimating the generalities and underestimating the specificity of trade and the biases imposed by market power. Any theory depicting markets as symmetrical between sellers and buyers will miss out the inequalities that are inherent in capitalism – from a Marxian perspective, it will help to project the façade of free and equal exchange (Marx, 1867, part 3; Junankar, 1982, chapter 2; Catephores, 1989, part 1; Lysandrou, 2000; Fine, 2012). The layered scheme can encompass variable historical circumstances, however, along with the inequalities seen in specific times and places. At the lower levels of generality (types of market, specific market cases), the details of actual trading will mark the realities of modern capitalism. Historical specificity comes about once the layered scheme is placed within the context of the total economy, a matter considered in the next chapter.

10 Markets within the total economy

Markets extend across a vast ocean of goods and services, so that everything may seem to be traded. Yet markets do not constitute all economic life. In examining the total economy, production and consumption should be distinguished from distribution. Markets, as a means of voluntary redistribution, are entwined with the rest of the economy while being conceptually separate. Outputs and inputs of production are traded in markets; items consumed are purchased on them; the route from production to consumption passes through them. Selling new products may stimulate technical changes with long-term ramifications for production methods. The desire of sellers to stimulate demand for their output induces advertising and marketing that guide consumer behaviour. Market trade bears upon production and consumption without being synonymous with them.

The current chapter sets markets within the context of the total economy. Two specific matters will be emphasised. The first is the continued existence of non-market sectors in developed economies and the need to recognise them in economic analysis. National accounting procedures often forget unmarketed outputs because of measurement difficulties and give them a low implicit weighting that underestimates total economic activity (Kuznets, 1949; Eisner, 1988; Landefeld and McCulla, 2000). Removed from attention, they are overlooked in economic theory or at best treated as a specialist interest. Neglecting non-market sectors will, by accident or design, equate markets with all economic activity.

The second matter emphasised is the presence of a total economy requiring a different theoretical approach from its individual elements. Attempting to use the same theory will yield a fallacy of composition, as Keynesians have contended: the whole is more than the sum of the parts. Although Keynesian ideas should avoid the fallacy, their eclipse in recent times has reintroduced it. Modern orthodox macroeconomics relies on neoclassical microfoundations that bring back market-clearing equilibria and narrow the distance between micro and macro theories. Modelling the whole economy in a fashion similar to individual markets will revive pre-Keynesian attitudes and bolster the neoclassical obsession with exchange. A more even view will be obtainable only with due recognition of non-market sectors in the total economy and a macro-level of analysis liberated from the study of particular markets.

Market and non-market sectors

The relative size of market and non-market sectors in an economy varies over time and place. Capitalist economies have a large market sector, though the non-market sector is more prominent in some cases than others. Various puzzles beset the market/non-market split. Markets are diverse and poorly defined, so we face problems distinguishing market from non-market exchange. Unmarketed activities have no recorded outputs and no data from the national income accounts, so it will be hard to assess their extent. Interdependence between market and non-market sectors is a further complication, bearing in mind the social background to markets (Dolfsma, Finch and McMaster, 2005; Dolfsma, 2013, chapter 2). Disaggregating economies into market and non-market sectors can only be approximate and open to challenge. It remains useful, all the same, as it can illustrate the contribution of non-market arrangements. An obvious way to proceed is to begin with national accounts as a record of marketed outputs and then ask what is missing.

Assumptions about the primacy of the market sector seem to be justified by the chronic trend towards commodification. Non-market sectors are largest in less developed countries, with a shift towards markets during economic development. Capitalist economies have an augmented set of commodities and markets, often instead of earlier non-market arrangements (Carruthers and Babb, 2000; Ciscel and Heath, 2001; Gudeman, 2001). The drift towards total commodification may seem inexorable. If everything were to be bought and sold in the long run, then the orthodox preoccupation with markets would be vindicated. Such conclusions are wrong, for commodification is partial and will never reach the final stage of a pure market economy. Even the most capitalistic economies have large non-market sectors crucial to their functioning (Williams, 2004, 2005). These sectors are liable to serve capitalist interests and help maintain the capitalist system but are outside the realm of commodities.

The boundaries of an economy are usually defined politically and geographically, with the nation state the focus (though smaller or larger units are possible). Formal efforts to measure national economies are quite recent in the history of economics: the first national income accounts are accredited to Wesley Mitchell, Simon Kuznets and others in the 1920s and 1930s, and international standards for national accounting date only from the 1940s, during the period when Keynesian macroeconomics came to the fore (Ruggles, 1993; Vanoli, 2005; De Beelde, 2009; Coyle, 2014). In the initial discussions on national accounting it was unclear what should be classified as economic and included in the accounts. Goods bought and sold could easily be included; housework and other welfare-promoting activities without a marketed product could not. Debates arose about whether the accounts should ascribe a value to outputs that are not marketed, which would increase the risks of inaccuracy but offer a better summary of total economic activity.

Pressure to publish national accounts as an empirical foundation for Keynesian macroeconomics encouraged simpler and narrower methods. In the end it was decided to concentrate on items with monetary prices, an approach endorsed by the United Nations (1953, 2008). Although national accounts are often taken for granted, the criteria used have never been self-evident and always debatable. A Marxian outlook, for example, would bring a different verdict on productive and unproductive activities; the Soviet Union and its allies did not accept UN-approved accounting and devised their own system of national accounts (the material product system) (Árvay, 1994; Herrera, 2010). Critics of national accounting have lamented its narrowness and proposed alternative methods as a more reliable gauge of economic activity and well-being (Miles, 1985; Hueting, 1992; Shaikh and Tonak, 1996; England, 2001; Costanza et al., 2009; Fleurbaey and Blanchet, 2013). Any measure of the total economy will never be definitive, as it will be influenced by decisions on what to include and how to weight it.

Beginning with national income accounts, evaluation of the total economy must fill the gaps and consider what has been missed. Figure 10.1 shows the typical pattern for a developed economy. The total economy is made up of a market sector, where outputs are sold, and a non-market sector, where outputs are not for sale. Each sector can be subdivided

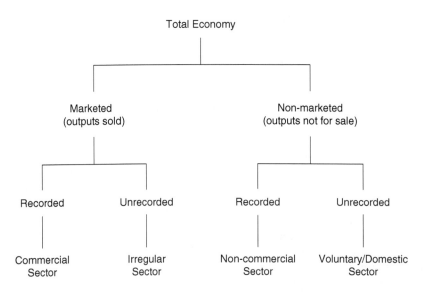

Figure 10.1 Market and non-market sectors of the economy.

according to whether activities are recorded and included in the national accounts, or unrecorded and given an implicit weighting of zero. Most macroeconomic discussion overlooks the informal, unrecorded activities, but they should be acknowledged. We thus have four sectors: commercial, irregular, non-commercial and voluntary/domestic.

Commercial sector

Outputs are sold at a monetary price and yield revenue for the seller. The firm or other selling organisation has a legal obligation to keep annual accounts, creating a formal record that can be aggregated. Along with sales revenues, the firm will have input costs (labour, raw materials) and profit returns. By the accounting identities, the recorded output values should equal the recorded costs and returns in any period: the scale of the firm's activities can be measured by either output budgeting or input budgeting, with equivalent results. The same goes for the aggregate level, so a country's national product (output-based) should equal its national income (input-based). The commercial sector in a capitalist economy is made up of private profit-making firms selling goods or services on markets, along with public or private not-for-profit organisations that sell their outputs and receive sales revenue.

Irregular sector

Outputs are marketed and yield monetary returns but go unrecorded in national accounts and lie outside the formal economy. Informal marketed outputs are illegal, since commerce is supposed to be recorded for taxation purposes. They constitute an irregular sector of black markets aimed at tax evasion or banned types of trade (in drugs, weapons, risky financial products, contraband, fake goods, etc.). Governments should, in principle, eliminate this illegal trading, though it will be unfeasible to eradicate all black markets and the costs of trying to do so may be prohibitive. A shadow economy emerges of unrecorded, marketed activities that coexist with their recorded counterparts. In less developed economies, the size of the irregular sector may indicate an economy at early stages of evolution and still with gaps in its accounting procedures. The irregular sector should diminish with further economic development, though it will not disappear. Cultural differences among countries lead to some tolerating a larger irregular sector than others.

Non-commercial sector

Outputs are not for sale and yield no sales revenue, so the organisations run on non-commercial lines. The chief example is tax-funded public bodies providing goods and services free of charge or at subsidised cost (such as state education, public health care and utilities in public ownership). With no priced outputs, these activities cannot be integrated into national accounts through output budgeting. They are nonetheless part of the formal economy as they have paid employees, and they pay for raw materials and other inputs. The standard method is to measure them through input budgeting. High input costs will not necessarily mean high outputs if an organisation is inefficient, so input budgeting can be queried as an output measure. It portrays the scale of activities but correlates precisely with outputs only when efficiency is held constant. Apart from public bodies, the non-commercial sector embraces large private or non-governmental charitable and not-for-profit organisations. These too have little or no sales revenue but do have employment and other costs recorded in accounts. As with public organisations, they can be included in the formal economy through input budgeting.

Voluntary/domestic sector

No monetary payments are made, for outputs or inputs. Most housework falls into this category, because household members perform it free of charge. Cooking, cleaning, washing, child care, care of the elderly, gardening, household repairs and other domestic tasks are all done mainly without payment. Despite their importance to the smooth running of the economy, they get zero weighting in national accounts and receive little attention in economic discussion. Unpaid voluntary work outside the household is also invisible to the national accounts and belongs to the informal economy – community services staffed by volunteers would be an example. Small charities with no employees will likewise fit into the voluntary sector. Larger charities may have formal business organisation, along with paid employees and other monetary costs or revenues. The formal element puts them in the non-commercial sector, even though they may carry out unpaid voluntary work.

Orthodox economics dwells on the commercial and non-commercial sectors in Figure 10.1. The two are not equal in status. Under capitalism the commercial sector dominates, with public/non-commercial activities in an ancillary, supportive role. The tacit rule is that activities should be private and commercial wherever possible and follow alternative principles only when absolutely necessary. This attitude has been reinforced in recent times by neoliberalism and its quest to marketise the economy (Peck and Tickell, 2002; Djelic, 2006; Molesworth, Scullion and Nixon, 2011; Ebner, 2015; Birch and Siemiatycki, 2016). Many activities previously public and non-commercial have been transferred into the commercial sector in a stalwart campaign to extend markets.

Even activities that stay in the public sector have been subjected to administrative reforms (internal markets, quasi-markets) that give them market-like features (Glennerster, 1991; Le Grand and Bartlett, 1993;

McMaster, 2001, 2002; Le Grand, 2007; Pollitt and Bouckaert, 2011). Mimicry of markets creates internal trading with commercial terminology (purchasers, providers, prices, vouchers, choice, competition, etc.). Outcomes may be little different from planning, especially if internal markets are highly regulated, and administrative costs will be high, but the terminology of markets has become self-justifying regardless of results. Similar trends towards the language and culture of markets are discernible in the voluntary and non-profit sectors (Salamon, 1993; Weisbrod, 1998; Eikenberry and Kluver, 2004; Evans, Richmond and Shields, 2005; Sanders and McClellan, 2014; Maier, Mayer and Steinbereithner, 2016). Imitating business practices is seen as a mark of professionalism, whether or not it meshes with the fundamental aims of a voluntary organisation. The ethos is commercial, promoting the commercial sector of the economy above all others as the blueprint for organisation and behaviour.

Enthralment with markets and commerce causes neglect of the other sectors in Figure 10.1. The public sector remains prominent in developed economies, its share of national income variable between countries but substantial (Tanzi and Schuknecht, 2000; Stiglitz and Rosengard, 2015, chapter 2). This prominence, which warrants a mixed economy label, reflects the need for public policies in guaranteeing universal health care, education and other services that would not come forth from commercial sources. Public welfare measures are vital to sustain aggregate demand and offset the unemployment and low incomes spawned by competitive markets. Far from being impediments to the economy, public expenditure and the attendant taxation underwrite its smooth operation. The very existence of capitalism rests on state backing, as Karl Polanyi (1944) observed. Only by legal approval of privately owned capital, tolerance of private wealth accumulation and advocacy of labour and financial markets could capitalism have come about.

The irregular sector of the economy has an ambivalent, market-but-not-market feel. It lies outside the formal economy and the failure to record incomes renders it illegal. Official attitudes are that it should be curtailed or brought within legal commerce (Thomas, 1992, part 3; Naylor, 2004; Oviedo, Thomas and Karakurum-Özmedir, 2009; Williams, 2014). Black markets are nevertheless a kind of market, as their name suggests. They rest on voluntary transfers of property rights in the same way as other markets and require organisation. Personal contacts are central, prices being excluded from open publication, but this personal element is widespread in legal commerce as well. Trading in the irregular sector is market exchange, even if not officially recognised and recorded as such (Beckert and Wehinger, 2013). It will benefit the traders, while often having adverse consequences for others. With no recorded accounts, the size of the informal sector is hard to assess; in developing countries it may be a large proportion of the economy; in developed countries it is a lower proportion but still significant (Williams and Windebank, 1998; Schneider and Enste,

2000, 2013; Gёrxhani, 2004; Williams and Schneider, 2016). Black markets confirm the impulse to trade, showing up its diversity and the obstacles to keeping it within formal boundaries.

The voluntary/domestic sector offers the starkest contrast with markets: outputs are neither marketed nor recorded. Much housework falls into this category, done by family members without monetary payment or any record of time elapsed (Wheelock, 1992; Himmelweit, 1995; Elson, 1998; Folbre and Nelson, 2000; Froud et al., 2000; Williams and Nadin, 2012). Invisible to the formal accounts, it is treated as costless and gets short shrift from economists. The same can be said for voluntary and charitable work outside the household, where no payments are made and nobody is employed. Again such activities go unremarked by most economic analysis. The apparent low value of voluntary/domestic work belies the huge opportunity costs from its time-intensiveness. If paid at similar rates to equivalent formal work, it would make up a major part of the formal economy.

Anything on this scale cannot safely be written off as negligible, yet it has been peripheral to economic discussion. Measurement difficulties are a reason for this, along with the orthodox fixation on markets. Only feminist economics has awarded the informal domestic sector its due credit, mainly in response to the gender bias in unpaid care and housework, most of which has been done by females (Donath, 2000; Elson, 2000a, 2017; Himmelweit, 2002; Power, 2004; Bakker, 2007; Campbell and Gillespie, 2016). The extensive female involvement, given the secondary status of women in the economy, has confirmed the low regard in which these tasks are held. Other than the feminist contribution, they are only occasionally studied by heterodox economics and the mainstream literature on economic appraisal. Their place in economics as a minority interest collides with their prominence in the total economy.

The market/non-market and recorded/unrecorded distinctions can set out the various economic sectors but may give a false impression. It may appear that the total economy in Figure 10.1 is just an aggregate of four separate, self-contained components that function independently. In practice the sectors are interrelated, such that the total economy is more than the sum of its parts. Rather than being alternatives, the sectors complement each other and contribute to the functioning of the economic system. Formal market trading depends on informal activity in order to be sustainable. Labour markets rely on the regular supply of working time from people supported by non-working family members. Without the unpaid domestic contribution, the smooth operation of labour markets (and the total economy) would no longer be feasible.

Interdependence of formal and informal sectors is hardly noticed in orthodox economics, which models labour supply as the outcome of individual preferences and omits the domestic sector. Heterodox economics has shown more appreciation of the interdependence: the role of the household in reproducing labour has long featured in analyses of social reproduction and provisioning (Himmelweit and Mohun, 1977; Jennings and Waller, 1990; Picchio, 1992; Folbre, 1994, 2006; Bakker and Silvey, 2008; LeBaron, 2010). As well as within households, informal and non-market activity occurs within firms and government, cutting across any simple market/non-market division. The commercial sector of Figure 10.1 includes the administrative, hierarchical organisation of private firms whose internal arrangements have nothing to do with markets. Many activities assigned by an output classification to one of the four sectors in Figure 10.1 will be an amalgam of traded and non-traded elements.

Any division between market and non-market sectors can only be approximate. A mixed economy goes well beyond a twofold market/non-market split or the fourfold scheme of Figure 10.1. The technical impossibility of pure competitive markets, together with the moral limits on what we should trade, ensures that markets do not have the supremacy predicated by orthodox theory. An accurate vision requires a fuller treatment of the informal, non-commercial parts of the economy and an awareness of the impurity of commerce. The total economy derives from complex interplay of trading and other behaviour – it will not be comprehended through an abstract technical account of trading alone. Theorising about the total economy must reach out to all of its several mingled components. Arguments for a separate analysis at the macro-level are associated with Keynesian economics (especially its heterodox, Post Keynesian version), so we should ask how markets relate to a Keynesian perspective.

Markets at the macro-level

The commercial sector has framed economists' perceptions of the total economy as the sum of traded goods and services. Everything else is nugatory or a means to the end of trading. Only by having traded outputs and inputs does anything get noticed. From this attitude it is a short step to depicting the whole economy as a colossal trading arena or market. Supply and demand can then be blown up to the aggregate level, brushing aside the aggregation problems. Market-clearing equilibria for product markets can supposedly be translated to whole economies, with price adjustments equating supply and demand. General equilibrium, in which markets are disaggregated, has existence and stability problems, so the temptation is to use aggregated partial-equilibrium models instead. Differences between product markets and the economy as a whole are skirted.

Pre-Keynesian thought treats both labour and capital markets in neoclassical style with stable equilibria that equate supply and demand. In labour markets, the equilibrium rules out involuntary unemployment, since supply equals demand for labour and everybody finds a job. In capital markets, supply and demand for capital are likewise equated

through changes in the price of capital (the interest rate), so that investment (demand for capital) falls into line with saving (supply of capital).
The whole economy adjusts efficiently through price movements that
equilibrate markets. Exactly the same arguments are made at all levels of
analysis, micro or macro. While these pre-Keynesian ideas receded in the
heyday of Keynesianism, they never disappeared and have returned since
the 1980s in the new classical macroeconomics and its offspring (Hoover,
1988; King, 2012, chapter 6; Vercelli, 2012; Toporowski, 2016). For new
classicists the desire for orthodox microfoundations is uppermost, and
neoclassical ideas are reintroduced into macroeconomics. Rational-choice
and market-clearing models extend the orthodox analysis of individual
markets to the whole economy.

Keynesianism asserts the need for a distinct macroeconomics (Davidson,
2011, chapter 2; King, 2015, chapter 2). Unlike neoclassical theory, which
appeals to the relative prices of real goods and services, Keynesian theory
takes a monetary form centred on income flows. The economy adjusts
not through relative prices but through shifts in income and employment
to attain a steady state where savings match investment. Market clearing plays no part in the analysis; supply seldom equals demand in product, labour or capital markets. Other things being equal, the economy can
remain in a steady state with involuntary unemployment and may require
government intervention to avoid a slump. We get the Keynesian distrust
of *laissez-faire* and case for fiscal measures to boost aggregate demand
(Keynes, 1936, chapter 24). Relative prices are less prominent than in
neoclassical economics, even though a Keynesian model depends on the
commercial transactions recorded in national income accounts. Analysis
is conducted in aggregates at the level of the whole rather than the parts,
and particular markets are relevant only if large enough to impact on
national income.

The ambiguous micro/macro relationship complicates the landscape
of macroeconomics. Various attitudes coexist, from complete micro/
macro separation to a macroeconomics with neoclassical foundations. The
treatment of markets differs accordingly. There are three basic positions:
Post Keynesianism (or fundamentalist Keynesianism), the neoclassical
synthesis and new classical macroeconomics. Post Keynesian economics
sees Keynesian macroeconomics as separate from neoclassical microeconomics and incapable of being merged with it (King, 2002, 2015; Harcourt,
2006; Lavoie, 2006, 2014; Davidson, 2011). Theory starts at the macro-level
in monetary terms, assumes that uncertainty is rife and makes no appeal
to neoclassical rational-choice methods. A divide between Keynesian
and neoclassical economics must be preserved, otherwise the message of
Keynesianism will be lost. The neoclassical synthesis, reinvented as New
Keynesianism in more recent literature, argues that Keynesian aggregate
demand can be synthesised with neoclassical ideas, notably in the portrayal of market imperfections (Greenwald and Stiglitz, 1987; Gordon,

1990; Rotheim, 1998, part 1; Fine and Milonakis, 2009, chapter 4; Cornwall, 2012). Keynesian policy conclusions can be obtained from models that stay in touch with neoclassicism and do not reject orthodoxy. New classical macroeconomics is palpably neoclassical, with utility maximisation, representative agent models, rational expectations and market-clearing equilibria (Hoover, 1988; Vercelli, 2012; Galbács, 2015). The Keynesian element withers, and Keynesian policies become less likely.

In the evolution of macroeconomics, fundamentalist Keynesianism was always too radical for the orthodox establishment and remained a minority view, though championed by many of Keynes's co-workers. The mainstream plumped for the neoclassical synthesis, represented in orthodox textbooks as the IS-LM model and other Keynesian/neoclassical hybrids. With the rise of neoliberalism the political climate has become hostile to Keynesianism, and orthodox macroeconomics has switched towards the new classical school. The effect has been to consolidate neoclassical orthodoxy and quell the Keynesian challenge. Among macroeconomists the only real alternative to the orthodox view of markets comes from the heterodox macroeconomics of Post Keynesianism, which will be the focus of the current discussion.

Post Keynesian economics makes a clean break with neoclassicism and keeps away from market-clearing models. Macroeconomics exists in its own right, in aggregated monetary form. The economy does not equilibrate but reaches a short-run steady state determined by aggregate demand. As the most wayward component of spending, investment is arbiter of national income and employment, with saving falling into line as income changes. Contrary to neoclassical assumptions, the economy adjusts in the short run through income and output as against relative prices. Conventional microeconomic modelling of markets is missing from Post Keynesian theory, no attempt being made at a neoclassical synthesis. The equilibrating function of relative prices, so crucial for neoclassicism, never comes into play.

How, then, do markets fit into Post Keynesian theory? In an aggregated monetary model founded on national income, a 'market' is just the expenditure devoted to a particular product or industry. It indicates the volume of trading for certain goods or services without any assumption of market-clearing equilibrium. Trade could be constrained by demand (if industry has spare capacity and output goes unsold) or supply (if products are unavailable and demand goes unmet). Trading for different items may vary, so that some goods are in excess supply, others in excess demand. Modern capitalist economies rarely encounter capacity limits (Lavoie, 2006, chapter 2, 2014, chapter 3). Economic activity is demand-constrained and rests on aggregate demand not supply.

Excess capacity stems from the market power of the oligopolies that control most product markets. These cases are not market imperfections, as in orthodox theory, but the norm for modern developed economies.

Firms restrict their output so as to raise prices; operating below full capacity means that they can change output quickly to meet demand. Price-making behaviour prevails, and most short-run adjustments occur through changes in output.

Links between market power and Keynesian ideas are clearest in the work of Michał Kalecki (1971, 1990), sometimes described as a distinct Kaleckian economics (Sawyer, 1985b; Sebastiani, 1989; López and Assous, 2010; Toporowski and Mamica, 2015). Kalecki worked independently of Keynes on the cyclical behaviour of capitalist economies and came up with a version of Keynesian analysis before Keynes's *General Theory* was published (Robinson, 1977; Sawyer, 1985b, chapter 9). He recognised the ubiquity of market power, arguing that the degree of monopoly in product markets determines the surplus and the profit share in national income. Kaleckian macroeconomics marries Keynesian ideas with a classical/Marxian perspective incorporating factor shares in national income and classical saving behaviour, such that saving occurs primarily from profit incomes. Market power then enters macroeconomics because a rise in the profit share restricts aggregate spending through the higher saving by capitalists relative to workers. Compared with a Keynesian model, Kaleckian economics offers a fuller picture of product markets and income distribution, as well as drawing together Keynesian and classical/Marxian reasoning.

Kalecki's treatment of individual markets acknowledged variations among different cases. He distinguished between cost-determined prices in markets where sellers can adjust supply and demand-determined prices in markets where short-run supply is invariant (Kalecki, 1971, chapter 5; Sawyer, 1985b, chapter 2). Most manufactured goods have cost-determined prices, since producers operate within capacity and respond to demand by adjusting output; prices change little in the short run, set by price-making producers to cover costs and secure a regular profit. In other sectors such as agriculture and housing the supply conditions are different, for sellers cannot easily adjust supply. Demand shifts are no longer accommodated by output shifts and may lead to volatile prices. Modern capitalist economies trade mainly in manufactured goods and services rather than agricultural produce, land or buildings, so most prices are cost-determined. Post Keynesian and Kaleckian economics has studied pricing, in the belief that prices are set by producers/sellers and do not emerge spontaneously from market equilibria (Lee, 1998, 2013; Downward, 1999; Gu and Lee, 2012). The resulting price invariance fits neatly into Keynesian analysis based on income and output changes.

Heterodox macroeconomics in the Post Keynesian and Kaleckian traditions takes market power as the norm. Instead of being an aberration, profits from market power are part of the economic system and not eroded by price competition. Firms prefer non-price competition, which protects their profits and maintains the surplus, the driver of capital accumulation.

This harmonises with classical/Marxian theory and clashes with orthodox market-clearing arguments that remove any surplus through relative price adjustments. A neoclassical synthesis will not work, but a synthesis between Post Keynesian/Kaleckian and classical/Marxian economics makes sense. At the macro-level, such a synthesis can be seen in monopoly capital arguments that combine Kaleckian macroeconomics with a classical/Marxian surplus approach (Baran and Sweezy, 1966; Sawyer, 1988; Sweezy, 2004; Foster, 2014). Despite differences of emphasis – Kaleckians pay more attention to product markets as an influence on factor shares, Marxians to production and the labour process – the outlooks are broadly compatible.

Some theorists have tried to formalise classical notions of equilibrium, as in Sraffian economics (Sraffa, 1960; Mainwaring, 1984; Sawyer, 1989, chapter 8; Mongiovi, 2012). The ambition is to attain a formal mathematical expression of the Ricardian model, with classical equilibrium (profit-rate equalisation) in place of neoclassical (market clearing). Such modelling can have long-period equilibria that obviate market clearing and remain consistent with a surplus approach, yet the link with Post Keynesian economics and other heterodox schools has been vexed (Aspromourgos, 2004; Lavoie, 2011; Lee and Jo, 2011; Hart and Kriesler, 2016). The mathematical methods of Sraffians, reliant on simultaneous-equation models reminiscent of neoclassical analysis, stand at odds with the Post Keynesian stress on fundamental uncertainty and scepticism about any equilibrium beyond the weakest short-run steady state. Attempts have been made to bring Sraffian and Post Keynesian economics closer together within a larger theoretical vision (Robinson, 1978; Eatwell, 1983; Kurz, 1985, 2013; Nell, 1992, 1998; White, 1998; Arena and Blankenberg, 2013). These do not yet amount to a Post Keynesian/Sraffian synthesis, which may never be feasible. Even so, Post Keynesian and Sraffian economics convey the same image of capitalist economies – they have far more in common with each other than with neoclassical economics.

Abundance and shortage

Market-clearing equilibria seldom occur in individual markets; it follows *a fortiori* that they will not occur at the macro-level. The meaning of any such equilibrium is unclear, as the whole economy cannot be one gigantic market. There is no aggregate price or wage, nor do economic agents exist in aggregate form. An economy has myriad prices and wages, all in monetary terms, influenced by market power. To portray this as a single, stable equilibrium makes little sense. Post Keynesian economics has avoided market-clearing equilibria and turned towards weaker steady states from output and employment changes. Economic activity is usually demand constrained. Unemployment, excess capacity and unsold output are routine.

Markets in a modern developed economy vary in trading conditions, price setting, price volatility and quantity adjustments. Of the possible outcomes, the least likely is the textbook case of well-behaved supply and demand curves that yield continuous market clearing. Few markets come anywhere near this, and none attain the neoclassical ideal of perfect competition. In markets for natural produce and raw materials, sellers often have little control over supply, so prices are demand-determined; in markets for manufactured goods, producers operate with excess capacity and easily control supply, so prices are cost-determined (Kalecki, 1971, chapter 5). Neither case complies with the standard microeconomic model.

Developed economies are dominated by manufacturing and service industries, hence the market power and cost-determined prices. Supply and demand curves are hard to discern when prices are set by price-makers (normally the producers/sellers). Depending on their decisions, some markets could be demand constrained, with demand the short side of the market, and others supply constrained, with supply the short side. Demand-constrained trading happens when producers/sellers set prices high, restrict output and operate within capacity limits. Trade volumes rest on demand not supply. Supply-constrained trading happens when producers/sellers set prices low and operate at capacity limits, so that supply determines trading volumes. The two alternatives, not mutually exclusive, can coexist in the same economy. Price setting will decide the balance between them.

In a capitalist economy, production is controlled by private, profit-making firms that seek market power to make the regular surplus on which their survival hangs. The inbuilt bias is towards demand-constrained trading with high prices and restricted output, attained by manufacturers and service providers operating within capacity limits. For a typical capitalist economy the demand-constrained case will be the norm, as assumed in monopoly-capital theories and Post Keynesian/Kaleckian economics (Baran and Sweezy, 1966, chapters 2 and 3; Sawyer, 1985b, chapter 2; Shapiro, 2005; Lavoie, 2006, chapters 1 and 2). Producers shun price competition, which would harm their profits, and adopt cost-plus pricing to ensure a regular profit return.

The only major exception is in the welfare states of mixed economies. Creating a welfare state within a capitalist frame has entailed public provision and finance of services (notably health care and education) run on non-commercial lines (Esping-Anderson, 1990; Mishra, 1990; Pierson, 2006). With no need to make profits, prices can be low and production set close to full capacity to yield supply-constrained outcomes. Unlike a pure capitalist economy with a preponderance of demand-constrained trade, a mixed economy has a more even balance of demand-constrained and supply-constrained components, within what remains a capitalist setting.

A contrast between demand-constrained and supply-constrained trading shows up in the comparison of capitalist and socialist economies in the late twentieth century (Kalecki, 1970, 1972, chapter 2; Kornai, 1980, 1992, 2013; Nell, 1991). The capitalist economies were mixed, with extensive planned, non-profit sectors, but most industrial capital was in private ownership and making a regular surplus. Market power was the guardian of this surplus, resulting in high prices, restricted output and demand-constrained sales. Socialist economies on Marxian principles did not have private ownership of the means of production and had no compulsion to make profit in every industry. The economy was steered by central planners adhering to a strategy at the national level. To make goods accessible, planners could set low prices across the whole economy, not just in welfare enclaves such as health care and education. Low prices stimulated high demand and supply-constrained sales allocated by rationing schemes.

Table 10.1 lists the attributes of demand-constrained and supply-constrained economies. In many ways they are opposites: demand-constrained economies put demand on the short side of most markets, which gives producers a surplus but forces them to compete, advertise and innovate; supply-constrained economies put supply on the short side of most markets, which soothes the pressures on producers, who have no trouble selling their output (Kornai, 1979). Discussion of these matters is sparse in the general economic literature and resides chiefly in the specialised field of comparative economic systems (Zimbalist and Sherman, 1984; Carson, 1990; Conklin, 1991; Gardner, 1998; Gregory and Stuart, 2004). Systemic comparisons between capitalist and socialist economies have seldom been even-handed and are tarnished by the ideological stand-off of the Cold War. The discussion in the rest of this section will sidestep the political background to point out some advantages and disadvantages of demand-constrained and supply-constrained economies.

Table 10.1 Demand-constrained and supply-constrained economies

	Demand-constrained	Supply-constrained
Prices	High	Low
Short side	Demand	Supply
Product availability	Abundance	Shortage
Unsold output	Yes	No
Profit/surplus	High	Low
Excess capacity	Yes	No
Allocation method	Rationing by price	Non-price rationing
Product duplication	Much	Little
Product innovation	Frequent	Rare
Non-price competition	High	Low
Advertising	Extensive	Limited
Marketing	Essential	Peripheral
Product branding	General	Occasional
Consumer choice	High	Low

Demand-constrained arrangements give an impression of abundance whatever the availability of goods for sale: supply (or the capacity to supply) exceeds demand and goods or services never seem to be scarce. Shelves in the shops are full, people can buy goods or services if they have the purchasing power and rationing schemes are unnecessary. Demand is curtailed through high prices (rationing by price), with no further restrictions on those willing and able to pay. Buyers like this open access to goods and services, subject only to pricing, compared with the added barriers imposed by a rationing scheme. Producers/sellers possess market power and make profits that allow them to subsist as private firms. They eschew price competition (a threat to profits) and preserve their share of the price-limited demand through non-price competition in the form of advertising, marketing and branding. The need to sustain demand and profitability brings incentives towards product innovation and cost reductions, which should improve living standards in the long run. Desire to innovate bestows on the economy a dynamic quality that would otherwise be missing (Kornai, 2013). Anyone with a decent income has freedom to make choices, so the atmosphere is one of consumerism and indulgence of buyers, who are active and engaged, even though market power lies with the sellers.

Beside their positive features, demand-constrained arrangements have various disadvantages. High prices restrict access to goods and services, making them affordable to the rich but excluding those on lower incomes. Inequalities in income will be mirrored by inequalities in consumption, with no means to redress them. Market power for the producers/sellers yields a surplus that may not be invested and under private ownership of capital may be distributed as dividends to wealthy shareholders: outcomes are again regressive and unequal. With price competition minimised, the surplus will not be competed away and becomes permanent. Non-price competition leaves the surplus intact and, if anything, causes it to grow if the producers/sellers consolidate their market power. Widespread use of advertising and marketing as promotional devices may distort information and manipulate people into buying. Brand imagery may obscure the true quality of products. Resources devoted to branding and marketing, which constitute new service industries, can be seen as wasted and better devoted to other things. Also wasteful are the unused productive capacity, the excess supply with products left unsold, and the trial of new products ultimately scorned by buyers. Goods and services are duplicated unnecessarily, as are productive facilities. At any given time the excess capacity, unemployment, unsold output and unsuccessful new products suggest a profligate, cavalier attitude to resources.

Supply-constrained arrangements set prices low so as to make goods and services cheaper and equalise access across consumers. They are atypical of capitalist economies as they cannot guarantee profits for private firms, though they do arise in the welfare states of mixed economies and under special circumstances when supply may be restricted (wartime and other crises). On a bigger scale they typify centrally planned economies in which profit motives are less relevant and planners set prices on social rather than commercial grounds. Efficiency and other arguments for planning are poorly represented in the orthodox economic literature but can be found elsewhere (Zimbalist and Sherman, 1984, parts 3 and 4; Mandel, 1986; Bottomore, 1990; Albert and Hahnel, 1991; Nove, 1991, parts 1 and 2; Cockshott and Cottrell, 1993; Gregory and Stuart, 2004, chapter 6; Ellman, 2014). Low prices reduce disparities in consumption and offset the influence of income differentials on living standards. With excess demand, almost all output gets sold and few resources are wasted. Producers readily find buyers for their output, so they can do without much branding, marketing and advertising – the effort and expense devoted to these can be redirected. Nor is there the constant urge to develop new products, many of which are of dubious value and prove to be commercial failures. Commercial 'successes' driven solely by clever branding and advertising are avoided. Production can meet genuine needs, not ephemeral fads and fashions induced by advertising and product promotion. Cutting back on unnecessary consumption will lessen any adverse effects on the environment.

Problems of supply-constrained arrangements are familiar from the critique of central planning as an economic system (Eatwell, Milgate and Newman, 1990; Nove, 1991; Ellman, 2014). Because goods and services are in chronic shortage, the authorities must implement permanent rationing schemes, which could be organised with equity in mind, but the simple option is random access by queuing (first come, first served). While queuing has a demotic hue, it is arbitrary and may not yield an equitable resource allocation. Buyers may spend many hours queuing, a waste of their time, and are liable to find this irritating compared with the demand-constrained alternative. Empty shelves and rationing make a poor contrast with full shelves and buying opportunities; shortages are less attractive than apparent abundance. Consumers seem to prefer an allocation method that offers the possibility of purchase, even when high prices prevent them from buying. Reduced incentives for product innovation diminish the diversity of products on offer and limit the choices available. Producers have little need to maintain quality, since bad products can still find buyers – deteriorating quality becomes a danger unless steps are taken to monitor it. Reduced product innovation hampers entrepreneurship and economic expansion, depressing growth rates. In the long run, growth slower than demand-constrained economies will lead to a cumulative disadvantage and adverse judgements on economic performance.

Comparison of demand-constrained and supply-constrained arrangements shows that neither can be proffered as ideal. Choosing between them is not an obvious decision. Orthodox economics upholds market-clearing equilibrium as the ideal compromise, with demand equal to supply and no constraint on either side. Markets that equilibrate would attain balanced outcomes characterised by Pareto efficiency, complete information, production at full capacity, no rationing schemes, no resources wasted and homogeneous products without branding or marketing. Selecting demand constraints or supply constraints would be redundant, as they both evaporate in the self-regulation of equilibrating markets. The problem with this viewpoint, as noted in Chapter 2, is that markets can never match the hypothetical ideal. Prices are set by price-makers who must decide the appropriate level: the choice is almost certain to call forth demand or supply constraints. Any compromise will be reached not by *laissez-faire* and general equilibrium, but by conscious decisions of price setters in a mixture of demand-constrained and supply-constrained cases.

Under capitalism, private ownership of capital ensures that demand-constrained arrangements pertain to most goods and services in order to buttress profits and keep private companies afloat. Compromise is reached in a mixed economy by taking certain services (health care, education, housing, public utilities) out of the commercial sector and having supply-constrained arrangements under different ownership structures. A balanced outcome is achieved without any part of the economy reaching market-clearing equilibrium. In a socialist economy with public ownership of capital, the choice of price level and trading patterns is open to further supply-constrained arrangements if desired. Here again the outcomes depend on price-setting decisions rather than spontaneous equilibria. All the various possibilities involve markets in the sense of organised and institutionalised exchange. A dichotomy between markets and planning is unfounded, as 'market economies' (capitalist) have large segments of planning and 'planned economies' (socialist) rely heavily on trading. Whatever the decisions about ownership and distribution in the economy as a whole, the practical consequences will be a blend of markets and planning.

Complexity of the total economy

Economies demonstrate complexity through the ordered plenitude of behaviour and institutions within a structured setting (Rosser, 1999; Hodgson, 2003a). No pure system of markets, planning or anything else will determine all economic outcomes in a clockwork manner. The real world is too intricate for that. According to the 'law of requisite variety' (Ashby's Law), the diversity of the real world cannot be contained by narrow rules and models – it requires a parallel diversity of response (Ashby, 1968; Boisot and McKelvey, 2011). Applied to the total economy, this leads to the 'impurity principle': all durable economic systems have necessary impurities that create variety and let the economy adapt (Hodgson, 1988, chapter 11, 1995). No system will ever extend markets into every corner of economic behaviour, which would terminate further change.

More than being outmoded remnants, the non-commercial and informal sectors of a developed economy are essential to its functioning. Firms and governments administer their internal organisation; planned welfare systems soften the harsher outcomes of competitive markets; informal provision within the domestic sector sustains the labour force and preserves social cohesion. The various sectors are complementary. A 'market economy' sits on a raft of non-market activities and would otherwise struggle to survive. Boundaries between market and non-market sectors are not always clear, given the problems in defining a market, and will be permeable. Arguments over commodification and the limits of trade are perennial and never fully resolved. Different arrangements may be suitable for different local circumstances. It would be unwise to draw sweeping conclusions, beyond the need for diverse organisation.

Complexity extends to the internal organisation of markets. The template of a pure competitive market never coincides with what we experience in the real world. Traders know each other, form trading relations, negotiate prices, differentiate their products and deploy marketing techniques. Every market has its own unique traits, as well as properties in common with other markets. Trading is never cast in stone, even if some details persist. Market power will ebb and flow, trading relations fade or revive, but they are unlikely to vanish. The demand-constrained trade in developed economies awards a handsome surplus to firms who avoid price competition and opt for non-price rivalries. Upkeep of the surplus is accompanied by leeway in how trade is conducted through trading relations, marketing, product innovation and other non-price competition. Whatever their shared attributes, markets embrace internal variety and complexity, in line with the complexity of the total economy. They are a complex part of a complex whole.

The tenor of the economy turns on the property rights and related institutions implemented by the state through the legal system. In a capitalist economy, the property rights permit private ownership of capital, along with tradability of this property. In a socialist economy, the property rights ban private ownership of capital but are consistent with other trading or markets. Various forms of property ownership are feasible as a basis for economic activity. Whatever the property rights may be, economic behaviour is not dictated by the institutional context and remains changeable. The multiplicity of capitalism is documented in the literature on its varieties and historical evolution (Albert, 1993; Groenewegen, 1997; Hall and Soskice, 2001; Trigilia, 2002, chapter 10; Amable, 2003; Peck and Theodore, 2007; Hancké, 2009). Although diverse organisation has often been viewed as a sign of an economy malfunctioning or being watered down, it is vital for adaptability. Efforts to reform a 'market system' by reducing diversity and returning to core principles will be counterproductive, hurting its capacity to evolve and making it vulnerable to breakdown. The same applies to socialist economies: there are varieties of socialism and gradual transformations over time. The place of markets under socialism, always contentious, remains an active area of debate (Brus and Laski, 1991; Nove, 1991; Roosevelt and Belkin, 1994; Ollman, 1998; Elson, 2000b; Yunker, 2001; Gregory and Stuart, 2004, chapter 7; Schweickart, 2011). Viable economic systems will combine the general characteristics imbued by their property rights and institutions with a good deal of internal diversity.

A capitalist economy tips the balance towards private ownership and for-profit trading, but their significance can shift as the economy evolves. One way to illustrate this is to use the formal/informal and demand-constrained/supply-constrained distinctions. Together they give the four alternative cases in Figure 10.2. The top-left case of commercial, profit-seeking activity will prevail under capitalism; the other cases are subordinate. Bottom-left is the public-service sector organised formally and pursuing non-profit welfare goals; bottom-right is its voluntary equivalent, informal in nature and also welfare motivated. Top-right is the irregular sector, commercially driven, usually illegal and covering the profit-seeking trade outside the formal economy. All four cases coexist within capitalist economies and shrink and expand as the economy evolves.

Figure 10.2 allows two directions of movement, vertical and horizontal. Upward movements correspond to commodification, whereby goods and services are produced to be traded for profit. Leftward movements correspond to formalisation, whereby economic activities are measured and recorded in accounts. At the earliest stages of economic development, societies had little trade and no formal accounts, so they were located at the bottom-right of the figure. Economic development has brought commodification and formalisation that have gradually moved activities out of the bottom-right case into the others. Whether commodification or formalisation came first can be left open, variable with historical circumstances, but the drift is towards the top-left of Figure 10.2.

Such trends, if they reached their limit, would converge all economies on a single, final stage of development with total commodification and formalisation. The apparently inevitable passage to the top-left of Figure 10.2 receives theoretical backing from orthodox economics, notably in the 'property rights' school (Alchian and Demsetz, 1972, 1973; Furubotn and Pejovich, 1972). Here the diffusion of tradable property rights across the whole economy is welcomed as a source of potential Pareto improvements. Economic rationality impels all societies to move towards tradable private property. These conclusions follow from the theoretical models adopted but are marred by the deficiencies of neoclassicism: they say more about orthodox economics than they do about the real world. In reality the movements within Figure 10.2 are far more tortuous.

The downward trend towards decommodification, even though it may seem to defy economic progress, has been much observed. It is bound up with nascent welfare states during the mid-twentieth century, a defining trend of that period (Esping-Andersen, 1990; Huber and Stephens, 2001;

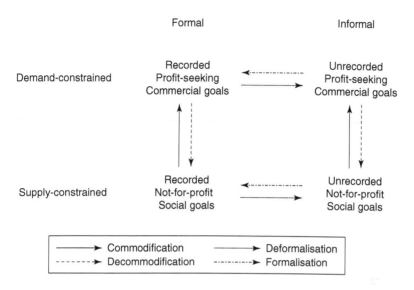

Figure 10.2 Evolutionary trends.

Arts and Gelissen, 2002; Swank, 2005). When welfare states were set up, health care and other services were removed from the market and provided publicly, financed from taxation. Public finance and provision were the only way to guarantee universal access and minimum standards for all citizens; commercial sale could never accomplish this. Decisions to take certain items out of the market were a political and ethical judgement to go for planned public services. Decommodification can also happen in 'bottom-up' versions from initiatives towards moral economy, fair trade, social enterprise and other resistance to commerce (Sayer, 2000, 2003, 2007; Bedore, 2010; Vail, 2010; Raynolds, 2012). Participants in trade may choose to move away from profit motives and production-for-sale towards social motives that include moral and distributive concerns.

The rightward trend towards deformalisation might seem improbable, as it swims against the tide of ever-greater formal organisation, whether commercial or non-commercial. Informal commerce tied to tax evasion or other illegal practices has been officially discouraged and penalised. Yet deformalisation is far from unknown. Many public services can be provided formally or informally. Governments often claim that social care should be informal ('community care') so as to improve its quality and reduce public spending (Means, Richards and Smith, 2008). A plea for the 'gift relationship' will support deformalisation in areas where markets have been over-extended (Titmuss, 1970; Archard, 2002). Trends towards the informal can be seen in 'untraded interdependencies' and the 'associational economy' (Storper, 1995; Cooke and Morgan, 1998; Scott and

Storper, 2003). Economic activities becoming less formal is not necessarily retrograde. Informality is the default option for economic or non-economic endeavours neglected in the formal economy. New activities may start informally before they become formalised, so a swing to the informal could arise from innovation.

To assume a single historical trend towards the top-left of Figure 10.2 would be oversimplified. Movements downwards and rightwards are possible at any time. Pure 'market economies' have never existed historically (see Part II) and will not exist in the future. Actual economies are a mixture of management/planning and trade, the two being intertwined. Markets could not function without management/planning, and the commercial character of modern capitalist economies depends on public services, management of firms and informal housework.

Instead of overemphasising markets at the expense of other economic arrangements, it is better to stress complexity. Even if commodification has spread far under capitalism, it remains a long way from penetrating every facet of economic life. If we are to understand markets we cannot focus on trading alone and must appreciate other elements of the economy. With a complex object of study, we should aim for theories and methods that recognise complexity. Most markets, local or global, will have social relations among buyers and sellers, trading by administered firms and other organisations, and public regulation. Diversity also extends across the macro-level of the total economy. Looking at markets and trade alone will be inadequate to understand economic affairs. We need a wider vision.

Markets at the macro-level present neither a single, complete system nor a bundle of uncoordinated special cases. Reality falls between the two extremes: markets have common properties as well as diversity. The task for theorists is how to capture the common properties while still being able to handle diversity. A universal scheme risks undue restrictiveness, yet specific cases may be too fragmentary. In searching for the middle ground, three broad guidelines pertain.

The first is that systemic arguments should be supple enough to include variety, refusing to impose a complete deterministic model. Markets do not encompass the whole economy, and they rely on other arrangements, often informal. One way to respect this is to be wary of total, overblown theories and prefer looser, less deterministic styles of theorising (Rousseas, 1989; Potts, 2000; Dopfer, 2005; Foster, 2005; Byrne and Callaghan, 2014). If systemic approaches are to be retained, they should acknowledge complexity and admit the multiplicity and layering of systems: this was appreciated in the original systems literature dating from the mid-twentieth century, although not always by later theorists (Bertalanffy, 1968, 1972; Boulding, 1985; Hodgson, 1987). The prospect of a general market system must be treated with caution.

The second guideline is that theorising about the total economy should be evolutionary, with the continuous possibility of change. There should be no fixed, timeless model of trade that adheres everywhere. As heterodox economists have argued, theories should be consistent with evolution (Hodgson, 1993; Nelson and Winter, 2002; Metcalfe, 2005; Dopfer and Potts, 2008; Nelson et al., 2018). Changes in the context of markets and in trading behaviour will be ongoing. The openness of markets and their capacity to receive innovations means that that they are frequently the conduit for economic evolution.

The third guideline is that theories should be alert to the total economy as a distinct level of analysis. Post Keynesian economics exemplifies this with its insistence on keeping macroeconomics separate from microeconomics (King, 2002, 2015; Davidson, 2011; Lavoie, 2006, 2014). Macroeconomic tendencies are permitted to emerge in their own right, escaping the fallacies of composition from misguided aggregation and false microfoundations. Markets have been a prime source of such fallacies through efforts to apply orthodox micro-models at the macro-level. The models, which have serious weaknesses even for single markets, shed no light on the economy as a whole.

Complexity of the total economy requires complex theory that denies a simple market model. Many alternative approaches are available, as surveyed in the current book. Their diversity should not be seen as incoherence or lack of rigour but as a reaction to the diverse markets in modern developed economies. The approaches are often compatible. Could they be merged into a unified scheme? The quest for a grand synthesis seems quixotic, but there is scope for finding common ground, exploring overlaps, building layered theory and seeking consistent terminology. Theorists could then work towards the requisite variety needed to portray markets while avoiding the superfluous variety from repetitions and duplication. A starting point, before dialogue can take place, is to be fully aware of the rich, ample theorising about markets.

Bibliography

Aaker, D.A. (1991), *Managing Brand Equity: Capitalizing on the Value of a Brand Name*, New York: Free Press.

Aaker, D.A., and Day, G.S. (eds.) (1982), *Consumerism: Search for the Consumer Interest*, 4th edn., New York: Free Press.

Abolafia, M.Y. (1996), *Making Markets: Opportunism and Restraint on Wall Street*, Cambridge, MA: Harvard University Press.

Ackerman, F. (1997), 'Consumed in theory: alternative perspectives on the economics of consumption', *Journal of Economic Issues*, 31(3): 651–664.

Ackerman, F. (2002), 'Still dead after all these years: interpreting the failure of general equilibrium theory', *Journal of Economic Methodology*, 9(2): 119–139.

Ackerman, F., and Nadal, A. (eds.) (2004), *The Flawed Foundations of General Equilibrium: Critical Essays on Economic Theory*, London: Routledge.

Adaman, F., and Madra, Y.M. (2002), 'Theorizing the "third sphere": a critique of the persistence of the "economistic fallacy"', *Journal of Economic Issues*, 36(4): 1045–1078.

Adams, D., and Tiesdell, S. (2010), 'Planners as market actors: rethinking state-market relations in land and property', *Planning Theory and Practice*, 11(2): 187–207.

Adorno, T.W. (1991), *The Culture Industry: Selected Essays on Mass Culture*, edited by J.M. Bernstein, London: Routledge.

Agnello, L., and Schuknecht, L. (2011), 'Booms and busts in housing markets: determinants and implications', *Journal of Housing Economics*, 20(3): 171–190.

Ahrne, G., Aspers, P., and Brunsson, N. (2015), 'The organization of markets', *Organization Studies*, 36(1): 7–27.

Aimar, T. (2009), *The Economics of Ignorance and Coordination: Subjectivism and the Austrian School of Economics*, Cheltenham, UK: Edward Elgar.

Akerlof, G.A. (1970), 'The market for "lemons": quality uncertainty and the market mechanism', *Quarterly Journal of Economics*, 84(3): 488–500.

Albert, M. (1993), *Capitalism Against Capitalism*, London: Whurr.

Albert, M., and Hahnel, R. (1991), *The Political Economy of Participatory Economics*, Princeton, NJ: Princeton University Press.

Albritton, R. (2012), 'Commodification and commodity fetishism', in B. Fine, and A. Saad-Filho (eds.), *The Elgar Companion to Marxist Economics*, Cheltenham, UK: Edward Elgar, pp. 66–71.

Alchian, A.A., and Demsetz, H. (1972), 'Production, information costs, and economic organization', *American Economic Review*, 62(5): 777–795.

Alchian, A.A., and Demsetz, H. (1973), 'The property right paradigm', *Journal of Economic History*, 33(1): 16–27.

Alexander, J.C. (ed.) (1985), *Neo-Functionalism*, London: Sage.

Alexander, J.C., and Colomy, P. (1985), 'Toward neo-functionalism', *Sociological Theory*, 3(2): 11–23.

Alter, M. (1990), *Carl Menger and the Origins of Austrian Economics*, Boulder, CO: Westview Press.

Alvey, J.E. (2000), 'An introduction to economics as a moral science', *International Journal of Social Economics*, 27(12): 1231–1252.

Amable, B. (2003), *The Diversity of Modern Capitalism*, Oxford, UK: Oxford University Press.

Amemiya, T. (2007), *Economy and Economics of Ancient Greece*, London: Routledge.

Amin, A. (ed.) (1994), *Post-Fordism: A Reader*, Oxford, UK: Blackwell.

Amin, A., and Thrift, N.J. (1995), 'Institutional issues for the European regions: from markets and plans to socioeconomics and powers of association', *Economy and Society*, 24(1): 41–66.

Amin, A., and Thrift, N.J. (2000), 'What kind of economic theory for what kind of economic geography?', *Antipode*, 32(1): 4–9.

Andereck, W.S. (2007), 'Commodified care', *Cambridge Quarterly of Healthcare Ethics*, 16(4): 398–406.

Anderson, E. (1990), 'The ethical limitations of the market', *Economics and Philosophy*, 6(2): 179–205.

Anderson, E. (1993), *Value in Ethics and Economics*, Cambridge, MA: Harvard University Press.

Anderson, J.P. (2018), *Insider Trading: Law, Ethics, and Reform*, Cambridge, UK: Cambridge University Press.

Andre, J. (1992), 'Blocked exchanges: a taxonomy', *Ethics*, 103(1): 29–47.

Annas, J. (2007), 'Virtue ethics', in D. Copp (ed.), *The Oxford Handbook of Ethical Theory*, Oxford, UK: Oxford University Press, pp. 515–536.

Applbaum, K. (2005), 'The anthropology of markets', in J.G. Carrier (ed.), *A Handbook of Economic Anthropology*, Cheltenham, UK: Edward Elgar, pp. 275–289.

Araujo, L. (2007), 'Markets, market-making and marketing', *Marketing Theory*, 7(3): 211–226.

Araujo, L., Finch, J., and Kjellberg, H. (eds.) (2010), *Reconnecting Marketing to Markets*, Oxford, UK: Oxford University Press.

Archard, D. (2002), 'Selling yourself: Titmuss's argument against a market in blood', *Journal of Ethics*, 6(1): 87–103.

Archer, M.S. (1995), *Realist Social Theory: The Morphogenetic Approach*, Cambridge, UK: Cambridge University Press.

Archer, M.S. (1996), *Culture and Agency: The Place of Culture in Social Theory*, revised edn., Cambridge, UK: Cambridge University Press.

Archer, M.S. (2003), *Structure, Agency and the Internal Conversation*, Cambridge, UK: Cambridge University Press.

Archer, M.S., Bhaskar, R., Collier, A., Lawson, T., and Norrie, A. (eds.) (1998), *Critical Realism: Essential Readings*, London: Routledge.

Arena, R., and Blankenberg, S. (2013), 'Sraffa, Keynes, and Post-Keynesians: suggestions for a synthesis in the making', in G.C. Harcourt, and P. Kriesler (eds.), *The Oxford Handbook of Post-Keynesian Economics, Volume 1: Theory and Origins*, Oxford, UK: Oxford University Press, pp. 74–100.

Aristotle (1953), *The Nicomachean Ethics*, translated by J.A.K. Thomson, Harmondsworth, UK: Penguin.

Aristotle (1962), *The Politics*, translated by T.A. Sinclair, Harmondsworth, UK: Penguin.

Arndt, J. (1979), 'Toward a concept of domesticated markets', *Journal of Marketing*, 43(4): 69–75.

Arndt, J. (1981), 'The political economy of marketing systems: reviving the institutional approach', *Journal of Macromarketing*, 1(2): 36–47.

Arnsperger, C., and Varoufakis, Y. (2006), 'What is neoclassical economics?', *Post-Autistic Economics Review*, 38: article 1.

Arthur, W.B. (2010), 'Complexity, the Santa Fe approach, and non-equilibrium economics', *History of Economic Ideas*, 18(2): 149–166.

Arthur, W.B. (ed.) (2015), *Complexity and the Economy*, Oxford, UK: Oxford University Press.

Arts, W., and Gelissen, J. (2002), 'Three worlds of welfare capitalism or more? A state-of-the-art report', *Journal of European Social Policy*, 12(2): 137–158.

Árvay, J. (1994), 'The Material Product System (MPS): a retrospective', in Z. Kenessey (ed.), *The Accounts of Nations*, Amsterdam: IOS Press, pp. 218–236.

Ashby, W.R. (1968), 'Variety, constraint, and the law of requisite variety', in W. Buckley (ed.), *Modern Systems Research for the Behavioral Scientist*, Chicago, IL: Aldine, pp. 129–136.

Ashton, T.S. (1997), *The Industrial Revolution 1760–1830*, new edn., Oxford, UK: Oxford University Press.

Aspers, P. (2007), 'Theory, reality, and performativity in markets', *American Journal of Economics and Sociology*, 66(2): 379–398.

Aspers, P. (2009), 'How are markets made?', *MPifG* Working Paper 09/2.

Aspers, P. (2011), *Markets*, Cambridge, UK: Polity Press.

Aspromourgos, T. (2004), 'Sraffian research programmes and unorthodox economics', *Review of Political Economy*, 16(2): 179–206.

Atkinson, A.B. (2008), *The Changing Distribution of Earnings in OECD Countries*, Oxford: Oxford University Press.

Atkinson, A.B. (2015), *Inequality: What Can Be Done?*, Cambridge, MA: Harvard University Press.

Atkinson, A.B., and Piketty, T. (eds.) (2010), *Top Incomes: A Global Perspective*, Oxford, UK: Oxford University Press.

Aubet, M.E. (2001), *The Phoenicians and the West: Politics, Colonies, and Trade*, translated by M. Turton, Cambridge, UK: Cambridge University Press.

Auger, P., and Devinney, T.M. (2007), 'Do what consumers say matter? The misalignment of preferences with unconstrained ethical intentions', *Journal of Business Ethics*, 76(4): 361–383.

Augier, M., and March, J.G. (2008), 'A retrospective look at *A Behavioral Theory of the Firm*', *Journal of Economic Behavior and Organization*, 66(1): 1–6.

Austin, A.L. (1962), *How to Do Things with Words*, Oxford, UK: Clarendon Press.

Babb, S. (2013), 'The Washington Consensus as transnational policy paradigm: its origins, trajectory and likely successor', *Review of International Political Economy*, 20(2): 268–297.

Backhaus, J.G. (1999), 'Money and its economic and social functions: Simmel and European monetary integration', *American Journal of Economics and Sociology*, 58(4): 1075–1090.

Backhouse, R.E., and Medema, S.G. (2009), 'Retrospectives: on the definition of economics', *Journal of Economic Perspectives*, 23(1): 221–233.

Bain, J.S. (1959), *Industrial Organization*, New York: Wiley.

Bainbridge, S.M. (2000), 'Insider trading', in B. Bouckaert, and G. DeGeest (eds.), *Encyclopedia of Law and Economics*, Vol. 3, Cheltenham, UK: Edward Elgar, pp. 772–812.

Baker, W.E. (1984), 'The social structure of a national securities market', *American Journal of Sociology*, 89(4): 775–811.

Baker, W.E. (1992), 'The network organization in theory and practice', in N. Nohria, and R.G. Eccles (eds.), *Networks and Organizations: Structure, Form, and Action*, Boston, MA: Harvard Business School Press, pp. 397–429.

Bakker, I. (2007), 'Social reproduction and the constitution of a gendered political economy', *New Political Economy*, 12(4): 541–556.

Bakker, I., and Silvey, R. (eds.) (2008), *Beyond States and Markets: The Challenges of Social Reproduction*, London: Routledge.

Baldwin, J.W. (1959), 'The medieval theories of the just price: Romanists, canonists, and theologians in the twelfth and thirteenth centuries', *Transactions of the American Philosophical Society*, 49(4): 1–92.

Banaji, J. (1976), 'The peasantry in the feudal mode of production: towards an economic model', *Journal of Peasant Studies*, 3(3): 299–320.

Banaji, J. (2012), 'Mode of production', in B. Fine, and A. Saad-Filho (eds.), *The Elgar Companion to Marxist Economics*, Cheltenham, UK: Edward Elgar, pp. 227–232.

Baran, P.A., and Sweezy, P.M. (1966), *Monopoly Capital: An Essay on the American Economic and Social Order*, New York: Monthly Review Press.

Barberis, N., and Thaler, R. (2003), 'A survey of behavioural finance', in G.M. Constantinides, M. Harris, and R. Stulz (eds.), *Handbook of the Economics of Finance*, Vol. 1B, Amsterdam: Elsevier, pp. 1053–1128.

Barker, C., and Jane, E.A. (2016), *Cultural Studies: Theory and Practice*, 5th edn., London: Sage.

Barker, G. (2006), *The Agricultural Revolution in Prehistory: Why Did Foragers Become Farmers?*, Oxford, UK: Oxford University Press.

Barnard, A. (2000), *History and Theory in Anthropology*, Cambridge, UK: Cambridge University Press.

Barnes, T.J., Peck, J., and Sheppard, E. (eds.) (2012), *The Wiley-Blackwell Companion to Economic Geography*, Chichester, UK: Wiley-Blackwell.

Barrotta, P. (2018), 'Hume's "law" and the ideal of value-free science', in P. Barrotta, *Scientists, Democracy and Society: A Community of Inquirers*, Cham, Switzerland: Springer, pp. 1–19.

Baskin, J.B., and Miranti, P.J. (1997), *A History of Corporate Finance*, Cambridge, UK: Cambridge University Press.

Baudrillard, J. (1993), *Symbolic Exchange and Death*, translated by I.H. Grant, London: Sage.

Baudrillard, J. (2017), *The Consumer Society: Myths and Structures*, revised edn., London: Sage.

Bauman, Z. (2001), 'Consuming life', *Journal of Consumer Culture*, 1(1): 9–29.

Baumol, W.J. (2002), *The Free-Market Innovation Machine: Analysing the Growth Miracle of Capitalism*, Princeton, NJ: Princeton University Press.

Bausor, R. (1982), 'Time and the structure of economic analysis', *Journal of Post Keynesian Economics*, 5(2): 163–179.

Beasley, R., and Danesi, M. (2002), *Persuasive Signs: The Semiotics of Advertising*, New York: De Gruyter.

Beckert, J. (2009a), 'The great transformation of embeddedness: Karl Polanyi and the new economic sociology', in C. Hann, and K. Hart (eds.), *Market and Society: The Great Transformation Today*, Cambridge, UK: Cambridge University Press, pp. 38–55.

Beckert, J. (2009b), 'The social order of markets', *Theory and Society*, 38(3): 245–269.

Beckert, J., and Wehinger, F. (2013), 'In the shadow: illegal markets and economic sociology', *Socio-Economic Review*, 11(1): 5–30.

Bedore, M. (2010), 'Just urban food systems: a new direction for food access and urban social justice', *Geography Compass*, 4(9): 1418–1432.

Beinhocker, E.D. (2006), *The Origin of Wealth: Evolution, Complexity, and the Radical Remaking of Economics*, Cambridge, MA: Harvard Business School Press.

Belk, R.W. (1988), 'Possessions and the extended self', *Journal of Consumer Research*, 15(2): 139–168.

Belk, R.W. (2013), 'Extended self in a digital world', *Journal of Consumer Research*, 40(3): 477–500.

Belk, R.W., and Wallendorf, M. (1990), 'The sacred meanings of money', *Journal of Economic Psychology*, 11(1): 35–67.

Bell, S. (2001), 'The role of the state and the hierarchy of money', *Cambridge Journal of Economics*, 25(2): 149–163.

Benicourt, E., and Guerrien, B. (2008), 'Is anything worth keeping in microeconomics?', *Review of Radical Political Economics*, 40(3): 317–323.

Beny, L.N. (2005), 'Do insider trading laws matter? Some preliminary comparative evidence', *American Law and Economics Review*, 7(1): 144–183.

Berger, S. (ed.) (2009), *The Foundations of Non-Equilibrium Economics: The Principle of Circular and Cumulative Causation*, London: Routledge.

Berle, A.A., and Means, G.C. (1932), *The Modern Corporation and Private Property*, New York: Macmillan.

Bernstein, W.J. (2008), *A Splendid Exchange: How Trade Shaped the World*, London: Atlantic Books.

Bertalanffy, L. von (1968), *General System Theory: Foundations, Development, Applications*, New York: George Braziller.

Bertalanffy, L. von (1972), 'The history and status of general systems theory', *Academy of Management Journal*, 15(4): 407–426.

Beunza, D., and Stark, D. (2004), 'Tools of the trade: the socio-technology of arbitrage in a Wall Street trading room', *Industrial and Corporate Change*, 13(2): 369–400.

Bevan, D. (eds.) (2015), 'Ethics should not cloud business or financial decisions: the enduring power of the neoclassical paradigm', in P. O'Sullivan, N.F.B. Allington, and M. Esposito (eds.), *The Philosophy, Politics and Economics of Finance in the 21st Century: From Hubris to Disgrace*, London: Routledge, pp. 310–331.

Bhaskar, R. (1978), 'On the possibility of social scientific knowledge and the limits of naturalism', *Journal for the Theory of Social Behaviour*, 8(1): 1–28.

Bhaskar, R. (1983), 'Beef, structure and place: notes from a critical naturalist perspective', *Journal for the Theory of Social Behaviour*, 13(1): 81–96.

Bhaskar, R. (1986), *Scientific Realism and Human Emancipation*, London: Verso.

Bhaskar, R. (1989), *Reclaiming Reality: A Critical Introduction to Contemporary Philosophy*, London: Verso.

Bhaskar, R. (1994), *Plato Etc. The Problems of Philosophy and Their Resolution*, London: Verso.

Bhaskar, R. (2015), *The Possibility of Naturalism: A Philosophical Critique of the Contemporary Human Sciences*, 4th edn., London: Routledge.

Bhaskar, R. (2016), *Enlightened Common Sense: The Philosophy of Critical Realism*, edited with a preface by M. Hartwig, London: Routledge.

Biggart, N.W., and Beamish, T.D. (2003), 'The economic sociology of conventions: habit, custom, practice, and routine in market order', *Annual Review of Sociology*, 29(1): 443–464.

Biggart, N.W., and Delbridge, R. (2004), 'Systems of exchange', *Academy of Management Review*, 29(1): 28–49.

Bilginsoy, C. (2015), *A History of Financial Crises: Dreams and Follies of Expectations*, London: Routledge.

Billig, M.S. (2000), 'Institutions and culture: neo-Weberian economic anthropology', *Journal of Economic Issues*, 34(4): 771–788.

Birch, K., and Siemiatycki, M. (2016), 'Neoliberalism and the geographies of marketization: the entangling of state and markets', *Progress in Human Geography*, 40(2): 177–198.

Birken, L. (1988), 'From macroeconomics to microeconomics: the marginalist revolution in sociocultural perspective', *History of Political Economy*, 20(2): 251–264.

Bishop, J.D. (1995), 'Adam Smith's invisible hand argument', *Journal of Business Ethics*, 14(3): 165–180.

Blaug, M. (ed.) (1991a), *Pioneers in Economics: Aristotle (384–322 BC)*, Cheltenham, UK: Edward Elgar.

Blaug, M. (ed.) (1991b), *Pioneers in Economics: St Thomas Aquinas (1225–1274)*, Cheltenham, UK: Edward Elgar.

Blaug, M. (1992), *The Methodology of Economics, or How Economists Explain*, 2nd edn., Cambridge, UK: Cambridge University Press.

Blaug, M. (2001), 'No history of ideas, please, we're economists', *Journal of Economic Perspectives*, 15(1): 145–164.

Blaug, M. (2007), 'The fundamental theorems of modern welfare economics, historically contemplated', *History of Political Economy*, 39(2): 185–207.

Block, F. (1990), *Postindustrial Possibilities: A Critique of Economic Discourse*, Berkeley, CA: University of California Press.

Block, F. (1991), 'Contradictions of self-regulating markets', in M. Mendell, and D. Salée (eds.), *The Legacy of Karl Polanyi: Market, State and Society at the End of the Twentieth Century*, London: Macmillan, pp. 86–106.

Block, F. (2000), 'Deconstructing capitalism as a system', *Rethinking Marxism*, 12(3): 83–98.

Block, F. (2003), 'Karl Polanyi and the writing of *The Great Transformation*', *Theory and Society*, 32(3): 275–306.

Block, F., and Somers, M.R. (1984), 'Beyond the economistic fallacy: the holistic social science of Karl Polanyi', in T. Skocpol (ed.), *Vision and Method in Historical Sociology*, Cambridge, UK: Cambridge University Press, pp. 47–84.

Bloom, P. (2017), *The Ethics of Neoliberalism: The Business of Making Capitalism Moral*, London: Routledge.

Bloomfield, R. (2008), 'Behavioural finance', in S.N. Durlauf, and L.E. Blume (eds.), *The New Palgrave Dictionary of Economics*, 2nd edn., London: Palgrave Macmillan, pp. 438–444.

Blowfield, M.E. (1999), 'Ethical trade: a review of developments and issues', *Third World Quarterly*, 20(4): 753–770.

Blowfield, M.E., and Dolan, C. (2010), 'Fairtrade facts and fancies: what Kenyan fairtrade tea tells us about business' role as development agent', *Journal of Business Ethics*, 93: 143–162.

Boettke, P.J. (1997), 'Where did economics go wrong? Modern economics as a flight from reality', *Critical Review*, 11(1): 11–64.

Boettke, P.J. (2002), 'Information and knowledge: Austrian economics in search of its uniqueness', *Review of Austrian Economics*, 15(4): 263–274.

Boettke, P.J., and Coyne, C.J. (2009), 'Context matters: institutions and entrepreneurship', *Foundations and Trends® in Entrepreneurship*, 5(3): 135–209.

Boggs, J.S., and Rantisi, N.M. (2003), 'The "relational turn" in economic geography', *Journal of Economic Geography*, 3(2): 109–116.

Bohannan, P., and Dalton, G. (eds.) (1962), *Markets in Africa*, Evanston, IL: Northwestern University Press.

Boisot, M., and McKelvey, B. (2011), 'Complexity and organization-environment relations: revisiting Ashby's law of requisite variety', in P. Allen, S. Maguire, and B. McKelvey (eds.), *The Sage Handbook of Complexity and Management*, London: Sage, pp. 279–298.

Bolton, J.L. (1980), *Medieval English Economy*, London: Dent, pp. 1150–1500.

Bortis, H. (1997), *Institutions, Behaviour and Economic Theory: A Contribution to Classical-Keynesian Political Economy*, Cambridge, UK: Cambridge University Press.

Botsman, R., and Rogers, R. (2011), *What's Mine Is Yours: How Collaborative Consumption Is Changing the Way We Live*, London: Collins.

Bottomore, T. (1990), *The Socialist Economy: Theory and Practice*, Hemel Hempstead, UK: Harvester Wheatsheaf.

Boulding, K.E. (1985), *The World as a Total System*, Beverly Hills, CA: Sage.

Bourdieu, P. (1977), *Outline of a Theory of Practice*, translated by R. Nice, Cambridge, UK: Cambridge University Press.

Bourdieu, P. (1990), *The Logic of Practice*, translated by R. Nice, Cambridge, UK: Polity Press.

Bourdieu, P. (1996), *The Rules of Art: Genesis and Structure of the Literary Field*, translated by S. Emanuel, Cambridge, UK: Polity Press.

Bourdieu, P. (1998), *Practical Reason: On the Theory of Action*, translated by R. Nice, Cambridge, UK: Polity Press.

Bourdieu, P. (2000), *Pascalian Meditations*, translated by R. Nice, Cambridge, UK: Polity Press.

Bourdieu, P. (2002), 'The forms of capital', in N.W. Biggart (ed.), *Readings in Economic Sociology*, Oxford, UK: Blackwell, pp. 280–291.

Bourdieu, P. (2005), 'Principles of an economic anthropology', in N.J. Smelser, and R. Swedberg (eds.), *The Handbook of Economic Sociology*, 2nd edn., Princeton, NJ: Princeton University Press, pp. 75–89.

Bourdieu, P., and Wacquant, L.J.D. (1992), *An Invitation to Reflexive Sociology*, Cambridge, UK: Polity Press.

Bradley, J.L. (ed.) (1984), *Ruskin: The Critical Heritage*, London: Routledge and Kegan Paul.

Bradley, K., and Cartledge, P. (eds.) (2011), *The Cambridge World History of Slavery, Volume 1 : The Ancient Mediterranean World*, Cambridge, UK: Cambridge University Press.

Braudel, F. (1981), *Civilization and Capitalism, 15th – 18th Century, Volumes I-III*, translated by S. Reynolds, London: Collins.

Braun, B. (2016), 'From performativity to political economy: index investing, ETFs and asset manager capitalism', *New Political Economy*, 21(3): 257–273.

Braverman, H. (1974), *Labor and Monopoly Capital: The Degradation of Work in the Twentieth Century*, New York: Monthly Review Press.

Bray, J., Johns, N., and Kilburn, D. (2011), 'An exploratory study into the factors impeding ethical consumption', *Journal of Business Ethics*, 98(4): 597–608.

Broad, R. (ed.) (2002), *Global Backlash: Citizen Initiatives for a Just World Economy*, Lanham, MD: Rowman & Littlefield.

Brousseau, E., and Glachant, J.-M. (eds.) (2008), *New Institutional Economics: A Guidebook*, Cambridge, UK: Cambridge University Press.

Brown, A. (2007), 'Reorienting critical realism: a system-wide perspective on the capitalist economy', *Journal of Economic Methodology*, 14(4): 499–519.

Brown, A. (2014), 'Critical realism in social research: approach with caution', *Work, Employment and Society*, 28(1): 112–123.

Brown, V. (1994), *Adam Smith's Discourse: Canonicity, Commerce and Conscience*, London: Routledge.

Bruggeman, J. (2008), *Social Networks: An Introduction*, London: Routledge.

Brus, W., and Laski, K. (1991), *From Marx to the Market: Socialism in Search of an Economic System*, Oxford, UK: Oxford University Press.

Buchanan, J.M., and Vanberg, V.J. (1991), 'The market as a creative process', *Economics and Philosophy*, 7(2): 167–186.

Buckle, S. (1991), *Natural Law and the Theory of Property: Grotius to Hume*, Oxford, UK: Oxford University Press.

Burkitt, B. (1984), *Radical Political Economy: An Introduction to the Alternative Economics*, Brighton, UK: Wheatsheaf.

Burt, R.S. (1992), *Structural Holes: The Social Structure of Competition*, Cambridge, MA: Harvard University Press.

Burt, R.S. (2000), 'The network structure of social capital', *Research in Organizational Behaviour*, 22: 345–423.

Burt, R.S. (2002), 'The social capital of structural holes', in M.F. Guillén, R. Collins, P. England, and M. Meyer (eds.), *The New Economic Sociology*, New York: Russell Sage Foundation, pp. 148–192.

Burt, R.S. (2004), 'Structural holes and good ideas', *American Journal of Sociology*, 110(2): 349–399.

Butler, J. (2010), 'Performative agency', *Journal of Cultural Economy*, 3(2): 147–161.

Buttle, F. (2009), *Customer Relationship Management: Concepts and Technologies*, 2nd edn., Oxford, UK: Butterworth-Heinemann.

Byrne, D., and Callaghan, G. (2014), *Complexity Theory and the Social Sciences: The State of the Art*, London: Routledge.

Çalışkan, K., and Callon, M. (2009), 'Economization, part 1: shifting attention from the economy towards processes of economization', *Economy and Society*, 38(3): 369–398.

Çalışkan, K., and Callon, M. (2010), 'Economization, part 2: a research programme for the study of markets', *Economy and Society*, 39(1): 1–32.

Callinicos, A.T. (1989), *Against Postmodernism: A Marxist Critique*, Cambridge, UK: Polity Press.

Callinicos, A.T. (2009), *Imperialism and Global Political Economy*, Cambridge, UK: Polity Press.

Callon, M. (1998), 'The embeddedness of economic markets in economics', in M. Callon (ed.), *The Laws of the Markets*, Oxford, UK: Blackwell, pp. 1–57.

Callon, M. (1999), 'Actor-network theory – the market test', *Sociological Review*, 47(1): 181–195.

Callon, M. (2016), 'Revisiting marketization: from interface markets to market-agencement', *Consumption Markets and Culture*, 19(1): 17–37.

Callon, M., and Latour, B. (1981), 'Unscrewing the big leviathan: how actors macro-structure reality and how sociologists help them to do so', in K. Knorr-Cetina, and A. Cicourel (eds.), *Advances in Social Theory and Methodology: Toward an Integration of Micro- and Macro-Sociologies*, London: Routledge and Kegan Paul, pp. 276–303.

Callon, M., Méadel, C., and Rabeharisoa, V. (2002), 'The economy of qualities', *Economy and Society*, 31(2): 194–217.

Callon, M., and Muniesa, F. (2005), 'Economic markets as calculative collective devices', *Organization Studies*, 26(8): 1229–1250.

Camerer, C.F., and Loewenstein, G. (2004), 'Behavioural economics: past, present, future', in C.F. Camerer, G. Loewenstein, and M. Rabin (eds.), *Advances in Behavioral Economics*, Princeton, NJ: Princeton University Press, pp. 3–52.

Cameron, R.E. (1993), *A Concise Economic History of the World: From Palaeolithic Times to the Present*, 2nd edn., Oxford, UK: Oxford University Press.

Campbell, J., and Gillespie, M. (eds.) (2016), *Feminist Economics and Public Policy*, London: Routledge.

Carlyle, T. (1829), 'Signs of the times', in A. Shelston (ed.), *Thomas Carlyle: Selected Writings*, Harmondsworth, UK: Penguin, 1971, pp. 59–85.

Carlyle, T. (1843), *Past and Present*, Oxford, UK: Oxford University Press, 1918.

Carrigan, M., Szmigin, I., and Wright, J. (2004), 'Shopping for a better world? An interpretive study of the potential for ethical consumption within the older market', *Journal of Consumer Marketing*, 21(6): 401–417.

Carroll, A.B. (2015), 'Corporate social responsibility: the centerpiece of competing and complementary frameworks', *Organizational Dynamics*, 44(2): 87–96.

Carruthers, B.G., and Babb, S.L. (2000), *Economy/Society: Markets, Meanings, and Social Structure*, Thousand Oaks, CA: Pine Forge Press.

Carson, R.L. (1990), *Comparative Economic Systems*, Armonk, NY: M.E. Sharpe.

Cartledge, P. (2002), 'The economy (economies) of ancient Greece', in W. Scheidel, and S. Von Reden (eds.), *The Ancient Economy*, New York: Routledge, pp. 11–32.

Carvalho, L.F., and Rodrigues, J. (2006), 'On markets and morality: revisiting Fred Hirsch', *Review of Social Economy*, 64(3): 331–348.

Carvalho, L.F., and Rodrigues, J. (2008), 'Are markets everywhere? Understanding contemporary processes of commodification', in J.B. Davis, and W. Dolfsma (eds.), *The Elgar Companion to Social Economics*, Cheltenham, UK: Edward Elgar, pp. 267–286.

Casson, M., and Lee, J.S. (2011), 'The origin and development of markets: a business history perspective', *Business History Review*, 85(1): 9–37.

Castells, M. (2000), *The Rise of the Network Society*, 2nd edn., Oxford: Blackwell.

Catephores, G. (1989), *An Introduction to Marxist Economics*, London: Macmillan.

Cedrini, M., and Fontana, M. (2018), 'Just another niche in the wall? How specialization is changing the face of mainstream economics', *Cambridge Journal of Economics*, 42(2): 427–451.

Cerni, P. (2012), 'Consumerism', in B. Fine, and A. Saad-Filho (eds.), *The Elgar Companion to Marxist Economics*, Cheltenham, UK: Edward Elgar, pp. 78–83.

Chaffey, D., and Ellis-Chadwick, F. (2016), *Digital Marketing: Strategy, Implementation and Practice*, 6th edn., London: Pearson.

Chambers, J.D., and Mingay, G.E. (1966), *The Agricultural Revolution 1750–1880*, London: Batsford.

Chandler, P. (2006), 'Fair trade and global justice', *Globalizations*, 3(2): 255–257.

Chang, H.-J. (2002a), 'Breaking the mould: an institutionalist political economy alternative to the neo-liberal theory of the market and the state', *Cambridge Journal of Economics*, 26(5): 539–559.

Chang, H.-J. (2002b), *Kicking Away the Ladder: Development Strategy in Historical Perspective*, London: Anthem Press.

Chang, H.-J. (ed.) (2003), *Rethinking Development Economics*, London: Anthem Press.

Chang, H.-J. (2004), 'What is wrong with the "official history of capitalism"?', in E. Fullbrook (ed.), *A Guide to What's Wrong with Economics*, London: Anthem Press, pp. 279–288.

Chang, H.-J. (2007), *Bad Samaritans: The Myth of Free Trade and the Secret History of Capitalism*, New York: Bloomsbury Press.

Chapman, A. (1980), 'Barter as a universal mode of exchange', *L'Homme*, 20(3): 33–83.

Charles, S. (2016), 'Is Minsky's financial instability hypothesis valid?', *Cambridge Journal of Economics*, 40(2): 427–436.

Chase-Dunn, C., and Grimes, P. (1995), 'World-systems analysis', *Annual Review of Sociology*, 21(1): 387–417.

Chaudhuri, A., and Holbrook, M.B. (2001), 'The chain of effects from brand trust and brand affect to brand performance: the role of brand loyalty', *Journal of Marketing*, 65(2): 81–93.

Chen, I.J., and Popovich, K. (2003), 'Understanding customer relationship management (CRM): people, process and technology', *Business Process Management Journal*, 9(5): 672–688.

Chevalier, M., and Mazzalovo, G. (2008), *Luxury Brand Management: A World of Privilege*, Chichester, UK: Wiley.

Chiles, T.H., Bluedorn, A.C., and Gupta, V.K. (2007), 'Beyond creative destruction and entrepreneurial discovery: a radical Austrian approach to entrepreneurship', *Organization Studies*, 28(4): 467–493.

Christainsen, G.B. (1994), 'Methodological individualism', in P.J. Boettke (ed.), *The Elgar Companion to Austrian Economics*, Aldershot: Edward Elgar, pp. 11–16.

Christophers, B. (2014), 'From Marx to market and back again: performing the economy', *Geoforum*, 57: 12–20.

Ciccone, R. (1994), 'Surplus approach', in P. Arestis, and M.C. Sawyer (eds.), *The Elgar Companion to Radical Political Economy*, Cheltenham, UK: Edward Elgar, pp. 389–393.

Cipolla, C.M. (1978), *The Economic History of World Population*, 7th edn., Harmondsworth, UK: Penguin.

Cirillo, R. (1984), 'Léon Walras and social justice', *American Journal of Economics and Sociology*, 43(1): 53–60.

Ciscel, D.H., and Heath, J.A. (2001), 'To market, to market: imperial capitalism's destruction of social capital and the family', *Review of Radical Political Economics*, 33(4): 401–414.

Clark, G.L., Feldman, M.P., and Gertler, M.S. (eds.) (2000), *The Oxford Handbook of Economic Geography*, Oxford, UK: Oxford University Press.

Clarke, D. (1987), 'Trade and industry in barbarian Europe till Roman times', in M.M. Postan, and E. Miller (eds.), *Cambridge Economic History of Europe, II Trade and Industry in the Middle Ages*, 2nd edn., Cambridge, UK: Cambridge University Press, pp. 1–70.

Coase, R.H. (1937), 'The nature of the firm', *Economica*, 4(16): 386–405.

Cockshott, W.P., and Cottrell, A. (1993), *Towards a New Socialism*, Nottingham, UK: Spokesman.

Cohen, I.G. (2003), 'The price of everything, the value of nothing: reframing the commodification debate', *Harvard Law Review*, 117(689): 689–710.

Cohen, M.N. (1989), *Health and the Rise of Civilization*, New Haven, CT: Yale University Press.

Colander, D.C., Holt, R.P.F., and Rosser, B. (2004), 'The changing face of mainstream economics', *Review of Political Economy*, 16(4): 485–499.

Collier, A. (1994), *Critical Realism: An Introduction to Roy Bhaskar's Philosophy*, London: Verso.

Commons, J.R. (1924), *Legal Foundations of Capitalism*, New York: Macmillan.

Commons, J.R. (1931), 'Institutional economics', *American Economic Review*, 21(4): 648–657.

Conklin, D.W. (1991), *Comparative Economic Systems: Objectives, Decision Modes, and the Process of Choice*, Cambridge, UK: Cambridge University Press.

Cook, S. (1966), 'The obsolete "anti-market" mentality: a critique of the substantive approach to economic anthropology', *American Anthropologist*, 68(2): 323–345.

Cooke, P.N., and Morgan, K.J. (1998), *The Associational Economy: Firms, Regions and Innovation*, Oxford, UK: Oxford University Press.

Cornwall, W. (2012), 'New Keynesian economics', in J.E. King (ed.), *The Elgar Companion to Post Keynesian Economics*, 2nd edn., Cheltenham, UK: Edward Elgar, pp. 425–429.

Coşgel, M.M. (1997), 'Consumption institutions', *Review of Social Economy*, 55(2): 153–171.

Coşgel, M.M. (2008), 'The socio-economics of consumption: solutions to the problems of interest, knowledge and identity', in J.B. Davis, and W. Dolfsma (eds.), *The Elgar Companion to Social Economics*, Cheltenham, UK: Edward Elgar, pp. 121–136.

Costanza, R., Hart, M., Posner, S., and Talberth, J. (2009), *Beyond GPD: The Need for New Measures of Progress*, The Pardee Papers No. 4, Boston, MA: Boston University.

Coulborn, R. (ed.) (1956), *Feudalism in History*, Princeton, NJ: Princeton University Press.

Couper, A.D. (1972), *The Geography of Sea Transport*, London: Hutchinson.

Coyle, D. (2014), *GDP: A Brief but Affectionate History*, Princeton, NJ: Princeton University Press.

Crafts, N.F.R. (1997), 'Some dimensions of the "quality of life" during the British Industrial Revolution', *Economic History Review*, 50(4): 617–639.

Craib, I. (1992), *Modern Social Theory: From Parsons to Habermas*, Hemel Hempstead, UK: Harvester Wheatsheaf.

Crespo, R. (2009), 'Aristotle', in J. Peil, and I. Van Staveren (eds.), *Handbook of Economics and Ethics*, Cheltenham, UK: Edward Elgar, pp. 14–20.

Crotty, J. (2003), 'The neoliberal paradox: the impact of destructive product market competition and impatient finance on nonfinancial corporations in the neoliberal era', *Review of Radical Political Economics*, 35(3): 271–279.

Crotty, J. (2009), 'Structural causes of the global financial crisis: a critical assessment of the "new financial architecture"', *Cambridge Journal of Economics*, 33(4): 563–580.

Crouch, C., and Streeck, W. (eds.) (1997), *Political Economy of Modern Capitalism: Mapping Convergence and Diversity*, Thousand Oaks, CA: Sage.

Cummins, R. (1975), 'Functional analysis', *Journal of Philosophy*, 72(20): 741–765.

Curtin, P.D. (1984), *Cross-Cultural Trade in World History*, Cambridge, UK: Cambridge University Press.

Curtis, M. (2001), *Trade for Life: Making Trade Work for Poor People*, London: Christian Aid.

Cyert, R.M., and March, J.G. (1963), *A Behavioral Theory of the Firm*, Englewood Cliffs, NJ: Prentice-Hall.

Dale, G. (2010), *Karl Polanyi: The Limits of the Market*, Cambridge, UK: Polity Press.

Dalton, G. (1961), 'Economic theory and primitive society', *American Anthropologist*, 63(1): 1–25.

Dalton, G. (1982), 'Barter', *Journal of Economic Issues*, 16(1): 181–190.

Danermark, B., Ekström, M., Jakobsen, L., and Karlsson, J.C. (2002), *Explaining Society: Critical Realism in the Social Sciences*, London: Routledge.

Dant, T. (2006), 'Material civilization: things and society', *British Journal of Sociology*, 57(2): 289–308.

Davidoff, S.M., and Zaring, D.T. (2009), 'Regulation by deal: the government's response to the financial crisis', *Administrative Law Review*, 61(3): 463–541.

Davidson, M.P. (1992), *The Consumerist Manifesto: Advertising in Postmodern Times*, London: Routledge.

Davidson, P. (2011), *Post Keynesian Macroeconomic Theory*, 2nd edn., Cheltenham, UK: Edward Elgar.

Davies, G. (2002), *A History of Money*, 3rd edn., Cardiff, UK: University of Wales Press.

Davis, J. (1992), *Exchange*, Buckingham, UK: Open University Press.

Davis, J. (2012), *Medieval Market Morality: Life, Law and Ethics in the English Marketplace, 1200–1500*, Cambridge, UK: Cambridge University Press.

Davis, J.B. (2003), *The Theory of the Individual in Economics: Identity and Value*, London: Routledge.

Davis, J.B. (2006), 'The turn in economics: neoclassical dominance to mainstream pluralism?', *Journal of Institutional Economics*, 2(1): 1–20.

Davis, J.B. (2007), 'The turn in economics and the turn in economic methodology', *Journal of Economic Methodology*, 14(3): 275–290.

Davis, J.B. (2011), *Individuals and Identity in Economics*, Cambridge, UK: Cambridge University Press.

Davis, J.B., and Dolfsma, W. (2008), 'Social economics: an introduction', in J.B. Davis, and W. Dolfsma (eds.), *The Elgar Companion to Social Economics*, Cheltenham, UK: Edward Elgar, pp. 1–7.

Davis, K. (1959), 'The myth of functional analysis as a special method in sociology and anthropology', *American Sociological Review*, 24(6): 757–772.

Davis, N. (1952), 'The proximate etymology of "market"', *Modern Language Review*, 47(2): 152–155.

Davis, O.A., and Whinston, A.B. (1965), 'Welfare economics and the theory of second best', *Review of Economic Studies*, 32(1): 1–14.

Davis, O.A., and Whinston, A.B. (1967), 'Piecemeal policy in the theory of second best', *Review of Economic Studies*, 34(3): 323–331.

Davison, M. (ed.) (2015), 'Financialisation', in P. O'Sullivan, N.F.B. Allington, and M. Esposito (eds.), *The Philosophy, Politics and Economics of Finance in the 21st Century: From Hubris to Disgrace*, London: Routledge, pp. 47–73.

De Beelde, I. (2009), 'National accounting', in J.R. Edwards, and S.P. Walker (eds.), *The Routledge Companion to Accounting History*, London: Routledge, pp. 354–368.

De Moraes Farias, P.F. (1974), 'Silent trade: myth and historical evidence', *History in Africa*, 1: 9–24.

De Roover, R. (1958), 'The concept of the just price: theory and economic policy', *Journal of Economic History*, 18(4): 418–434.

De Roover, R. (1963), 'The organization of trade', in M.M. Postan, E.E. Rich, and E. Miller (eds.), *Cambridge Economic History of Europe, III Economic Organization and Policies in the Middle Ages*, Cambridge, UK: Cambridge University Press, pp. 42–118.

De Vroey, M. (1975), 'The transition from classical to neoclassical economics: a scientific revolution', *Journal of Economic Issues*, 9(3): 415–439.

Deakin, S. (2006), '"Capacitas": contract law and the institutional preconditions of a market economy', *European Review of Contract Law*, 2(3): 317–341.

Deakin, S. (2009), 'Legal origin, juridical form and industrialization in historical perspective: the case of the employment contract and the joint-stock company', *Socio-Economic Review*, 7(1): 35–65.

Deakin, S., Gindis, D., Hodgson, G.M., Huang, K., and Pistor, P. (2017), 'Legal institutionalism: capitalism and the constitutive role of the law', *Journal of Comparative Economics*, 45(1): 188–200.

Deane, P.M. (1979), *The First Industrial Revolution*, 2nd edn., Cambridge, UK: Cambridge University Press.

Deardorff, A.V. (1980), 'The general validity of the law of comparative advantage', *Journal of Political Economy*, 88(5): 941–957.

Deardorff, A.V. (2005), 'How robust is comparative advantage?', *Review of International Economics*, 13(5): 1004–1016.

Deleplace, G., and Nell, E.J. (eds.) (1996), *Money in Motion: The Post Keynesian and Circulation Approaches*, London: Macmillan.

Delgado-Ballester, E., and Luis Munuera-Alemán, J.L. (2001), 'Brand trust in the context of consumer loyalty', *European Journal of Marketing*, 35(11–12): 1238–1258.

DellaVigna, S. (2009), 'Psychology and economics: evidence from the field', *Journal of Economic Literature*, 47(2): 315–372.

Demerath, N.J., and Peterson, R.A. (eds.) (1967), *System, Change and Conflict: A Reader on Contemporary Sociological Theory and the Debate over Functionalism*, New York: Free Press.

Dequech, D. (2007), 'Neoclassical, mainstream, orthodox, and heterodox economics', *Journal of Post Keynesian Economics*, 30(2): 279–302.

Dick, A.S., and Basu, K. (1994), 'Customer loyalty: toward an integrated conceptual framework', *Journal of the Academy of Marketing Science*, 22(2): 99–113.

Dierksmeier, C., and Pirson, M. (2009), '*Oikonomia* versus *chrematistike*: learning from Aristotle about the future orientation of business management', *Journal of Business Ethics*, 88(3): 417–430.

Diller, H. (2000), 'Customer loyalty: *fata morgana* or realistic goal? Managing relationships with customers', in T. Hennig-Thurau, and U. Hansen (eds.), *Relationship Marketing*, Berlin: Springer, 29–48.

Djelic, M.-L. (2006), 'Marketization: from intellectual agenda to global policy-making', in M.-L. Djelic, and K. Sahlin-Andersson (eds.), *Transnational Governance: Institutional Dynamics of Regulation*, Cambridge, UK: Cambridge University Press, pp. 53–73.

Dobb, M.H. (1973), *Theories of Value and Distribution Since Adam Smith: Economics and Ideology*, Cambridge, UK: Cambridge University Press.

Dodd, N. (2014), *The Social Life of Money*, Princeton, NJ: Princeton University Press.

Doeringer, P.B., and Piore, M.J. (1985), *Internal Labor Markets and Manpower Analysis*, 2nd edn., Armonk, NY: M.E. Sharpe.

Dolfsma, W. (2002), 'Mediated preferences – how institutions affect consumption', *Journal of Economic Issues*, 36(2): 449–457.

Dolfsma, W. (2004), *Institutional Economics and the Formation of Preferences: The Advent of Pop Music*, Cheltenham, UK: Edward Elgar.

Dolfsma, W. (2013), *Government Failure: Society, Markets and Rules*, Cheltenham, UK: Edward Elgar.

Dolfsma, W., Finch, J., and McMaster, R. (2005), 'Market and society: how do they relate, and how do they contribute to welfare?', *Journal of Economic Issues*, 39(2): 347–356.

Dolfsma, W., and Spithoven, A. (2008), '"Silent trade" and the supposed continuum between OIE and NIE', *Journal of Economic Issues*, 42(2): 517–526.

Donath, S. (2000), 'The other economy: a suggestion for a distinctively feminist economics', *Feminist Economics*, 6(1): 115–123.

Dopfer, K. (2005), 'Evolutionary economics: a theoretical framework', in K. Dopfer (ed.), *The Evolutionary Foundation of Economics*, Cambridge, UK: Cambridge University Press, pp. 3–55.

Dopfer, K., and Potts, J. (2008), *The General Theory of Economic Evolution*, London: Routledge.

Dore, R.P. (1961), 'Function and cause', *American Sociological Review*, 26(6): 843–853.

Dore, R.P. (1983), 'Goodwill and the spirit of market capitalism', *British Journal of Sociology*, 34(4): 459–482.

Dos Santos, P.L. (2012), 'Money', in B. Fine, and A. Saad-Filho (eds.), *The Elgar Companion to Marxist Economics*, Cheltenham, UK: Edward Elgar, pp. 233–239.

Douglas, A.X. (2016), *The Philosophy of Debt*, London: Routledge.

Douglas, M., and Isherwood, B. (1996), *The World of Goods: Towards an Anthropology of Consumption*, new edn., London: Routledge.

Dow, G.K. (1987), 'The function of authority in transaction cost economics', *Journal of Economic Behavior and Organization*, 8(1): 13–38.

Dowd, D.F. (2004), *Capitalism and Its Economics: A Critical History*, London: Pluto Press.

Downward, P. (1999), *Pricing Theory in Post Keynesian Economics: A Realist Approach*, Cheltenham, UK: Edward Elgar.

Downward, P. (ed.) (2003), *Applied Economics: A Critical Realist Approach*, London: Routledge.

Downward, P. (2009), 'Prices', in J. Peil, and I. Van Staveren (eds.), *Handbook of Economics and Ethics*, Cheltenham, UK: Edward Elgar, pp. 399–406.

Dugger, W.M. (1977), 'Social economics: one perspective', *Review of Social Economy*, 35(3): 299–310.

Dugger, W.M. (1989), 'Instituted process and enabling myth: the two faces of the market', *Journal of Economic Issues*, 23(2): 607–615.

Dugger, W.M. (1990), 'The new institutionalism: new but not institutionalist', *Journal of Economic Issues*, 24(2): 423–431.

Dugger, W.M. (1996), 'Redefining economics: from market allocation to social provisioning', in C. Whalen (ed.), *Political Economy for the 21st Century: Contemporary Views on the Trends of Economics*, Armonk, NY: M.E. Sharpe, pp. 31–43.

Dugger, W.M. (1998), 'Against inequality', *Journal of Economic Issues*, 32(2): 286–303.

Dugger, W.M. (2000), 'Deception and inequality: the enabling myth concept', in R. Pollin (ed.), *Capitalism, Socialism, and Radical Political Economy*, Cheltenham, UK: Edward Elgar, pp. 66–80.

Dulbecco, P., and Dutraive, V. (2001), 'The meaning of market: comparing Austrian and institutional economics', in P. Garrouste, and S. Ioannides (eds.), *Evolution and Path Dependence in Economic Ideas, Past and Present*, Cheltenham, UK: Edward Elgar, pp. 41–70.

Dunn, S.P. (1982), *The Fall and Rise of the Asiatic Mode of Production*, London: Routledge and Kegan Paul.

Durkheim, É. (1893), *The Division of Labour in Society*, translated by W.D. Halls, London: Macmillan, 1984.

Durkheim, É. (1895), *The Rules of Sociological Method*, translated by W.D. Halls, London: Macmillan, 1982.

Dwyer, F.R., Schurr, P.H., and Oh, S. (1987), 'Developing buyer-seller relationships', *Journal of Marketing*, 51(2): 11–27.

Eagleton-Pierce, M. (2016), *Neoliberalism: the Key Concepts*, London: Routledge.

Easterly, W. (2001), 'The lost decades: developing countries' stagnation in spite of policy reform 1980–1998', *Journal of Economic Growth*, 6(2): 135–157.

Eatwell, J. (1983), 'Theories of value, output and employment', in J. Eatwell, and M. Milgate (eds.), *Keynes's Economics and the Theory of Value and Distribution*, London: Duckworth, pp. 93–128.

Eatwell, J. (1987a), 'Competition: classical conceptions', in J. Eatwell, P. Newman, and M. Milgate (eds.), *The New Palgrave: A Dictionary of Economics*, Vol. 1, London: Macmillan, pp. 537–540.

Eatwell, J. (1987b), 'Imperfectionist models', in J. Eatwell, P. Newman, and M. Milgate (eds.), *The New Palgrave: A Dictionary of Economics*, Vol. 2, London: Macmillan, pp. 726–728.

Eatwell, J., and Milgate, M. (1983), 'Introduction', in J. Eatwell, and M. Milgate (eds.), *Keynes's Economics and the Theory of Value and Distribution*, London: Duckworth, pp. 1–17.

Eatwell, J., Milgate, M., and Newman, P. (eds.) (1990), *Problems of the Planned Economy*, London: Macmillan.

Ebeling, R.M. (1986), 'Toward a hermeneutical economics: expectations, prices and the role of interpretation in a theory of the market process', in I.M. Kirzner (ed.),

Subjectivism, Intelligibility and Economic Understanding, London: Macmillan, pp. 39–55.

Ebeling, R.M. (1990), 'What is a price? Explanation and understanding', in D. Lavoie (ed.), *Economics and Hermeneutics*, London: Routledge, pp. 174–191.

Ebner, A. (2015), 'Marketization: theoretical reflections building on the perspectives of Polanyi and Habermas', *Review of Political Economy*, 27(3): 369–389.

Eikenberry, A.M., and Kluver, J.D. (2004), 'The marketization of the non-profit sector: civil society at risk?', *Public Administration Review*, 64(2): 132–140.

Eisner, R. (1988), 'Extended accounts for national income and product', *Journal of Economic Literature*, 26(4): 1611–1684.

Ekelund, R.B., and Tollison, R.D. (1980), 'Mercantilist origins of the corporation', *Bell Journal of Economics*, 11(2): 715–720.

Ekins, P., and Max-Neef, M. (eds.) (1992), *Real-Life Economics: Understanding Wealth Creation*, London: Routledge.

Elder-Vass, D. (2010), *The Causal Power of Social Structures: Emergence, Structure and Agency*, Cambridge, UK: Cambridge University Press.

Ellen, R. (1994), 'Modes of subsistence: hunting and gathering to agriculture and pastoralism', in T. Ingold (ed.), *Companion Encyclopedia of Anthropology*, London: Routledge, pp. 197–225.

Elliott, J.E. (1980), 'Marx and Schumpeter on capitalism's creative destruction: a comparative restatement', *Quarterly Journal of Economics*, 95(1): 45–68.

Elliott, J.E. (2000), 'Adam Smith's conceptualization of power, markets, and politics', *Review of Social Economy*, 58(4): 429–454.

Ellman, M. (2014), *Socialist Planning*, 3rd edn., Cambridge, UK: Cambridge University Press.

Elson, D. (1998), 'The economic, the political and the domestic: businesses, states and households in the organisation of production', *New Political Economy*, 3(2): 189–208.

Elson, D. (2000a), 'Gender at the macroeconomic level', in J. Cook, J. Roberts, and G. Waylen (eds.), *Towards a Gendered Political Economy*, London: Palgrave Macmillan.

Elson, D. (2000b), 'Socialising markets, not market socialism', *Socialist Register*, 36: 67–85.

Elson, D. (2017), 'Recognize, reduce, and redistribute unpaid care work: how to close the gender gap', *New Labor Forum*, 26(2): 52–61.

Emirbayer, M., and Goodwin, J. (1994), 'Network analysis, culture, and the problem of agency', *American Journal of Sociology*, 99(6): 1411–1454.

Emmett, R.B. (ed.) (2010), *The Elgar Companion to the Chicago School of Economics*, Cheltenham, UK: Edward Elgar.

England, R.W. (2001), 'Alternatives to gross domestic product: a critical survey', in C.J. Cleveland, D.I. Stern, and R. Costanza (eds.), *The Economics of Nature and the Nature of Economics*, Cheltenham, UK: Edward Elgar, pp. 218–237.

Epstein, G.A. (ed.) (2005), *Financialization and the World Economy*, Cheltenham, UK: Edward Elgar.

Epstein, S.R. (1994), Regional fairs, institutional innovation, and economic growth in late medieval Europe', *Economic History Review*, 47(3): 459–482.

Epstein, S.R. (2008), 'Craft guilds in the pre-modern economy: a discussion', *Economic History Review*, 61(1): 155–174.

Eriksen, T.H. (2004), *What Is Anthropology?*, London: Pluto Press.

Eriksen, T.H., and Nielsen, F.S. (2001), *A History of Anthropology*, London: Pluto Press.

Esping-Andersen, G. (1990), *The Three Worlds of Welfare Capitalism*, Cambridge, UK: Polity Press.

Evans, B., Richmond, T., and Shields, J. (2005), 'Structuring neoliberal governance: the non-profit sector, emerging new modes of control and the marketisation of service delivery', *Policy and Society*, 24(1): 73–97.

Fabozzi, F.J., Mann, S.V., and Choudhry, M. (2002), *The Global Money Markets*, Hoboken, NJ: Wiley.

Farber, L. (2006), *An Anatomy of Trade in Medieval Writing: Value, Consent, and Community*, Ithaca, NY: Cornell University Press.

Farjoun, M. (2010), 'Beyond dualism: stability and change as a duality', *Academy of Management Review*, 35(2): 202–225.

Farquhar, P.H. (1989), 'Managing brand equity', *Marketing Research*, 1(3): 24–33.

Fehl, U. (1994), 'Spontaneous order', in P.J. Boettke (ed.), *The Elgar Companion to Austrian Economics*, Aldershot, UK: Edward Elgar, pp. 197–205.

Felin, T., and Foss, N.J. (2009), 'Social reality, the boundaries of self-fulfilling prophecy, and economics', *Organization Science*, 20(3): 654–668.

Fennis, B.M., and Stroebe, W. (2016), *The Psychology of Advertising*, 2nd edn., London: Routledge.

Fernández-Huerga, E. (2013), 'The market concept: a characterization from institutional and post-Keynesian economics', *American Journal of Economics and Sociology*, 72(2): 361–385.

Fernández-Huerga, E. (2019), 'The labour demand of firms: an alternative conception based on the capabilities approach', *Cambridge Journal of Economics*, 43(1): 37–60.

Fernández-Huerga, E., García-Arias, J., and Salvador, A. (2017), 'Labor supply: toward the construction of an alternative conception from post Keynesian and institutional economics', *Journal of Post Keynesian Economics*, 40(4): 576–599.

Ferraro, F., Pfeffer, J., and Sutton, R.I. (2005), 'Economics language and assumptions: how theories can become self-fulfilling', *Academy of Management Review*, 30(1): 8–24.

Fforde, A. (2013), *Understanding Development Economics: Its Challenge to Development Studies*, London: Routledge.

Fine, B. (1992), *Women's Employment and the Capitalist Family*, London: Routledge.

Fine, B. (1998), *Labour Market Theory: A Constructive Reassessment*, London: Routledge.

Fine, B. (2001), *Social Capital Versus Social Theory: Political Economy and Social Science at the Turn of the Millennium*, London: Routledge.

Fine, B. (2002), *The World of Consumption: The Material and Cultural Revisited*, 2nd edn., London: Routledge.

Fine, B. (2003), 'Callonistics: a disentanglement', *Economy and Society*, 32(3): 478–484.

Fine, B. (2004), 'Addressing the critical and the real in critical realism', in P. Lewis (ed.), *Transforming Economics: Perspectives on the Critical Realist Project*, London: Routledge, pp. 202–226.

Fine, B. (2005), 'From actor-network theory to political economy', *Capitalism Nature Socialism*, 16(4): 91–108.

Fine, B. (2006), 'Debating critical realism in economics', *Capital and Class*, 30(2): 121–129.

Fine, B. (2012), 'Exploitation and surplus value', in B. Fine, and A. Saad-Filho (eds.), *The Elgar Companion to Marxist Economics*, Cheltenham, UK: Edward Elgar, pp. 118–124.

Fine, B., and Milonakis, D. (2009), *From Economics Imperialism to Freakonomics: The Shifting Boundaries Between Economics and Other Social Sciences*, London: Routledge.

Fine, B., and Saad-Filho, A. (2016), *Marx's Capital*, 6th edn., London: Pluto Press.

Finley, M.I. (1970), 'Aristotle and economic analysis', *Past and Present*, 47(1): 3–25.

Finley, M.I. (1999), *The Ancient Economy*, updated edn., Berkeley, CA: University of California Press.

Firth, R. (1951), *Elements of Social Organization*, London: Watts.

Firth, R. (1955), 'Function', in W.L. Thomas Jr. (ed.), *Yearbook of Anthropology*, Chicago, IL: University of Chicago Press, pp. 237–258.

Fisher, F.M. (1989), 'Adjustment processes and stability', in J. Eatwell, M. Milgate, and P. Newman (eds.), *General Equilibrium*, London: Macmillan, pp. 36–42.

Fitzmaurice, C.J., Ladegaard, I. et al. (2018), 'Domesticating the market: moral exchange and the sharing economy', *Socio-Economic Review*, https://doi.org/10.1093/ser/mwy003.

Fleetwood, S. (ed.) (1999), *Critical Realism in Economics: Development and Debate*, London: Routledge.

Fleetwood, S. (2006), 'Rethinking labour markets: a critical-realist-socioeconomic perspective', *Capital and Class*, 30(2): 59–89.

Fleetwood, S. (2011), 'Sketching a socio-economic model of labour markets', *Cambridge Journal of Economics*, 35(1): 15–38.

Fleetwood, S. (2016), 'Reflections upon neoclassical labour economics', in J. Morgan (ed.), *What Is Neoclassical Economics? Debating the Origins, Meaning and Significance*, London: Routledge, pp. 273–310.

Fleetwood, S. (2017), 'From labour market institutions to an alternative model of labour markets', *Forum for Social Economics*, 46(1): 78–103.

Fleurbaey, M., and Blanchet, D. (2013), *Beyond GDP: Measuring Welfare and Assessing Sustainability*, Oxford, UK: Oxford University Press.

Fligstein, N. (1996), 'Markets as politics: a political-cultural approach to market institutions', *American Sociological Review*, 61(4): 656–673.

Fligstein, N. (2001), *The Architecture of Markets: An Economic Sociology of Twenty-First-Century Capitalist Societies*, Princeton, NJ: Princeton University Press.

Fligstein, N., and Calder, R. (2015), 'Architecture of markets', in R.A. Scott, and S.M. Kosslyn (eds.), *Emerging Trends in the Social and Behavioral Sciences*, Hoboken, NJ: Wiley, pp. 1–14.

Fligstein, N., and Dauter, L. (2007), 'The sociology of markets', *Annual Review of Sociology*, 33(1): 105–128.

Fligstein, N., and Freeland, R. (1995), 'Theoretical and comparative perspectives on corporate organization', *Annual Review of Sociology*, 21(1): 21–43.

Fligstein, N., and Mara-Drita, I. (1996), 'How to make a market: reflections on the attempt to create a single market in the European Union', *American Journal of Sociology*, 102(1): 1–33.

Fligstein, N., and McAdam, D. (2011), 'Toward a general theory of strategic action fields', *Sociological Theory*, 29(1): 1–26.

Fligstein, N., and McAdam, D. (2012), *A Theory of Fields*, Oxford, UK: Oxford University Press.

Flinn, M.W. (1966), *Origins of the Industrial Revolution*, London: Longman.

Folbre, N. (1994), *Who Pays for the Kids? Gender and the Structures of Constraint*, London: Routledge.

Folbre, N. (2006), 'Measuring care; gender, empowerment, and the care economy', *Journal of Human Development*, 7(2): 183–199.

Folbre, N., and Nelson, J.A. (2000), 'For love or money – or both?', *Journal of Economic Perspectives*, 14(4): 123–140.

Foley, D.K. (2004), 'Rationality and ideology in economics', *Social Research*, 71(2): 329–342.

Foss, N.J., and Klein, P.G. (eds.) (2002), *Entrepreneurship and the Firm: Austrian Perspectives on Economic Organization*, Cheltenham, UK: Edward Elgar.

Foster, J. (2005), 'From simplistic to complex systems in economics', *Cambridge Journal of Economics*, 29(6): 873–892.

Foster, J.B. (2014), *The Theory of Monopoly Capitalism: An Elaboration of Marxian Political Economy*, 2nd edn., New York: Monthly Review Press.

Fourcade, M. (2007), 'Theories of markets and theories of society', *American Behavioral Scientist*, 50(8): 1015–1034.

Fourcade, M., and Healy, K. (2007), 'Moral views of market society', *Annual Review of Sociology*, 33(1): 285–311.

Fourcade, M., and Healy, K. (2017), 'Seeing like a market', *Socio-Economic Review*, 15(1): 9–29.

Fourie, F.C.v.N. (1991), 'The nature of the market: a structural analysis', in G.M. Hodgson, and E. Screpanti (eds.), *Rethinking Economics: Markets, Technology and Economic Evolution*, Aldershot, UK: Edward Elgar, pp. 40–57.

Frank, A.W. (2002), 'What's wrong with medical consumerism?', in S. Henderson, and A. Petersen (eds.), *Consuming Health: The Commodification of Health Care*, London: Routledge, pp. 13–30.

Frankel, T. (1993), 'The legal infrastructure of markets: the role of contract and property law', *Boston University Law Review*, 73(3): 389–405.

Fraser, N. (2014), 'Can society be commodities all the way down? Post-Polanyian reflections on capitalist crisis', *Economy and Society*, 43(4): 541–558.

Freedland, M.R. (2005), *The Personal Employment Contract*, Oxford, UK: Oxford University Press.

Fridell, G. (2006), 'Fair trade and neoliberalism: assessing emerging perspectives', *Latin American Perspectives*, 33(6): 8–28.

Fridell, G. (2007), 'Fair-trade coffee and commodity fetishism: the limits of market-driven social justice', *Historical Materialism*, 15(4): 79–104.

Friedman, M. (1962), *Capitalism and Freedom*, Chicago, IL: University of Chicago Press.

Frisby, D. (2002), *Georg Simmel*, 2nd edn., London: Routledge.

Froud, J., Haslam, C., Johal, S., and Williams, K. (2000), 'Representing the household: in and after national income accounting', *Accounting, Auditing and Accountability Journal*, 13(4): 535–560.

Fuat Firat, A., Dholakia, N., and Venkatesh, A. (1995), 'Marketing in a postmodern world', *European Journal of Marketing*, 29(1): 40–56.

Fuchs, S. (2001), 'Beyond agency', *Sociological Theory*, 19(1): 24–40.

Fujita, N. (2007), 'Myrdal's theory of cumulative causation', *Evolutionary and Institutional Economics Review*, 3(2): 275–284.

Furubotn, E.G., and Pejovich, S. (1972), 'Property rights and economic theory: a survey of recent literature', *Journal of Economic Literature*, 10(4): 1137–1162.

Gage, T.B., and DeWitte, S. (2009), 'What do we know about the agricultural demographic transition?', *Current Anthropology*, 50(5): 649–655.

Galbács, P. (2015), *The Theory of New Classical Macroeconomics: A Positive Critique*, Cham: Springer.

Galbraith, J.K. (1969), *The Affluent Society*, 2nd edn., Boston, MA: Houghton Mifflin.

Galbraith, J.K. (1975), *Money: Whence It Came, Where It Went*, London: André Deutsch.

Gallegati, M., and Kirman, A.P. (2012), 'Reconstructing economics: agent based models and complexity', *Complexity Economics*, 1(1): 5–31.

Gardiner, J. (1976), 'Political economy of domestic labour in capitalist society', in D.L. Barker, and S. Allen (eds.), *Dependence and Exploitation in Work and Marriage*, London: Longman, pp. 109–120.

Gardner, H.S. (1998), *Comparative Economic Systems*, 2nd edn., Fort Worth, TX: Dryden Press.

Garegnani, P. (1987), 'Surplus approach to value and distribution', in J. Eatwell, P. Newman, and M. Milgate (eds.), *The New Palgrave: A Dictionary of Economics*, Vol. 4, London: Macmillan, pp. 560–573.

Garegnani, P. (1998), 'Sraffa: the theoretical world of the "old classical economists"', *European Journal of the History of Economic Thought*, 5(3): 415–429.

Garlan, Y. (1988), *Slavery in Ancient Greece*, translated by J. Lloyd, Ithaca, NY: Cornell University Press.

Gartzke, E. (2007), 'The capitalist peace', *American Journal of Political Science*, 51(1): 166–191.

Gasper, D. (2008), 'From "Hume's Law" to problem- and policy-analysis for human development. Sen after Dewey, Myrdal, Streeten, Stretton and Haq', *Review of Political Economy*, 20(2): 233–256.

Gay, R., Charlesworth, A., and Esen, R. (2007), *Online Marketing: A Customer-Led Approach*, Oxford, UK: Oxford University Press.

Gemici, K. (2008), 'Karl Polanyi and the antinomies of embeddedness', *Socio-Economic Review*, 6(1): 5–33.

George, D. (2001), *Preference Pollution: How Markets Create the Desires We Dislike*, Ann Arbor, MI: University of Michigan Press.

George, V., and Wilding, P. (1994), *Welfare and Ideology*, Hemel Hempstead, UK: Harvester Wheatsheaf.

Geras, N. (1985), 'The controversy about Marx and justice', *New Left Review*, 150: 47–85.

Gerrard, B. (1993), 'The significance of interpretation in economics', in W. Henderson, T. Dudley-Evans, and R. Backhouse (eds.), *Economics and Language*, London: Routledge, pp. 51–63.

Gërxhani, K. (2004), 'The informal sector in developed and less developed countries: a literature survey', *Public Choice*, 120(3–4): 267–300.

Gibbs, P. (2001), 'Higher education as a market: a problem or solution?', *Studies in Higher Education*, 26(1): 85–94.

Gibson-Graham, J.K. (2000), 'Poststructural interventions', in E. Sheppard, and T.J. Barnes (eds.), *A Companion to Economic Geography*, Oxford, UK: Blackwell, pp. 95–110.

Gibson-Graham, J.K. (2006), *A Postcapitalist Politics*, Minneapolis, MN: University of Minnesota Press.

Gibson-Graham, J.K. (2008), 'Diverse economies: performative practices for "other worlds"', *Progress in Human Geography*, 32(5): 613–632.

Giddens, A. (1984), *The Constitution of Society: Outline of the Theory of Structuration*, Cambridge, UK: Polity Press.

Gindis, D. (2009), 'From fictions and aggregates to real entities in the theory of the firm', *Journal of Institutional Economics*, 5(1): 25–46.

Ginsburg, N. (1979), *Class, Capital and Social Policy*, London: Macmillan.

Gintis, H. (2000), Beyond *homo economicus*: evidence from experimental economics', *Ecological Economics*, 35(3): 311–322.

Glennerster, H. (1991), 'Quasi-markets for education?', *Economic Journal*, 101(408): 1268–1276.

Gloria-Palermo, S. (1999), *The Evolution of Austrian Economics: from Menger to Lachmann*, London: Routledge.

Godson, M. (2009), *Relationship Marketing*, Oxford, UK: Oxford University Press.

Goldberg, V.P. (1976), 'Toward an expanded economic theory of contract', *Journal of Economic Issues*, 10(1): 45–61.

Goldberg, V.P. (1980), 'Relational exchange: economics and complex contracts', *American Behavioral Scientist*, 23(3): 337–352.

Goldschmidt-Clermont, L. (1992), 'Measuring households' non-monetary production', in P. Ekins, and M. Max-Neef (eds.), *Real-Life Economics: Understanding Wealth Creation*, London: Routledge, pp. 265–283.

Goldstein, M.M., and Bowers, D.G. (2015), 'The patient as consumer: empowerment or commodification? Currents in contemporary bioethics', *Journal of Law, Medicine and Ethics: A Journal of the American Society of Law, Medicine and Ethics*, 43(1): 162–165.

Golub, S.S., and Hsieh, C.-T. (2000), 'Classical Ricardian theory of comparative advantage revisited', *Review of International Economics*, 8(2): 221–234.

Goode, R. (1994), 'Gardiner Means on administered prices and administrative inflation', *Journal of Economic Issues*, 28(1): 173–186.

Goodstein, E.S. (2002), 'Style as substance: Georg Simmel's phenomenology of culture', *Cultural Critique*, 52(1): 209–234.

Gordon, B. (1975), *Economic Analysis Before Adam Smith: Hesiod to Lessius*, London: Macmillan.

Gordon, D.M., Edwards, R., and Reich, M. (1982), *Segmented Work, Divided Workers*, Cambridge, UK: Cambridge University Press.

Gordon, R.J. (1990), 'What is new-Keynesian economics?', *Journal of Economic Literature*, 28(3): 1115–1171.

Gore, C. (2000), 'The rise and fall of the Washington Consensus as a paradigm for developing countries', *World Development*, 28(5): 789–804.

Gough, I. (1979), *The Political Economy of the Welfare State*, London: Macmillan.

Goux, J.-J. (2001), 'Ideality, symbolicity, and reality in postmodern capitalism', in S. Cullenberg, J.L. Amariglio, and D.F. Ruccio (eds.), *Postmodernism, Economics and Knowledge*, London: Routledge, pp. 166–181.

Gowdy, J.M. (ed.) (1998), *Limited Wants, Unlimited Means: A Reader on Hunter-Gatherer Economics and the Environment*, Washington, DC: Island Press.

Goyal, S. (2007), *Connections: An Introduction to the Economics of Networks*, Princeton, NJ: Princeton University Press.

Goyal, S. (2011), 'Social networks in economics', in J. Scott, and P.J. Carrington (eds.), *The Sage Handbook of Social Network Analysis*, London: Sage, pp. 67–79.

Graetz, F., and Smith, A.C.T. (2008), 'The role of dualities in arbitrating continuity and change in forms of organizing', *International Journal of Management Reviews*, 10(3): 265–280.

Graham, S., and Marvin, S. (2001), *Splintering Urbanism: Networked Infrastructures, Technological Mobilities and the Urban Condition*, London: Routledge.

Granovetter, M.S. (1983), 'The strength of weak ties: a network theory revisited', *Sociological Theory*, 1: 201–233.

Granovetter, M.S. (1985), 'Economic action and social structure: the problem of embeddedness', *American Journal of Sociology*, 91(3): 481–510.

Granovetter, M.S. (1992), 'Economic institutions as social constructions: a framework for analysis', *Acta Sociologica*, 35(1): 3–11.

Granovetter, M.S. (1995), *Getting a Job: A Study of Contacts and Careers*, 2nd edn., Chicago, IL: University of Chicago Press.

Granovetter, M.S. (2005), 'The impact of social structure on economic outcomes', *Journal of Economic Perspectives*, 19(1): 33–50.

Granovetter, M.S. (2017), *Society and Economy: Framework and Principles*, Cambridge, MA: Harvard University Press.

Greco, T.H. (2001), *Money: Understanding and Creating Alternatives to Legal Tender*, White River Junction, VT: Chelsea Green.

Greenwald, B., and Stiglitz, J.E. (1987), 'Keynesian, New Keynesian and New Classical economics', *Oxford Economic Papers*, 39(1): 119–133.

Gregory, C.A. (1982), *Gifts and Commodities*, London: Academic Press.

Gregory, P.R., and Stuart, R.C. (2004), *Comparing Economic Systems in the Twenty-First Century*, 7th edn., Mason, OH: South-Western.

Groenewegen, J. (1997), 'Institutions of capitalisms: American, European, and Japanese systems compared', *Journal of Economic Issues*, 31(2): 333–348.

Grönroos, C. (1994), 'From marketing mix to relationship marketing: towards a paradigm shift in marketing', *Management Decision*, 32(2): 4–20.

Grube, L.E., and Storr, V.H. (eds.) (2015), *Culture and Economic Action*, Cheltenham, UK: Edward Elgar.

Gruchy, A.G. (1987), *The Reconstruction of Economics: An Analysis of the Fundamentals of Institutional Economics*, New York: Greenwood Press.

Gu, G.C., and Lee, F.S. (2012), 'Prices and pricing', in J.E. King (ed.), *The Elgar Companion to Post Keynesian Economics*, 2nd edn., Cheltenham, UK: Edward Elgar, pp. 456–463.

Guala, F. (2001), 'Building economic machines: the FCC auctions', *Studies in History and Philosophy of Science Part A*, 32(3): 453–477.

Gudeman, S.F. (1986), *Economics as Culture: Models and Metaphors of Livelihood*, London: Routledge.

Gudeman, S.F. (2001), *The Anthropology of Economy: Community, Market, and Culture*, Oxford, UK: Blackwell.

Gudeman, S.F. (2016), *Anthropology and Economy*, Cambridge, UK: Cambridge University Press.

Gummesson, E. (2008), *Total Relationship Marketing*, 3rd edn., London: Routledge.

Hahn, F.H. (1987), 'The foundations of monetary theory', in M. De Cecco, and J.-P. Fitoussi (eds.), *Monetary Theory and Economic Institutions*, London: Macmillan, pp. 21–43.

Hahnel, R. (2007), 'The case against markets', *Journal of Economic Issues*, 41(4): 1139–1159.

Hall, P.A., and Soskice, D. (2001), *Varieties of Capitalism: The Institutional Foundations of Comparative Advantage*, Oxford, UK: Oxford University Press.

Halteman, J., and Noell, E. (2012), *Reckoning with Markets: Moral Reflection in Economics*, Oxford, UK: Oxford University Press.

Hamilton, A. (2000), 'Max Weber's *Protestant ethic and the spirit of capitalism*', in S. Turner (ed.), *The Cambridge Companion to Weber*, Cambridge, UK: Cambridge University Press, pp. 151–171.

Hamilton, D. (1991), 'The meaning of anthropology for economic science: a case for intellectual reciprocity', *Journal of Economic Issues*, 25(4): 937–949.

Hancké, B. (ed.) (2009), *Debating Varieties of Capitalism: A Reader*, Oxford, UK: Oxford University Press.

Hannibal, B., and Ono, H. (2017), 'Relationships of collapse: network brokerage, opportunism and fraud in financial markets, *International Journal of Social Economics*, 44(12): 2097–2111.

Harcourt, G.C. (2006), *The Structure of Post-Keynesian Economics: the Core Contributions of the Pioneers*, Cambridge, UK: Cambridge University Press.

Hargreaves Heap, S. (1989), *Rationality in Economics*, Oxford: Basil Blackwell.

Harris, M. (2001a), *Cultural Materialism: The Struggle for a Science of Culture*, updated edn., Walnut Creek, CA: Altamira Press.

Harris, M. (2001b), *The Rise of Anthropological Theory: A History of Theories of Culture*, updated edn., Walnut Creek, CA: Altamira Press.

Harrison, R., Newholm, T., and Shaw, D. (eds.) (2005), *The Ethical Consumer*, London: Sage.

Hart, N., and Kriesler, P. (2016), 'Keynes, Kalecki, Sraffa: coherence within pluralism?', in J. Courvisanos, J. Doughney, and A. Millmow (eds.), *Reclaiming Pluralism in Economics*, London: Routledge, pp. 186–202.

Hartwell, R.M. (ed.) (1967), *The Causes of the Industrial Revolution in England*, London: Methuen.

Harvey, D. (1982), *The Limits to Capital*, Oxford, UK: Basil Blackwell.

Harvey, D. (2003), *The New Imperialism*, Oxford, UK: Oxford University Press.

Havighurst, A.F. (ed.) (1976), *The Pirenne Thesis: Analysis, Criticism, and Revision*, 3rd edn., Boston, MA: D.C. Heath.

Hayek, F.A. (1948), *Individualism and Economic Order*, London: Routledge and Kegan Paul.

Hayek, F.A. (1960), *The Constitution of Liberty*, London: Routledge and Kegan Paul.

Hayek, F.A. (1979), *Law, Legislation and Liberty*, Volumes 1–3, London: Routledge and Kegan Paul.

Hayek, F.A. (1989), 'The pretence of knowledge', *American Economic Review*, 79(6): 3–7.

Heady, P. (2005), 'Barter', in J.G. Carrier (ed.), *A Handbook of Economic Anthropology*, Cheltenham, UK: Edward Elgar, pp. 262–274.

Healy, S. (2009), 'Alternative economies', in R. Kitchin, and N.J. Thrift (eds.), *The International Encyclopedia of Human Geography*, Oxford, UK: Elsevier, pp. 338–344.

Heath, R.G. (2012), *Seducing the Subconscious: The Psychology of Emotional Influence in Advertising*, Chichester, UK: Wiley-Blackwell.

Hegre, H., Oneal, J.R., and Russett, B. (2010), 'Trade does promote peace: new simultaneous estimates of the reciprocal effects of trade and conflict', *Journal of Peace Research*, 47(6): 763–774.

Heinrichs, H. (2013), 'Sharing economy: a potential new pathway to sustainability', *Gaia – Ecological Perspectives for Science and Society*, 22(4): 228–231.

Helman, D., and De Chernatony, L.D. (1999), 'Exploring the development of lifestyle retail brands', *Service Industries Journal*, 19(2): 49–68.

Hempel, C.G. (1959), 'The logic of functional analysis', in L. Gross (ed.), *Symposium on Sociological Theory*, New York: Harper and Row, pp. 271–307.

Herbruck, W. (1929), 'Forestalling, regrating and engrossing', *Michigan Law Review*, 27(4): 365–388.

Herrera, Y.M. (2010), *Mirrors of the Economy: National Accounts and International Norms in Russia and Beyond*, Ithaca, NY: Cornell University Press.

Herskovits, M.J. (1952), *Economic Anthropology*, New York: Knopf.

Hesse, M.B. (1970), *Forces and Fields: The Concept of Action at a Distance in the History of Physics*, Westport, CT: Greenwood Press.

Heydebrand, W.V. (1989), 'New organizational forms', *Work and Occupations*, 16(3): 323–357.

Hill, E. (2018), 'The informal economy in theory and policy: prospects for well-being', in T.-H. Jo, L. Chester, and C. D'Ippoliti (eds.), *The Routledge Handbook of Heterodox Economics*, London: Routledge, pp. 276–289.

Himmelweit, S.F. (1995), 'The discovery of "unpaid work": the social consequences of the expansion of "work"', *Feminist Economics*, 1(2): 1–19.

Himmelweit, S.F. (1998), 'Accounting for caring', *Radical Statistics*, 70: 3–7.

Himmelweit, S.F. (2002), 'Making visible the hidden economy: the case for gender-impact analysis of economic policy, *Feminist Economics*, 8(1): 49–70.

Himmelweit, S.F. (2007), 'The prospects for caring: economic theory and policy analysis', *Cambridge Journal of Economics*, 31(4): 581–599.

Himmelweit, S.F., and Mohun, S. (1977), 'Domestic labour and capital', *Cambridge Journal of Economics*, 1(1): 15–31.

Hindess, B., and Hirst, P.Q. (1975), *Pre-capitalist Modes of Production*, London: Routledge and Kegan Paul.

Hirsch, F. (1977), *Social Limits to Growth*, London: Routledge and Kegan Paul.

Hirschman, A.O. (1982), 'Rival interpretations of market society: civilizing, destructive, or feeble?', *Journal of Economic Literature*, 20(4): 1463–1484.

Hodgson, G.M. (1987), 'Economics and systems theory', *Journal of Economic Studies*, 14(4): 65–86.

Hodgson, G.M. (1988), *Economics and Institutions: A Manifesto for a Modern Institutional Economics*, Cambridge, UK: Polity Press.

Hodgson, G.M. (1989), 'Institutional economic theory: the old versus the new', *Review of Political Economy*, 1(3): 249–269.

Hodgson, G.M. (1991), 'Hayek's theory of cultural evolution: an evaluation in the light of Vanberg's critique', *Economics and Philosophy*, 7(1): 67–82.

Hodgson, G.M. (1993), *Economics and Evolution: Bringing Life Back into Economics*, Cambridge, UK: Polity Press.

Hodgson, G.M. (1995), 'The political economy of utopia', *Review of Social Economy*, 53(2): 195–214.

Hodgson, G.M. (1998), 'The approach of institutional economics', *Journal of Economic Literature*, 36(1): 166–192.

Hodgson, G.M. (1999), *Economics and Utopia: Why the Learning Economy Is Not the End of History*, London: Routledge.

Hodgson, G.M. (2000), 'What is the essence of institutional economics?', *Journal of Economic Issues*, 34(2): 317–329.

Hodgson, G.M. (2001), *How Economics Forgot History: The Problem of Historical Specificity in Social Science*, London: Routledge.

Hodgson, G.M. (2002), 'The legal nature of the firm and the myth of the firm-market hybrid', *International Journal of the Economics of Business*, 9(1): 36–60.

Hodgson, G.M. (2003a), 'Capitalism, complexity, and inequality', *Journal of Economic Issues*, 37(2): 471–478.

Hodgson, G.M. (2003b), 'The hidden persuaders: institutions and individuals in economic theory', *Cambridge Journal of Economics*, 27(2): 159–175.

Hodgson, G.M. (2004a), 'Some claims made for critical realism in economics: two case studies', *Journal of Economic Methodology*, 11(1): 53–73.

Hodgson, G.M. (2004b), *The Evolution of Institutional Economics: Agency, Structure and Darwinism in American Institutionalism*, London: Routledge.

Hodgson, G.M. (2006), 'What are institutions?', *Journal of Economic Issues*, 40(1): 1–25.

Hodgson, G.M. (2007), 'Institutions and individuals: interaction and evolution', *Organization Studies*, 28(1): 95–116.

Hodgson, G.M. (2008), 'Markets', in J.B. Davis, and W. Dolfsma (eds.), *The Elgar Companion to Social Economics*, Cheltenham, UK: Edward Elgar, pp. 251–266.

Hodgson, G.M. (2017), 'Karl Polanyi on economy and society: a critical analysis of core concepts', *Review of Social Economy*, 75(1): 1–25.

Holcombe, R.G. (2014), *Advanced Introduction to the Austrian School of Economics*, Cheltenham, UK: Edward Elgar.

Hollander, S. (1965), 'On the interpretation of the just price', *Kyklos*, 18(4): 615–634.

Hollingsworth, J.R., and Boyer, R. (eds.) (1997), *Contemporary Capitalism: The Embeddedness of Institutions*, Cambridge, UK: Cambridge University Press.

Holmwood, J. (2014), *Founding Sociology? Talcott Parsons and the Idea of General Theory*, London: Routledge.

Holton, R.J. (1985), *The Transition from Feudalism to Capitalism*, London: Macmillan.

Holton, R.J. (1986), *Cities, Capitalism and Civilization*, London: Allen and Unwin.

Hoover, K.D. (1988), *The New Classical Macroeconomics: A Sceptical Inquiry*, Oxford, UK: Basil Blackwell.

Hopkins, K. (1980), 'Taxes and trade in the Roman Empire (200 b.c.–a.d. 400)', *Journal of Roman Studies*, 70: 101–125.

Howells, P., and Bain, K. (2000), *Financial Markets and Institutions*, 3rd edn., Harlow, UK: Prentice Hall.

Howgego, C. (1995), *Ancient History from Coins*, London: Routledge.

Huang, M.-H. (2001), 'The theory of emotions in marketing', *Journal of Business and Psychology*, 16(2): 239–247.

Huber, E., and Stephens, J.D. (2001), *Development and Crisis of the Welfare State: Parties and Policies in Global Markets*, Chicago, IL: University of Chicago Press.

Hudson, M. (2004), 'The archaeology of money: debt versus barter theories of money's origins', in L.R. Wray (ed.), *Credit and State Theories of Money: The Contributions of A. Mitchell Innes*, Cheltenham, UK: Edward Elgar, pp. 99–127.

Hudson, P. (1992), *The Industrial Revolution*, London: Edward Arnold.

Hudson, R. (2005), *Economic Geographies: Circuits, Flows and Spaces*, London: Sage.

Hueting, R. (1992), 'Growth, environment and national income: theoretical problems and a practical solution', in P. Ekins, and M. Max-Neef (eds.), *Real-Life Economics: Understanding Wealth Creation*, London: Routledge, pp. 255–263.

Humphrey, C. (1985), 'Barter and economic disintegration', *Man*, 20(1): 48–72.

Humphrey, C., and Hugh-Jones, S. (eds.) (1992), *Barter, Exchange and Value: An Anthropological Approach*, Cambridge, UK: Cambridge University Press.

Humphreys, S.C. (1969), 'History, economics, and anthropology: the work of Karl Polanyi', *History and Theory*, 8(2): 165–212.

Hunt, B.C. (1936), *The Development of the Business Corporation in England*, Cambridge, MA: Harvard University Press, pp. 1800–1867.

Hussain, A. (1990), 'Commodity fetishism', in J. Eatwell, M. Milgate, and P. Newman (eds.), *Marxian Economics*, London: Macmillan, pp. 85–86.

Ikeda, S. (1994), 'Market process', in P.J. Boettke (ed.), *The Elgar Companion to Austrian Economics*, Cheltenham, UK: Edward Elgar, pp. 23–32.

Ingham, G.K. (1996a), 'Money is a social relation', *Review of Social Economy*, 54(4): 507–529.

Ingham, G.K. (1996b), 'Some recent changes in the relationship between economics and sociology', *Cambridge Journal of Economics*, 20(2): 243–275.

Ingham, G.K. (2000), '"Babylonian madness": on the historical and sociological origins of money', in J. Smithin (ed.), *What Is Money?*, London: Routledge, pp. 16–41.

Ingham, G.K. (2004), *The Nature of Money*, Cambridge, UK: Polity Press.

Inkpen, A.C., and Tsang, E.W.K. (2005), 'Social capital, networks, and knowledge transfer', *Academy of Management Review*, 30(1): 146–165.

Ioannides, S. (1992), *The Market, Competition and Democracy: A Critique of Neo-Austrian Economics*, Aldershot, UK: Edward Elgar.

Isaac, B.L. (1993), 'Retrospective on the formalist-substantivist debate', in B.L. Isaac (ed.), *Research in Economic Anthropology*, Vol. 14, Greenwich, CT: JAI Press, pp. 213–233.

Isard, P. (1977), 'How far can we push the "law of one price"?', *American Economic Review*, 67(5): 942–948.

Isard, W. (1975), *An Introduction to Regional Science*, Englewood Cliffs, NJ: Prentice-Hall.

Itoh, M., and Lapavitsas, C. (1999), *Political Economy of Money and Finance*, London: Macmillan.

Jackson, W.A. (1991), 'On the treatment of population ageing in economic theory', *Ageing and Society*, 11(1): 59–68.

Jackson, W.A. (1993), 'Culture, society and economic theory', *Review of Political Economy*, 5(4): 453–469.

Jackson, W.A. (1995), 'Naturalism in economics', *Journal of Economic Issues*, 29(3): 761–780.

Jackson, W.A. (1996), 'Cultural materialism and institutional economics', *Review of Social Economy*, 54(2): 221–244.

Jackson, W.A. (1998), *The Political Economy of Population Ageing*, Cheltenham, UK: Edward Elgar.

Jackson, W.A. (1999), 'Dualism, duality and the complexity of economic institutions', *International Journal of Social Economics*, 26(4): 545–558.

Jackson, W.A. (2002), 'Functional explanation in economics: a qualified defence', *Journal of Economic Methodology*, 9(2): 169–189.

Jackson, W.A. (2003), 'Social structure in economic theory', *Journal of Economic Issues*, 37(3): 727–746.

Jackson, W.A. (2005), 'Capabilities, culture and social structure', *Review of Social Economy*, 63(1): 101–124.

Jackson, W.A. (2007a), 'Economic flexibility: a structural analysis', in S. Ioannides, and K. Nielsen (eds.), *Economics and the Social Sciences: Boundaries, Interaction and Integration*, Cheltenham, UK: Edward Elgar, pp. 215–232.

Jackson, W.A. (2007b), 'On the social structure of markets', *Cambridge Journal of Economics*, 31(2): 235–253.

Jackson, W.A. (2009), *Economics, Culture and Social Theory*, Cheltenham, UK: Edward Elgar.

Jackson, W.A. (2013), 'The desocialising of economic theory', *International Journal of Social Economics*, 40(9): 809–825.

Jackson, W.A. (2014), 'External capabilities and the limits to social policy', in H.-U. Otto, and H. Ziegler (eds.), *Critical Social Policy and the Capability Approach*, Opladen, Germany: Barbara Budrich, pp. 125–142.

Jackson, W.A. (2015a), 'Distributive justice with and without culture', *Journal of Cultural Economy*, 8(6): 673–688.

Jackson, W.A. (2015b), 'Markets and the meaning of flexibility', *Economic Issues*, 20(2): 45–65.

Jackson, W.A. (2018), 'Strategic pluralism and monism in heterodox economics', *Review of Radical Political Economics*, 50(2): 237–251.

Jackson, W.A. (2019), 'Active and passive trading relations', *Journal of Economic Issues*, 53(1): 98–114.

Jaffé, W. (1975), 'Léon Walras, an economic advisor manqué', *Economic Journal*, 85(4): 810–823.

Jennings, A.L., and Waller, W. (1990), 'Constructions of social hierarchy: the family, gender, and power', *Journal of Economic Issues*, 24(2): 623–631.

Jhally, S. (1990), *The Codes of Advertising: Fetishism and the Political Economy of Meaning in the Consumer Society*, London: Routledge.

Jo, T.-H. (2011), 'Social provisioning process and socio-economic modeling', *American Journal of Economics and Sociology*, 70(5): 1094–1116.

Jo, T.-H. (2016), 'What if there are no conventional price mechanisms?', *Journal of Economic Issues*, 50(2): 327–344.

Jo, T.-H., and Todorova, Z. (2018), 'Social provisioning process: a heterodox view of the economy', in T.-H. Jo, L. Chester, and C. D'Ippoliti (eds.), *The Routledge Handbook of Heterodox Economics*, London: Routledge, pp. 29–40.

Johnston, J. (2002), 'Consuming global justice: fair trade shopping and alternative development', in J. Goodman (ed.), *Protest and Globalisation: Prospects for Transnational Solidarity*, Annandale, Australia: Pluto Press, pp. 38–56.

Jolink, A. (1996), *The Evolutionist Economics of Léon Walras*, London: Routledge.

Jones, A.H.M. (1956), 'Slavery in the ancient world', *Economic History Review*, 9(2): 185–199.

Joseph, J., and Kennedy, S. (2000), 'The structure of the social', *Philosophy of the Social Sciences*, 30(4): 508–527.

Junankar, P.N. (1982), *Marx's Economics*, Oxford, UK: Philip Allan.

Kahneman, D. (2003), 'Maps of bounded rationality: psychology for behavioral economics', *American Economic Review*, 93(5): 1449–1475.

Kahneman, D., Slovic, P., and Tversky, A. (eds.) (1982), *Judgement Under Uncertainty: Heuristics and Biases*, New York: Cambridge University Press.

Kaldor, N. (1972), 'The irrelevance of equilibrium economics', *Economic Journal*, 82(328): 1237–1255.

Kaldor, N. (1985), *Economics Without Equilibrium*, Cardiff, UK: University College Cardiff Press.

Kalecki, M. (1970), 'Theories of growth in different social systems', *Scientia*, 105 (5–6): 311–316.

Kalecki, M. (1971), *Selected Essays on the Dynamics of the Capitalist Economy*, Cambridge, UK: Cambridge University Press.

Kalecki, M. (1972), *Selected Essays on the Economic Growth of the Socialist and the Mixed Economy*, Cambridge, UK: Cambridge University Press.

Kalecki, M. (1990), *Capitalism: Business Cycles and Full Employment (Collected Works Volume I)*, edited by J. Osiatyński, Oxford, UK: Clarendon Press.

Kalleberg, A.L. (2000), 'Nonstandard employment relations: part-time, temporary and contract work', *Annual Review of Sociology*, 26(1): 341–365.

Kamenka, E. (1969), *Marxism and Ethics*, London: Macmillan.

Karacuka, M., and Zaman, A. (2012), 'The empirical evidence against neoclassical utility theory: a review of the literature', *International Journal of Pluralism and Economics Education*, 3(4): 366–414.

Katzner, D.W. (2001), The significance, success, and failure of microeconomic theory', *Journal of Post Keynesian Economics*, 24(1): 41–58.

Katzner, D.W. (2008), 'On the analytical and methodological significance of microeconomic theory', *Review of Radical Political Economics*, 40(3): 324–330.

Katzner, D.W. (2016), 'Time and the analysis of economic decision making', *Real-World Economics Review*, 77: 64–72.

Kaufman, B.E. (2007), 'The impossibility of a perfectly competitive labour market', *Cambridge Journal of Economics*, 31(5): 775–787.

Keen, S. (1995), 'Finance and economic breakdown: modelling Minsky's "financial instability hypothesis"', *Journal of Post Keynesian Economics*, 17(4): 607–635.

Keen, S. (2011), *Debunking Economics: The Naked Emperor Dethroned?*, 2nd edn., London: Zed Books.

Keister, L.A. (2002), 'Financial markets, money, and banking', *Annual Review of Sociology*, 28(1): 39–61.

Keller, K.L. (2001), 'Building customer-based brand equity: a blueprint for creating strong brands', *Marketing Management*, 28(1): 35–41.

Keller, K.L. (2003), 'Understanding brands, branding and brand equity', *Interactive Marketing*, 5(1): 7–20.

Kellner, D.M. (1983), 'Critical theory, commodities and the consumer society', *Theory, Culture and Society*, 1(3): 66–83.

Kennedy, L. (1982), 'The first agricultural revolution: property rights in their place', *Agricultural History*, 56(2): 379–390.

Keynes, J.M. (1931), 'The end of *laissez-faire*', in J.M. Keynes, *Essays in Persuasion*, London: Macmillan, 1972, pp. 272–294.

Keynes, J.M. (1936), *The General Theory of Employment, Interest and Money*, London: Macmillan.

Khalil, E.L. (1994), 'Trust', in G.M. Hodgson, W.J. Samuels, and M.R. Tool (eds.), *The Elgar Companion to Institutional and Evolutionary Economics*, Vol. 2, Aldershot, UK: Edward Elgar, pp. 339–346.

Kincaid, H. (1990), 'Assessing functional explanations in the social sciences', *PSA: Proceedings of the Biennial Meeting of the Philosophy of Science Association*, 1: 341–354.

Kindleberger, C.P. (1984), *A Financial History of Western Europe*, London: George Allen & Unwin.

Kindleberger, C.P., and Aliber, R.Z. (2011), *Manias, Panics and Crashes: A History of Financial Crises*, 5th edn., Basingstoke, UK: Palgrave Macmillan.

King, J.E. (1983), 'Utopian or scientific? A reconsideration of the Ricardian socialists', *History of Political Economy*, 15(3): 345–373.

King, J.E. (2002), *A History of Post Keynesian Economics Since 1936*, Cheltenham, UK: Edward Elgar.

King, J.E. (2003), 'Non-Marxian socialism', in W.J. Samuels, J.E. Biddle, and J.B. Davis (eds.), *A Companion to the History of Economic Thought*, Oxford, UK: Blackwell, pp. 184–200.

King, J.E. (2012), *The Microfoundations Delusion: Metaphor and Dogma in the History of Macroeconomics*, Cheltenham, UK: Edward Elgar.

King, J.E. (2015), *Advanced Introduction to Post Keynesian Economics*, Cheltenham, UK: Edward Elgar.

Kirman, A.P. (1989), 'The intrinsic limits of modern economic theory: the emperor has no clothes', *Economic Journal*, 99(395) (conference papers): 126–139.

Kirman, A.P. (2006), 'Demand theory and general equilibrium: from explanation to introspection, a journey down the wrong road', *History of Political Economy*, 38(5): 246–280.

Kirman, A.P. (2011), *Complex Economics: Individual and Collective Rationality*, London: Routledge.

Kirzner, I.M. (1973), *Competition and Entrepreneurship*, Chicago, IL: University of Chicago Press.

Kirzner, I.M. (1992), *The Meaning of Market Process: Essays in the Development of Modern Austrian Economics*, London: Routledge.

Kirzner, I.M. (1997), 'Entrepreneurial discovery and the competitive market process: an Austrian approach', *Journal of Economic Literature*, 35(1): 60–85.

Kjellberg, H., and Helgesson, C.-F. (2006), 'Multiple versions of markets: multiplicity and performativity in market practice', *Industrial Marketing Management*, 35(7): 839–855.

Kjellberg, H., and Helgesson, C.-F. (2010), 'Political marketing: multiple values, performativities and modes of engaging', *Journal of Cultural Economy*, 3(2): 279–297.

Klamer, A. (2011), 'Cultural entrepreneurship', *Review of Austrian Economics*, 24(2): 141–156.

Klein, P.G., and Bylund, P.L. (2014), 'The place of Austrian economics in contemporary entrepreneurship research', *Review of Austrian Economics*, 27(3): 259–279.

Klemperer, P. (2004), *Auctions: Theory and Practice*, Princeton, NJ: Princeton University Press.

Knapp, G.F. (1924), *The State Theory of Money*, 4th edn., London: Macmillan.

Knights, D., and Willmott, H. (eds.) (1990), *Labour Process Theory*, London: Macmillan.

Knorr Cetina, K. (2006), 'The market', *Theory, Culture and Society*, 23(2–3): 551–556.

Knorr Cetina, K., and Bruegger, U. (2002), 'Global microstructures: the virtual societies of financial markets', *American Journal of Sociology*, 107(4): 905–950.

Koehler, B. (2016), 'The thirteenth-century economics of Thomas Aquinas', *Economic Affairs*, 36(1): 56–63.

Koehn, D., and Wilbratte, B. (2012), 'A defense of a Thomistic concept of the just price', *Business Ethics Quarterly*, 22(3): 501–526.

Kornai, J. (1979), 'Resource-constrained versus demand-constrained systems', *Econometrica*, 47(4): 801–819.

Kornai, J. (1980), *Economics of Shortage*, Amsterdam: North-Holland.

Kornai, J. (1992), *The Socialist System: The Political Economy of Communism*, Oxford, UK: Clarendon Press.

Kornai, J. (2013), *Dynamism, Rivalry, and the Surplus Economy: Two Essays on the Nature of Capitalism*, Oxford, UK: Oxford University Press.

Kornberger, M. (2010), *Brand Society: How Brands Transform Management and Lifestyle*, Cambridge, UK: Cambridge University Press.

Kotler, P.T., and Keller, K.L. (2016), *Marketing Management*, 15th edn., London: Pearson.

Kotz, D.M. (2009), 'The financial and economic crisis of 2008: a systemic crisis of neoliberal capitalism', *Review of Radical Political Economics*, 41(3): 305–317.

Kregel, J. (2011), 'Evolution versus equilibrium', *Journal of Economic Issues*, 45(2): 269–275.

Krippner, G.R. (2001), 'The elusive market: embeddedness and the paradigm of economic sociology', *Theory and Society*, 30(6): 775–810.

Krippner, G.R. (2005), 'The financialization of the American economy', *Socio-Economic Review*, 3(2): 173–208.

Krishna, V. (2010), *Auction Theory*, 2nd edn., San Diego, CA: Academic Press.

Kristal, T. (2010), 'Good times, bad times: postwar labor's share of national income in capitalist democracies', *American Sociological Review*, 75(5): 729–763.

Krugman, P.R. (1987), 'Is free trade passé?', *Journal of Economic Perspectives*, 1(2): 131–144.

Krugman, P.R. (1998), 'What's new about the new economic geography?', *Oxford Review of Economic Policy*, 14(2): 7–17.

Kumar, V., and Reinartz, W. (2012), *Customer Relationship Management: Concept, Strategy, and Tools*, 2nd edn., Heidelberg, Germany: Springer.

Kurz, H.D. (1985), 'Effective demand in a "classical" model of value and distribution: the multiplier in a Sraffian framework', *Manchester School of Economic and Social Studies*, 53(2): 121–137.

Kurz, H.D. (2006), 'Whither the history of economic thought? Going nowhere rather slowly?', *European Journal of the History of Economic Thought*, 13(4): 463–488.

Kurz, H.D. (2013), 'Sraffa, Keynes, and post-Keynesianism', in G.C. Harcourt, and P. Kriesler (eds.), *The Oxford Handbook of Post-Keynesian Economics, Volume 1: Theory and Origins*, Oxford, UK: Oxford University Press, pp. 51–73.

Kurz, H.D. (2016), 'Adam Smith on markets, competition and violations of natural liberty', *Cambridge Journal of Economics*, 40(2): 615–638.

Kuttner, R. (1999), *Everything for Sale: The Virtues and Limits of Markets*, Chicago, IL: University of Chicago Press.

Kuznets, S. (1949), 'National income and industrial structure', *Econometrica*, 17 (Supplement): 205–241.

Lachmann, L.M. (1976), 'From Mises to Shackle: an essay on Austrian Economics and the kaleidic society', *Journal of Economic Literature*, 14(1): 54–62.

Lachmann, L.M. (1986), *The Market as an Economic Process*, Oxford, UK: Basil Blackwell.

Lamartina, S., and Zaghini, A. (2011), 'Increasing public expenditure: Wagner's Law in OECD countries', *German Economic Review*, 12(2): 149–164.

Lamb, R.B. (1974), 'Adam Smith's system: sympathy not self-interest', *Journal of the History of Ideas*, 35(4): 671–682.

Lambe, C.J., Spekman, R.E., and Hunt, S.D. (2000), 'Interimistic relational exchange: conceptualization and propositional development', *Journal of the Academy of Marketing Science*, 28(2): 212–225.

Landefeld, J.S., and McCulla, S.H. (2000), 'Accounting for nonmarket household production within a national accounts framework', *Review of Income and Wealth*, 46(3): 289–307.

Lane, C., and Wood, G. (2009), 'Capitalist diversity and diversity within capitalism', *Economy and Society*, 38(4): 531–551.

Lapavitsas, C. (2003), *Social Foundations of Markets, Money and Credit*, London: Routledge.

Lapavitsas, C. (2005), 'The emergence of money in commodity exchange, or money as monopolist of the ability to buy', *Review of Political Economy*, 17(4): 549–569.

Lash, S., and Urry, J. (1994), *Economies of Signs and Space*, London: Sage.

Lau, G.T., and Lee, S.H. (1999), 'Consumers' trust in a brand and the link to brand loyalty', *Journal of Market-Focused Management*, 4(4): 341–370.

Lavoie, D. (ed.) (1990), *Economics and Hermeneutics*, London: Routledge.

Lavoie, D. (1994), 'The interpretive turn', in P.J. Boettke (ed.), *The Elgar Companion to Austrian Economics*, Aldershot, UK: Edward Elgar, pp. 54–62.

Lavoie, D. (2011), 'The interpretive dimension of economics: science, hermeneutics and praxeology', *Review of Austrian Economics*, 24(2): 91–128.

Lavoie, M. (2006), *Introduction to Post-Keynesian Economics*, Basingstoke, UK: Palgrave Macmillan.

Lavoie, M. (2011), 'Should Sraffian economics be dropped out of the Post-Keynesian school?', *Economies et Sociétés*, 45(7): 1027–1059.

Lavoie, M. (2012), 'Financialization, neo-liberalism, and securitization', *Journal of Post Keynesian Economics*, 35(2): 215–233.

Lavoie, M. (2014), *Post-Keynesian Economics: New Foundations*, Cheltenham, UK: Edward Elgar.

Lawson, T. (1997), *Economics and Reality*, London: Routledge.

Lawson, T. (2001), 'Evaluating trust, competition and cooperation', in Y. Shionoya, and K. Yagi (eds.), *Competition, Trust, and Cooperation: A Comparative Study*, Berlin: Springer, pp. 42–76.

Lawson, T. (2003), *Reorienting Economics*, London: Routledge.

Lawson, T. (2005), 'The nature of institutional economics', *Evolutionary and Institutional Economics Review*, 2(1): 7–20.

Lawson, T. (2012), 'Ontology and the study of social reality: emergence, organisation, community, power, social relations, corporations, artefacts and money', *Cambridge Journal of Economics*, 36(2): 345–385.

Lawson, T. (2013), 'What is this "school" called neoclassical economics?', *Cambridge Journal of Economics*, 37(5): 947–983.

Lawson, T. (2015), *Essays on the Nature and State of Modern Economics*, London: Routledge.

Lawson, T. (2016), 'Social positioning and the nature of money', *Cambridge Journal of Economics*, 40(4): 961–996.

Layder, D. (1987), 'Key issues in structuration theory: some critical remarks', *Current Perspectives in Social Theory*, 8: 25–46.

Layder, D. (2006), *Understanding Social Theory*, 2nd edn., London: Sage.

Layton, R.A. (2007), 'Marketing systems – a core macromarketing concept', *Journal of Macromarketing*, 27(3): 227–242.

Layton, R.A. (2011), 'Towards a theory of marketing systems', *European Journal of Marketing*, 45(1–2): 259–276.

Lazonick, W. (1990), 'Labour process', in J. Eatwell, M. Milgate, and P. Newman (eds.), *Marxian Economics*, London: Macmillan, pp. 225–232.

Lazonick, W. (1991), *Business Organization and the Myth of the Market Economy*, Cambridge, UK: Cambridge University Press.

Le Grand, J. (2007), *The Other Invisible Hand: Delivering Public Services Through Choice and Competition*, Princeton, NJ: Princeton University Press.

Le Grand, J., and Bartlett, W. (eds.) (1993), *Quasi-Markets and Social Policy*, London: Macmillan.

Le Mare, A. (2008), 'The impact of fair trade on social and economic development: a review of the literature', *Geography Compass*, 2(6): 1922–1942.

LeBaron, G. (2010), 'The political economy of the household: neoliberal restructuring, enclosures, and daily life', *Review of International Political Economy*, 17(5): 889–912.

LeClair, E.E.L. (1962), 'Economic theory and economic anthropology', *American Anthropologist*, 64(6): 1179–1203.

Lee, F.S. (1998), *Post Keynesian Price Theory*, Cambridge, UK: Cambridge University Press.

Lee, F.S. (2013), 'Post-Keynesian price theory: from pricing to market governance to the economy as a whole', in G.C. Harcourt, and P. Kriesler (eds.), *The Oxford Handbook of Post-Keynesian Economics, Volume 1: Theory and Origins*, Oxford, UK: Oxford University Press, pp. 467–484.

Lee, F.S., and T.-H. Jo. (2011), 'Social surplus approach and heterodox economics', *Journal of Economic Issues*, 45(4): 857–876.

Lee, F.S., and Keen, S. (2004), 'The incoherent emperor: a heterodox critique of neoclassical microeconomic theory', *Review of Social Economy*, 62(2): 169–199.

Lee, R., and Wills, J. (eds.) (1997), *Geographies of Economies*, London: Arnold.

Leifer, E.M., and White, H.C. (1987), 'A structural approach to markets', in M.S. Mizruchi, and M. Schwartz (eds.), *Intercorporate Relations: The Structural Analysis of Business*, Cambridge, UK: Cambridge University Press, pp. 85–108.

Leontaridi, M.R. (1998), 'Segmented labour markets: theory and evidence', *Journal of Economic Surveys*, 12(1): 103–109.

Leung, C. (2004), 'Macroeconomics and housing: a review of the literature', *Journal of Housing Economics*, 13(4): 249–267.

Levi, M., and Linton, A. (2003), 'Fair trade: a cup at a time?', *Politics and Society*, 31(3): 407–432.

Lev-Yadun, S., Gopher, A., and Abbo, S. (2000), 'The cradle of agriculture', *Science*, 288(5471): 1602–1603.

Lewis, M. (1993), *The Culture of Inequality*, 2nd edn., Amherst, MA: University of Massachusetts Press.

Lewis, P. (ed.) (2004), *Transforming Economics: Perspectives on the Critical Realist Project*, London: Routledge.

Lewis, T., and Potter, E. (eds.) (2011), *Ethical Consumption: A Critical Introduction*, London: Routledge.

Lewison, M. (1999), 'Conflicts of interest? The ethics of usury', *Journal of Business Ethics*, 22(4): 327–339.

Leyshon, A., Lee, R., McDowell, L., and Sunley, P. (eds.) (2011), *The Sage Handbook of Economic Geography*, London: Sage.

Leyshon, A., Lee, R., and Williams, C.C. (eds.) (2003), *Alternative Economic Spaces*, London: Sage.

Lie, J. (1991), 'Embedding Polanyi's market society', *Sociological Perspectives*, 34(2): 219–235.

Lie, J. (1997), 'Sociology of markets', *Annual Review of Sociology*, 23(1): 341–360.

Lindert, P.H., and Williamson, J.G. (1983), 'English workers' living standards during the Industrial Revolution: a new look', *Economic History Review*, 36(1): 1–25.

Linton, A. (2008), 'Ethical trade initiatives', *Globalizations*, 5(2): 227–229.

Linton, A. (2012), *Fair Trade from the Ground Up: New Markets for Social Justice*, Seattle, WA: University of Washington Press.

Lipsey, R.G. (2007), 'Reflections on the general theory of second best at its golden jubilee', *International Tax and Public Finance*, 14(4): 349–364.

Lipsey, R.G., and Lancaster, K. (1956), 'The general theory of second best', *Review of Economic Studies*, 24(1): 11–32.

List, F. (1841), *The National System of Political Economy*, translated by S.S. Lloyd, London: Longmans, Green, 1885.

Littler, J. (2011), 'What's wrong with ethical consumption?', in T. Lewis, and E. Potter (eds.), *Ethical Consumption: A Critical Introduction*, London: Routledge, pp. 27–39.

Litvan, G. (1991), 'Democratic and socialist values in Karl Polanyi's thought', in M. Mendell, and D. Salée (eds.), *The Legacy of Karl Polanyi*, London: Macmillan, pp. 251–271.

Lo, A.W. (2008), 'Efficient markets hypothesis', in S.N. Durlauf, and L.E. Blume (eds.), *The New Palgrave Dictionary of Economics*, 2nd edn., London: Palgrave Macmillan, pp. 782–794.

Lodewijks, J. (1994), 'Anthropologists and economists: conflict or cooperation?', *Journal of Economic Methodology*, 1(1): 81–104.

López, J., and Scott, J. (2000), *Social Structure*, Buckingham, UK: Open University Press.

López, J.G., and Assous, M. (2010), *Michał Kalecki*, London: Palgrave Macmillan.

Lopez, R.S. (1976), *The Commercial Revolution of the Middle Ages*, Cambridge, UK: Cambridge University Press, pp. 950–1350.

Lopez, R.S. (1979), 'The dawn of medieval banking', in Center for Medieval and Renaissance Studies, UCLA (ed.), *The Dawn of Modern Banking*, New Haven, CT: Yale University Press, pp. 1–18.

Lorenz, C. (2012), 'If you're so smart, why are you under surveillance? Universities, neoliberalism, and new public management', *Critical Inquiry*, 38(3): 599–629.

Lorenz, E. (1999), 'Trust, contract and economic cooperation', *Cambridge Journal of Economics*, 23(3): 301–315.

Louzek, M. (2011), 'The battle of methods in economics: the classical *Methodenstreit* – Menger vs Schmoller', *American Journal of Economics and Sociology*, 70(2): 439–463.

Lowry, S.T. (1979), 'Recent literature on ancient Greek economic thought', *Journal of Economic Literature*, 17(1): 65–86.

Lowry, S.T. (1987), 'The Greek heritage in economic thought', in S.T. Lowry (ed.), *Pre-Classical Economic Thought: From the Greeks to the Scottish Enlightenment*, Boston, MA: Kluwer, pp. 7–42.

Lowry, S.T. (1994), 'Institutionalist view of the market', in G.M. Hodgson, W.J. Samuels, and M.R. Tool (eds.), *The Elgar Companion to Institutional and Evolutionary Economics*, Vol. 2, Aldershot, UK: Edward Elgar, pp. 47–53.

Löwy, M. (1987), 'The Romantic and the Marxist critique of modern civilization', *Theory and Society*, 16(6): 891–904.

Löwy, M., and Sayre, R. (2001), *Romanticism Against the Tide of Modernity*, translated by C. Porter, Durham, NC: Duke University Press.

Loxley, J. (2007), *Performativity*, London: Routledge.

Lucas, J.R. (1972), 'Justice', *Philosophy*, 47(181): 229–248.

Lukes, S. (1985), *Marxism and Morality*, Oxford, UK: Clarendon Press.

Lutz, M.A. (1999), *Economics for the Common Good: Two Centuries of Social Economic Thought in the Humanistic Tradition*, London: Routledge.

Lutz, M.A. (2002), 'Social economics, justice and the common good', *International Journal of Social Economics*, 29(1–2): 26–44.

Lutz, M.A. (2009), 'Social economics', in J. Peil, and I. Van Staveren (eds.), *Handbook of Economics and Ethics*, Cheltenham, UK: Edward Elgar, pp. 516–522.

Lynch, K. (2006), 'Neo-liberalism and marketisation: the implications for higher education', *European Educational Research Journal*, 5(1): 1–17.

Lyon, D. (1988), *The Information Society: Issues and Illusions*, Cambridge, UK: Polity Press.

Lysandrou, P. (2000), 'The market and exploitation in Marx's economic theory: a reinterpretation', *Cambridge Journal of Economics*, 24(3): 325–347.

Macdonald, K., and Marshall, S. (eds.) (2016), *Fair Trade, Corporate Accountability and Beyond: Experiments in Globalizing Justice*, London: Routledge.

MacKenzie, D. (2004), 'The big, bad wolf and the rational market: portfolio insurance, the 1987 crash and the performativity of economics', *Economy and Society*, 33(3): 303–334.

MacKenzie, D. (2006a), *An Engine, Not a Camera: How Financial Models Shape Markets*, Cambridge, MA: MIT Press.

MacKenzie, D. (2006b), 'Is economics performative? Option theory and the construction of derivatives markets', *Journal of the History of Economic Thought*, 28(1): 29–55.

MacKenzie, D. (2009), *Material Markets: How Economic Agents Are Constructed*, Oxford, UK: Oxford University Press.

MacKenzie, D., and Millo, Y. (2003), 'Constructing a market, performing theory: the historical sociology of a financial derivatives exchange', *American Journal of Sociology*, 109(1): 107–145.

MacKenzie, D., Muniesa, F., and Siu, L. (eds.) (2007), *Do Economists Make Markets? On the Performativity of Economics*, Princeton, NJ: Princeton University Press.

Mackinnon, D., and Cumbers, A. (2011), *Introduction to Economic Geography: Globalization, Uneven Development and Place*, 2nd edn., Harlow, UK: Prentice Hall.

MacMullen, R. (1970), 'Market-days in the Roman Empire', *Phoenix*, 24(4): 333–341.

Macneil, I.R. (1981), 'Economic analysis of contractual relations', in P. Burrows, and C.J. Veljanowski (eds.), *The Economic Approach to Law*, London: Butterworths, pp. 61–92.

Macneil, I.R. (2000), 'Relational contract theory: challenges and queries', *Northwestern University Law Review*, 94(3): 877–907.

Maier, F., Meyer, M., and Steinbereithner, M. (2016), 'Nonprofit organizations becoming business-like: a systematic review', *Nonprofit and Voluntary Sector Quarterly*, 45(1): 64–86.

Mainwaring, L. (1984), *Value and Distribution in Capitalist Economies: An Introduction to Sraffian Economics*, Cambridge, UK: Cambridge University Press.

Maisels, C.K. (1990), *The Emergence of Civilization: From Hunting and Gathering to Agriculture, Cities, and the State in the Near East*, London: Routledge.

Mandel, E. (1986), 'In defence of socialist planning', *New Left Review*, 159: 5–37.

Marcuse, H. (1991), *One–Dimensional Man: Studies in the Ideology of Advanced Industrial Society*, 2nd edn., Boston, MA: Beacon Press.

Marshall, A. (1890–1920), *Principles of Economics*, 9th (Variorum) edn., London: Macmillan, 1961.

Marti, E., and Gond, J.-P. (2018), 'When do theories become self-fulfilling? Exploring the boundary conditions of performativity', *Academy of Management Review*, 43(3): 487–508.

Martin, C.J. (2016), 'The sharing economy: a pathway to sustainability or a nightmarish form of neoliberal capitalism?', *Ecological Economics*, 121: 149–159.

Martin, J.E. (1983), *Feudalism to Capitalism: Peasant and Landlord in English Agrarian Development*, London: Macmillan.

Martin, J.L. (2003), 'What is field theory?', *American Journal of Sociology*, 109(1): 1–49.

Martin, M. (2000), *Verstehen: The Uses of Understanding in Social Science*, New Brunswick, NJ: Transaction Publishers.

Martin, R. (1999), 'The new "geographical turn" in economics: some critical reflections', *Cambridge Journal of Economics*, 23(1): 65–91.

Martin, R. (2000), 'Institutional approaches in economic geography', in E. Sheppard, and T.J. Barnes (eds.), *A Companion to Economic Geography*, Oxford, UK: Blackwell, pp. 77–94.

Martins, N.O. (2014), *The Cambridge Revival of Political Economy*, London: Routledge.

Martins, N.O. (2018), 'The social surplus approach: historical origins and present state', in T.-H. Jo, L. Chester, and C. D'Ippoliti (eds.), *The Routledge Handbook of Heterodox Economics*, London: Routledge, pp. 41–53.

Marx, K. (1857–8), *Pre-Capitalist Economic Formations*, translated by J. Cohen, London: Lawrence & Wishart, 1964.

Marx, K. (1859), *A Contribution to the Critique of Political Economy*, translated by S.W. Ryazanskaya, London: Lawrence & Wishart, 1971.

Marx, K. (1867), *Capital: A Critique of Political Economy, Volume I*, translated by B. Fowkes, Harmondsworth, UK: Penguin, 1976.

Marx, K., and Engels, F. (1846), *The German Ideology*, edited by C.J. Arthur, London: Lawrence & Wishart, 1970.

Mason, R. (2002), 'Conspicuous consumption in economic theory and thought', in E. Fullbrook (ed.), *Intersubjectivity in Economics: Agents and Structures*, London: Routledge, pp. 85–104.

Mathias, P. (2001), *The First Industrial Nation: An Economic History of Britain 1700–1914*, 2nd edn., London: Routledge.

Mauss, M. (1925), *The Gift: Forms and Functions of Exchange in Archaic Societies*, translated by I. Cunnison, London: Cohen & West, 1966.

May, C. (2002), *The Information Society: A Sceptical View*, Cambridge: Polity Press.

Mayhew, A. (1987), 'Culture: core concept under attack', *Journal of Economic Issues*, 21(2): 586–603.

Mayhew, A. (1994), 'Culture', in G.M. Hodgson, W.J. Samuels, and M.R. Tool (eds.), *The Elgar Companion to Institutional and Evolutionary Economics*, Vol. 1, Aldershot, UK: Edward Elgar, pp. 115–119.

Mayhew, A. (2002), 'All consumption is conspicuous', in E. Fullbrook (ed.), *Intersubjectivity in Economics: Agents and Structures*, London: Routledge, pp. 43–55.

McAfee, R.P., and McMillan, J. (1987), 'Auctions and bidding', *Journal of Economic Literature*, 25(2): 699–738.

McChesney, R.W., Foster, J.B., Stole, I.L., and Holleman, H. (2009), 'The sales effort and monopoly capital', *Monthly Review*, 60(11): 1–23.

McCulloh, I.A., Armstrong, H.L., and Johnson, A.N. (2013), *Social Network Analysis with Applications*, Hoboken, NJ: Wiley.

McDermott, J.F.M. (2015), 'Perfect competition, methodologically contemplated', *Journal of Post Keynesian Economics*, 37(4): 687–703.

McFall, L. (2004), *Advertising: A Cultural Economy*, London: Sage.

McGee, R.W. (1990), 'Thomas Aquinas: a pioneer in the field of law and economics', *Western State University Law Review*, 18(1): 471–438.

McMaster, R. (2001), 'A Veblenian-inspired critique of the "quasi-markets" concept', *International Journal of Social Economics*, 28(9): 710–724.

McMaster, R. (2002), 'The analysis of welfare state reform: why the "quasi-markets" narrative is descriptively inadequate and misleading', *Journal of Economic Issues*, 36(3): 769–794.

McMaster, R. (2008), 'The welfare state and privatization', in J.B. Davis, and W. Dolfsma (eds.), *The Elgar Companion to Social Economics*, Cheltenham, UK: Edward Elgar, pp. 519–536.

McMillan, J. (2002), *Reinventing the Bazaar: A Natural History of Markets*, New York: Norton.

McPake, B., Normand, C., and Smith, S. (2013), *Health Economics: An International Perspective*, 3rd edn., London: Routledge.

Means, G.C. (1935), *Industrial Prices and Their Relative Inflexibility*, Senate Document No. 13. 74th Congress, 1st sess., Washington, DC: Government Printing Office.

Means, G.C. (1939), *The Structure of the American Economy, Part I: Basic Characteristics*, Washington, DC: Government Printing Office.

Means, R., Richards, S., and Smith, R. (2008), *Community Care: Policy and Practice*, 4th edn., Basingstoke, UK: Palgrave Macmillan.

Meenaghan, T. (1995), 'The role of advertising in brand image development', *Journal of Product and Brand Management*, 4(4): 23–34.

Meikle, S. (1997), *Aristotle's Economic Thought*, Oxford, UK: Oxford University Press.

Ménard, C., and Shirley, M.M. (eds.) (2005), *Handbook of New Institutional Economics*, New York: Springer.

Menger, C. (1892), 'On the origin of money', *Economic Journal*, 2(6): 239–255.

Merton, R.K. (1948), 'The self-fulfilling prophecy', *Antioch Review*, 8(2): 193–210.

Merton, R.K. (1968a), *Social Theory and Social Structure*, Enlarged edn., New York: Free Press.

Merton, R.K. (1968b), 'The Matthew effect in science', *Science*, 159(3810): 56–63.

Metcalfe, J.S. (1998), *Evolutionary Economics and Creative Destruction*, London: Routledge.

Metcalfe, J.S. (2005), 'Evolutionary concepts in relation to evolutionary economics', in K. Dopfer (ed.), *The Evolutionary Foundation of Economics*, Cambridge, UK: Cambridge University Press, pp. 391–430.

Mews, C.J., and Abraham, I. (2007), 'Usury and just compensation: religious and financial ethics in historical perspective', *Journal of Business Ethics*, 72(1): 1–15.

Mey, H. (1972), *Field Theory: A Study of Its Applications in the Social Sciences*, New York: St Martin's Press.

Migone, A. (2007), 'Hedonistic consumerism: patterns of consumption in contemporary capitalism', *Review of Radical Political Economics*, 39(2): 173–200.

Miles, I. (1985), *Social Indicators for Human Development*, London: Frances Pinter.

Miles, S. (1998), *Consumerism as a Way of Life*, London: Sage.

Milgrom, P. (1989), 'Auctions and bidding: a primer', *Journal of Economic Perspectives*, 3(3): 3–22.

Miljkovic, D. (1999), 'The law of one price in international trade: a critical review', *Review of Agricultural Economics*, 21(1): 126–139.

Miller, D. (2002), 'Turning Callon the right way up', *Economy and Society*, 31(2): 218–233.

Miller, F.D. (1997), *Nature, Justice, and Rights in Aristotle's Politics*, Oxford, UK: Clarendon Press.

Milner, A.J. (1993), *Cultural Materialism*, Carlton, Australia: Melbourne University Press.

Milner, A.J. (2002), *Re-Imagining Cultural Studies: The Promise of Cultural Materialism*, London: Sage.

Milonakis, D., and Fine, B. (2009), *From Political Economy to Economics: Method, the Social and the Historical in the Evolution of Economic Theory*, London: Routledge.

Minsky, H.P. (1985), 'The financial instability hypothesis: a restatement', in P. Arestis, and T. Skouras (eds.), *Post Keynesian Economic Theory*, Brighton, UK: Wheatsheaf, pp. 24–55.

Minsky, H.P. (1994), 'The financial instability hypothesis', in P. Arestis, and M.C. Sawyer (eds.), *The Elgar Companion to Radical Political Economy*, Aldershot, UK: Edward Elgar, pp. 153–158.

Mirowski, P. (2002), *Machine Dreams: Economics Becomes a Cyborg Science*, Cambridge, UK: Cambridge University Press.

Mirowski, P. (2007), 'Markets come to bits: evolution, computation and markomata in economic science', *Journal of Economic Behavior and Organization*, 63(2): 209–242.

Mirowski, P., and Nik-Khah, E. (2007), 'Markets made flesh: performativity, and a problem in science studies, augmented with consideration of the FCC auctions', in D. MacKenzie, F. Muniesa, and L. Siu (eds.), *Do Economists Make Markets? On the Performativity of Economics*, Princeton, NJ: Princeton University Press, pp. 190–224.

Mises, L. von (1949), *Human Action: A Treatise on Economics*, New Haven, CT: Yale University Press.

Mises, L. von (1978), *The Ultimate Foundation of Economic Science: An Essay on Method*, 2nd edn., Kansas City, MO: Sheed Andrews and McMeel.

Mishkin, F.S. (2011), 'Over the cliff: from the subprime to the global financial crisis', *Journal of Economic Perspectives*, 25(1): 49–70.

Mishkin, F.S. (2016), *The Economics of Money, Banking and Financial Markets*, 11th edn., London: Pearson.

Mishra, R. (1981), *Society and Social Policy: Theoretical Perspectives on Welfare*, London: Macmillan.

Mishra, R. (1990), *The Welfare State in Capitalist Society*, Hemel Hempstead, UK: Harvester Wheatsheaf.

Miyazaki, H. (2007), 'Between arbitrage and speculation: an economy of belief and doubt', *Economy and Society*, 36(3): 396–415.

Moenjak, T. (2014), *Central Banking: Theory and Practice in Sustaining Monetary and Financial Stability*, Hoboken, NJ: Wiley.

Mohun, S. (2006), 'Distributive shares in the US economy, 1964–2001', *Cambridge Journal of Economics*, 30(3): 347–370.

Mokyr, J. (1998), 'The new economic history and the Industrial Revolution', in J. Mokyr (ed.), *The British Industrial Revolution: An Economic Perspective*, Boulder, CO: Westview Press, pp. 1–131.

Mokyr, J. (2008), 'The institutional origins of the Industrial Revolution', in E. Helpman (ed.), *Institutions and Economic Performance*, Cambridge, MA: Harvard University Press, pp. 64–119.

Molesworth, M., Nixon, E., and Scullion, R. (2009), 'Having, being and higher education: the marketisation of the university and the transformation of the student into consumer', *Teaching in Higher Education*, 14(3): 277–287.

Molesworth, M., Scullion, R., and Nixon, E. (eds.) (2011), *The Marketization of Higher Education and the Student as Consumer*, London: Routledge.

Mongiovi, G. (2012), 'Sraffian economics', in J.E. King (ed.), *The Elgar Companion to Post Keynesian Economics*, 2nd edn., Cheltenham: Edward Elgar, pp. 499–505.

Montes, L. (2004), *Adam Smith in Context: A Critical Reassessment of Some Central Components of His Thought*, Basingstoke, UK: Palgrave Macmillan.

Montgomery, J.D. (1991), 'Social networks and labor-market outcomes: toward an economic analysis', *American Economic Review*, 81(5): 1408–1418.

Mooij, M.K. de (2011), *Consumer Behavior and Culture: Consequences for Global Marketing and Advertising*, 2nd edn., London: Sage.

Mooij, M.K. de (2014), *Global Marketing and Advertising: Understanding Cultural Paradoxes*, 4th edn., London: Sage.

Moore, G. (2004), 'The Fair Trade movement: parameters, issues and future research', *Journal of Business Ethics*, 53(1–2): 73–86.

Morgan, J. (ed.) (2016), *What Is Neoclassical Economics? Debating the Origins, Meaning and Significance*, London: Routledge.

Morgan, K. (1997), 'The learning region: institutions, innovation and regional renewal', *Regional Studies*, 31(5): 491–503.

Morgan, R.M., and Hunt, S.D. (1994), 'The commitment-trust theory of relationship marketing', *Journal of Marketing*, 58(3): 20–38.

Morris, I., and Manning, J.G. (2005), 'The economic sociology of the ancient Mediterranean world', in N.J. Smelser, and R. Swedberg (eds.), *The Handbook of Economic Sociology*, 2nd edn., Princeton, NJ: Princeton University Press, pp. 131–159.

Mosini, V. (ed.) (2007), *Equilibrium in Economics: Scope and Limits*, London: Routledge.

Mousseau, M. (2000), 'Market prosperity, democratic consolidation, and democratic peace', *Journal of Conflict Resolution*, 44(4): 472–507.

Mouzelis, N. (1989), 'Restructuring structuration theory', *Sociological Review*, 37(4): 613–635.

Mouzelis, N. (1995), *Sociological Theory: What Went Wrong? Diagnosis and Remedies*, London: Routledge.

Munch, R., and Smelser, N. (1987), 'Relating the micro and macro', in J.C. Alexander, B. Giesen, R. Munch, and N. Smelser (eds.), *The Micro-Macro Link*, Berkeley, CA: University of California Press, pp. 356–387.

Muniesa, F. (2007), 'Market technologies and the pragmatics of prices', *Economy and Society*, 36(3): 377–395.

Myrdal, G. (1957), *Economic Theory and Underdeveloped Regions*, London: Duckworth.

Nagel, E. (1961), *The Structure of Science: Problems in the Logic of Scientific Explanation*, London: Routledge and Kegan Paul.

Narotzky, S. (1997), *New Directions in Economic Anthropology*, London: Pluto Press.

Natale, S.M., and Doran, C. (2012), 'Marketization of education: an ethical dilemma', *Journal of Business Ethics*, 105(2): 187–196.

Naylor, R.T. (2004), *Wages of Crime: Black Markets, Illegal Finance, and the Underworld Economy*, revised edn., Ithaca, NY: Cornell University Press.

Neal, L. (1994), *The Rise of Financial Capitalism: International Capital Markets in the Age of Reason*, Cambridge, UK: Cambridge University Press.

Neale, W.C. (1987), 'Institutions', *Journal of Economic Issues*, 21(3): 1177–1206.

Neale, W.C., and Mayhew, A. (1983), 'Polanyi, institutional economics, and economic anthropology', in S. Ortiz (ed.), *Economic Anthropology*, Lanham, MD: University Press of America, pp. 11–20.

Neary, J.P. (2001), 'Of hype and hyperbolas: introducing the new economic geography', *Journal of Economic Literature*, 39(2): 536–561.

Nee, V., and Ingram, P. (1998), 'Embeddedness and beyond: institutions, exchange, and social structure', in M. Brinton, and V. Nee (eds.), *The New Institutionalism in Sociology*, New York: Russell Sage Foundation, pp. 19–45.

Nell, E.J. (1980), 'The revival of political economy', in E.J. Nell (ed.), *Growth, Profits and Property: Essays in the Revival of Political Economy*, Cambridge, UK: Cambridge University Press, pp. 19–31.

Nell, E.J. (1991), 'Capitalism, socialism and effective demand', in E.J. Nell, and W. Semmler (eds.), *Nicholas Kaldor and Mainstream Economics*, London: Macmillan, pp. 577–611.

Nell, E.J. (1992), *Transformational Growth and Effective Demand: Economics After the Capital Critique*, London: Macmillan.

Nell, E.J. (1998), *The General Theory of Transformational Growth: Keynes After Sraffa*, Cambridge, UK: Cambridge University Press.

Nelson, P. (1974), 'Advertising as information', *Journal of Political Economy*, 82(4): 729–754.

Nelson, R.R. et al. (eds.) (2018), *Modern Evolutionary Economics: An Overview*, Cambridge, UK: Cambridge University Press.

Nelson, R.R., and Winter, S.G. (1982), *An Evolutionary Theory of Economic Change*, Cambridge, MA: Harvard University Press.

Nelson, R.R., and Winter, S.G. (2002), 'Evolutionary theorizing in economics', *Journal of Economic Perspectives*, 16(2): 23–46.

Newell, F. (2001), *Loyalty.com: Customer Relationship Management in the New Era of Internet Marketing*, New York: McGraw-Hill.

Newholm, T., and Shaw, D. (2007), 'Studying the ethical consumer: a review of research', *Journal of Consumer Behaviour*, 6(5): 253–270.

Nicholls, A. (2010), 'Fair Trade: towards an economics of virtue', *Journal of Business Ethics*, 92(S2): 241–255.

Nicholls, A., and Opal, C. (2005), *Fair Trade: Market-Driven Ethical Consumption*, London: Sage.

Nielsen, P. (2002), 'Reflections on critical realism in political economy', *Cambridge Journal of Economics*, 26(6): 727–738.

Nik-Khah, E. (2006), 'What the FCC auctions can tell us about the performativity thesis', *Economic Sociology - European Electronic Newsletter*, 7(2): 15–21.

Nik-Khah, E. (2008), 'A tale of two auctions', *Journal of Institutional Economics*, 4(1): 73–97.

Nolan, P. (1994), 'Fordism and post-Fordism', in P. Arestis, and M.C. Sawyer (eds.), *The Elgar Companion to Radical Political Economy*, Aldershot, UK: Edward Elgar, pp. 162–166.

Noonan, J.T. (1957), *The Scholastic Analysis of Usury*, Cambridge, MA: Harvard University Press.

Nooteboom, B. (2002), *Trust: Forms, Foundations, Functions, Failures and Figures*, Cheltenham, UK: Edward Elgar.

Nooteboom, B. (2009), 'Trust', in J. Peil, and I. Van Staveren (eds.), *Handbook of Economics and Ethics*, Cheltenham, UK: Edward Elgar, pp. 547–554.

Nooteboom, B. (2014), *How Markets Work and Fail, and What to Make of Them*, Cheltenham, UK: Edward Elgar.

North, D.C., and Thomas, R.P. (1977), 'The first economic revolution', *Economic History Review*, 30(2): 229–241.

Nove, A. (1991), *The Economics of Feasible Socialism Revisited*, 2nd edn., London: Harper Collins.

O'Driscoll, G.P., and Rizzo, M.J. (1996), *The Economics of Time and Ignorance*, London: Routledge.

O'Connor, J. (2002), *The Fiscal Crisis of the State*, 2nd edn., New Brunswick, NJ: Transaction Publishers.

O'Leary, B. (1989), *The Asiatic Mode of Production: Oriental Despotism, Historical Materialism and Indian History*, Oxford, UK: Basil Blackwell.

O'Neill, J. (1998), *The Market: Ethics, Knowledge and Politics*, London: Routledge.

O'Neill, J. (2009), 'Market', in J. Peil, and I. Van Staveren (eds.), *Handbook of Economics and Ethics*, Cheltenham, UK: Edward Elgar, pp. 317–324.

Obstfeld, M., and Taylor, A.M. (2004), 'Globalization and capital markets', in M.D. Bordo, A.M. Taylor, and J.G. Williamson (eds.), *Globalization in Historical Perspective*, Chicago, IL: University of Chicago Press, pp. 121–187.

Offe, C. (1984), *Contradictions of the Welfare State*, edited by. J. Keane, London: Hutchinson.

Offer, A. (1997), 'Between the gift and the market: the economy of regard', *Economic History Review*, 50(3): 450–476.

Ollman, B. (ed.) (1998), *Market Socialism: The Debate Among Socialists*, London: Routledge.

Oly Ndubisi, N. (2007), 'Relationship marketing and customer loyalty', *Marketing Intelligence and Planning*, 25(1): 98–106.

Orhangazi, Ö. (2008), *Financialization and the US Economy*, Cheltenham, UK: Edward Elgar.

Oswald, L.R. (2012), *Marketing Semiotics: Signs, Strategies, and Brand Value*, Oxford, UK: Oxford University Press.

Outhwaite, W. (1986), *Understanding Social Life: The Method Called Verstehen*, 2nd edn., Lewes: Jean Stroud.

Overton, M. (1996), *Agricultural Revolution in England: The Transformation of the Agrarian Economy 1500–1850*, Cambridge, UK: Cambridge University Press.

Oviedo, A.M., Thomas, M.R., and Karakurum-Özmedir, K. (2009), *Economic Informality: Causes, Costs, and Policies – A Literature Survey*, Washington, DC: World Bank.

Pack, S.J. (2008), 'Aristotle's difficult relationship with modern economic theory', *Foundations of Science*, 13(3–4): 265–280.

Packard, V. (1991), *The Hidden Persuaders*, Harmondsworth, UK: Penguin.

Palley, T.I. (2013), *Financialization: The Economics of Finance Capital Domination*, Basingstoke, UK: Palgrave Macmillan.

Parsons, S.D. (2003), *Money, Time and Rationality in Max Weber: Austrian Connections*, London: Routledge.

Parsons, T. (1949), *The Structure of Social Action*, 2nd edn., Glencoe, IL: Free Press.

Parsons, T. (1951), *The Social System*, New York: Free Press.

Patsiaouras, G., and Fitchett, J.A. (2012), 'The evolution of conspicuous consumption', *Journal of Historical Research in Marketing*, 4(1): 154–176.

Payne, A., and Frow, P. (2005), 'A strategic framework for customer relationship management', *Journal of Marketing*, 69(4): 167–176.

Peacock, M.S. (2013), *Introducing Money*, London: Routledge.

Peacock, M.S. (2017), 'The ontology of money', *Cambridge Journal of Economics*, 41(5): 1471–1487.

Peck, J., and Theodore, N. (2007), 'Variegated capitalism', *Progress in Human Geography*, 31(6): 731–772.

Peck, J., and Tickell, A. (2002), 'Neoliberalizing space', *Antipode*, 34(3): 380–404.

Pellegrino, E.D. (1999), 'The commodification of medical and health care: the moral consequences of a paradigm shift from a professional to a market ethic', *Journal of Medicine and Philosophy*, 24(3): 243–266.

Penrose, E. (1959), *The Theory of the Growth of the Firm*, Oxford, UK: Blackwell.

Perry, M. (2002), *Marxism and History*, Basingstoke, UK: Palgrave Macmillan.

Persky, J. (1995), 'The ethology of homo economicus', *Journal of Economic Perspectives*, 9(2): 221–231.

Persky, J. (2007), 'From usury to interest', *Journal of Economic Perspectives*, 21(1): 227–236.

Pheby, J. (1988), *Methodology and Economics: A Critical Introduction*, London: Macmillan.

Pianta, M. (2014), 'Slowing trade: global activism against trade liberalization', *Global Policy*, 5(2): 214–221.

Picchio, A. (1992), *Social Reproduction: the Political Economy of the Labour Market*, Cambridge, UK: Cambridge University Press.

Pierson, C. (2006), *Beyond the Welfare State? The New Political Economy of Welfare*, 3rd edn., Cambridge, UK: Polity Press.

Pietrykowski, B. (2009), *The Political Economy of Consumer Behavior: Contesting Consumption*, London: Routledge.

Piketty, T., and Saez, E. (2003), 'Income inequality in the United States, 1913–1998', *Quarterly Journal of Economics*, 118(1): 1–39.

Pilbeam, K. (2018), *Finance and Financial Markets*, 4th edn., Basingstoke, UK: Palgrave Macmillan.

Pirenne, H. (1925), *Medieval Cities: Their Origins and the Revival of Trade*, translated by F.D. Halsey, Princeton, NJ: Princeton University Press.

Pirenne, H. (1936), *Economic and Social History of Medieval Europe*, translated by I.E. Clegg, London: Routledge and Kegan Paul.

Podolny, J.M., and Page, K.L. (1998), 'Network forms of organization', *Annual Review of Sociology*, 24: 57–76.

Polachek, S.W. (1980), 'Conflict and trade', *Journal of Conflict Resolution*, 24(1): 55–78.

Polanyi, K. (1944), *The Great Transformation: The Political and Economic Origins of Our Time*, New York: Farrar & Rinehart.

Polanyi, K. (1947), 'On belief in economic determinism', *Sociological Review*, 39(1): 96–102.

Polanyi, K. (1957), 'The economy as instituted process', in K. Polanyi, C.M. Arensberg, and H.W. Pearson (eds.), *Trade and Market in the Early Empires: Economies in History and Theory*, Glencoe, IL: Free Press, pp. 243–270.

Polanyi, K. (1963), 'Ports of trade in early societies', *Journal of Economic History*, 23(1): 30–45.

Polanyi, K. (1977), 'The economistic fallacy', *Review, Fernand Braudel Center*, 1(1): 9–18.

Polanyi, K., Arensberg, C.M., and Pearson, H.W. (eds.) (1957), *Trade and Market in the Early Empires: Economies in History and Theory*, Glencoe, IL: Free Press.

Polanyi-Levitt, K. (2013), 'The great financialization', in K. Polanyi-Levitt, *From the Great Transformation to the Great Financialization*, London: Zed Books, pp. 181–192.

Pollard, S. (1963), 'Factory discipline in the Industrial Revolution', *Economic History Review*, 16(2): 254–271.

Pollitt, C., and Bouckaert, G. (2011), *Public Management Reform: A Comparative Analysis – New Public Management, Governance, and the Neo-Weberian State*, 3rd edn., Oxford, UK: Oxford University Press.

Porpora, D.V. (1989), 'Four concepts of social structure ', *Journal for the Theory of Social Behaviour*, 19(2): 195–211.

Postan, M.M. (1972), *The Medieval Economy and Society: An Economic History of Britain in the Middle Ages*, London: Weidenfeld & Nicolson.

Postan, M.M. (1973), *Medieval Trade and Finance*, Cambridge, UK: Cambridge University Press.

Potts, J. (2000), *The New Evolutionary Microeconomics: Complexity, Competence and Adaptive Behaviour*, Cheltenham, UK: Edward Elgar.

Powell, W.W. (1990), 'Neither market nor hierarchy: network forms of organization', *Research in Organizational Behavior*, 12: 295–336.

Power, M. (2004), 'Social provisioning as a starting point for feminist economics', *Feminist Economics*, 10(3): 3–19.

Prasch, R.E. (1995), 'Toward a "general theory" of market exchange', *Journal of Economic Issues*, 29(3): 807–828.

Prasch, R.E. (1996), 'Reassessing the theory of comparative advantage', *Review of Political Economy*, 8(1): 37–56.

Prasch, R.E. (2004), 'How is labor distinct from broccoli? Some unique characteristics of labor and their importance for economic analysis and policy', in D.P. Champlin, and J.T. Knoedler (eds.), *The Institutionalist Tradition in Labor Economics*, Armonk, NY: M.E. Sharpe, pp. 146–158.

Prasch, R.E. (2008), *How Markets Work: Supply, Demand and the 'Real World'*, Cheltenham, UK: Edward Elgar.

Pratt, A.C. (2004), 'The cultural economy: a call for spatialized "production of culture" perspectives', *International Journal of Cultural Studies*, 7(1): 117–128.

Pratten, S. (ed.) (2015), *Social Ontology and Modern Economics*, London: Routledge.

Prebisch, R. (1950), *The Economic Development of Latin America and Its Principal Problems*, New York: United Nations.

Preda, A. (2007), 'The sociological approach to financial markets', *Journal of Economic Surveys*, 21(3): 506–533.

Prell, C. (2012), *Social Network Analysis: History, Theory and Methodology*, London: Sage.

Prychitko, D.L. (ed.) (1995), *Individuals, Institutions, Interpretations: Hermeneutics Applied to Economics*, Aldershot, UK: Avebury.

Prychitko, D.L., and Storr, V.H. (2007), 'Communicative action and the radical constitution: the Habermasian challenge to Hayek, Mises and their descendants', *Cambridge Journal of Economics*, 31(2): 255–274.

Pryke, M., and Du Gay, P. (2007), 'Take an issue: cultural economy and finance', *Economy and Society*, 36(3): 339–354.

Purdy, D. (1988), *Social Power and the Labour Market: A Radical Approach to Labour Economics*, London: Macmillan.

Quigley, J.M. (2003), 'Transaction costs and housing markets', in T. O'Sullivan, and K. Gibb (eds.), *Housing Economics and Public Policy*, Oxford, UK: Blackwell, pp. 56–66.

Quinn, K., and Green, T.R. (1998), 'Hermeneutics and libertarianism: an odd couple', *Critical Review*, 12(3): 207–223.

Radin, M.J. (1989), 'Justice and the market domain', in J.W. Chapman, and J.R. Pennock (eds.), *Markets and Justice*, New York: New York University Press, pp. 165–197.

Radin, M.J. (1996), *Contested Commodities*, Cambridge, MA: Harvard University Press.

Rapaczynski, A. (1996), 'The roles of the state and the market in establishing property rights', *Journal of Economic Perspectives*, 10(2): 87–103.

Rauch, J.E. (2001), 'Business and social networks in international trade', *Journal of Economic Literature*, 39(4): 1177–1203.

Ravasi, D., and Rindova, V.P. (2008), 'Symbolic value creation', in D. Barry, and H. Hansen (eds.), *The Sage Handbook of New Approaches in Management and Organization*, London: Sage, pp. 270–284.

Ravenhill, J. (ed.) (2017), *Global Political Economy*, 5th edn., Oxford, UK: Oxford University Press.

Raynolds, L.T. (2012), 'Fair trade: social regulation in global food markets', *Journal of Rural Studies*, 28(3): 276–287.

Raynolds, L.T., and Bennett, E.A. (eds.) (2015), *Handbook of Research on Fair Trade*, Cheltenham, UK: Edward Elgar.

Raynolds, L.T., Murray, D.L., and Wilkinson, J. (eds.) (2007), *Fair Trade: The Challenges of Transforming Globalization*, London: Routledge.

Reagans, R., and McEvily, B. (2003), 'Network structure and knowledge transfer: the effects of cohesion and range', *Administrative Science Quarterly*, 48(2): 240–267.

Rebitzer, J.B. (1993), 'Radical political economy and the economics of labor markets', *Journal of Economic Literature*, 31(3): 1394–1434.

Redmond, W.H. (1989), 'Domesticated markets as barriers to new competition', *Journal of Macromarketing*, 9(1): 35–41.

Redmond, W.H. (2013), 'Three modes of competition in the marketplace', *American Journal of Economics and Sociology*, 72(2): 423–446.

Reed, C.M. (2003), *Maritime Traders in the Ancient Greek World*, Cambridge, UK: Cambridge University Press.

Reed, M.I. (1997), 'In praise of duality and dualism: rethinking agency and structure in organizational analysis', *Organization Studies*, 18(1): 21–42.

Reinert, E.S. (2007), *How Rich Countries Got Rich and Why Poor Countries Stay Poor*, London: Constable.

Reinert, H., and Reinert, E.S. (2006), 'Creative destruction in economics: Nietzsche, Sombart, Schumpeter', in J.G. Backhaus, and W. Drechsler (eds.), *Friedrich Nietzsche (1844–1900): Economy and Society*, Boston, MA: Springer, pp. 55–85.

Richardson, G. (2001), 'A tale of two theories: monopolies and craft guilds in medieval England and modern imagination', *Journal of the History of Economic Thought*, 23(2): 217–242.

Richardson, G. (2004), 'Guilds, laws, and markets for manufactured merchandise in late-medieval England', *Explorations in Economic History*, 41(1): 1–25.

Richardson, G.B. (1972), 'The organisation of industry', *Economic Journal*, 82(327): 883–896.

Richardson, J.D. (1978), 'Some empirical evidence on commodity arbitrage and the law of one price', *Journal of International Economics*, 8(2): 341–351.

Rigby, S.H. (1998), *Marxism and History: A Critical Introduction*, 2nd edn., Manchester, UK: Manchester University Press.

Rigney, D. (2010), *The Matthew Effect: How Advantage Begets Further Advantage*, New York: Columbia University Press.

Riley, J. (2016), 'The definition of the contract of employment and its differentiation from other contracts and other work relations', in M.R. Freedland (ed.), *The Contract of Employment*, Oxford, UK: Oxford University Press, pp. 321–340.

Rima, I.H. (2009), *Development of Economic Analysis*, 7th edn., London: Routledge.

Rizvi, S.A.T. (1994), 'The microfoundations project in general equilibrium theory', *Cambridge Journal of Economics*, 18(4): 357–377.

Robbins, L. (1932), *An Essay on the Nature and Significance of Economic Science*, London: Macmillan.

Roberts, J. (2003), 'The manufacture of corporate social responsibility: constructing corporate sensibility', *Organization*, 10(2): 249–265.

Roberts, J.M. (2012), 'Poststructuralism against poststructuralism: actor-network theory, organizations and economic markets', *European Journal of Social Theory*, 15(1): 35–53.

Robinson, J. (1933), *The Economics of Imperfect Competition*, London: Macmillan.

Robinson, J. (1953), 'Imperfect competition revisited', *Economic Journal*, 63(251): 579–593.

Robinson, J. (1977), 'Michał Kalecki on the economics of capitalism', *Oxford Bulletin of Economics and Statistics*, 39(1): 7–17.

Robinson, J. (1978), 'Keynes and Ricardo', *Journal of Post Keynesian Economics*, 1(1): 12–18.

Robinson, J. (1980), 'Time in economic theory', *Kyklos*, 33(2): 219–229.

Roosevelt, F., and Belkin, D. (eds.) (1994), *Why Market Socialism? Voices from Dissent*, Armonk, NY: M.E. Sharpe.

Rosenbaum, E.F. (2000), 'What is a market? On the methodology of a contested concept', *Review of Social Economy*, 58(4): 455–482.

Rosser, J.B. (1999), 'On the complexities of complex economic dynamics', *Journal of Economic Perspectives*, 13(4): 169–192.

Rotheim, R.J. (ed.) (1998), *New Keynesian Economics/Post Keynesian Alternatives*, London: Routledge.

Rousseas, S. (1989), 'Anti systems', *Journal of Post Keynesian Economics*, 11(3): 385–398.

Rousseas, S. (1998), *Post Keynesian Monetary Economics*, 3rd edn., London: Macmillan.

Rowe, J.K. (2005), 'Corporate social responsibility as business strategy', in R.D. Lipschutz, and J.K. Rowe (eds.), *Globalization, Governmentality and Global Politics: Regulation for the Rest of Us?*, London: Routledge, pp. 122–160.

Rowlands, M., Larsen, M., and Kristiansen, K. (eds.) (1987), *Centre and Periphery in the Ancient World*, Cambridge, UK: Cambridge University Press.

Rubery, J., Ward, K., Grimshaw, D., and Beynon, H. (2005), 'Working time, industrial relations and the employment relationship', *Time and Society*, 14(1): 89–111.

Ruffin, R.J. (2002), 'David Ricardo's discovery of comparative advantage', *History of Political Economy*, 34(4): 727–748.

Ruggles, R. (1993), 'National income accounting: concepts and measurement. Economic theory and practice', *Economic Notes by Monte Dei Paschi di Siena*, 22(2): 235–264.

Ruskin, J. (1862), 'Unto this last: four essays on the first principles of political economy', in C. Wilmer (ed.), *John Ruskin: Unto This Last and Other Writings*, Harmondsworth: Penguin, 1985, pp. 155–228.

Ruskin, J. (1863), 'Munera Pulveris: Six Essays on the Elements of Political Economy', in E.T. Cook, and A. Wedderburn (eds.), *The Works of John Ruskin*, Vol. XVII, London: George Allen, 1905, pp. 115–293.

Rutherford, M.H. (1983), 'J.R. Commons's institutional economics', *Journal of Economic Issues*, 17(3): 721–744.

Rutherford, M.H. (1994), *Institutions in Economics: The Old and the New Institutionalism*, Cambridge, UK: Cambridge University Press.

Rutherford, M.H. (1997), 'American institutionalism and the history of economics', *Journal of the History of Economic Thought*, 19(2): 178–195.

Rutherford, M.H. (2001), 'Institutional economics: then and now', *Journal of Economic Perspectives*, 15(3): 173–194.

Ryan, A. (1984), *Property and Political Theory*, Oxford, UK: Blackwell.

Ryan, C.C. (1981), 'The fiends of commerce: Romantic and Marxist criticisms of classical political economy', *History of Political Economy*, 13(1): 80–94.

Sahlins, M.D. (1965), 'On the sociology of primitive exchange', in M. Banton (ed.), *The Relevance of Models for Social Anthropology*, London: Tavistock, pp. 139–236.

Sahlins, M.D. (1974), *Stone Age Economics*, London: Tavistock.

Sahlins, M.D. (2000), 'The original affluent society', in S.K. Sanderson (ed.), *Sociological Worlds: Comparative and Historical Readings on Society*, Chicago, IL: Fitzroy Dearborn, pp. 2–14.

Salamon, L.M. (1993), 'The marketization of welfare: changing non-profit and for-profit roles in the American welfare state', *Social Service Review*, 67(1): 16–39.

Sallaz, J.J. (2013), *Labor, Economy, and Society*, Cambridge, UK: Polity Press.

Salvadori, N., and Signorino, R. (2013), 'The classical notion of competition revisited', *History of Political Economy*, 45(1): 149–175.

Samuels, W.J. (1994), 'Property', in G.M. Hodgson, W.J. Samuels, and M.R. Tool (eds.), *The Elgar Companion to Institutional and Evolutionary Economics*, Vol. 1, Aldershot, UK: Edward Elgar, pp. 180–184.

Sandel, M.J. (2012), *What Money Can't Buy: The Moral Limits to Markets*, London: Allen Lane.

Sandel, M.J. (2013), 'Market reasoning as moral reasoning: why economists should re-engage with political philosophy', *Journal of Economic Perspectives*, 27(4): 121–140.

Sanders, M.L., and McClellan, J.G. (2014), 'Being business-like while pursuing a social mission: acknowledging the inherent tensions in US non-profit organizing', *Organization*, 21(1): 68–89.

Sandler, T., and Hartley, K. (1995), *The Economics of Defense*, Cambridge, UK: Cambridge University Press.

Santos, A.C. (2011), 'Behavioural and experimental economics: are they really transforming economics?', *Cambridge Journal of Economics*, 35(4): 705–728.

Santos, A.C., and Rodrigues, J. (2009), 'Economics as social engineering? Questioning the performativity thesis', *Cambridge Journal of Economics*, 33(5): 985–1000.

Sassen, S. (2005), 'The embeddedness of electronic markets: the case of global capital markets', in K. Knorr Cetina, and A. Preda (eds.), *The Sociology of Financial Markets*, Oxford, UK: Oxford University Press, pp. 17–37.

Satz, D. (2010), *Why Some Things Should Not Be for Sale: The Moral Limits of Markets*, Oxford, UK: Oxford University Press.

Sautet, F. (2010), 'The competitive market is a process of entrepreneurial discovery', in P.J. Boettke (ed.), *Handbook on Contemporary Austrian Economics*, Cheltenham, UK: Edward Elgar, pp. 87–108.

Sautet, F. (2015), 'Market theory and the price system', in P.J. Boettke, and C.J. Coyne (eds.), *The Oxford Handbook of Austrian Economics*, Oxford, UK: Oxford University Press, pp. 65–93.

Sawyer, M.C. (1985a), *The Economics of Industries and Firms: Theories, Evidence and Policy*, 2nd edn., London: Croom Helm.

Sawyer, M.C. (1985b), *The Economics of Michał Kalecki*, London: Macmillan.

Sawyer, M.C. (1988), 'Theories of monopoly capitalism', *Journal of Economic Surveys*, 2(1): 47–76.

Sawyer, M.C. (1989), *The Challenge of Radical Political Economy: An Introduction to the Alternatives to Neo-classical Economics*, Hemel Hempstead, UK: Harvester Wheatsheaf.

Sawyer, M.C. (1993), 'The nature and role of the market', in C.N. Pitelis (ed.), *Transaction Costs, Markets and Hierarchies*, Oxford, UK: Blackwell, pp. 20–40.

Sawyer, R.K. (2005), *Social Emergence: Societies as Complex Systems*, Cambridge, UK: Cambridge University Press.

Sayer, A. (1982), 'Explanation in economic geography: abstraction versus generalization', *Progress in Human Geography*, 6(1): 68–88.

Sayer, A. (1995), *Radical Political Economy: A Critique*, Oxford, UK: Blackwell.

Sayer, A. (1997), 'Critical realism and the limits to critical social science', *Journal for the Theory of Social Behaviour*, 27(4): 473–488.

Sayer, A. (2000), 'Moral economy and political economy', *Studies in Political Economy*, 61(1): 79–103.

Sayer, A. (2003), '(De-)commodification, consumer culture, and moral economy', *Environment and Planning D: Society and Space*, 21(3): 341–357.

Sayer, A. (2007), 'Moral economy as critique', *New Political Economy*, 12(2): 261–270.

Sayer, A. (2010), *Method in Social Science: A Realist Approach*, revised 2nd edn., London: Routledge.

Sayre, R., and Löwy, M. (1984), 'Figures of Romantic anti-capitalism', *New German Critique*, 32(32): 42–92.

Schaps, D.M. (2004), *The Invention of Coinage and the Monetization of Ancient Greece*, Ann Arbor, MI: University of Michigan Press.

Scherer, F.M. (1980), *Industrial Market Structure and Economic Performance*, 2nd edn., Boston, MA: Houghton Mifflin.

Schmitt, B. (1999), 'Experiential marketing', *Journal of Marketing Management*, 15 (1–3): 53–67.

Schmitthoff, M. (1939), 'The origin of the joint-stock company', *University of Toronto Law Journal*, 3(1): 74–96.

Schneider, F., and Enste, D.H. (2000), 'Shadow economies: size, causes, and consequences', *Journal of Economic Literature*, 38(1): 77–114.

Schneider, F., and Enste, D.H. (2013), *The Shadow Economy: An International Survey*, 2nd edn., Cambridge, UK: Cambridge University Press.

Schneider, H.K. (1974), *Economic Man: The Anthropology of Economics*, New York: Free Press.

Schneider, J. (1977), 'Was there a pre-capitalist world system?', *Peasant Studies*, 6(1): 20–29.

Schor, J.B. (2016), 'Debating the sharing economy', *Journal of Self-Governance and Management Economics*, 4(3): 7–22.

Schumpeter, J.A. (1954), *History of Economic Analysis*, London: Allen & Unwin.

Schumpeter, J.A. (1987), *Capitalism, Socialism and Democracy*, 6th edn., London: Unwin Hyman.

Schweickart, D. (2011), *After Capitalism*, 2nd edn., Lanham, MD: Rowman & Littlefield.

Scott, A.J., and Storper, M. (2003), 'Regions, globalization, development', *Journal of Regional Studies*, 37(6-7): 579–593.

Scott, J. (2017), *Social Network Analysis*, 4th edn., London: Sage.

Screpanti, E. (1999), 'Capitalist forms and the essence of capitalism', *Review of International Political Economy*, 6(1): 1–26.

Screpanti, E., and Zamagni, S. (2005), *An Outline of the History of Economic Thought*, 2nd edn., Oxford, UK: Oxford University Press.

Sebastiani, M. (ed.) (1989), *Kalecki's Relevance Today*, New York: St Martin's Press.

Sent, E.-M. (2004), 'Behavioral economics: how psychology made its (limited) way back into economics', *History of Political Economy*, 36(4): 735–760.

Setterfield, M. (1995), 'Historical time and economic theory', *Review of Political Economy*, 7(1): 1–27.

Setterfield, M. (1998), 'History versus equilibrium: Nicholas Kaldor on historical time and economic theory', *Cambridge Journal of Economics*, 22(5): 521–537.

Shackle, G.L.S. (1972), *Epistemics and Economics: A Critique of Economic Doctrines*, Cambridge, UK: Cambridge University Press.

Shaikh, A.M., and Tonak, E.A. (1996), *Measuring the Wealth of Nations: the Political Economy of National Accounts*, Cambridge, UK: Cambridge University Press.

Shamir, R. (2005), 'Mind the gap: the commodification of corporate social responsibility', *Symbolic Interaction*, 28(2): 229–253.

Shamir, R. (2008), 'The age of responsibilization: on market-embedded morality', *Economy and Society*, 37(1): 1–19.

Shand, A.H. (1984), *The Capitalist Alternative: An Introduction to Neo-Austrian Economics*, New York: New York University Press.

Shapiro, N. (2005), 'Competition and aggregate demand', *Journal of Post Keynesian Economics*, 27(3): 541–549.

Shatzmiller, J. (1990), *Shylock Reconsidered: Jews, Moneylending, and Medieval Society*, Berkeley, CA: University of California Press.

Shleifer, A. (2000), *Inefficient Markets: An Introduction to Behavioural Finance*, Oxford, UK: Oxford University Press.

Siddiqui, K. (2015), 'Trade liberalization and economic development: a critical review', *International Journal of Political Economy*, 44(3): 228–247.

Sillitoe, P. (2006), 'Why spheres of exchange?', *Ethnology*, 45(1): 1–23.

Silver, M. (1994), *Economic Structures of Antiquity*, Westport, CT: Greenwood Press.

Simmel, G. (1907), *The Philosophy of Money*, 2nd edn., translated by T. Bottomore, and D. Frisby, London: Routledge, 1990.

Simon, H.A. (1951), 'A formal theory of the employment relationship', *Econometrica*, 19(3): 293–305.

Simon, H.A. (1959), 'Theories of decision-making in economics and behavioural science', *American Economic Review*, 49(3): 253–283.

Simon, H.A. (1986), 'Rationality in psychology and economics', *Journal of Business*, 59(S4): S209–S224.

Simon, H.A. (1997), *Administrative Behavior: A Study of Decision-Making Processes in Administrative Organizations*, 4th edn., New York: Free Press.

Singer, H.W. (1950), 'The distribution of gains between investing and borrowing countries', *American Economic Review*, 40(2): 473–485.

Singer, H.W. (1975), 'The distribution of gains from trade and investment – revisited', *Journal of Development Studies*, 11(4): 376–382.

Singh, A. (2011), 'Comparative advantage, industrial policy and the World Bank: back to first principles', *Policy Studies*, 32(4): 447–460.

Singh, S. (2016), 'What is relational structure? Introducing history to the debates on the relation between fields and social networks', *Sociological Theory*, 34(2): 128–150.

Sismondi, J.C.L. Simonde de (1827), *New Principles of Political Economy*, translated by R. Hyse, London: Transaction Publishers, 1991.

Sison, A.J.G., and Fontrodona, J. (2012), 'The common good of the firm in the Aristotelian-Thomist tradition', *Business Ethics Quarterly*, 22(2): 211–246.

Slater, D.R. (2002a), 'Capturing markets from the economists', in P. du Gay, and M. Pryke (eds.), *Cultural Economy: Cultural Analysis and Commercial Life*, London: Sage, pp. 59–77.

Slater, D.R. (2002b), 'From calculation to alienation: disentangling economic abstractions', *Economy and Society*, 31(2): 234–249.

Slater, D.R. (2002c), 'Markets, materiality and the "new economy"', in S.J. Metcalfe, and A. Warde (eds.), *Market Relations and the Competitive Process*, Manchester, UK: Manchester University Press, pp. 95–113.

Slater, D.R. (2005), 'The sociology of consumption and lifestyle', in C. Calhoun, C. Rojek, and B. Turner (eds.), *The Sage Handbook of Sociology*, London: Sage, pp. 174–187.

Slater, D.R., and Tonkiss, F. (2001), *Market Society: Markets and Modern Social Theory*, Cambridge, UK: Polity Press.

Smith, A. (1759), *The Theory of Moral Sentiments*, edited by D.D. Raphael, and A.L. Macfie, Oxford, UK: Oxford University Press, 1976.

Smith, A. (1776), *An Inquiry into the Nature and Causes of the Wealth of Nations*, edited by R.H. Campbell, and A.S. Skinner, Oxford, UK: Oxford University Press, 1976.

Smith, B.D. (1995), *The Emergence of Agriculture*, New York: Scientific American Library.

Smith, C. (2016), 'Rediscovery of the labour process', in S. Edgell, H. Gottfried, and E. Granter (eds.), *The Sage Handbook of the Sociology of Work and Employment*, London: Sage, pp. 205–224.

Smith, C.W. (1993), 'Auctions: from Walras to the real world', in R. Swedberg (ed.), *Explorations in Economic Sociology*, New York: Russell Sage Foundation, pp. 176–192.

Smith, R.L. (2009), *Premodern Trade in World History*, London: Routledge.

Smith, V.L. (1989), 'Auctions', in J. Eatwell, M. Milgate, and P. Newman (eds.), *Allocation, Information and Markets*, London: Macmillan, pp. 39–53.

Smith-Doerr, L., and Powell, W.W. (2005), 'Networks and economic life', in N.J. Smelser, and R. Swedberg (eds.), *The Handbook of Economic Sociology*, 2nd edn., Princeton, NJ: Princeton University Press, pp. 379–402.

Southgate, G.W. (1970), *English Economic History*, London: Dent.

Spencer, J. (2009), 'Formalism and substantivism', in A. Barnard, and J. Spencer (eds.), *The Routledge Encyclopedia of Social and Cultural Anthropology*, 2nd edn., London: Routledge, p. 142.

Spillman, L. (1999), 'Enriching exchange: cultural dimensions of markets', *American Journal of Economics and Sociology*, 58(4): 1047–1071.

Spooner, B. (ed.) (1972), *Population Growth: Anthropological Implications*, Cambridge, MA: MIT Press.

Spufford, P. (2002), *Power and Profit: The Merchant in Medieval Europe*, London: Thames & Hudson.

Sraffa, P. (1960), *Production of Commodities by Means of Commodities: Prelude to a Critique of Economic Theory*, Cambridge, UK: Cambridge University Press.

Stanfield, J.R. (1980), 'The institutional economics of Karl Polanyi', *Journal of Economic Issues*, 14(3): 593–614.

Stanfield, J.R. (1986), *The Economic Thought of Karl Polanyi*, London: Macmillan.

Stanfield, J.R., and Stanfield, J.B. (1980), 'Consumption in contemporary capitalism: the backward art of living', *Journal of Economic Issues*, 14(2): 437–451.

Starr, M.A. (2009), 'The social economics of ethical consumption: theoretical considerations and empirical evidence', *Journal of Socio-Economics*, 38(6): 916–925.

Starr, M.A. (2016), 'The economics of ethical consumption', in D. Shaw, M. Carrington, and A. Chatzidakis (eds.), *Ethics and Morality in Consumption: Interdisciplinary Perspectives*, London: Routledge, pp. 42–56.

Staveren, I. van (2001), *The Values of Economics: an Aristotelian Perspective*, London: Routledge.

Staveren, I. van (2009), 'Virtue ethics', in J. Peil, and I. van Staveren (eds.), *Handbook of Economics and Ethics*, Cheltenham, UK: Edward Elgar, pp. 570–577.

Stearns, L.B., and Mizruchi, M.S. (2005), 'Banking and financial markets', in N.J. Smelser, and R. Swedberg (eds.), *The Handbook of Economic Sociology*, 2nd edn., Princeton, NJ: Princeton University Press, pp. 284–306.

Stearns, P.N. (2006), *Consumerism in World History: The Global Transformation of Desire*, 2nd edn., London: Routledge.

Stehr, N. (2008), *Moral Markets: How Knowledge and Affluence Change Consumers and Products*, Boulder, CO: Paradigm Publishers.

Stehr, N., and Adolf, M. (2010), 'Consumption between market and morals: a socio-cultural consideration of moralized markets', *European Journal of Social Theory*, 13(2): 213–228.

Stehr, N., Henning, C., and Weiler, B. (eds.) (2006), *The Moralization of the Markets*, New Brunswick, NJ: Transaction Publishers.

Stigler, G.J. (1957), 'Perfect competition, historically contemplated', *Journal of Political Economy*, 65(1): 1–17.

Stigler, G.J., and Becker, G.S. (1977), 'De gustibus non est disputandum', *American Economic Review*, 67(2): 76–90.

Stiglitz, J.E., and Rosengard, J.K. (2015), *Economics of the Public Sector*, 4th edn., New York: Norton.

Stilwell, F. (2011), *Political Economy: The Contest of Economic Ideas*, 3rd edn., Oxford, UK: Oxford University Press.

Stinchcombe, A.L. (1989), 'An outsider's view of network analyses of power', in R. Perrucci, and H.R. Potter (eds.), *Networks of Power*, New York: Aldine de Gruyter, pp. 119–133.

Storbacka, K., and Nenonen, S. (2011a), 'Markets as configurations', *European Journal of Marketing*, 45(1–2): 241–258.

Storbacka, K., and Nenonen, S. (2011b), 'Scripting markets: from value propositions to market propositions', *Industrial Marketing Management*, 40(2): 255–266.

Storper, M. (1995), 'The resurgence of regional economies, ten years later: the region as a nexus of untraded interdependencies', *European Urban and Regional Studies*, 2(3): 191–221.

Storper, M. (1997), *The Regional World: Territorial Development in a Global Economy*, New York: Guilford Press.

Storr, V.H. (2010a), 'The facts of the social sciences are what people believe and think', in P.J. Boettke (ed.), *Handbook on Contemporary Austrian Economics*, Cheltenham, UK: Edward Elgar, pp. 30–40.

Storr, V.H. (2010b), 'The social construction of the market', *Society*, 47(3): 200–206.

Storr, V.H. (2013), *Understanding the Culture of Markets*, London: Routledge.

Stovel, K., and Shaw, L. (2012), 'Brokerage', *Annual Review of Sociology*, 38: 139–158.

Strasser, S. (ed.) (2003), *Commodifying Everything: Relationships of the Market*, London: Routledge.

Strathern, A., and Stewart, P.J. (2005), 'Ceremonial exchange', in J.G. Carrier (ed.), *A Handbook of Economic Anthropology*, Cheltenham, UK: Edward Elgar, pp. 230–245.

Strauss, J., and Frost, R. (2016), *E-Marketing*, London: Routledge.

Sugden, R. (1989), 'Spontaneous order', *Journal of Economic Perspectives*, 3(4): 85–97.

Sutherland, F., and Smith, A.C.T. (2011), 'Duality theory and the management of the change–stability paradox', *Journal of Management and Organization*, 17(4): 534–547.

Svetlova, E. (2012), 'On the performative power of financial models', *Economy and Society*, 41(3): 418–434.

Swank, D. (2005), 'Globalisation, domestic politics, and welfare state retrenchment in capitalist democracies', *Social Policy and Society*, 4(2): 183–195.

Swedberg, R. (1998), *Max Weber and the Idea of Economic Sociology*, Princeton, NJ: Princeton University Press.

Swedberg, R. (2003), *Principles of Economic Sociology*, Princeton, NJ: Princeton University Press.

Sweezy, P.M. (2004), 'Monopoly capitalism', *Monthly Review*, 56(5): 78–85.

Sweezy, P.M. et al. (2006), *The Transition from Feudalism to Capitalism*, introduced by R. Hilton, Delhi: Aakar Books.

Tadelis, S., and Williamson, O.E. (2013), 'Transaction cost economics', in R. Gibbons, and J. Roberts (eds.), *The Handbook of Organizational Economics*, Princeton, NJ: Princeton University Press, pp. 159–191.

Tallontire, A. (2002), 'Challenges facing fair trade: which way now?', *Small Enterprise Development*, 13(3): 12–24.

Tallontire, A. (2009), 'Top heavy? Governance issues and policy decisions for the fair trade movement', *Journal of International Development*, 21(7): 1004–1014.

Tan, X., Yen, D.C., and Fang, X. (2002), 'Internet integrated customer relationship management: a key success factor for companies in the e-commerce arena', *Journal of Computer Information Systems*, 42(3): 77–86.

Tanzi, V., and Schuknecht, L. (2000), *Public Spending in the 20th Century: A Global Perspective*, Cambridge, UK: Cambridge University Press.

Tawney, R.H. (1926), *Religion and the Rise of Capitalism: A Historical Study*, London: Murray.

Temin, P. (2001), 'A market economy in the early Roman empire', *Journal of Roman Studies*, 91: 169–181.

Temin, P. (2004), 'Financial intermediation in the early Roman Empire', *Journal of Economic History*, 64(3): 705–733.

Temin, P. (2006), 'The economy of the early Roman Empire', *Journal of Economic Perspectives*, 20(1): 133–151.

Temin, P. (2013), *The Roman Market Economy*, Princeton, NJ: Princeton University Press.

Thaler, R.H. (2017), 'Behavioral economics', *Journal of Political Economy*, 125(6): 1799–1805.

Thirlwall, A.P., and Pacheco-López, P. (2017), *Economics of Development*, 10th edn., Basingstoke, UK: Palgrave Macmillan.

Thomas, B. (1991), 'Alfred Marshall on economic biology', *Review of Political Economy*, 3(1): 1–14.

Thomas, J.J. (1992), *Informal Economic Activity*, Hemel Hempstead, UK: Harvester Wheatsheaf.

Thomas, K.V. (1964), 'Work and leisure in pre-industrial society', *Past and Present*, 29: 50–66.

Thompson, E.P. (1967), 'Time, work discipline, and industrial capitalism', *Past and Present*, 38: 56–97.

Thompson, G.F. (2003), *Between Hierarchies and Markets: The Logic and Limits of Network Forms of Organization*, Oxford, UK: Oxford University Press.

Thompson, G.F., Frances, J., Levačić, R., and Mitchell, J. (eds.) (1991), *Markets, Hierarchies and Networks: The Coordination of Social Life*, London: Sage.

Thompson, P., and McHugh, D. (2009), *Work Organisations: A Critical Approach*, 4th edn., Basingstoke, UK: Palgrave Macmillan.

Thompson, W.E. (1982), 'The Athenian entrepreneur', *L'Antiquité Classique*, 51(1): 53–85.

Thorelli, H.B. (1986), 'Networks: between markets and hierarchies', *Strategic Management Journal*, 7(1): 37–51.

Thrift, N.J. (2000), 'Pandora's box: cultural geographies of economics', in G.L. Clark, M.P. Feldman, and M.S. Gertler (eds.), *The Oxford Handbook of Economic Geography*, Oxford, UK: Oxford University Press, pp. 689–704.

Throsby, D. (2001), *Economics and Culture*, Cambridge, UK: Cambridge University Press.

Thrupp, S.L. (1963), 'The gilds', in M.M. Postan, E.E. Rich, and E. Miller (eds.), *Cambridge Economic History of Europe, III Economic Organization and Policies in the Middle Ages*, Cambridge, UK: Cambridge University Press, pp. 230–280.

Thünen, J.H. von (1826), *The Isolated State*, translated by C.M. Wartenberg, Oxford, UK: Pergamon Press, 1966.

Tinel, B. (2012), 'Labour, labour power and the division of labour', in B. Fine, and A. Saad-Filho (eds.), *The Elgar Companion to Marxist Economics*, Cheltenham, UK: Edward Elgar, pp. 187–193.

Titmuss, R.M. (1970), *The Gift Relationship: From Human Blood to Social Policy*, London: George Allen & Unwin.

Titmuss, R.M. (2001), *Welfare and Wellbeing*, edited by P. Alcock, H. Glennerster, A. Oakley, and A. Sinfield, Bristol, UK: Policy Press.

Tittenbrun, J. (2014), 'Talcott Parsons' economic sociology', *International Letters of Social and Humanistic Sciences*, 13: 20–40.

Tönnies, F. (1887), *Community and Society*, translated and edited by C.P. Loomis, Mineola, NY: Dover, 2002.

Toporowski, J. (2015), 'Neologism as theoretical innovation in economics: the case of "financialisation"', in P. O'Sullivan, N.F.B. Allington and M. Esposito (eds.), *The Philosophy, Politics and Economics of Finance in the 21st Century: From Hubris to Disgrace*, London: Routledge, pp. 254–266.

Toporowski, J. (2016), 'Microfoundations, Minsky and classical political economy', *Review of Political Economy*, 28(1): 92–98.

Toporowski, J., and Mamica, Ł. (eds.) (2015), *Michał Kalecki in the 21st Century*, London: Palgrave Macmillan.

Toye, J., and Toye, R. (2003), 'The origins and interpretation of the Prebisch-Singer thesis', *History of Political Economy*, 35(3): 437–467.

Tribe, K. (2003), 'Historical schools of economics: German and English', in W.J. Samuels, J.E. Biddle, and J.B. Davis (eds.), *A Companion to the History of Economic Thought*, Oxford, UK: Blackwell, pp. 215–230.

Trigg, A.B. (2001), 'Veblen, Bourdieu, and conspicuous consumption', *Journal of Economic Issues*, 35(1): 99–115.

Trigilia, C. (2002), *Economic Sociology: State, Market, and Society in Modern Capitalism*, Oxford: Blackwell.

Tullock, G. (1975), 'Competing monies', *Journal of Money, Credit and Banking*, 7(4): 491–497.

Tversky, A., and Kahneman, D. (1974), 'Judgement under uncertainty: heuristics and biases', *Science*, 185(4157): 1124–1131.

Tversky, A., and Kahneman, D. (1981), 'The framing of decisions and the psychology of choice', *Science*, 211(4481): 453–458.

Tymoigne, É., and Wray, L.R. (2006), 'Money: an alternative story', in P. Arestis, and M.C. Sawyer (eds.), *A Handbook of Alternative Monetary Economics*, Cheltenham, UK: Edward Elgar, pp. 1–16.

United Nations (1953), *A System of National Accounts and Supporting Tables*, New York: United Nations.

United Nations (2008), *System of National Accounts 2008*, New York: United Nations.

Utting, K. (2009), 'Assessing the impact of Fair Trade coffee: towards an integrative framework', *Journal of Business Ethics*, 86: 127–149.

Uzzi, B. (1999), 'Embeddedness in the making of financial capital: how social relations and networks benefit firms seeking financing', *American Sociological Review*, 64(4): 481–505.

Vail, J. (2010), 'Decommodification and egalitarian political economy', *Politics and Society*, 38(3): 310–346.

Van Daal, J., and Jolink, A. (1993), *The Equilibrium Economics of Léon Walras*, London: Routledge.

Van Dijk, J.A.G.M. (2006), *The Network Society: Social Aspects of New Media*, 2nd edn., London: Sage.

Van Horn, R., and Mirowski, P. (2009), 'The rise of the Chicago School of Economics and the birth of neoliberalism', in P. Mirowski, and D. Plehwe (eds.), *The Road from Mont Pelerin*, Cambridge, MA: Harvard University Press, pp. 139–178.

Vanberg, V.J. (1986), 'Spontaneous market order and social rules: a critical examination of F.A. Hayek's theory of cultural evolution', *Economics and Philosophy*, 2(1): 75–100.

Vanoli, A. (2005), *A History of National Accounting*, translated by M.P. Libreros, and G.H. Partmann, Amsterdam: IOS Press.

Vargo, S.L. (2007), 'On a theory of markets and marketing: from positively normative to normatively positive', *Australasian Marketing Journal*, 15(1): 53–60.

Veblen, T.B. (1898), 'Why is economics not an evolutionary science?', *Quarterly Journal of Economics*, 12(4): 373–397.

Veblen, T.B. (1899), *The Theory of the Leisure Class: An Economic Study of Institutions*, New York: Macmillan.

Veblen, T.B. (1900), 'The preconceptions of economic science III', *Quarterly Journal of Economics*, 14(2): 240–269.

Velthuis, O. (2004), 'An interpretive approach to meanings of prices', *Review of Austrian Economics*, 17(4): 371–386.

Venables, A.J. (2010), 'New economic geography', in S.N. Durlauf, and L.E. Blume (eds.), *Economic Growth*, Berlin: Springer, pp. 207–214.

Venkatesh, A., Penaloza, L., and Faut Firat, A. (2006), 'The market as a sign system and the logic of the market', in R.F. Lusch, and S.L. Vargo (eds.), *The Service-Dominant Logic of Marketing: Dialog, Debate and Directions*, Armonk, NY: M.E. Sharpe, pp. 251–265.

Vercelli, A. (2012), 'New classical economics', in J.E. King (ed.), *The Elgar Companion to Post Keynesian Economics*, 2nd edn., Cheltenham, UK: Edward Elgar, pp. 420–425.

Verlinden, C. (1963), 'Markets and fairs', in M.M. Postan, E.E. Rich, and E. Miller (eds.), *Cambridge Economic History of Europe, III Economic Organization and Policies in the Middle Ages*, Cambridge, UK: Cambridge University Press, pp. 119–153.

Vromen, J.J. (1995), *Economic Evolution: An Enquiry into the Foundations of New Institutional Economics*, London: Routledge.

Wade, R.H. (2003), 'What strategies are viable for developing countries today? The World Trade Organization and the shrinking of "development space"', *Review of International Political Economy*, 10(4): 621–644.

Wade, R.H. (2004a), 'Is globalization reducing poverty and inequality?', *World Development*, 32(4): 567–589.

Wade, R.H. (2004b), 'On the causes of increasing world poverty and inequality, or why the Matthew effect prevails', *New Political Economy*, 9(2): 163–188.

Wade, R.H. (2017), 'The American paradox: ideology of free markets and the hidden practice of directional thrust', *Cambridge Journal of Economics*, 41(3): 859–880.

Waldrop, M.M. (1992), *Complexity: the Emerging Science at the Edge of Order and Chaos*, New York: Simon and Schuster.

Wallerstein, I.M. (1974), *The Modern World-System: Capitalist Agriculture and the Origins of the European World Economy in the Sixteenth Century*, New York: Academic Press.

Wallerstein, I.M. (2004), *World-Systems Analysis: An Introduction*, Durham, NC: Duke University Press.

Walras, L. (1926), *Elements of Pure Economics*, translated by W. Jaffé, New York: Kelley, 1954.

Walsh, A. (2004), 'The morality of the market and the medieval schoolmen', *Politics, Philosophy and Economics*, 3(2): 241–259.

Walsh, A., and Lynch, T. (2002), 'The very idea of justice in pricing', *Business and Professional Ethics Journal*, 21(3–4): 3–25.

Walzer, M. (1983), *Spheres of Justice: A Defence of Pluralism and Equality*, New York: Basic Books.

Waters, W.R. (1988), 'Social economics: a solidarist perspective', *Review of Social Economy*, 46(2): 113–143.

Waters, W.R. (1993), 'A review of the troops: social economics in the twentieth century', *Review of Social Economy*, 51(3): 262–286.

Weber, A. (1909), *Theory of the Location of Industries*, translated by C.J. Friedrich, Chicago, IL: University of Chicago Press, 1929.

Weber, M. (1904–5), *The Protestant Ethic and the Spirit of Capitalism*, translated by S. Kalberg, Oxford, UK: Blackwell, 2002.

Weber, M. (1909), *The Agrarian Sociology of Ancient Civilizations*, London: New Left Books, 1976.

Weber, M. (1921), *The City*, edited and translated by D. Martindale and G. Neuwirth, Glencoe, IL.: Free Press, 1958.

Weber, M. (1922), *Economy and Society: An Outline of Interpretive Sociology*, edited by G. Roth, and C. Wittich, New York: Bedminster Press, 1968.

Weber, M. (1923), *General Economic History*, translated by F.H. Knight, New Brunswick, NJ: Transaction Publishers, 1981.

Weber, M. (1946), *From Max Weber: Essays in Sociology*, translated and edited by H.H. Gerth, and C.W. Mills, New York: Oxford University Press.

Weber, M. (1981), 'Some categories of interpretive sociology', *Sociological Quarterly*, 22(2): 151–180.

Webster, F. (2014), *Theories of the Information Society*, 4th edn., London: Routledge.

Weisbrod, B.A. (ed.) (1998), *To Profit or Not to Profit: The Commercial Transformation of the Nonprofit Sector*, Cambridge, UK: Cambridge University Press.

Weisdorf, J.L. (2005), 'From foraging to farming: explaining the Neolithic Revolution', *Journal of Economic Surveys*, 19(4): 561–586.

Wheelock, J. (1992), 'The household in the total economy', in P. Ekins, and M. Max-Neef (eds.), *Real-Life Economics: Understanding Wealth Creation*, London: Routledge, pp. 124–136.

Wheelock, J., and Oughton, E. (1996), 'The household as a focus for research', *Journal of Economic Issues*, 30(1): 143–159.

White, G. (1998), 'Disequilibrium pricing and the Sraffa-Keynes synthesis', *Review of Political Economy*, 10(4): 459–475.

White, H.C. (1981), 'Where do markets come from?', *American Journal of Sociology*, 87(3): 517–547.

White, H.C. (1993), 'Markets in production networks', in R. Swedberg (ed.), *Explorations in Economic Sociology*, New York: Russell Sage Foundation, pp. 161–175.

White, H.C. (2002), *Markets from Networks: Socioeconomic Models of Production*, Princeton, NJ: Princeton University Press.

Whitfield, L. (2012), 'How countries become rich and reduce poverty: a review of heterodox explanations of economic development', *Development Policy Review*, 30(3): 239–260.

Wilk, R.R., and Cliggett, L.C. (2007), *Economies and Cultures: Foundations of Economic Anthropology*, 2nd edn., Boulder, CO: Westview Press.

Wilkinson, J. (2007), 'Fair trade: dynamic and dilemmas of a market oriented global social movement', *Journal of Consumer Policy*, 30(3): 219–239.

Williams, C.C. (2004), 'The myth of marketization: an evaluation of the persistence of non-market activities in advanced economies', *International Sociology*, 19(4): 437–449.

Williams, C.C. (2005), *A Commodified World? Mapping the Limits of Capitalism*, London: Zed Books.

Williams, C.C. (2014), *Confronting the Shadow Economy: Evaluating Tax Compliance and Behaviour Policies*, Cheltenham, UK: Edward Elgar.

Williams, C.C., and Nadin, S. (2012), 'Work beyond employment: representations of informal economic activities', *Work, Employment and Society*, 26(2): 1–10.

Williams, C.C., and Schneider, F. (2016), *Measuring the Global Shadow Economy: the Prevalence of Informal Work and Labour*, Cheltenham, UK: Edward Elgar.

Williams, C.C., and Windebank, J. (1998), *Informal Employment in the Advanced Economies: Implications for Work and Welfare*, London: Routledge.

Williams, J.C., and Zelizer, V.A. (2005), 'To commodify or not to commodify: that is not the question', in M.M. Ertman, and J.C. Williams (eds.), *Rethinking Commodification: Cases and Readings in Law and Culture*, New York: New York University Press, pp. 362–382.

Williams, M. (2000), 'Why Marx neither has nor needs a commodity theory of money', *Review of Political Economy*, 12(4): 435–451.

Williams, R. (1958), *Culture and Society: Coleridge to Orwell*, London: Chatto and Windus.

Williams, R. (1977), *Marxism and Literature*, Oxford, UK: Oxford University Press.

Williams, R. (1980), 'Base and superstructure in Marxist cultural theory', in R. Williams, *Problems in Materialism and Culture: Selected Essays*, London: Verso, pp. 31–49.

Williams, R. (1981), *Culture*, London: Fontana Press.

Williams, R. (1988), *Keywords: A Vocabulary of Culture and Society*, 2nd edn., London: Fontana Press.

Williamson, J. (1978), *Decoding Advertisements: Ideology and Meaning in Advertising*, London: Marion Boyars.

Williamson, O.E. (1979), 'Transaction-cost economics: the governance of contractual relations', *Journal of Law and Economics*, 22(2): 233–261.

Williamson, O.E. (1985), *The Economic Institutions of Capitalism: Firms, Markets, Relational Contracting*, New York: Free Press.

Williamson, O.E. (2000), 'The new institutional economics: taking stock, looking ahead', *Journal of Economic Literature*, 38(3): 595–613.

Wilson, G.W. (1975), 'The economics of the just price', *History of Political Economy*, 7(1): 56–74.

Winer, R.S. (2001), 'A framework for customer relationship management', *California Management Review*, 43(4): 89–105.

Witt, U. (2001), 'Learning to consume: a theory of wants and the growth of demand', *Journal of Evolutionary Economics*, 11(1): 23–36.

Wood, E.M. (2012), 'Capitalism', in B. Fine, and A. Saad-Filho (eds.), *The Elgar Companion to Marxist Economics*, Cheltenham, UK: Edward Elgar, pp. 34–39.

Wood, S. (1982), *The Degradation of Work? Skill, Deskilling, and the Labour Process*, London: Hutchinson.

Wray, L.R. (2012), 'Money', in J.E. King (ed.), *The Elgar Companion to Post Keynesian Economics*, Cheltenham, UK: Edward Elgar, pp. 401–409.

Wray, L.R. (2014), *From the State Theory of Money to Modern Money Theory: An Alternative to Economic Orthodoxy*, Levy Economics Institute of Bard College, Working Paper No. 792.

Yan, Y. (2005), 'The gift and gift economy', in J.G. Carrier (ed.), *A Handbook of Economic Anthropology*, Cheltenham, UK: Edward Elgar, pp. 246–261.

Yang, S., Keller, F.B., and Zheng, L. (2017), *Social Network Analysis: Methods and Examples*, London: Sage.

Yeung, H.W. (2003), 'Practicing new economic geographies: a methodological examination', *Annals of the Association of American Geographers*, 93(2): 442–462.

Yunker, J.A. (2001), *On the Political Economy of Market Socialism: Essays and Analyses*, Aldershot, UK: Ashgate.

Zafirovski, M. (2001), *Exchange, Action and Social Structure: Elements of Economic Sociology*, Westport, CT: Greenwood Press.

Zafirovski, M. (2003a), 'Human rational behavior and economic rationality', *Electronic Journal of Sociology*, 7(2).

Zafirovski, M. (2003b), 'Orthodoxy and heterodoxy in analyzing institutions: original and new institutional economics re-examined', *International Journal of Social Economics*, 30(7): 798–826.

Zak, P.J. (ed.) (2008), *Moral Markets: The Critical Role of Values in the Economy*, Princeton, NJ: Princeton University Press.

Zak, P.J. (2011), 'Moral markets', *Journal of Economic Behavior and Organization*, 77(2): 212–233.

Zakia, R.D., and Nadin, M. (1987), 'Semiotics, advertising and marketing', *Journal of Consumer Marketing*, 4(2): 5–12.

Zelizer, V.A. (1988), 'Beyond the polemics on the market: establishing a theoretical and empirical agenda', *Sociological Forum*, 3(4): 614–634.

Zelizer, V.A. (1989), 'The social meaning of money: "special monies"', *American Journal of Sociology*, 95(2): 342–377.

Zelizer, V.A. (1994), *The Social Meaning of Money*, New York: Basic Books.

Zimbalist, A., and Sherman, H.J. (1984), *Comparing Economic Systems: A Political-Economic Approach*, Orlando, FL: Academic Press.

Index

evolutionary trends 183–4
excess capacity 173, 176, 178
exchange 4–5; network theories 86–9;
    relational exchange 83–5; transfer or
    property 28–9; *see also* trade
exchange theory of money 29–30
exchange value 121
extended credit 47
external pluralism 22

fair trade: moral regulation and 124–9
fairs 36
feminist economics 170
feudalism 36–7, 41, 43
fictitious commodities 68
field theories 93–5
financial crises 18, 47, 125–6
financial instability hypothesis 48, 126
financial markets: capitalism 46–8;
    moral regulation and fair trade
    125–6; performativity 90–1
financial products 146, 167
financialisation 48, 91
Firth, Raymond 105
fiscal crisis of the state 131
fixed preferences: orthodox approach
    13, 17, 24, 86, 117
Fligstein, Neil 94–5
formal structure of markets 79–83
formalisation 182
formalism/substantivism 56–9
free trade 39, 62, 68, 127, 138
functional approaches 101–18, 148
functionalism 101, 105
functionalists 101
functions: of markets 109–13; of money
    106–9; of trade 102–6

general equilibrium 157, 171, 180;
    orthodox approach 15
generalised reciprocity 57–8
geography: economic geography 59–62
German historical school:
    institutionalism 62
gift economies 29, 58
gift relationship 134–5, 183
gifts 4, 29, 32, 58, 84
global trading environment 127
Granovetter, Mark 86
Greeks: householding 120;
    householding and profit-making 66;
    markets 33; money 34
guilds: medieval world 37–8, 48, 61, 122

habits 17, 22, 63, 76, 85
habitual trade 160
habitus 93–4
Harris, Marvin 75
health care 50, 69, 84, 91, 133, 158,
    168, 176
heterodox economics: moral regulation
    and fair trade 125
heterodox macroeconomics 174
historical materialism 70–4
historical time 136
householding 66, 120, 129
housework 50, 168, 170
housing markets 145
human agency 92; field theories
    93–5; stratified and critical realist
    theories 96
Hume, David 123
Hume's Law 119
hunting/gathering 27–8

ideal type 67
idealism 65–6, 68, 92
illusio 94
imitating business practices 169
imperfect competition 19–20
imperfectionism: orthodox approach
    19–21, 24
impurity principle 180
individualism 13, 23, 56, 66, 96, 123,
    150; Austrian economics 116–17
industrial location 59
Industrial Revolution 41, 43
inequalities 135–8
information technology:
    network theories 88; relational
    exchange 85
innovation 76, 88, 104, 113,
    116–18, 151
input budgeting 167–8
institutional: backgrounds 150–1;
    economics 62–4
institutionalism 62–4, 116; new
    institutionalism 23–4
interest 38, 46, 122
internal markets 168–9
international commerce 127;
    cumulative causation 137–8
internet 6, 85, 137
interpretative methods 65, 117
invisible hand 18, 64, 123, 154
involuntary transfers 5
irregular sector 167, 169